Nation, Empire, Colony

Nation, Empire, Colony
Historicizing Gender and Race

EDITED BY
Ruth Roach Pierson
AND
Nupur Chaudhuri

With the Assistance of Beth McAuley

Indiana University Press

BLOOMINGTON AND INDIANAPOLIS

This book is a publication of

Indiana University Press
601 North Morton Street
Bloomington, Indiana 47404-3797 USA

http://www.indiana.edu/~iupress

Telephone orders 800-842-6796
Fax orders 812-855-7931
Orders by e-mail iuporder@indiana.edu

The paper used in this publication meets the minimum requirements
of American National Standard for Information Sciences—Perma-
nence of Paper for Printed Library Materials, ANSI Z39.48-1984.

MANUFACTURED IN THE UNITED STATES OF AMERICA

Library of Congress Cataloging-in-Publication Data

Nation, empire, colony : historicizing gender and race / edited by
    Ruth Roach Pierson and Nupur Chaudhuri ; with the assistance
    of Beth McAuley.
        p.   cm.
Includes index.
ISBN 0-253-33398-9 (cloth : alk. paper). — ISBN 0-253-21191-3 (pbk. :
    alk. paper)
1. Women—Europe—Colonies—History. 2. Women—America—
    Colonies—History. 3. Sex Role—Europe—Colonies—History.
    4. Sex role—America—Colonies—History. 5. Imperialism
    —History—19th century. 6. Imperialism—History—20th cen-
    tury.   I. Pierson, Ruth Roach, date.   II. Chaudhuri, Nupur.
    III. McAuley, Beth.
HQ 1587.N28   1998
305.4'09—dc21   98-19966

1 2 3 4 5 03 02 01 00 99 98

Any royalties generated by the sale of this book
will go toward supporting the future work of the
International Federation for Research in Women's History/
Fédération internationale pour la recherche en histoire des femmes
IFRWH/FIRHF

CONTENTS

ACKNOWLEDGMENTS

We wish, first of all, to express our profound gratitude to the four Rapportrices of the 1995 IFRWH/FIRHF conference in Montréal on "Women, Colonialisms, Imperialisms, and Nationalisms through the Ages," Micheline Dumont, Susan Geiger, Catherine Hall, and Nakanyike Musisi. Their reports' insightful commentaries on, and analyses and assessments of, the papers prepared for that conference established the foundation on which we based the selection of the chapters for this book. Second, we also wish to acknowledge our great debt to Andrée Lévesque for her help with the vetting of the conference paper proposals and for her enormous contribution to the organization of the Montréal conference's evening events. We are also grateful to all those whose papers were presented at the conference as well as to all those who attended and participated in the lively general discussions. And we especially want to thank the contributors to this book for their patience with the long and arduous process of compiling, editing, and overseeing this international anthology through to publication.

The manuscript has benefited significantly from the highly perceptive and knowledgeable readings given it, in whole or in part, at various stages in its development. For this invaluable work we would like to acknowledge Franca Iacovetta, Margaret Kamau, Adele Perry, and Sherene Razack, as well as the anonymous reviewers of the manuscript for Indiana University Press.

To Elizabeth Fear, secretary in the Department of Theory and Policy Studies in Education at the Ontario Institute for Studies in Education of the University of Toronto, we also owe a vote of thanks for the work she performed of inputting a number of the chapters for this volume. And we are greatly in the debt of Larry Brookwell for his patience in solving a host of problems caused by computer glitches at the last minute. Finally we would like to express our appreciation to our editor at Indiana University Press, Joan Catapano, and her assistant, Grace Profatilov, for their faith in this project.

Ruth Roach Pierson, Nupur Chaudhuri, and Beth McAuley

Nation, Empire, Colony

Introduction

RUTH ROACH PIERSON

Histories of nationalism, imperialism, and colonialism have, as has so much other historical writing, traditionally neglected the experiences of women. And those theorizing nationalism, imperialism, and colonialism have, until recently, paid little critical attention to gender relations, even when their theories abound with figurations of women and metaphors of gender.[1] This book has as one of its purposes to further the projects both of restoring women to, and of ferreting out the workings of gender in, histories of the construction of nation, empire, and colony. Unifying the book's contributions is a critical awareness of power: that the power relations of gender have intertwined with those of class, race, and sexuality and that these technologies of power have been at the heart of the histories of imperialism, colonialism, and nationalism shaping our modern world. But the lines of power transmit in both directions, and so a further purpose of the book is to uncover the crucial importance of constructions of nation, empire, and colony in the construction of race and gender. Women's history in the modern era occurs within a matrix of these interlocking categories.

The essays collected in this volume have been selected from those presented at the conference entitled "Women, Colonialisms, Imperialisms, and Nationalisms through the Ages" and sponsored by the International Federation for Research in Women's History at the Eighteenth International Congress of Historical Sciences in Montréal, August 30–31, 1995. This was the fourth conference organized by the International Federation for Research in Women's History / Fédération internationale pour la recherche en histoire des femmes (IFRWH / FIRHF) since its founding in 1987. As its title indicates, the International Federation is dedicated to furthering research on the history of women throughout the world. But the Federation eschews both the divisive dichotomy between women's history and gender history[2] and the assumption that gender is synonymous with women. To advocate a focus on women that is not merely additive but rather reconfiguring is to recognize the great diversity of women and the instability of the category women and its perpetual constitution and reconstitution in and through other categories of difference. As "women of color" theorists have argued, the ways one becomes a woman or a man are much more complex than in simple opposition to members of the other sex. To quote Norma Alarcón, "In cultures in which 'asymmetric race and class relations are a central organizing principle of society,' one may also 'become a woman' in opposition to other women."[3] A conception of the interlocking and mutually constitutive character of social categories, then, also explodes the notion that gender rotates simply around a single axis of bipolar opposites. Instead it makes visible the plurality of genders, that gender is, for instance, classed and raced. Leonore Davidoff and Catherine Hall have shown how bourgeois femininity and masculinity emerged in England through constitutive differentiation from aristocratic and working-class femininities and masculinities.[4] And Evelyn Brooks Higginbotham and Patricia Hill Collins, along with a host of other African American feminist scholars and historians of African North American experience, have shown how Black femaleness, white femaleness, Black maleness, and white maleness are all intricately intertwined in the constitution of one another.[5]

A relative newcomer on the stage of feminist historical scholarship, the Federation has moved steadily in the direction of internationalizing women's history. The specific topics taken up in the papers reported on at the Montréal conference were culled from records from almost every major land mass in the world. But to avoid what Gayatri Spivak has called "pretentious internationalism,"[6] the editors of this present volume have sought not only to preserve a multinational scope but also to aspire to a global[7] perspective[8] that captures the asymmetrical power relations between and among nations. "International" implies communication and interaction between more or less equal and similarly constituted "nation states." The term "global," in contrast, can be construed to encompass power relations between and among radically unequal political/social units at opposite ends of the earth. More importantly, it gestures toward the notion that, in a world crisscrossed with relations of imperialism and neoimperialism, colonialism and neocolonialism, the metropole and the periphery are inescapably interconnected. As Inderpal Grewal argues, "[t]o focus merely on what happens to the colony is . . . to leave out a major factor in the discourse of colonization."[9] She reminds us that what Mary Louise Pratt has termed "contact zones," that is, the "space of colonial encounters,"[10] occur "not just in the so-called peripheries, but in the colonial metropolis itself."[11] We understand a global perspective, then, to rest on the assumption that to comprehend developments in the metropolitan center, one needs to grasp how its formation and sense of self have been shaped by its relationship with the imperialized and colonized margins.[12] The reverse of this formulation, i.e., that center affects margin, has usually been taken as self-evident, although the physical coercion and psychical violence intrinsic to these encounters have all too often been elided.[13] Yet if we applaud with Ann Laura Stoler the growth of a scholarship that attempts to bring together "metropole and colony in a single analytic field,"[14] we also concede with her the enormous difficulty of this project for any one individual. Books of the present sort[15] attempt to overcome that difficulty by joining together the work of many scholars, all bringing different angles of vision to bear on the phenomena of nationalism, colonialism, and imperialism and their power politics of race, sexuality, gender, and identity. By the very act of juxtaposition we hope to dismantle the brackets separating the imperialists' history from that of the imperialized, the colonists' from that of the colonized, the narrative of the nation's core from that of its excluded margins.

The periods looked at in these essays date from the time we now think of as the Grand Era of European and later American imperialism, from sometime in the eighteenth century until after the Second World War. The heyday of European imperialist expansion coincided with the emergence of the Enlightenment quest for encyclopedic knowledge of the world—the fervid desire to map every nook and cranny of the earth's surface, to plumb the depths of its every body of water, to collect specimens of every plant, animal, mineral, human, and humanoid. Hand-in-hand with European conquerors, explorers, slave traders, merchants, missionaries, and imperial and colonial administrators, European cartographers, botanists, biologists, and budding anthropologists fanned out over the globe, returning home with the booty that fueled the mania for classification and categorization. These were at the heart of the great urge to control, the will to power, through the creation of "a new global order of cultural knowledge," which Anne McClintock calls one of "the governing themes of Western imperialism."[16] But the Enlightenment's claim to universalism, uttered contemporaneously with social and political revolutionary cries for freedom, equality, and tolerance, was spurious. The revolutionary shibboleth "brotherhood" gives away the gendered limitation, the fact that the social contract into which equal men freely entered was predicated on a prior, sexual contract that subordinated women.[17] Similarly, as David Theo Goldberg argues, European liberalism's idealization of liberty, equality, and fraternity hides its inherent drive to hegemony and racial (and class) exclusivity.[18] The autonomy of European liberalism's free man rests on property and on the domination and exploitation of other classes and races—the colonized populations abroad and the working masses at home. The late eighteenth century onward was, moreover, also the period of the emergence of the nation-state. The universal claims of the Enlightenment chafed uneasily against the competing militaries and capitalist imperialisms of the so-called European Great Powers—culminating in the scramble for Africa of the 1880s and the outbreak of the First World War. As for internal tolerance, the formation of national identities was predicated on an imagined community of shared sameness (sameness of language, culture, blood, soil, economic interest), but the achievement of that unity entailed the violent suppression, exclusion, or denial of difference and conflict (difference of dialect, belief, ancestry; conflicting property and economic interests). The philosophers and politicians of the Enlightenment had to go to considerable lengths to manage the contradictions between their ostensibly universalist claims and their European elite white male determination to set limits on equality and liberty in order to maintain their social and political preeminence. In their strategies to preserve dominance over women in general, including those from their own milieus, over the "lower" orders within Europe, as well as over the conquered peoples abroad, lay the seeds of "scientific" racism and a sociobiology-based gender ideology. The Enlightenment appeal to Natural Law to ground its claim that all people are by nature created equal was countered by its search for natural differences within and among peoples, the fabrication and elaboration of anatomies of difference.[19]

A body-based, biological dimorphism was advanced by gender theorists to underpin their assertions of almost inseparable difference between women and men.[20] The "scientists" of race labored to divide the vast diversity of the human species into a small number of separate and distinct races, reducing, in the end, the number of major racial types to four or five, depending on the theorist.[21] While the theorists of race and sex differences proceeded often in apparent independence from one another, the interchange of metaphors between the one discourse and the other betrays their mutuality, as conquered territories and their male inhabitants became feminized[22] and the marginalized of the metropole became racialized.[23] And the mutuality between the racism and sexism resounding within Europe's capitalist and epistemological expansionism was material as well as metaphoric. The success and prosperity of the European bourgeoisie with its gender ideology of separate spheres depended on colonialism and imperialism, just as the imperialist and colonialist enterprises took shape around the bourgeois Victorian cult of domesticity. Or, as McClintock has succinctly put it in her discussion of the relationship between the imperial home country and the colonies, "as domestic space became racialized, colonial space became domesticated."[24] In other words, as keeping "dirt" within bourgeois homes at bay acquired associations with erecting barriers against the racially unclean, so the strategies of colonial and imperial administrators for securing "white prestige" and maintaining "white" control rested not only on the policing of rigid boundaries between colonizer and contamination from the colonized but also on the imposition of western bourgeois ideals of cleanliness and gender difference on native peoples.[25]

Both racist and sexist thought would eventually make use of Darwinist evolutionary theory and an evolutionized discourse of civilization. The notion of a Great Chain of Being, once conceived as a static hierarchy stretching from animal to angel,[26] was reconfigured by evolutionism and the idea of progress to have more of a temporal than a spatial dimension. Races were now placed in a progressive chronology from the primitive stages of "savagery" and "barbarism" through decadent civilizations to culminate in white, European (and later American) civilization.[27] The bearers of this civilization were male, and one measure of the advance of European civilization over "earlier" ones was the large degree of differentiation and separation achieved between the sexes within the dominant classes of Europe. Only among primitive peoples and the lower classes were males and females similar. The great fear activated by the discourse of civilization and its concomitant notions of racial and gender superiority was the fear of degeneration.[28] That there were savage and barbaric primitive peoples still existing on the face of the earth, and older decayed civilizations still surviving into the present, was an anachronism. Those whose development was construed as arrested in some prehistoric or premodern stage—women, colonized peoples, the laboring masses—were relegated in the European and North American discourse of manliness and civilization to what McClintock has dubbed "anachronistic space."[29] But these exemplars of earlier stages in the development of "the family of man" could serve as lessons to the current carriers of civilization in their struggle to stave off racial and cultural degeneration.

To study critically the complex phenomena of colonialisms, imperialisms, and nationalisms is, as Himani Bannerji suggests in the concluding chapter of this book, to try "to study a wave as a stable form, as an arc of water, and yet to be attentive to the vast mass of liquid from which it formed and into which it will decompose." The chapters in this book are endeavors toward that end. The authors strive to take into account as many axes of difference, angles of vision, triangulations of power as they can in their excavation and explication of the historical evidence. While seeking to avoid the commission of "epistemic violence,"[30] they take on the challenge, wherever possible, of recovering voices, subaltern voices, women's voices, while fully aware of the extent to which the violences of colonialism, imperialism, and nationalism have depleted the archive and severely curtailed our abilities to access data about women, much less direct testimonies by women.

Patricia Grimshaw's contribution to the book, Chapter 1, illustrates the difficulties of reconstructing the "experiences" of colonized women, when those women's societies were preliterate and the only surviving records are the texts written by the colonizing Europeans, mostly men. Grimshaw has found differences in the (mis)representations of Maori women in Aotearoa/New Zealand as compared with those of Aboriginal women in southeastern Australia at the hands of British invaders, occupiers, and proselytizers starting at the end of the eighteenth century and continuing into the nineteenth. As her chapter indicates, subject races, while all seen as stagnating in premodernity, were also seen as occupying different rungs of the temporal ladder from barbarism to civilization. Both groups of indigenous women in her study were viewed through the distorting lens of British gender and class systems and the emerging discourses of race and empire that held the European bourgeoisie and its ways to be the expression of civilization at its most advanced. Surprise was hence voiced at the authority, strength, and courage evinced by Maori women, particularly chiefly women. For, according to European evolutionist sociobiology, the passionless, frail, and retiring femininity of the Victorian "angel" of the house was the bipolar opposite of ideal Victorian manhood, that extreme difference in the sexes being the mark of the highest degree of civilization. A note of actual awe crept into accounts of the heroic deeds of Maori warrior women in battle and of their willing commission of suicide, by hanging or drowning, when their "husbands died or were killed in warfare." Grimshaw reads the European men's accounts in general as more positive in evaluation of the agriculturalist and stratified Maori than of the hunter-and-gatherer Aboriginals. But even with regard to the relatively more respected Maori, the European recorders sought out telltale signs of this people's primitiveness: the institution of polygamy; the "swift, brutal, barbaric murder" of adulterous wives by husbands; the incidence of infanticide; the heavy labor performed by Maori women; the lack of "distinction of sex" in child-rearing practices; the "masculinization" of Maori women's bodies. (Mis)representations of the hunter / gatherer Aboriginals were even more negative. The prevalent theme was the "great degradation" of Aboriginal women at the hands of Aboriginal men. The emphasis on the victim status of Aboriginal women was related to the depiction of Aboriginal men as vicious, and both delineations served to justify British interventions, particularly the "massive colonial determination to transform [Aboriginal women] into domestic servants and housewives on a British model."[31]

Those underdeveloped occupants of "anachronistic space" in European imperialist discourse—women, colonized peoples, the laboring masses—were stripped by that same discourse of historical agency.[32] In this way, the making of History became the monopoly of European bourgeois men at the pinnacle of civilization. While contesting men's privileged place in history, white western feminists in the early stages of the contemporary resurgence of women's history bought into the notion that European women and women of European descent in the Americas and the Antipodes were exempt from imperialism.[33] Women of color and "post-colonial" theorists and scholars have done much to expose the imperializing and colonializing inherent in the adoption of such an "innocent" stance.[34] Current white western feminist scholarship has sought to distance itself from its former collusion in the creation of a unitary category of Woman.[35] More recently a body of historical scholarship has emerged that, scrutinizing the workings of power closely, implicates white western feminism in imperialism and colonialism and establishes clearly that women, too, bear "Burdens of History."[36] A number of authors in this volume contribute to this revisioning.

In Chapter 2, Rosalyn Terborg-Penn's research reveals white American suffragists acting as "agents of imperialism" in their efforts, if not to restrain, then, in the role of beneficent custodian, to control the suffrage struggle of Caribbean women. Contesting the sexism but not the racism of the discourse of civilization, the white elite women of the American National Woman's Party defined themselves as equal to the leading white men of the United States but morally, racially, and culturally superior to their "little colored sisters" in the Caribbean.

In Chapter 3, Dolores Janiewski presents a more contradictory figure in her examination of the career of U.S. government agent, anthropologist, and feminist Alice Fletcher in the last decades of the twentieth century. Following Margaret Strobel's finding with respect to

European women in the colonial setting,[37] Janiewski defines her Euramerican subject both as an agent of cultural imperialism and as a critic
of the colonizing and imperialist project of the expansionist republic. As
a U.S. Indian agent, Fletcher worked to implement a culturally annihi-
lating policy of assimilation, as an anthropologist she sought to preserve remnants of the culture she was helping to eliminate, and as a
white feminist she was looking in Indian culture for traces of matriarchy with which to critique the patriarchy of her own "civilized" society
at the same time as she worked to bring Indian women under the
separate-spheres rule of "civilization."

One way in which white western feminism has produced its own
colonial discourse and participated in the perpetuation of a racist
discourse of civilization has been grandly and blinkeredly to assume
that the West has been and continues to be the fount of all feminist
thought and action. Cheryl Johnson-Odim challenges this imperialist
assumption in Chapter 4, in her study of two women's protest groups
active during the colonial era in Lagos, the capital city of Nigeria.
Johnson-Odim argues that both the grass-roots Lagos Market Wom-
en's Association and the more elite-led Nigerian Women's Party derived their feminism not from western models, but from indigenous
traditions. And she traces the autochthony of both groups' feminism in
their methods of organizing, in their theories of rights, and in their
strategies of protest.

According to the British imperialist world view, civilization emanated out from centers of learning and culture in England, located at the
heart of civilization, to the outposts of civilization, Britain's colonies. In
Australia, Marilyn Lake points out in Chapter 5, the frontier, on the
extreme border of the outskirts of civilization, has figured as definitional of Australian nationality. At the same time the frontier has been
perceived as a quintessentially masculine terrain where white "marauding" frontiersmen roamed free. This context, of a settler colony on
the imperial frontier, Lake argues, gave white Australian feminism of
the late nineteenth and early twentieth centuries its particular contours.
Taking her lead from Adele Perry's work on white women in the
backwoods of British Columbia,[38] Lake finds quite ordinary white
women in Australia drawing on the discursive distinction "between
primitive/barbarous societies and civilized/Christian ones" to position themselves "as the agents of civilization and custodians of the
[white] race." It is only by considering the centrality of racist and
masculinist colonialism to their feminism, Lake maintains, that one can
account for Australian feminists' fixation on "sexuality as inherently
degrading" and their preoccupation with protection—of white women

and of the white race—from the uncontrolled sexual transgressions of unsettled white men.

This position had implications for Australian feminists' relationship to and role in Australian state formation. In Gabriela Cano's analysis in Chapter 6, Mexican feminism played a similarly crucial but different role in the creation of the Mexican national identity. For Cano, the concept of "the Mexican woman" and its relationship to feminism became "a battlefield" on which different definitions of Mexican statehood were contested. For the prerevolutionary conservative government, feminism represented an alien and "double" threat—a threat to "the Mexican woman," imaged as conservative, Catholic, and maternal, and, by its alienizing and masculinizing force, a genocidal threat to Mexican nationhood. Backers of the revolution, in contrast, conceived of "the Mexican woman" as an enemy of rationality and progress and hence of the revolutionary nation in formation. For instrumental reasons, the anticlerical revolutionaries welcomed feminism as a useful weapon in their struggle against the Catholic Church. But neither the politics of conservatism nor the politics of revolution, according to Cano, was free of misogyny. And for all three parties to the question— conservatives, revolutionaries, and feminists alike—their *criollo* identification rested on the violent excision of Indian history and reality from the creation of Mexican national identity.

In Chapter 7, Breda Gray and Louise Ryan read the Irish struggle against British colonialism as more hospitable to feminist activism than the post-1920 nation building of the Irish Free State. The concept of Irish "race" and an insider/outsider dichotomy were used to develop national identity and cultural cohesion in the new republic. Not only did this maneuver have "the effect," in Gray's and Ryan's view, "of underestimating the heterogeneity of Irish people in the 1920s and overestimating the uniqueness of the Irish 'race,'" a focus on Catholic "family values" placed regulation of female sexuality and reproduction at the center of nationalist discourse—as crucial to the sameness the Irish shared and the difference that marked them off from others. The symbolic role that Irish women were assigned in the "family values" script rendered invisible the sexual violence and sexual abuse suffered by women "that were part and parcel of Irish society," and silenced as anti-Irish any feminist demands for women's control over their own sexuality and fertility.

As Gray and Ryan observe, the frequent failure to analyze the positioning and figuration of women in nationalisms is remarkable given the central role women play in the "biological, social, cultural, and symbolic reproduction of nations." In Chapter 8, Joanna de Groot studies women and nationalisms in nineteenth- and twentieth-century Iran. By focusing on the mutual construction of gender identities and the ethnic-cultural identity of "Iranianness," de Groot seeks to illuminate both "the role of nationalism in the political experience of Iranian women, and the constitutive place of women and gender in the history of Iranian nationalism." In the political contestations out of which the Iranian nation-state would emerge, not only were modernist, nationalist, and anti-imperialist discourses shot through with gender and sexual themes, the "woman question" was often at the center of the debates. Lata Mani has argued in her examination of the debate on Sati in colonial India that, "whether viewed as weak, deluded creatures who must be reformed through legislation and education" or as "the valiant keepers" of a religious and ethnic/cultural tradition that must be protected against the corrupting incursions of western modernity, Hindu women came to represent "tradition" for all the debate's participants. Looking at a wide spectrum of views in the nineteenth- and twentieth-century debates in Iran over what would be best for the Iranian nation, de Groot has found Iranian "women" serving a similar symbolic function. As she traces the shifting political fortunes of both Europeanizing "modernizers" and those more concerned with fending off foreign threats to the culture and politics of an Islamic Iran, de Groot detects "women" and "gender issues" operating as "key signifiers of the 'best' outcomes for Iranian social and political life," "women" being linked sometimes with "tradition," sometimes with modernity. Moreover, while Mani found Hindu women to occupy the position of "neither subject, nor object, but ground"[39] in the debate on Sati in India, de Groot's study reveals Iranian women to have occupied all three positions—that of agent, target, and shifting terrain—within both secular and religious conversations in Iran about "Iranianness" and Iranian nationhood. The position of agent, however, was least secured, for, according to de Groot, "the distinctions between 'religious' and 'secular' views were less important" in terms of women's political agency "than the power of discourses" to entrench gender at the core of political language while marginalizing women as political actors in their own right.

Tanika Sarkar in Chapter 9 traces the recent rise to political militancy of women in India who self identify with the cultural nationalism of the Hindu Right. It took eleven years after its founding in 1925 for the Rashtriya Swayamsevak Sangh (RSS), the all-male, umbrella organization of the Hindu Right, to allow the formation of the Rashtrasevika Samiti for women in 1936. Until about ten years ago, the major function of Rashtrasevikas, according to Sarkar, was to provide cadres of Samiti-trained mothers and wives of RSS families to instill the values and self-discipline of Hindu revivalism and supremacism within their own family circles and to proselytize those within their urban, upper-caste, middle-class neighborhoods. The revivalist Hindu supremacist movement of self-reform has survived the many vicissitudes of the twentieth century, Sarkar contends, by endlessly inventing and reinventing the Muslim as the common enemy of the Hindus. What is striking in the last ten years is the emergence of women within the Hindu Right at the forefront of violent campaigns against Indian Muslims. What is also striking is their increasing assumption of a powerful public identity at the same time as they do not contest the Right's conservative prescriptions for gender relations within the domestic sphere. Sarkar concludes that Hindu women on the Right have exchanged the suppression of a politics addressing gender issues for an enlargement of their political space and voice. What Hindu fundamentalist women have exchanged, she believes, is any "individualism based on notions of gender rights or social justice" for a self-individuation based in the new consumerism.

Nation building involves simultaneous processes of identification and differentiation, and these are not necessarily benign in their operations. In Chapter 10, Karen Adler examines the violent underside of these processes as they wreaked havoc with the lives of French Jewish women survivors of Nazism, caught between the murderous racism of the Nazis and the homogenizing forces of postwar French republican nationalism. These women were among the few European Jews to escape the not merely exclusionary but determinedly exterminationist[40] antisemitism of the Nazi attempt to build a racially pure "Volksgemeinschaft."[41] But they returned to a liberated France intent on constructing "the French" as identical with "the Resistance" and on leveling all distinctions in degree of persecution and suffering at the hands of the Nazi occupiers. In this homogenization, the particular histories of Jewish women survivors were tragically misrepresented, and their assimilation to the French republican nationalist identity was called into question. How could Jewish mothers who "passively" gave up their children in order to preserve their lives claim membership in the Resistance? How could one be identified as a Resister when to flee for one's life was seen as cowardly running away? Adler explores the "matrix of ambivalence" Jewish women survivors negotiated in France after the Liberation.

In Chapter 11, in a study of the processes of identification and differentiation in nationality formation, Johanna Gehmacher zeroes in on the gendered deployment of antisemitism in German-Nationalist and National Socialist discursive constructions of Austro-German national identity in the 1920s and 1930s. She discovers non-Jewish women as well as non-Jewish men managing not only class conflicts but also gender antagonisms by displacing them onto "race." In a context of sexual violence against women, "Aryan" Austrian women projected fears of rape and other forms of sexual oppression onto the Jewish man. Economically and psychologically insecure "Aryan" Austrian men, meanwhile, resolved their ambivalent attitudes toward female independence by dividing women into "the sisterly 'pure'" on one side and "those 'polluted' by Jews," i.e., the emancipated, on the other. Gehmacher, then, finds non-Jewish Austro-German women as implicated as non-Jewish Austro-German men in the construction of "the Jew" as the demonized and pathologized "Other," the one whom it was necessary to expel "in order to erect a *Volksgemeinschaft*," a homogenized racial / national community.

From the eighteenth century onward, the European "sciences" of race and gender difference, as already noted, were usually pursued in apparent independence of one another. Bourgeois Europeans, male and female, were the focus of disquisitions on the differences between the sexes, while the male body predominated in studies of race.[42] Salient metaphorically and rhetorically as the female figure was in imperialist and colonialist conceptualizations, women of non-European descent tended to be left out of the main articulations of both race and sex theory and of the "empirical" studies on which those theories claimed to be based, except in one important area: that of sexuality. Here, the female racialized "Other" made a strong appearance, not as a rational being but as a sexualized body. The murky depths of the psychosexual dimensions of imperialism, colonialism, and nationalism have begun to be plumbed.[43] These reveal the prurience of the male European gaze, the displacement of sexual fears and desires onto the colonized "Other," the voyeuristic and fetishized fascination with the genitalia and secondary sex characteristics of women of vanquished "races."

European imperialism is replete with accounts of explorers, conquerors, and traders returning to Europe with "specimens" of the subjugated peoples to be put on display. None is more horrific than the case of the Khoisan woman from the Cape of South Africa who was brought to England in 1810, renamed Sara Bartman, and exhibited to the general public as an exotic specimen of exaggerated female sexuality. For Yvette Abrahams, the author of Chapter 12 and a contemporary South African of Khoisan descent, to examine the degradation visited on one of her female ancestors, both during her life and after her death, by members of the cultural and "scientific" elite of Europe is to see the European claim to civilization and humane progress explode into shattered images of barbaric cruelty. The contrived "bestial sexuality" of Sara Bartman served to justify the savagery of colonial conquest and to constrast sharply with desexualized and domesticated white English womanhood, in the process of being turned at the time into a symbol of civilized refinement.

Imperialism has not been, not even in the modern world, an exclusively European phenomenon. In Asia in the 1860s, partly in reaction to incursions from European imperialists, Japan embarked on its own course of modernization and empire building. As in the case of European nationalisms and imperialisms, unequal gender dynamics and myths of race also served to secure and maintain Japanese nationalist and imperialist enterprises. In Chapter 13, Sayoko Yoneda examines the intersection and imbrication of these two systems, the system of racial/ ethnic discrimination and the system of gender abuse, in her study of the Japanese military's sexual exploitation of so-called "comfort women" during the Second World War. For Yoneda, the policy of forcing Korean and Southeast Asian women into prostitution for the pleasure of Japan's men in uniform did not end with Japan's military defeat. Rather, she claims, it has persisted into the postwar world, metamorphosed into the "sex tourism" enjoyed by Japanese businessmen today in the Philippines and other economically impoverished regions. Resisting the notion of Japanese women's "exemption from imperialism," and refusing the division of women into Japanese and Other, Yoneda insists that Japanese women themselves are implicated in both the racist and sexist power relations that created and perpetuate the existence of "comfort women."

In Chapter 14, Karen Dubinsky uncovers the commodification of race and sex in the imperialist dynamics at work in Niagara Falls tourism of the late nineteenth and early twentieth centuries. This was a time when Europe's "scientific" racism was transmogrifying into commodity racism, and photography was facilitating the marketing of European imperialism and colonialism as commodity spectacle. Similar developments were taking place in North America. As Dubinsky discloses, Niagara Falls tourism cashed in on "the appropriation of indigenous cultures as spectacle and souvenir." The existence of a Native community not far from the Falls offered the spectacle of race, often a disappointment to the tourists for whom "Indians" were supposed to be frozen in "anachronistic space." The brisk sales in often fake "Indian" artifacts reveals the coexistence of contempt for the racial "Other" with enchantment—a romanticized fascination satisfied through the act of possessing homogenized fabrications of the "Other's" cultural trappings, an example of what Renato Rosaldo has termed "imperialist nostalgia."[44] White North American women participated alongside their men in these rites of purchase that rendered the culture of the Other kitsch and reinscribed the power relations between triumphing tourist and subordinate Other. The reading of a sexually alluring Native woman into the Falls was a version of the eroticization of the unfamiliar, the feminization of Nature, common among European explorers and adventurers. While not in possession of this male gaze, female tourists, according to Dubinsky, were no different from male tourists in their disdain for the racialized and economically marginalized others whose subservient labor made the very experience of tourism possible.[45]

In our talk about commodity racism and commodity imperialism, it is important to remember that in nationalist and imperialist conflicts actual women have been turned into commodities, to be bought and sold, to be raped and discarded. In Chapter 15, Aparna Basu draws our attention to the fate of women, both Hindu and Muslim, at the time of the Partition of the Indian subcontinent in 1947 into Pakistan and India. Her study reveals the violence at the core of the politics of sexuality in national/cultural consolidation and differentiation. As the signifiers of national identity, and of cultural/ethnic purity, women became the targets of the brutality of their group's opponents, for in such an economy of signs, "wounds inflicted on" a community's women "scarred and tainted" the entire community. That abductions of women would occur was apparently anticipated by both sides to the Partition with the passage of legislation requiring the return of abducted women and the establishment of machinery of rescue and recovery. Basu's study of this rescue and recovery work reveals, however, that the boundaries drawn by the taboo against hybridization were transgressed not exclusively out of retribution but also out of desire.

The reflections of historical sociologist/sociological historian Himani Bannerji in Chapter 16 serve as a conclusion to this collection as they served to conclude the Montréal conference. As it is not the role of introductions to summarize conclusions, no such summary will be offered here. But a cluster of issues raised by Bannerji merit pre-iteration. Writing history, Bannerji reminds us, entails the responsibilities of political/ontological representation as well as aesthetic/epistemological re-presentation.[46] And the history we write as feminist historians is as discursive a practice, as much an act of knowledge production with power political effects, as any other history writing. The Federation has been rather more successful in bringing a global perspective to bear at the level of re-presentation than at the level of political/ontological representation. Although our sixteen contributors come from eleven different countries around the world, the white-dominated areas of Europe, North America, and Australia are most heavily represented. The Federation has been able to recruit national committee memberships more easily from the more affluent, westernized, and "developed" parts of the world, and from the white majority populations in those lands, than from Africa, Asia, or Latin America. While the International Federation is striving to become more global, the fact that our internationalism remains so heavily European, North American, and Australian in composition reflects the persistence into the present day of the very systems of empire, colony, and nation and the resulting global inequalities in power and resource distribution that the Montréal conference and now this book seek to address. Yet is it not in itself historically significant that the International Federation for Research in Women's History/Fédération internationale pour la recherche en histoire des femmes has turned to histories of nationalisms, colonialisms, and imperialisms in the second half of the 1990s? And, true to the tradition of critical concern for the connections between the past and the present that has been the hallmark of the best of feminist women's history, many of the contributors to this book use their investigations of imperialist, colonialist, and nationalist processes in history to shed light on the relations of power in global and local politics and culture today. We recognize that the writing of history is not ideologically innocent and that there is no way, individually or collectively, that we could have avoided all epistemological traps and pitfalls. But within those constraints, not the least of which is writing in the language of the colonizer in the case of many of us, we have striven to produce historical re-presentations responsibly and by so doing to contribute our feminist analyses to the growing interrogations of the implications of empire, colony, and nation for gender and race and of gender and race for imperialism, colonialism, and nationalism.

NOTES

This introduction owes much to the challenging questions and stunning insights of the students in my graduate seminar, "Women, Colonialisms, Imperialisms, and Nationalisms in History," over the last two years.

1. See, for example, Frantz Fanon, *The Wretched of the Earth* (New York: Grove Press, 1963); Edward W. Said, *Orientalism* (New York: Vintage Books, 1978); Ernest Gellner, *Nations and Nationalism* (Oxford: Blackwell, 1983); Benedict Anderson, *Imagined Communities: Reflections on the Origin and Spread of Nationalism*, rev. ed. (London: Verso, 1991); Partha Chatterjee, *Nationalist Thought and the Colonial World: A Derivative Discourse* (Tokyo: Zed Books for United Nations University, 1986); V. G. Kiernan, *Imperialism and Its Contradictions*, ed. Harvey J. Kaye (New York: Routledge, 1995).

2. This disagreement has principally exercised Anglo–North American feminist historians, for, as the European feminist theorist Rosi Braidotti points out, "the notion of 'gender' is a vicissitude of the *English language*, one which bears little or no relevance to theoretical traditions in the Romance languages," or in other language groups, for that matter. For a European feminist statement of opposition to gender theory, see the interview of Rosi Braidotti with Judith Butler, "Feminism by Any Other Name," *Differences: A Journal of Feminist Cultural Studies* 6, nos. 2 and 3 (1994): 27–61.

For examples of contributions to the Anglo–North American debate, see Laura Lee Downs, "If 'Woman' Is Just an Empty Category, Then Why Am I Afraid to Walk Alone at Night? Identity Politics Meets the Post-modern Subject"; Joan W. Scott, "'The Tip of the Volcano,'" and Laura Downs, "Reply to Joan Scott," *Comparative Studies in Society and History* 35, no. 2 (April 1993): 414–37, 438–43, 444–51; Joan Hoff, "Gender as a Postmodern Category of Paralysis," *Women's History Review* 3, no. 2 (1994): 149–68; Joan Sangster, "Re-assessing Gender History and Women's History in Canada," *Left History: An Interdisciplinary Journal of Historical Inquiry & Debate* 3, no. 1 (Spring–Summer 1995), 109–21; Karen Dubinsky and Lynne Marks, "Beyond Purity: A Response to Sangster," Franca Iacovetta and Linda Kealey, "Women's History, Gender History and Debating Dichotomies," and Joan Sangster, "Reconsidering Dichotomies," *Left History* 3–4, nos. 2–1 (Fall 1995–Spring 1996), 205–20, 221–37, 239–48.

3. Norma Alarcón, "The Theoretical Subject(s) of This Bridge Called My Back and Anglo-American Feminism," in Gloria Anzaldúa, ed., *Making Face, Making Soul* Haciendo Caras: *Creative and Critical Perspectives by Women of Color* (San Francisco: Aunt Lute Foundation, 1990), 360.

4. Leonore Davidoff and Catherine Hall, *Family Fortunes: Men and Women of the English Middle Class 1780–1850* (Chicago: University of Chicago Press, 1987).

5. See, inter alia, Evelyn Brooks Higginbotham, "African-American Women's History and the Metalanguage of Race," *Signs: Journal of Women in Culture and Society* 17, no. 2 (Winter 1992): 251–74; Patricia Hill Collins, *Black Feminist Thought: Knowledge, Consciousness, and the Politics of Empowerment* (Boston: Unwin Hyman, 1990); Patricia Morton, *Disfigured Images: The Historical Assault on Afro-American Women* (New York: Praeger, 1991); Dolores E. Janiewski, *Sisterhood Denied: Race, Gender, and Class in a New South Community* (Philadelphia: Temple University Press, 1985); Darlene Clark Hine, *Black Women in White: Racial Conflict and Cooperation in the Nursing Profession, 1890–1950* (Bloomington: Indiana University Press, 1989); Dionne Brand, "Bread Out of Stone," in Libby Scheier, Sarah Sheard and Eleanor Wachtel, eds., *Language in Her Eye: Writing and Gender* (Toronto: Coach House Press, 1990), 45–53.

6. Gayatri Chakravorty Spivak, *The Post-Colonial Critic: Interviews, Strategies, Dialogues*, ed. Sarah Harasym (New York: Routledge, 1990), 5.

7. The term "global" is not being used here in the sense of the slogan "sisterhood is global," which has been considered to be a western hegemonic construction. See, for example, Inderpal Grewal and Caren Kaplan, eds., "Introduction," *Scattered Hegemonies: Postmodernity and Transnational Feminist Practices* (Minneapolis: University of Minnesota Press, 1994).

8. As Nupur Chaudhuri and Cheryl Johnson-Odim have written, "A global perspective on women's activity is a necessary corrective to a Eurocentric view of feminism." Chaudhuri and Johnson-Odim, "Introduction," *Special Issue: Global Perspectives*, ed. Nupur Chaudhuri and Cheryl Johnson-Odim, *NWSA [National Women's Studies Association] Journal* 8, no. 1 (Spring 1996): 1.

9. Inderpal Grewal, *Home and Harem: Nation, Gender, Empire and the Cultures of Travel* (Durham: Duke University Press, 1996), 9.

10. Mary Louise Pratt, *Imperial Eyes: Travel Writing and Transculturation* (New York: Routledge, 1992), 6.

11. Grewal, *Home and Harem*, 4.

12. See Edward W. Said, *Culture and Imperialism* (New York: Alfred A. Knopf, 1993). As Mary Louise Pratt has written, "While the imperial metropolis tends to understand itself as determining the periphery (in the emanating glow of the civilizing mission or the cash flow of development, for example), it habitually blinds itself to the ways in which the periphery determines the metropolis . . ." *Imperial Eyes*, 6.

13. For instance, the movement of western medicine and public health into the colonized world is perceived by the imperial mind-set as producing nothing but good for the "natives." See, for example, Nancy Rose Hunt, "'Le bébé en brousse': European Women, African Birth Spacing, and Colonial Intervention in Breast Feeding in the Belgian Congo," in Frederick Cooper and Ann Laura Stoler, eds., *Tensions of Empire: Colonial Cultures in a Bourgeois World* (Berkeley and Los Angeles: University of California Press, 1997), 287–321.

14. "Dismantling the careful bracketing that contained metropolitan and colonial history . . . has not only become unwieldy as an individual effort, but difficult for either fledgling graduate student or seasoned scholar to sustain." Ann Laura Stoler, *Race and the Education of Desire: Foucault's History of Sexuality and the Colonial Order of Things* (Durham: Duke University Press, 1995), xii.

15. For example, Cheryl Johnson-Odim and Margaret Strobel, eds., *Expanding the Boundaries of Women's History* (Bloomington: Indiana University Press, 1992).

16. Anne McClintock, *Imperial Leather: Race, Gender and Sexuality in the Colonial Context*, 1, 3. Londa Schiebinger argues that "the explosion of knowledge associated with the rise of modern [western] science," involving as it frequently did the exclusion of knowledge not generated and controlled by Europeans and occurring in tandem with massive cultural extinction through colonialisms, imperialisms, and nationalisms, might well have "resulted in a loss of knowledge in the long run." L. Schiebinger, *Nature's Body: Gender in the Making of Modern Science* (Boston: Beacon Press, 1993), 209.

17. Carole Pateman, *The Sexual Contract* (Stanford: University of Stanford Press, 1988).

18. David Theo Goldberg, *Racist Culture: Philosophy and the Politics of Meaning* (Oxford: Blackwell, 1993), 3–8.

19. Londa Schiebinger attributes this move only to those "in conservative quarters," whereas theorists such as Goldberg and Pateman would argue that the gendered and racialized structures of difference, dominance, and subordination were integral to liberalism's project. Schiebinger, *Nature's Body*, 9.

20. See Thomas Laqueur, *Making Sex: Body and Gender from the Greeks to Freud* (Cambridge: Harvard University Press, 1990). A gender ideology based in a notion of biological bipolarity became fully elaborated during the Victorian era. See, for example, Mary Poovey, *Uneven Developments: The Ideological Work of Gender in Mid-Victorian England* (Chicago: University of Chicago Press, 1988), and Deirdre David, *Women, Empire, and Victorian Writing* (Ithaca: Cornell University Press, 1995).

21. See Schiebinger, *Nature's Body*, and George L. Mosse, *Toward the Final Solution: A History of European Racism* (New York: Howard Fertig, Inc., 1978).

22. See Mrinalina Sinha, *Colonial Masculinity: The 'Manly Englishman' and the 'Effeminate Bengali' in the Late Nineteenth Century* (Manchester: Manchester

University Press, 1995). Feminine attributes, regarded as inferior to the masculine attributes, were also ascribed to male members of excluded, despised, and discriminated-against racial minorities within the European "mother" country or the *Vaterland*, such as Jews. See Otto Weininger, *Geschlecht und Charakter* (Wien, 1903), discussed in Solomon Liptzin, *Germany's Stepchildren* (Philadelphia: Jewish Publication Society of America, 1944), passim, and in Mosse, *Toward the Final Solution*, 101, 108–11.

23. See Leonore Davidoff, "Class and Gender in Victorian England: The Case of Hannah Cullwick and A. J. Munby," in *Worlds Between: Historical Perspectives on Gender & Class* (New York: Routledge, 1995), 103–50, reprinted from *Feminist Studies* 5, no. 1 (Spring 1979).

24. McClintock, *Imperial Leather*, 36. See, also, Karen Hansen, ed., *African Encounters with Domesticity* (New Brunswick, NJ: Rutgers University Press, 1992).

25. See, inter alia, Luise White, "Separating the Men from the Boys: Constructions of Gender, Sexuality, and Terrorism in Central Kenya, 1939–1959," *International Journal of African Historical Studies* 23, no. 1 (1990): 1–25; Ann L. Stoler, "Making Empire Respectable: The Politics of Race and Sexual Morality in 20th Century Colonial Cultures," *American Ethnologist* 16, no. 4 (1989): 634–60; and Ann L. Stoler, "Carnal Knowledge and Imperial Power: Gender, Race, and Morality in Colonial Asia," in Michaela di Leonardo, ed., *Gender at the Crossroads of Knowledge* (Berkeley and Los Angeles: University of California Press, 1991), 51–101.

26. Arthur Lovejoy, *The Great Chain of Being* (New York: Harper Torchbooks, 1960).

27. See Gail Bederman, *Manliness and Civilization: A Cultural History of Gender and Race in the United States, 1880–1917* (Chicago: University of Chicago Press, 1995).

28. Mosse, *Toward the Final Solution*, 83–87; McClintock, *Imperial Leather*, 52–56; Ann L. Stoler, "Carnal Knowledge and Imperial Power," 72–80.

29. McClintock, *Imperial Leather*, 40.

30. Gayatri Chakravorty Spivak, "Can the Subaltern Speak?" in Cary Nelson and Lawrence Grossberg, eds., *Marxism and the Interpretation of Culture* (Urbana: University of Illinois Press, 1988), 280–81.

31. The reshaping of gender dynamics and gender identities was also critical to the imperialist and colonialist project of subjugating Native peoples in Canada, particularly through the domestication of Native women. Karen Anderson, *Chain Her by One Foot: The Subjugation of Native Women in Seventeenth-Century New France* (New York: Routledge, 1991).

32. McClintock, *Imperial Leather*, 40.

33. Antoinette Burton refers to the influence of Virginia "Woolf, who claimed white English women's exemption from imperialism." A. Burton, "Recapturing Jane Eyre: Reflections on Historicizing the Colonial Encounter in Victorian Britain," *Radical History Review* 64 (Winter 1996): 64, 70, cited the following passage from Virginia Woolf, *A Room of One's Own* (New York: Harcourt Brace Jovanovich, 1929/1981), 50: "It is one of the great advantages of being a woman that one can pass even a very fine Negress without wanting to make an Englishwoman of her."

34. Chandra Talpade Mohanty, "Under Western Eyes: Feminist Scholarship and Colonial Discourses," in C. T. Mohanty, Ann Russo, and Lourdes Torres, eds., *Third World Women and the Politics of Feminism* (Bloomington: Indiana University Press, 1991), 51–80; Valerie Amos and Pratibha Parmar, "Challenging Imperial Feminism," *Feminist Review* 17 (July 1984): 3–19; bell hooks,

"Feminism and Militarism: A Comment," in *Talking Back: Thinking Feminist, Thinking Black* (Toronto: Between the Lines, 1988), 92– 97; Mary Louise Fellows and Sherene Razack, *The Race to Innocence: Hierarchical Relations among Women, Iowa Law Review*, forthcoming.

35. Catherine Hall, *White, Male and Middle Class: Explorations in Feminism and History* (New York: Routledge, 1992).

36. Antoinette Burton, *Burdens of History: British Feminists, Indian Women, and Imperial Culture, 1865–1915* (Chapel Hill: University of North Carolina Press, 1994). See, also, Vron Ware, *Beyond the Pale: White Women, Racism and History* (London: Verso, 1992); Nupur Chaudhuri and Margaret Strobel, eds., *Western Women and Imperialism: Complicity and Resistance* (Bloomington: Indiana University Press, 1992); and Billie Melman, *Women's Orients: English Women and the Middle East, 1718–1918: Sexuality, Religion and Work* (Ann Arbor: University of Michigan Press, 1992).

37. Margaret Strobel, "Gender and Race in the Nineteenth- and Twentieth-Century British Empire, " in Renate Bridenthal, Claudia Koonz, and Susan Stuard, eds. *Becoming Visible: Women in European History* (Boston: Houghton Mifflin Co., 1987), 375–95. These ideas are more fully developed in Margaret Strobel, *European Women and the Second British Empire* (Bloomington: Indiana University Press, 1991).

38. Adele Perry, "'How Influential a Few Men and a Few Families Become': White Women, Families, and Colonialism in Nineteenth-Century British Columbia," paper presented at the 18th International Congress of Historical Sciences, Montréal, Québec, August 1995, revised as "'Fair Ones of a Pure Caste': White Women and Colonialism in Nineteenth-Century British Columbia," *Feminist Studies* 23, no. 3 (Fall 1997).

39. Lata Mani, "Contentious Traditions: The Debate on Sati in Colonial India," in Kumkum Sangari and Sudesh Vaid, eds., *Recasting Women: Essays in Indian Colonial History* (New Brunswick, NJ: Rutgers University Press, 1990), 117, 118.

40. See Daniel Jonah Goldhagen, *Hitler's Willing Executioners: Ordinary Germans and the Holocaust* (New York: Alfred A. Knopf, 1996), for an exposition of the pervasiveness in German culture of an "eliminationist" antisemitism before the Nazis came to power.

41. Literally translated as "community of the people." In the emerging German nationalist discourse of the late eighteenth and early nineteenth centuries, *Volk* stood for the people of the nation but, as George L. Mosse has argued, racism is a "scavenger ideology," and by the second half of the nineteenth century, German racism had annexed nationalism (as well as bourgeois respectability), racializing *Volk* in the process. Mosse, *Toward the Final Solution*, and George L. Mosse, *Nationalism and Sexuality: Middle-Class Morality and Sexual Norms in Modern Europe* (Madison: University of Wisconsin Press, 1985), 10.

42. Schiebinger, *Nature's Body*, 160.

43. See, for example, Sander Gilman, *The Jew's Body* (London: Routledge, 1991).

44. "Imperialist nostalgia uses a pose of 'innocent yearning' both to capture people's imaginations and to conceal its complicity with often brutal domination." Renato Rosaldo, "Imperialist Nostalgia," *Representations* 26 (1989): 108. See also bell hooks, "Eating the Other: Desire and Resistance," in *Black Looks: Race and Representation* (Toronto: Between the Lines, 1992), 21–39.

45. For a study that has laid some of the critical groundwork for our understanding of the relations between and among race, colonialism, and to

some extent gender within tourism in Canada, see Patricia Jasen, *Wild Things: Nature, Culture and Tourism in Ontario* (Toronto: University of Toronto Press, 1995).

46. Gayatri Chakravorty Spivak likens the difference between representation and re-presentation to that between "a proxy and a portrait." Basing her discussion of the difference on a reading of Karl Marx's *The Eighteenth Brumaire of Louis Bonaparte*, she points out that, in German, the two senses are conveyed by two different terms, namely *vertreten* and *darstellen*. Spivak, "Can the Subaltern Speak?" 275–80.

1

Maori Agriculturalists and Aboriginal Hunter-Gatherers

*Women and Colonial Displacement in Nineteenth-Century
Aotearoa/New Zealand and Southeastern Australia*

PATRICIA GRIMSHAW

Starting at the end of the eighteenth century and continuing
into the nineteenth, British migrants invaded and occupied lands of
Aborigines in southeastern Australia and of Maori in Aotearoa/New
Zealand. Aborigines and Maori of both sexes shared the trauma that
resulted from the killings, from aggravated internecine disputes, from
the resultant hunger, poverty, and diseases. Humanitarians and missionaries attempted to protect survivors and mitigate the harshness of
their lives, but pursued at the same time, with great insensitivity, their
conversion to western religious and social forms. The similarities between the fates of the two peoples were considerable as settler populations increased with rapidity. Compared with Maori, however, Aborigines faced more severe conditions of displacement, forced as they were
from their former lives as hunter-gatherers into virtual confinement on
reserves and mission stations, from the 1860s onward. Maori, defeated
in a full-scale war with the British in the 1860s, subsisted thereafter on
marginal land by farming and unskilled labor. Nevertheless, unlike
Aborigines, Maori sustained a place in the settler economy and its
public life, including exercising male voting rights and participating in
mainstream politics.

This chapter presents a comparative analysis of the experiences of
women in this drastic phase of colonial displacement. Given that both

societies were initially preliterate, developing a written language only gradually through mission education, few literary sources created by the women themselves survive from the period. The nature of Aboriginal and Maori women's traditional place in their own communities, and their responses to the processes of change, have been in large part constructed from texts written by those Europeans in closest contact with them: men—and a very few women—who were travelers and adventurers, colonial officials and missionaries. These observers did not offer "facts" or "information," but detail and anecdote couched in value-laden terms. These texts must be interrogated with caution if we wish to reconstruct indigenous women's lives in the early nineteenth century, and to understand the dominant colonial discourses shaping cultural attitudes about gender and race.[1]

Similar to the situation of women described by postcolonial feminist scholars for colonial India, representations of southeastern Aboriginal women emphasized their victimlike status at the hands of Aboriginal men. Representations of Maori women, however, were more highly contested, in part as a result of the more stratified nature of Maori society that endowed certain highborn women, as well as men, with ascriptive rights to authority. Observers were impressed with the power some Maori women exercised to offset the social disadvantages, as the British viewed it, of such practices as polygamy. Maori women and Aboriginal women alike were judged by an ideal of Victorian femininity, of dutiful housewifery and motherhood, and disparaged when they fell short of it. One important section of Maori women, however, commanded and sustained a respect arising from their elevated indigenous status—a status that the class-bound British themselves recognized, albeit grudgingly.

Discourses on gender in Aboriginal and Maori society were part of the many-layered processes of British settlers' drive for land and resources in both sites of colonization. Yet the comparative advantage of Maori women over Aboriginal women was significant and was crystalized in their civic status at the turn of the century. In 1893, Maori women became acknowledged citizens of Aotearoa/New Zealand when, along with white women, they were granted the vote. Aboriginal women, by contrast, shared the fate of Aboriginal men of debarment from citizenship in 1901 to 1902, at the time of the federation of the six Australian colonies into the Commonwealth of Australia. (Ironically, any New Zealand resident of Australia, whether Maori or European, woman or man, received, in principle, voting rights in this same Act.) The limits of citizenship could be found in the continuing health, educational, and material disadvantages that most Maori women, like Aboriginal women, sustained into the twentieth century.[2]

THE ARRIVAL OF THE BRITISH

Australia and New Zealand were first uncovered for European knowledge from the reports of the seventeenth-century Dutch explorer Captain Abel Tasman and the eighteenth-century Englishman Captain James Cook. Aborigines had dwelled on the Australian land mass for 40,000 years or more, Maori in the islands of Aotearoa/New Zealand probably since the fourteenth century A.D. The first white settlement in Australia was established in 1788 with the arrival in Sydney of a contingent of soldiers and a few hundred convicts, who were sent from overcrowded British jails to serve their term in a strange, distant land. Numbers increased rapidly over the next few decades, not only of felons but of free settlers, farmers, traders, colonial officials, and missionaries. Settlement fanned out into surrounding districts, to Port Phillip (later Victoria) and South Australia, and southeast to the island of Tasmania. Those who had ventured as far as southeastern Australia might also consider the attractions of Aotearoa/New Zealand, a thousand miles across the Tasman Sea. Sealers, whalers, adventurers, and missionaries gained a foothold at harbors around the coast. The Reverend Samuel Marsden, an Anglican from the Sydney settlement, preached the first Christian sermon to curious Maori in the Bay of Islands, north of Auckland, on Christmas Day, 1814. British intruders sought, above all, possession of land in order to exploit it in European style.[3]

Aborigines and Maori greeted the newcomers in a variety of ways. Southeastern Aborigines were hunter-gatherers, shifting seasonally in tribal and kin groups within their appropriate territories as they sought game, fish, shellfish, fruits, and edible plants. There were many groups, with a number of different languages and dialects, and with persistent enmities and affinities among them. Maori were part of the Polynesian peoples of the eastern and southern Pacific islands, including Hawaii, Tahiti, the Marquesas, Tonga, and Samoa. Like other Polynesians, Maori were horticulturalists, living in villages, farming and fishing, sustaining strong loyalties to family and tribal groups; they too engaged in sporadic hostilities with some tribes and sustained reciprocal support with others. Both Aborigines and Maori had oral cultures; written languages appeared only in the wake of European presence. Their material possessions were crafted from wood and stone, animals and feathers, and were often skillfully and beautifully made. Some of the first Aboriginal and Maori people to confront the new arrivals on their shores were hostile, some curious, some hospitable, some eager to engage in trade for mutual benefit. At first, the British, whatever their various purposes for stepping ashore, needed to negotiate for food, for places to erect shelter, and for freedom from assault.

As the number of white intruders increased, however, the delicacy of their negotiations declined. British settlers, though a tiny minority, were backed by the technical superiority of guns, and soldiers and sailors to wield them on their behalf in organized assault, where their individual efforts to gain political paramountcy failed. The conquest was swifter and more total in southeastern Australia. To make a good living, the more ambitious settlers sought large tracts of land for pastoralism, for sheep above all, since wool was the product that could be profitably transported back to England. Scattered bands of Aborigines stood in the way of this settlement, resisting by guerilla warfare tactics as best they could, but they were no match for the ruthless British entrepreneurs and their workers, who were often ex-convicts. By the 1850s, most of the land that Europeans could exploit for rural economic pursuits was occupied, thousands upon thousands of Aborigines were dead from violence or introduced diseases, and survivors were eking out a meager living on the margins of pastoral properties or rural towns. There were no treaties made. The 1860s witnessed the creation of rural missions and reserves for the survivors of the Aboriginal holocaust and the pressure of colonial governments to persuade Aborigines into these ghettoes of surveillance and regulation.[4]

In Aotearoa/New Zealand, the process of dispossession proceeded more slowly because a sizable population of Maori retained occupation of the desirable land, and Maori acquired and used guns effectively. In 1840, representatives of Queen Victoria and Maori chiefs signed the Treaty of Waitangi, an ambiguous document at best, but one which, however interpreted, certainly promised concessions to Maori land rights and livelihoods in exchange for acceptance of British sovereignty. When misunderstandings drove some Maori to combine forces in an effort to resist further settler encroachment, the pitched battles of the Maori wars of the 1860s brought conflict into the open. Defeated, their best land confiscated, Maori retreated to farming and rural labor, for the most part where settlers did not care to live. In contrast to Aborigines, however, Maori remained numerically stronger in relation to the settler population; they sustained livelihoods independent of state assistance and continued to present a more united (if no longer martial) challenge to successive governments in a developing democracy. That partial resistance to domination was facilitated in part by acceptance in some form of both Christianity and western education.[5]

Understanding the part that representations of gender played in these colonial displacements demands close attention to the texts created by those Europeans—almost entirely men—whose close descriptions of the indigenous people commanded public attention, both in

Britain and in the colonies. These significant writings came from the pens of travelers and settlers, missionaries and colonial officials. Many of these observers had a more than cursory acquaintance with indigenous groups, although this ranged from living in close association in the earliest phase of white incursion to encountering indigenous peoples after very considerable social dislocation had occurred. While the focus of this essay is on an analysis of colonial discourses, it recognizes that ethnohistorians from the turn of the century to the present have relied considerably on information from these very same texts to construct descriptions of these early-nineteenth-century societies. Alternative sources of understanding have lain in archaeological evidence and in the oral traditions of the indigenous peoples, but the latter have been slow to reach wider audiences: Maori and Aboriginal writers are now beginning to speak, write, and publish more freely than before, but this has been a relatively recent phenomenon.

Modern ethnohistorical accounts, then, must be viewed as themselves constructions by specifically situated scholars, almost all western in origin, largely relying on documents handed down from other specifically situated westerners writing 150 or more years before them. In the case of Australia, ethnohistorians also extrapolate from twentieth-century anthropological studies of Aborigines still living in remote areas far from centers of European settlement, and ethnohistorians of both peoples rely on comparative studies on a global scale. The deficiencies of sources accepted, one might, albeit schematically and briefly, offer the following summaries of how ethnohistorians have portrayed these indigenous women's social position. For Maori, ethnohistorians would emphasize the differentiation of women according to status within a highly stratified society. Maori society, like other Polynesian groups (especially Hawaiian), resembled feudal society, with a powerful chiefly group imbued with religious authority: chiefly women as well as men, from birth to death, commanded enormous respect from commoners. There were also slave women, usually hostages seized in battle, whose lives were miserable indeed. So while women as a whole might have been subject to some similar definition by virtue of sex, ascriptive power or lack of it rivaled gender scripts in shaping women's lives.[6]

Few specific extensive ethnohistorical accounts of southeastern Aboriginal women exist, and it is rather more to the generalizations of anthropologists that a historian must turn. Anthropologists have discovered Aboriginal women as possessing considerable influence, but within a society sharply divided on lines of gender. They suggest that women increased their status over the course of their life cycle, from the relatively powerless period of girlhood to a respected older age; and that women were integral and important to the material survival of the entire clan and valued accordingly; and that women were important within their families of origin as well as within their new kinship affiliations through marriage, and derived status and strength from this. The issue of women's overall power remains contested territory, with a debate concerning Aboriginal women's social status revolving around the nature and degree of their economic, spiritual, and child-rearing roles, but the overall image, particularly in the work of feminist scholars, is a positive one, suggesting mutual respect between women and men.[7]

But we return now to the past, and to the characterizations of women and of gender relations, which were placed before a colonial and a British readership by early male observers: first, to their attempts to make sense of the Maori.

THE BRITISH GAZE AND MAORI WOMEN

The visitors and early settlers who described Maori society pointed frequently and with surprise to the important place of Maori women and to the degree of influence and power they at times clearly possessed. Maori women, it seemed, were extremely significant socially as seen by their husbands, their children, their kin, and their tribal group. "The women are not held in bondage, but have a share of influence corresponding with the natural strength of their character,"[8] wrote one. Maori women were treated by men "with great consideration and kindness, enjoying the full exercise of their free will, and possessing a remarkable influence in all the affairs of the tribe,"[9] said another. And again, Maori women exercised "the greatest influence over their tribes; especially the widows of important chiefs, or aged women, some of whom are supposed to possess the power of witchcraft and sorcery."[10]

Maori women were not apathetic or reticent spectators of any major occasion, but were visible and volubly active participants: they organized resources, marshaled a labor force, and welcomed and entertained guests. "On feasts being given or when a fishing party is proposed, the first wife is accounted mistress of the ceremonies, and is looked up to with deference accordingly."[11] This pivotal role flowed from the active part women played in essential labor: in preparing soil for planting, sowing, and reaping; in cooking the food; and in weaving mats, cloaks, and baskets. Nonslave women appear to have undertaken similar work, whatever their age or standing. Many men reiterated the claim of the missionary Samuel Marsden of the Church Missionary

Society that female chiefs undertook physical labor, when on a visit in 1819 he observed the wife of the chief Hongi Heke digging a potato field. He expressed appreciation that "a woman of the first rank" would labor alongside her servants and children.[12]

The strength Maori women displayed in work was portrayed as a mirror image of their wider influence in their families and tribal groups. In European eyes the most remarkable demonstration of their courage, and their influence, was women's involvement on the battlefield. Wives accompanied husbands to battle, spurring them on to deeds of valor, singing, shouting, and supporting their men in every way. Sometimes, indeed, they entered the fray themselves. A naval officer noted one chiefly wife who displayed "the most undaunted spirit, rivalling the boldest men in deeds of heroism, and selecting for her antagonist the most formidable she could find." Such warrior women were, he hastened to add, only "certain ladies of more intrepid character than the rest."[13]

Augustus Earle, like so many writers, recorded the women's loyalty and devotion to their husbands. He described elderly couples who had married in youth, lived happily together all their lives, and "whose kind and friendly manner towards each other set an example well worth of imitation in many English families."[14] One described wives as their husbands' "constant companions." Another thought that married couples could sustain a disconcerting distance from each other, as though unrelated, and could be found sleeping separately quite soon after marriage. But it was rare, they agreed, for married couples to quarrel, and "still rarer for a husband to beat his wife."[15]

The depth of wives' attachment to husbands could be measured by their supreme bravery. When husbands died or were killed in warfare, their wives committed suicide, mostly by hanging or drowning themselves. This act Europeans distinguished from widow burning in India, since the wives themselves took courageous initiative, apparently driven by their overwhelming grief and desperate wish to follow their husbands to the grave: no prompting or persuasion was needed. Stories were told of dramatic, public acts of a wife's suicide at the news of her husband's death, and of agonized wives plaiting their suicide ropes as they kept watch at their husbands' deathbeds. "The ardour of affection or rather devotion, that has been exhibited by the sex in New Zealand, has never been surpassed in any period or in any country," thought one traveler.[16]

Writers of the same accounts that detailed the influence and status enjoyed by many Maori women frequently made starkly contradictory statements about women's status, especially when they moved from a description of the particular to attempting wider generalizations. Often, while claiming that unmarried women were equal to men in privileges and freedom, they added, "when married, their freedom is at an end; they become mere slaves, and sink gradually into domestic drudges to those who have the power of life and death over them."[17] They pointed most graphically to the dramatic feature of marriage that mesmerized observers: that the errant wife risked instant death at the hands of her vengeful husband when she was found in an adulterous relationship. Maori women were praised for holding fidelity in marriage in high esteem, but the sanction for transgression was certainly awful.

> The favours of a married woman in New Zealand are full as difficult of attainment as in any part of the world, the punishment of death being awarded as the penalty for an infringement of the nuptial bond, which is held by these people in as sacred a light as in the most civilised states.[18]

A traveler held that marriage was "regarded as a most solemn ordinance" in which "married women enjoy as much liberty and exercise as much influence as they do in Europe." But "crimes on their part are visited with the sternness and cruelty of Eastern despotism. Infidelity is invariably visited with death."[19]

And so, although casual domestic violence was rarely reported, writers emphasized that husbands sustained this overwhelmingly terrible right to kill outright an adulterous wife. There was no real reciprocity between the sexes in sexual restraint, since polygamy was said to prevail. European authors experienced a great deal of confusion about the extent of polygamy. Some authors said it only occurred among chiefs, and yet others denied that it was common at all. Most claimed that men had legitimate sexual access to several women or wives. The reasons for polygamy seemed, on the face of it, to prioritize a man's sexual interests, while sustaining a women's fidelity through draconian penalties.

But polygamy was seen by some observers as the cause of many evils, largely arising from the jealousy of co-wives: polygamy was "greatly abhorred by the females of the country" and it caused "unhappiness and incessant brawling."[20] Even if this was not always so, these writers asked, did not polygamy of itself imply a low status for women, whatever the justifications? Observers might occasionally note that if men had the power of life and death over wives in these circumstances, they might well suffer retribution at the hands of their wives' relatives. Overall, however, the emphasis was on tales of swift, brutal, barbaric murder.

European recorders placed Maori women most centrally as wives rather than mothers. Once again, however, when these observers did turn their attention to motherhood, they could write affirmatively of Maori women's maternal capacities. The women, one observer said, greatly desired children, and a woman was "usually held in respect according to the number of children with which she had strengthened the tribe."[21] Childless wives were inconsolable and engaged in ceremonies to intercede with the gods to aid conception. Women's health and strength were emphasized in descriptions of the ease with which they experienced childbirth. Another man reported that women sat in the open air, surrounded by men and women, and gave birth "without uttering a single groan." Thereupon the new mother cut the umbilical cord herself, and "rose up as if no such occurrence had taken place, and resumed her ordinary occupations."[22] Babies were nursed with affection and tenderness, and breast-feeding was said to extend into the child's third year. Mothers showed their young a fierce loyalty, and children traced their all-important descent lines through their mother's as well as their father's lineages. There was no suggestion, as in some other parts of the Pacific, that mothers were "unnatural" and unable to care for their children "properly."

But motherhood, like wifehood, had its terrible aspect, and the two were linked. At the feet of polygamy was laid the cause for a terrible act, perpetrated by mothers: infanticide. Jealous wives were said to kill their infants to spite the fathers when they took new wives, or when they had upset the wife in any way. An observer wrote that, "should a husband quarrel with his wife, she would not hesitate to kill her children merely to *annoy* him."[23]

In this case the wife's act was seen as one of defiance, implying power, not as an indication of servility or degradation. Indeed, one reason given for the surprising observation that fathers, even great chiefs, could be seen carrying infants around on their backs, nestled into their cloaks, for much of the day, was the fear that the child was in jeopardy from a revengeful mother. For others, the Maori fathers' care of infants and toddlers was in part touching and impressive, in part puzzling. Why did grown men devote so much time to the very young? The Europeans knew of wet nurses, but dubbed these fathers "dry nurses."[24] What did this imply for the notion of Maori motherhood? Truly, both parents seemed amazingly indulgent of young children, scarcely ever correcting them and leading them with great kindness into the knowledge and skills they would need in adult life. The Europeans looked askance at the "cheeky" questions and "pestering" behavior of children, but could certainly say that if babies survived their births, they could look forward to careful and loving nurture.

Infanticide, however, was by far the most widely discussed feature of Maori motherhood. Despite the fact that it was rare for observers to go so far as to claim that they had actually seen the act of infanticide, all claimed that it was common and confessed to by countless informants. (William Yate, who served with the Church Missionary Society in the Bay of Islands, was one of the few to claim that he witnessed several cases of infanticide, which he, too, blamed on women's jealousy of co-wives.)[25] Other reasons for infanticide were canvassed, although these were similarly related to the issue of women's status. Was infanticide weighted toward infant girls? Many observers, like the one quoted here, asserted this to be the case:

> The murder of the female infant after birth is, however, often perpetrated by its own mother under a smarting sense of the indignities and sufferings to which every female is exposed, long before she arrives at womanhood, and generally to the latest hour of her life. . . . the fortitude of women, proof against everything but man's neglect, may be overcome, until even natural affection cease to animate her, and the love of the mother be absorbed in the misery of the woman. A greater proof of the degraded estate of the female sex in New Zealand cannot exist, than that which their very crimes, stated above, supply.[26]

Some observers thought that because males were much more esteemed than females, "the latter are chiefly the victims, and are sacrificed that they may escape future miseries."[27] One claimed that the excuse women gave for killing baby girls was "that they were quite as much trouble to rear, and consumed just as much food, as a male child, and yet, when grown up, they were not fit to go to war as their boys were."[28] Another reported that mothers killed daughters in order to flee enemies unencumbered, but spared baby sons since they would in time be warriors.[29]

However, it should be noted that there were Europeans who denied that infanticide was prevalent, and others who denied there was a distinction made by sex. Despite these conflicting reports, and whatever the truth of the matter, the existence of so many graphic and emotive accounts of infanticide meant that assessments of Maori women as wives and mothers were inevitably influenced negatively, affecting popular perceptions of Maori women.

Even observers who described Maori women as well-treated, autonomous, and influential in tribal affairs could qualify their remarks with a description of the adverse physical consequences of their arduous work. Apart from the daughters of high chiefs, Maori women, they stressed, "are burdened with all the heavy work; they have to cultivate the fields, to carry from their distant plantations wood and provisions, and to bear heavy loads during their travelling excursions";[30] "early intercourse," "frequent abortions," and prolonged suckling of children contributed "to cause the early decay of their youth and beauty and are prejudicial to the full development of their frame." Most writers also found abhorrent the mature women's *moku*, or tattooing on the chin.

Observers were unanimous that Maori women, occasional highborn women excepted, aged rapidly: "women arrive very early at maturity, and as early become old and withered."[31] Girls married very early and had lost their youth by the age of thirty. For some, this rapid aging was blamed on the early "promiscuity"; other women were said to be worn down prematurely through the physical toll exacted by their bountiful giving and nurturing of the lives of children, kin, and tribal group. Amazons, these mature women were often called, even if at times "a good-looking, self-willed sort of Amazon," as when a woman saved a group of Europeans from death.

If women's labor was worthy, was it nice? Was it becoming? Women could be seen participating as equals with men in a canoe race and joining the vociferous singing at the race's end. Their exertions seemed violent, inappropriate; "the distinction of sex appearing no longer visible, was completely lost in their convulsive excesses."[32] Maori women may have often seemed to have some freedom of action in public domains, but even if this revealed power, did it go beyond acceptable limits for their sex? And could these public engagements all be justified if the end result was bodies marked by time, bodies that were masculinized?

This concern with women's rapid aging and their "masculine" appearance and behavior reflects the preoccupation of many of the male writers with women's sexuality. Women's appearance is discussed as a measure of their sexual attractiveness to the white male observers. This and other aspects of their sexuality, such as their chastity (or lack thereof), and the extent of women's control over their own bodies in sexual relations and in reproduction, were often the predominant foci of accounts of Maori women. Individual young girls with their fine figures, long flowing hair, laughing eyes, and delicate hands and feet were portrayed as lovely, indeed charming, potential sexual partners and protectors of European men's homes. But there was a problem here too, of course, when their availability was assessed within a context of women's status. Young women were not chaste, not chaste at all. They clearly had series of sexual encounters with Maori youth: "while they remain single they enjoy all the privileges of the other sex; they may rove where they please, and bestow their favours on whom they choose,

and are entirely beyond control or restraint."[33] Some observers depicted those young women living near ports as exchanging sexual favors
for European goods with apparent alacrity, although there was considerable disagreement among observers as to the extent of women's willing participation, and whether or not they were "naturally licentious."
Many early observers said that slave women were involved at first,
while others declared that any unmarried women, except chiefly wom-
en, were participating. Was this not sheer prostitution? And were not
prostitutes of low status? But the women who *were* chaste, their mothers
and grandmothers, were viewed as signally unattractive, unfeminine
in appearance and demeanor.

Representations of Maori women were, in these ways, contested,
partly as a result of the stratification of Maori society and the fact that
authority accrued to highborn women as well as to highborn men. The
impressive power exercised by some Maori women offset, in the eyes of
some British observers, the social disadvantages they associated with
polygamy.

While Aboriginal women were also judged by an ideal of Victorian
femininity (of dutiful housewifery and motherhood), in contrast to
depictions of their Maori counterparts, representations of Aboriginal
women more consistently emphasized their victimhood at the hands of
Aboriginal men.

THE BRITISH GAZE AND ABORIGINAL WOMEN

"The Government of the Aborigines is strictly Patriarchal";
"The position of the women is one of great degradation"; "The women
... are generally a most miserable and truly pitiable race of beings, over
whom the men exercise a cruel and tyrannical despotism"; "as regards
the females, they must obediently serve their masters in every season
and under all circumstances."[34] Writer after writer in the early white
colonies of Australia offered views in this mode, impervious to sources of Aboriginal women's power or to restrictions on Aboriginal male
autonomy, constructing a massive case for the women's oppressed
status. As writers provided examples to give substance to their generalizations, their emphasis on the structural underpinnings of this situation could, as with observers of Maori women, shift from Aboriginal
women's relationships to sexuality, to their work in reproduction, to
their material needs, and to their control of distribution of resources.
European readings of all elements of gender organization revealed,
perhaps, more about white cultural prejudices than about the realities
of Aboriginal life.

Most writers provided graphic illustration of women's presumed oppression in a misreading of sexual practices. Some simply proclaimed women to be the sexual property of all tribal men of a tribe. Alternatively, they wrote that "There is no such thing as marriage, in the proper sense of the word":

> The acts which precede matrimony are certainly not entitled to be regarded as rites. Men obtain wives by a convenient system of exchange, by conquest sometimes, and sometimes a woman is stolen. By what mode soever a man procures a bride, it is very seldom an occasion of rejoicing for the females.[35]

Another writer attempted to effect a crude jocularity in his estimation that "another instance of ignominy" to which Aboriginal women were subjected was the action of the young man procuring a wife:

> having seen a woman whose sable charms overcome him, he first asks her to run away with him, if she refused when opportunity favours, he inflicts a blow on her head with a heavy waddy or club which stuns her, and then carries her off to his own home, where she spends a life of drudgery and misery. . . .[36]

A man holding the position of Protector of Aborigines, ignorant of the complex intricacy of betrothal arrangements, described the existence of marriages of young girls to older men as "infant connubiancy" as he set out to eradicate it in his adopted district.[37] Another Protector saw women oppressed by the "gross sensuality" of Aboriginal men, manifested in the institution of polygamy:

> one great point of ambition in the Australian native was to get a number of wives. I have known as many as six appropriated to one man. Two were common among the middle-aged men. The unfortunate women had no voice in their own disposal. They were considered the property of their nearest male relative. . . .[38]

But what was worse, he continued, was that men could dispose of their wives as they wished: "the strongest mark of friendship that could be displayed by one man to another, was to present him with one of his superfluous wives."[39] Meanwhile, thought some, the wives fought jealously with one another to obtain their husband's favor. If the wife attempted to escape, so this disastrous tale went, "the probability is that she would be speared or beaten to death for her pains."[40] The physical violence of Aboriginal men toward wives was displayed as an image of Aboriginal men's violence toward other Aboriginal men, seen often to be based in conflicts over women and marriages.

This misrepresentation of Aboriginal life made Aboriginal women into victims, while it made Aboriginal men into vicious oppressors, giving legitimacy to white male attempts to "protect" Aboriginal women. That male violence occurred within Aboriginal society—as in most societies—prior to white contact is well established, but the controls on it were also strong. Now fact and fiction, in this context of alienation, became dangerously confused. Story after story was told, with scant regard to the source or interpretation of evidence, of Aboriginal men's violence toward women. Just one report gave details of a series of events, half-understood, but unambiguously reported, of women's oppression. One elderly man beat and burned his wife for opposing his wish to take a young woman, "a common prostitute evidently from her own choice," as his second wife. The wife, however, subsequently begged with tears in her eyes that her husband not be put in jail. In another story, a man speared two women, one in the back and another in the thigh, for offending him. When accosted and locked up, this man offered to allow his own wife to be speared to expiate his crime.[41] Such crudely observed and arrogantly described accounts were legion. Women could scarcely have been shown in a worse situation. Men could scarcely have been shown more cruel.

And so, European observers represented Aboriginal women as the sad and powerless victims of their men, who lacked the capacity for affection. What was worse in their construction of Aboriginal culture was the assertion that the men were lazy, and oppressed their wives further by keeping them hard at work. "The man, regarding them more as slaves than in any other light, employs them in every possible way to his own advantage. They are obliged to get him shell-fish, roots and eatable plants," went a typical interpretation of the gender division of labor.[42] Or, "the great value of a [wife] to one of these lazy fellows," might be best judged by considering "the industry and skill of their . . . wives . . . in making nets, sewing cloaks, mussel-fishing, rooting, etc."[43] The men, it was said, principally monopolized the animals, reptiles, birds, and fish, while the roots, grubs, and ants were the women's lot; for her services, a wife was "usually rewarded with the part of any food which the husband cannot gourmandize."[44]

In line with many writers, one noted that when clans moved about, the women carried the groups' material possessions. He observed "these poor enduring creatures":

> toiling on a burning hot day through the bush, laden with a heterogeneous assemblage of pots, blankets, rugs, bags containing charms, etc., skins, baskets, and perhaps mounted on all these articles will be a child from three

days to six years old, and this is not for a walk of an hour but probably for the whole day.[45]

The shifting of the clan and the carriage of goods, others noted, was not delayed if a woman who had a newborn baby had to halt her journey to suckle the baby at frequent intervals.

Motherhood, they said, oppressed Aboriginal women in further ways. Insufficient concern and respect was shown the woman at the time of birth, or immediately afterward. (We might otherwise say, of course, that Aboriginal women, until smitten with European diseases, were strong, active, and healthy and bore childbirth stoically.) Even worse and more terribly, numerous writers portrayed the women as forced to kill their young if new babies were seen as a threat to their clan's mobility. The "will of the tribe" demanded it. Within Aboriginal laws, wrote one, "infanticide is a necessary practice, and one which, if disregarded, would, under certain circumstances, be disapproved of; and the disapproval would be marked by punishment."[46] Infanticide was first assumed, and then, once again, ascribed to male callousness, for Aboriginal women were portrayed as very affectionate mothers, indeed. The death of a child was a time of fearful distress: "It has been an occasional custom . . . for the mother to carry about for weeks the body of their lost one."[47] Again, "stronger than the maternal love of the tigress or the lioness is that of the Australian Aboriginal woman for a favourite child. She will die in an effort to preserve it, and as willingly suffer the pangs of hunger, and the prolonged misery of hard travel, to secure it from injury."[48] Wrote another, "they never desert their children; as soon as they are able to walk the mothers endeavour to induce them to look out for their own food . . . and never think of leaving them for any length of time until well able to provide for themselves."[49] This apparent praise, of course, for the women's mothering qualities was once again constructed to contrast with the cruelty of the men.

Aboriginal women might well love their offspring, but the burdens of births and child-rearing took their toll under the conditions of life which the writers constructed. And the result? The appearance of these very women was portrayed in the most appalling terms, by men who not only were unused to confronting female nakedness, but who drew their comparisons from racial stereotypes of degraded physical countenance and inferior mental capacity. Just as the British nineteenth-century urban poor were depicted by the middle class as savages and "a race apart," Aboriginal culture felt the full force of racial prejudices. "If the men are ugly, the women are hideous," wrote one. He foreshadowed a link between nonwhite races and animals that would become prominent in nineteenth-century racist discourse. The women's appearance was, in part, he said, because they became mothers so early: "their hands, arms, feet, and legs being more like the paws and claws of the lower animals. . . ."[50] Thought another, "Brutal treatment, frequent privations, and too early marital associations, combine to impoverish and deteriorate the constitution of the aboriginal female."[51]

It would be a mistake to assume that the subject positions from which these self-appointed authorities spoke was always a stable one. When describing specific women, and specific events involving women, their descriptions could acknowledge more favorable contexts, although they drew on sexist rather than racist stereotypes. "The female Aborigines have their amusements as well as the males, and simple and innocent they are," conceded one observer of young women:

> they are particularly fond of dancing in the Spring and Autumn especially. . . . they decorate their heads with flowers, and round their wrists like bracelets and round the ankles, and very gay the black lasses look, they dance away as merrily as our country girls round the May Pole, they chase their own leader who is young like themselves.[52]

Another wrote of Gippsland women, "In affairs of moment the women have a voice, and it is not without weight." Of traveling parties another wrote, "the women stayed close to their men, who supported them when descending gullies or climbing hills, either by the arm or by the whole body." And yet another, "Men show strong affection towards each other; they love their wives; women are faithful, and die on the graves of their husbands."[53] On a man who grieved for his dead wife: "we subsequently inter his faithful lubra [wife] . . . the old man wept bitterly, the kindness of all around to this lubra would scarce be credited." Again, "they have great natural affection." In many respects, "in the bush," they were depicted as a well-ordered, affectionate community: "there is no complaining in the streets of a Native Encampment[;] all partake of the fortune of the day and share among each other what providence has been pleased to give them."[54] But this positive observation surfaces only fitfully in the mass of writing about Aboriginal women and gender relations. The overall evaluation was negative, and destructive.

THE AFTERMATH

The nineteenth-century displacement of Aboriginal and Maori peoples, both men and women, was a result of the drive of British settlers for the land and resources of indigenous peoples. These indigenous peoples found various ways of resisting and evading oppression within the sharp boundaries posed by British and (eventually) colonial political structures, backed up the coercive powers of their armies and their legal systems. Stories of resistance and of the continuities in Maori and Aboriginal culture are important narratives in their own right, but neither can be understood outside of the discursive frameworks established by the invaders. Central to such frameworks was the settlers' projection of ideas of why they intruded on others' territories, the nature of their new society, and the likely outcomes of white settlement for the original occupants. Codes of representing Aboriginal or Maori "traditional" societies in ways that legitimated the new white domination were a significant part of that process, and this included readings of women's lives and gender relations.

Although colonial representations of gender were constructed among writers on Maori society and among writers on Aboriginal society, nevertheless the negative descriptions dominated the writing on Aborigines far more hegemonically than those on Maori. To account for this is a complex task, but one might point to some bases for this different treatment. In the first place, the British found more formidable resistance to domination from Maori groups than from Aboriginal groups, related to their different social organization as agriculturalists and hunter-gatherers. The geographical dislocation occurred more slowly in Aotearoa/New Zealand than in southeastern Australia, and more British people lived with Maori tribal groups, thus facilitating closer observation of Maori over extended periods of time. Writers on Maori women and gender were likely, therefore, to have had time to be more than swiftly reactive in their responses, and to air ambiguities, even if they could not reconcile the apparent contradictions they experienced. Secondly, the British, fresh from their own class-bound society, were impressed with the power and authority of chiefly Maori women, as of men, and hence accorded young and old female chiefs respect, if often grudgingly. By contrast, Aboriginal society did not accord power on ascriptive basis of rank, but on age and sex: The British understood and respected this less easily, if at all, and perceived women as always subordinate, even victims, of men. Thirdly, after the British had finally imposed containment in missions and reserves on the Aboriginal survivors of invasion, Aboriginal women, while remaining utterly significant to their own kin and community, faced massive colonial determination to transform them into domestic servants and housewives on a British model. But Maori eluded such incarceration in institutions, retaining some space of their own, however impoverished they might be. Highborn Maori women retained negotiating power with white settler society as well as their own, and accommodation or otherwise to colonial cultural norms remained at least partly in Maori hands.

Yet Maori women enjoyed a significant comparative advantage over Aboriginal women that was crystallized in their attainment of civic status at the turn of the century. The 1893 granting of the vote to women in Aotearoa/New Zealand embraced Maori women as well as white European women. In contrast, Aboriginal women were, as were their men, debarred from citizenship in 1901 and 1902 within the newly formed Commonwealth of Australia.[55]

The advantage in citizenship Maori women enjoyed, however, did not protect them from suffering the sort of health, educational, and material disadvantages that Aboriginal women sustained far into the twentieth century. But that is another story.

NOTES

I acknowledge with gratitude the assistance of Helen Morton and Andrew May in the research for this chapter.

1. See Lata Mani, "Multiple Mediations: Feminist Scholarship in the Age of Multinational Reception," *Feminist Review* 35 (1992): 24–41; Chandra Talpade Mohanty, "Under Western Eyes: Feminist Scholarship and Colonial Discourses," in C. T. Mohanty, Ann Russo, and Lourdes Torres, eds., *Third World Women and the Politics of Feminism* (Bloomington: Indiana University Press, 1991), 51–80; Nupur Chaudhuri and Margaret Strobel, eds., *Western Women and Imperialism* (Bloomington: Indiana University Press, 1992).

2. See Audrey Oldfield, *Woman Suffrage in Australia: Gift or Struggle?* (Sydney: Cambridge University Press, 1992); Patricia Grimshaw, *Women's Suffrage in New Zealand*, rev. ed. (Auckland: Auckland University Press, 1987); Patricia Grimshaw, *Colonialism, Gender and Representations of Race: Issues in Writing Women's History in Australia and the Pacific* (Melbourne: Melbourne University History Occasional Papers No. 4, 1994).

3. Keith Sinclair, *A History of New Zealand*, rev. ed. (Harmondsworth, England: Penguin, 1990); P. Grimshaw, M. Lake, A. McGrath, and M. Quartly, *Creating a Nation* (Melbourne: McPhee-Gribble, 1994).

4. Jan Critchett, *A Distant Field of Murder: Western District Frontiers, 1834–1848* (Melbourne: Allen and Unwin, 1990); Bain Attwood, *The Making of the Aborigines* (Sydney: Allen and Unwin, 1989); M. F. Christie, *Aborigines in Colonial Victoria, 1835–1886* (Sydney: Allen and Unwin, 1979); Henry Reynolds, *Frontier: Aborigines, Settlers and Land* (Sydney: Allen and Unwin, 1987).

5. Keith Sinclair, *The Origin of the Maori Wars* (Wellington: University of Auckland Press, New Zealand University Press, 1957); W. H. Oliver, ed., *The Oxford History of New Zealand* (Wellington: Oxford University Press, 1981).

6. Berys Heuer, *Maori Women* (Wellington: A. H. and A. W. Reed, 1972); Bruce Biggs, *Maori Marriage* (Wellington: A. H. and A. W. Reed, 1960).

7. See Diane Bell, *Daughters of the Dreaming* (Sydney: Allen and Unwin, 1983); Kay Saunders and R. Evans, eds., *Gender Relations in Australia: Domination and Negotiation* (Sydney: Allen and Unwin, 1992).

8. William Brown, *New Zealand and Its Aborigines* (London: Smith Elder and Co., 1845), 38.

9. Ernest Dieffenbach, *Travels in New Zealand*, vol. 2 (London: John Murray, 1843), 11.

10. George Angas, *Savage Life and Scenes in Australia*, vol. 1 (1847; reprint, New York: Johnson Reprint Corporation, 1967), 317.

11. Joel Polack, *Manners and Customs of the New Zealanders*, 2 vols. (London: James Madden and Co., 1840), 1:155.

12. J. R. Elder, ed., *Letters and Journals of Samuel Marsden* (Dunedin: Coylls, Somerville, Wilkie and Read, 1932), 166.

13. John Nicholas, *Narrative of a Voyage to New Zealand*, vol. 1 (London: James Black and Son, 1817), 199.

14. Augustus Earle, *Narrative of Residence in New Zealand* (1832; reprint, Oxford: Clarendon Press, 1966), 180.

15. Brown, *New Zealand and Its Aborigines*, 33.

16. Polack, *Manners and Customs of the New Zealanders*, 1:156.

17. Nicholas, *Narrative of a Voyage to New Zealand*, 1:180.

18. Joel Polack, *New Zealand: Being a Narrative of Travels and Adventures*, 2 vols. (1838; reprint Christchurch, New Zealand: Capper Press, 1974), 369.

19. Samuel Martin, *New Zealand in a Series of Letters* (London: Simmonds and Ward, 1845), 304.

20. Polack, *Manners and Customs*, 1:147.

21. Francis Fenton, *Observations on the State of the Aboriginal Inhabitants of New Zealand* (Auckland: New Zealand Government, 1859), 27.

22. Nicholas, *Narrative of a Voyage to New Zealand*, 1:41.

23. Brown, *New Zealand and Its Aborigines*, 41.

24. Polack, *New Zealand*, 2:273.

25. William Yate, *An Account of New Zealand* (1835; reprint, Shannon: Irish University Press, 1970), 98.

26. William Marshall, *A Personal Narrative of Two Visits to New Zealand* (London: James Nisbett and Co., 1836), 14.

27. Brown, *New Zealand and Its Aborigines*, 41.

28. Earle, *Narrative of Residence in New Zealand*, 179.

29. Fenton, *Observations*, 30.

30. Dieffenbach, *Travels in New Zealand*, 12.

31. Brown, *New Zealand and Its Aborigines*, 38.

32. Nicholas, *Narrative of a Voyage*, 1:364.

33. Earle, *Narrative of Residence in New Zealand*, 180.

34. William Thomas, "Brief Remarks on the Aborigines of Victoria, 1838–1839," La Trobe Library, State Library of Victoria, MS 7838, p.10; *Report of the Select Committee of the Legislative Council on Aborigines*, Victorian Parliamentary Papers, 1858–59, p. 236; J. C. Symons, *Life of the Rev. Daniel James Draper* (Melbourne: Wesleyan Book Depot, 1870), 356; R. B. Smyth, *The Aborigines of Victoria*, vol. 1 (1876; reprint, Melbourne: John Currey, O'Neil, 1972), 46.

35. Smyth, *The Aborigines of Victoria*, 1:76.

36. G. H. Haydon, *Five Years' Experience in Australia Felix*, vol. 2 (London: Hamilton, Adams and Co., 1846), 43.

37. William Thomas, "Quarterly Report 1 March 1847," Public Record Office of Victoria, Series VPRS 4410, Unit 4, Item 96.

38. E. S. Parker, *The Aborigines of Australia* (Melbourne: Hugh McColl, 1854), 22.

39. Ibid., 23.

40. Haydon, *Five Years' Experience in Australia Felix*, 2:43.

41. E. S. Parker, "Quarterly Journal, 1 December 1841–42 February 1842," Public Record Office of Victoria, Series VPRS 4410, Unit 2, Item 60.

42. H. E. A. Meyer, "Manners and Customs of the Encounter Bay Tribe" (1846), as quoted in Smyth, *The Aborigines of Victoria*, 1:85.

43. T. L. Mitchell, "Three Expeditions into the Interior of Eastern Australia" (1838), as quoted in Smyth, *The Aborigines of Victoria*, 1:85.

44. Haydon, *Five Years' Experience in Australia Felix*, 2:43.

45. Ibid., 2:41.

46. Smyth, *The Aborigines of Victoria*, 2:xxi.

47. Parker, *The Aborigines of Australia*, 23.

48. Smyth, *The Aborigines of Victoria*, 2:98.

49. Haydon, *Five Years' Experience in Australia Felix*, 2:42.

50. C. Griffith, *The Present State and Prospects of the Port Phillip District* (Dublin: William Curry, Jun. and Company, 1845), 148.

51. Parker, *The Aborigines of Australia*, 2.

52. Thomas, "Brief Remarks on the Aborigines of Victoria, 1838- 1839," 43–44.

53. L. Fison and A. W. Howitt, *Kamilaroi and Kurnai* (Melbourne: George Robertson, 1880), 212; C. Paclt, *Wide World Travels of Cenek Paclt* (1888; reprint, Brisbane: John Oxley Library, 1986), 17; and Smyth, *The Aborigines of Victoria*, 2:138.

54. William Thomas, "Quarterly Report 25 May 1859," Public Record Office of Victoria, Series VPRS 2896, Unit 3, B 1859/2707; ibid., 7 November 1840.

55. Grimshaw, *Colonialism, Gender and Representations of Race*.

2

Enfranchising Women of Color

Woman Suffragists as Agents of Imperialism

ROSALYN TERBORG-PENN

Imperialist agency appears continually in my most recent research on woman suffrage movements in the Caribbean. The manifestation is similar to the relation I found in researching Black and white
woman suffragists in the United States. As a result, I have embarked on
a comparative study of African American and Caribbean woman suffragists, as well as their relationship to the socially and politically
dominant suffragists in the United States. This essay conveys some of
my findings concerning comparative history of woman suffrage movements, specifically with reference to the relationship between white
elite women in the United States and their effect on African American,
Puerto Rican, and St. Thomian woman suffragists. Although the concept of race was constructed differently among the people of the United
States, in contrast to people in the Caribbean, the dominant political
forces in the United States—the agents of imperialism—polarized race
into Black and white and imposed this view on those they encountered
in the Caribbean. As a result, the woman suffrage movements in the
United States, in Puerto Rico, and in St. Thomas were affected by racist
assumptions prevalent among women who were connected to the
powerful white elite in the United States.

Imperialism and colonialism are apparent constructs for describing
the relationship of Puerto Ricans and St. Thomians to those white
individuals of power born in the United States. I apply the definitions

for imperialism, in particular, that Nupur Chaudhuri and Margaret Strobel use in the introduction to their anthology *Western Women and Imperialism*. They define imperialism as "a concept that signifies any relationship of dominance and subordination between nations, including the modern form of economic control."[1]

Although African Americans living in the United States are not officially considered to be among the colonized, in figurative ways we are, as literary and dramatic figures in our communities have noted for many years. "The Last Colony," for example, was the name of a 1960s repertory theater in the District of Columbia, a territory of primarily African Americans, which lost its home rule in the 1870s. The theater's name symbolized the political victimization of the Black people who lived in the nation's capital. In the United States, African Americans, like Latinos and Native people, function in a reality quite similar to the circumstance of colonized people abroad, where often women are third class to their men, who are treated as second-class citizens by the society as a whole.

The intersection of race, class, culture, and gender is significant in reconstructing the history of woman suffrage campaigns in both the United States and in the Caribbean. In my scholarly research and writing over the last twenty years in African American women suffrage, I have discussed the reasons why Black women became suffragists from the early years of the mid-nineteenth-century movement through the push to ratify the Nineteenth Amendment, the seventy-fifth anniversary of which was celebrated in the United States on August 26, 1995. I have looked also at the strategies African American women used to convince the people in their own communities to support the movement, and their strategies to protest against white women's attempts to keep Black women from gaining the right to vote. In my research, I found significant pockets of strong woman suffrage activities among Black women living in the Northeast, especially in New York City, and in the District of Columbia. The majority of African American woman suffragists were educated and from the middle class, although there were working-class Black suffragists also. I argue that African American women were determined to gain the right to vote in order to improve conditions in their own communities as well as to improve their own status. Twenty years ago when I began this research, there were many who doubted whether I would find anything. However, now the word is out, and feminist scholars have acknowledged the Black presence in the U.S. woman suffrage movement.

Similarly, feminist scholars in the United States had been reluctant to research women's movements in the Caribbean, because of the belief that females in the Western Hemisphere outside of the United States and Canada have thicker layers of oppression to overcome; hence, their struggles for political empowerment have been retarded and more difficult than those of women in the West. The assumption that there were virtually no woman suffrage movements to speak of in the Caribbean was common into the 1980s, causing feminist scholars to dismiss even looking for organized women's political activities in Caribbean states. The organization called the Latin American and Caribbean Women's Collective substantiated this assumption when, in 1977, they first published their book *Slaves of Slaves: The Challenge of Latin American Women*.[2]

In discussing the absence of woman suffrage movements, the Collective argued that there was no equivalent of nineteenth-century European and North American suffrage movements in Latin America and the Caribbean. Perhaps this statement is true, but the question of its truth remains unresolved until further research is attempted. I suspect that one of the overlooked reasons was the invisibility of women in the Southern Hemisphere.

Western feminists focused their woman suffrage struggles inward, not outward. The struggle was for their own enfranchisement, not the political empowerment of invisible women outside of the network, living in the colonies. This should not be surprising for those of us who study woman suffrage history in the United States, because middle-class white suffragists in the States more often than not focused their movement among themselves, ignoring working-class white and Latina women, and attempting to exclude Black women. It is significant that the organized anti–Black woman suffrage strategy developed in the 1890s, around the time that the United States became a major imperialist nation and Puerto Rico became a U.S. colony.

Since the late 1980s, Caribbean women historians have tested the assumptions and set out to revise the historiography which excludes them from woman suffrage history. As a result, graduate students and scholars, some from Caribbean states such as Puerto Rico, Cuba, Jamaica, and Trinidad, have written dissertations, articles, and books that have challenged previous assumptions. In fact, some of them writing in the 1990s have even challenged earlier works written about women's movements in Cuba and Puerto Rico, primarily because, while the pioneering works broke new ground, they did not include a comprehensive class or race analysis.[3]

In placing the Caribbean within a global context, we see that successful twentieth-century woman suffrage movements appeared first in western nations, which controlled colonies in other areas of the globe, and in white-dominated or white-colonized colonies. In contrast, the women living in the heavily mixed-race colonies, and colonies in which white administrators formed a tiny minority, were not enfranchised at the time women received the ballot in the so-called "mother country" and her white colonies. What may be surprising to feminist historians is the fact that colonial Caribbean women, some from the elite and some from the working classes, lobbied in a variety of ways to earn the right to vote during the early years of the twentieth century. At times, class or race status determined the strategies used by organized woman suffragists. As a result, either conflicting political motivations for suffrage were found among differing classes of women, or racism masked the class and status differences among women of color and fused their political interests, as was the case in the U.S. Virgin Islands. Events in the United States, where the woman suffrage struggle was won for women on the mainland in 1920, influenced several of the Caribbean states, where women did not gain the vote until the 1930s.[4]

There appear to be but two historical monographs published in English or Spanish about women's rights movements in the Caribbean, both of which have revisionist challenges. One book, written in Spanish by Yamila Azize, is about Puerto Rico, and the other, written in English by K. Lynn Stoner, is about Cuba. Each book has at least one chapter on woman suffrage.[5] These two Caribbean states were among the first in the region to enfranchise women, with the Puerto Rican legislature passing a restricted literate suffrage bill in 1929. Cuba followed Puerto Rico in 1934, after a long organized struggle among elite women. Unlike their Puerto Rican sisters, however, all Cuban women won the right to vote by executive order; nonetheless, elite women were in the vanguard of the movement. Neither Azize nor Stoner focuses upon both the class and race conflicts among women in these two suffrage movements.

To return to the hypothesis put forth by the Latin American and Caribbean Women's Collective, the authors admit that they did not know why woman suffrage movements were absent during the nineteenth century. They suggest reasons, however, citing the persistence of slavery and the independence struggles that took first priority, and the undereducation of even elite women who were bound by religion and centered on the home.[6] A significant missing factor in the Collective's hypothesis was the belief among white women leaders of the western woman suffrage movements that women of Latin America and the Caribbean were not prepared to exercise the vote.

An example of this prejudice occurred during the 1920s when Cuban suffragists sought help from North American feminists. Former

U.S. suffragists refused to appeal to their government to support the constitutional reform in Cuba, which was needed to enfranchise women. Their refusal was not based upon anti-imperialist convictions. Acting on what Stoner called "their own cultural and political biases," feminists representing the United States at the 1926 Inter-American Women's Congress in Panama disdainfully argued that Latin American women were not ready to exercise political rights, and abstained from voting for a resolution to bring women's suffrage to all American nations. This decision is just one example of white American women acting as agents of imperialism.[7]

Nonetheless, elite Caribbean women appeared not to be aware of this prejudice and believed that the North American feminists were truly concerned for their movement. But such concern not only coexisted with, it formed an integral part of U.S.-born suffragists' own bid for national citizenship within a growing imperial power. Take the case of Doris Stevens, who represented the National Woman's Party (NWP) and met with elite Cuban women in efforts to bridge the activities of woman suffragists on an international level. She, like other suffragist leaders from the United States I discuss later, spoke in the imperialist voice of the more advanced civilization extending a helping hand to its colonial inferiors. At home, Stevens's feminism was interlaced with racism. *Jailed for Freedom*, the book she published in 1920, described the treatment she and other National Woman's Party members experienced when they were arrested and jailed during a 1917 protest march in the District of Columbia. Stevens and other elite women seemed more indignant about being jailed with Black women than they were about other prison experiences. This consensus was apparent in their expressions of contempt. One cover drawing of *The Suffragist*, the official magazine of the National Woman's Party, depicted an elite woman dressed in prison clothing, with a list of indignities printed beside her image. The list included being "thrown in the workhouse with Negroes and criminals," apparently the ultimate insult.[8]

Puerto Rican historian Gladys Jimenez-Munoz also questions the good intentions of the postsuffrage U.S. women, and challenges the historiography describing the Puerto Rican woman suffrage movement. She says, "The most famous act of cooperation performed by the post-suffrage woman's movement in the United States was the National Woman's Party campaign to have the U.S. Congress impose women's suffrage over the express will of the Puerto Rican legislature."[9] In discussing the existing historiography of the Puerto Rican movement, she notes that the studies reference how most U.S. federal government interventions in the local affairs of the island were "inherently colonialist." Jimenez-Munoz then asks why the historiography fails to raise the question about how acts of solidarity among woman suffragists interplayed with the colonialist character attributed to U.S. interventions during that time? She raises a final, most important question, "In what ways did this solidarity also contain colonialist and racist practices?"[10]

Jimenez-Munoz sees a contradiction in the interplay between the U.S. members of the NWP, basically elite white North American women living in the United States, and the middle-class woman suffragists living in Puerto Rico. The North American women may have espoused solidarity with Brown women living abroad, but they did not practice solidarity at home among African American, Mexican, and Native women. She notes two significant factors that could very well have had an effect on the two differing realities for elite North American women in their interactions with women of color at home and abroad. First, Puerto Rican women as voters could never decide public policy in the United States. Their voting habits would never be threatening, whereas enfranchised women of color in the United States could directly affect the legislative composition of the U.S. Congress. This factor I find to be especially true for the South where, in some areas, Blacks were in the majority during the early years of the twentieth century. Second, Jimenez-Munoz interprets the women of the NWP, in both portraying and authorizing the woman suffrage struggle in Puerto Rico, as attempting to speak for colonized women. These two realities, she concludes, make the cry for universal womanhood "a facile guise," because the women of the NWP defined themselves in terms of moral, racial, and cultural superiority and as the custodians of what "they apparently saw as their little colored sisters . . . infantilized colonized women," who were lost without the aid of their "more civilized" white North American sisters.[11]

The Jimenez-Munoz analysis supports my characterization of many postsuffrage white women of the United States as agents of imperialism. Nonetheless, some North American feminists reject my analysis as they defend the women of the NWP as powerless victims of patriarchy.[12]

Jimenez-Munoz develops her argument further as she describes the NWP participation in the Sixth Pan-American Conference held in 1928 in Havana, Cuba. Two women representing the National Woman's Party—Doris Stevens and Muna Lee de Munoz Marin—spoke at that conference. Although Muna Lee was Mississippi-born and a former NWP member in the United States, she had married a prominent Puerto Rican legislator and moved to the island, and she taught at the University of Puerto Rico. As a result, she represented the Puerto Rican chapter of the NWP as well as the university at the Pan-American Conference. Despite her credentials, other NWP women in the United States questioned her image as a National Woman's Party representative, doubting whether she would have the same influence as a representative sent from the United States.[13]

Significantly, Jimenez-Munoz analyzed both Steven's and Lee's presentations, finding the language to be similar in that they both attempted to represent all Latin American women, depicting them bound together by a common culture determined via the Euro-American experience. Of course in this context, even Lee could not speak for all women of Latin America, nor of Puerto Rico, because not all of the women were descendants of Europeans, or, as Jimenez notes, "claimed to be protagonists of colonialism or of the establishment of these republics."[14]

The North American women of the NWP were not the only agents of imperialism. In 1929, Carrie Chapman Catt was the director of the Women's Struggle for World Peace and Friendship with South America. A decade before, Catt had been one of the national leaders of the U.S. woman suffrage movement. She was the president of the largest group, the National American Woman Suffrage Association, at the time the Nineteenth Amendment was ratified. One would think that Catt understood the struggle and the broad-based membership of her former organization, which included women from a diversity of races, classes, and ethnicities. Nonetheless, she criticized Latin American suffragists' demands for the vote, arguing that they had not "fought long enough to appreciate" the responsibilities that came with the right to use the ballot.[15] This imperialist stance was quite similar to that held by many white middle-class women suffragists at the turn of the twentieth century. Catt represented feminism in the United States, but she also represented imperialist agency. She saw no contradiction in her belief in political equity for middle-class educated women with white men of the United States, yet not for women in the southern region of the Western Hemisphere. Ironically, many of the women Catt dismissed as not ready for enfranchisement were wives and daughters of the white ruling elite of their respective nations, women such as Muna Lee. Catt's views reflected the argument of some other white women suffragists in her class, who would have preferred to see only "educated" American women vote, hence eliminating working-class and poorer women among the enfranchised.

This colonializing and imperializing view, i.e., that others were further back on the evolutionary scale and required more time to develop before they could speak and act in their own right, had existed among woman suffrage leaders in the United States on the eve of the Nineteenth Amendment victory in 1920. Such beliefs caused African American suffragists to be ignored and discriminated against by members of the mainstream movement. As a result of similar biases among U.S. feminist leaders of the late nineteenth and early twentieth centuries, the history of the movement they left for posterity was distorted, rendering African American woman suffragists invisible.[16] I have found that studies about Caribbean women and politics, some written by North American women, often include similar lacunae.[17]

Two historiographical problems result when constructing woman suffrage movements cross-culturally. Either written histories of suffrage movements in the Caribbean do not focus upon women's issues or, when they do, the studies fail to include in the accounts the names of the women who have been involved in political action and the explicit roles the women have played. In addition, the connection between woman suffragists in the United States and their effect on their Caribbean counterparts has not been fully developed and needs further study. Hence, I have begun to investigate the positive and the negative results of the connection.

My research has brought me to look at the history of the suffrage victories for literate women in Puerto Rico and for propertied women in St. Thomas, because both are U.S. territories. In analyzing the events, for St. Thomas particularly, race, class, and the sociopolitical influence of the United States are important factors in reconstructing the woman suffrage victories. Conversely, the frequent avoidance of issues about race or color in Puerto Rican culture makes these factors difficult to trace.

Now let us return to the presuffrage years in the United States and look at the effect North American suffragists had on St. Thomian and Puerto Rican woman suffragists before and after the ratification of the woman suffrage amendment to the U.S. Constitution.

In 1917, during the midst of the woman suffrage debate in the United States, Puerto Ricans were granted U.S. citizenship, and the Danish West Indies became U.S. possessions. As a result, when the Nineteenth Amendment was ratified in 1920, the United States was an imperialist nation like most of her allies in western Europe.

According to historian William W. Boyer, when the United States took over the Danish islands, Americans inherited "a legacy of neglect," because the Danes made no real effort to assume responsibility for the people's social problems. Unfortunately, the U.S. government remained indifferent to the plight of Virgin Islanders for fourteen years, establishing military rule that lasted until 1931. Not surprisingly, the all-white U.S. Navy ruled over a largely Black and impoverished population, imposing racial policies that fostered segregation. Despite the neglect of the islands by the Danes, there had been minimal overt racial discrimination against Black islanders before the coming of the Americans. As in Puerto Rico, before the coming of the U.S. troops, discrimination had been based more on class than race, although color often determined class. In the meantime, white supremacy was being infused into the mores of Virgin Islanders.[18]

Questions about constitutional rights for Puerto Ricans and Virgin Islanders had surfaced shortly after the United States acquired the Danish islands, and whites at home became more fearful of the encroaching numbers of individuals of color who had been added to the U.S. jurisdiction. The issue was debated until one year after the United States ratified the Nineteenth Amendment. In 1921, the U.S. Supreme Court ruled that rights protected by the Constitution did not extend to residents of either Puerto Rico or the Virgin Islands. Instead, residents of Puerto Rico were bound by the 1900 Organic Act, and those in the Virgin Islands were bound by the Danish Colonial Law of 1906. The 1906 law had set qualifications that extremely limited suffrage.[19]

Suffragists in the United States should not have been surprised at the decision that would prevent women in the territories from gaining the right to vote. In 1917, at the time the Danish West Indies became U.S. possessions, some of them had assumed erroneously that women in the Danish colonies had already been enfranchised when, in 1915, Denmark had extended suffrage to women in the mother country. There appears, however, to have been no effort by the Danes to extend even limited suffrage to women in their colonies. Not only had women suffragists in the United States been ill informed about the political problems between Denmark and the Danish West Indies, U.S. suffragists had also naively believed that once the Virgin Islands became U.S. possessions, the women there would be enfranchised.[20]

In Puerto Rico, woman suffragists were appalled by the 1921 U.S. Supreme Court ruling. Elite women assumed that the Nineteenth Amendment had enfranchised them as well as all women on the mainland. In fact, according to Yamila Azize, it was the U.S. women's victory that re-ignited the woman suffrage campaign among both the working class and the elite feminists of Puerto Rico. Of the two classes, the working-class suffragists had initiated the movement at the turn of the century, when the U.S. Congress passed the first Organic Act governing the island. Nonetheless, Azize does not focus on the class differences among suffragists, and avoids any mention of race or color.

In Puerto Rico, working-class suffragists were radical and confrontational, as indicated by Genara Pagan, an activist in the Free Federation of Workers, who had attempted unsuccessfully to register as a voter in 1920. Conflicting strategies and aspirations reflected the class differences among women who sought the vote. On the one hand, the union-affiliated women felt they should seize the opportunity before it was too late to obtain the suffrage; on the other hand, the elite women were confident that they would receive the franchise as U.S. citizens. The 1921 Supreme Court ruling killed those hopes.[21]

Azize did not indicate whether race was a factor that differentiated the elite from at least some of the working-class women, but I have suspected for some time that it was. In the meantime, the Puerto Rican legislature remained silent, and the conservative wing of the Catholic Church led an antifeminist campaign. Feminist anger over the court ruling, however, united the elite and the working-class women briefly. The new coalition was more conservative than the working-class women's movement had been, yet it gained support from the Socialist Party and from the Republican Party members of the legislature, the founder of which was a Black physician, Jose Celso Barbosa.[22] However, the majority in the legislature, the Union Party, opposed enfranchising women. The struggle continued for several years, with suffragists creating new strategies, including an elitist drive for literate suffrage, similar to the elitist strategy conservative U.S. suffragists had adopted in the late nineteenth and early twentieth centuries. It soon became clear also that Washington politicians thwarted Puerto Rican universal suffrage goals for fear that the illiterate masses would elect the Socialist Party to control the Puerto Rican legislature. I have discovered many of those party members to be Black.[23]

In the meantime, Puerto Rican women living in New York City organized the Puerto Rican and Hispanic League to support their sisters' efforts on the island. Mainland encouragement helped the Puerto Rican suffrage movement, but by the close of the late 1920s, they witnessed the debate between the universal suffrage and the restricted suffrage proponents.[24] Despite the continued pressure from groups such as the Teachers Association of Puerto Rico, the Association of Women Suffragists, the Puerto Rican and Hispanic League of New York, and the New York–based Puerto Rican Women Defense League, the legislature passed neither bill. When delegates from the Women's Pan-American Congress met in the District of Columbia during 1926 and Puerto Rican women living in the United States lobbied the U.S. Senate, renewed political pressure from Washington was placed on the Puerto Rican legislature. A bill for restricted suffrage finally passed both Puerto Rican legislative houses in April 1929, a consequence, as we have noted, of intervention from imperialist agency. Suffrage was granted to literate women over the age of twenty-one.[25] The conservative forces who needed to maintain the status quo and protect their neocolonialist interests had won, obviously by exploiting the working-class supporters of woman suffrage, then sacrificing them for an elite political victory.

Although in the Virgin Islands women had long been active in political and social reform, it appears that not until the United States granted the residents a civilian government in 1931 did women voice their desire for the right to vote. At the time, there was a small middle class of Blacks in St. Thomas—educators, civil servants, and businesspeople—the Black elite. The majority of educators were women, most of whom owned property. Hence, gender was what restricted them from the suffrage. For the most part, these were the women who organized to decry their disfranchisement. They protested, then sued, and finally, in 1935, won the right to vote. How they became radical suffragists and why it took until the mid-1930s for them to win the vote became the focus of my recent research.

The answer was elusive and not found in published studies of St. Thomas political history. Only through asking questions from the women keepers of the community history could I find the answers. In 1984, I interviewed the late Edith Williams, who was 97 years old at the time. After forty-five years of teaching in the Moravian and later the public schools, she had retired in 1945. According to Williams, Virgin Islands suffragists felt, as had Puerto Rican suffragists in 1920, that because women in the United States voted, and Virgin Islanders were U.S. citizens, they should vote also.[26]

Although Williams's explanation about the woman suffrage movement may appear simple and plausible enough, I still had questions. I wondered what had invoked her feminism, and since the U.S. Congress had granted citizenship to the Virgin Islanders in 1932, why it took the suffragists until 1935 to confront the political powers in St. Thomas. Like the Puerto Rican women, St. Thomian women maintained continual communication about women's status with other jurisdictions. There were contacts with Puerto Rico and the mainland through newspaper reports, such as in 1935 when Puerto Rico removed the literacy requirement for women's voting. There was also contact through women's interactions. In both jurisdictions, women had gained the right to vote before the women in the Virgin Islands.

In addition, several of the St. Thomas woman suffragists had visited or lived in Black communities in the United States, where they had earlier contacts with African Americans, some of whom may have been suffragists. Edith Williams herself had visited New York City several times as a youth, when she played cricket with a team called the Harlem Virgin Islands Girls. Another prominent St. Thomas suffragist, Eulalie Stevens, had been born in New York City. She migrated to St. Thomas in the late 1920s. She had been eighteen years old in 1917, the year when New York State women finally won the vote they had been struggling to obtain. In addition, during the 1920s a third suffragist, Bertha Boschulte, had been a student at Hampton Institute, a Black institution for higher education in Virginia. A native Virgin Islander, she returned to St. Thomas to teach in 1929. Boschulte said that she learned about the woman suffrage movement when living in the States. It appears that for St. Thomian woman suffragists, the question was not where are the role models, but when would the opportunity be right.[27]

The opportunity appeared to be near in 1931 when the appointed civilian government replaced the U.S. Navy as the governing agency in the Virgin Islands. This was the year before U.S. citizenship was granted. Ella Gifft, a Black entrepreneur, encouraged the women of St. Thomas to fight for the franchise on the basis of the U.S. Woman Suffrage Amendment. Gifft believed, as did other politically astute women, that once Virgin Islanders became U.S. citizens, all constitutional rights should apply to them. According to Edith Williams, Gifft was one of the earliest suffragists. However, Williams did not believe Gifft was part of an organized movement, as she was.[28]

What opportunity did Edith Williams and her network of women of color discover that propelled them to victory? A look at the way in which Williams and others functioned in educational and civic affairs may give some additional clues to the historical reconstruction of this case. Considered the "mother" of public education in St. Thomas, Williams was a single woman, who early in her career established a network of women working to better the conditions for students and teachers. Although Virgin Islands teachers earned low salaries, Williams struggled until she acquired enough funds to purchase her own property, as did several of the other female teachers.[29]

The 1935 victory involved a process of petitioning and court battles, led by a network of respected teachers like Williams, mainly women in the St. Thomas Teachers Association and their male supporters. Their opportunity had come with the appointment of Judge Albert Levitt to the St. Thomas District Court. A New Dealer, he came to the island from New York City with his wife, Elsie Hill, a former woman suffragist and leader in the NWP. According to Bertha Boschulte, who at the time was a young teacher and the secretary of the St. Thomas Teachers Association, Mrs. Levitt (as Boschulte called Elsie Hill) was outraged to learn that Virgin Islands women could not vote and convinced the Association members that her husband would be sympathetic to their cause if they attempted to register to vote. By November of 1935, the Teachers Association had successfully won a legal suit wherein the question was raised about women's right to vote under the Nineteenth Amendment. Judge Levitt ruled that the Danish Colonial Law was unconstitutional because it violated the Nineteenth Amendment to the U.S. Constitution.[30]

Subsequently, in December 1935, Edith Williams became the first female suffrage applicant. Within a week, twenty-three women had applied to vote. Local officials, however, were quite disturbed by the ruling, and on December 18, the Board of Elections rejected all the female applicants on the ground that female suffrage was not in accord with the Danish Colonial Law or the Act of Congress of 1917. Within a few days before Christmas, the teachers announced that they had obtained a writ of mandamus to be issued to the electoral board to permit qualified St. Thomian women to vote.[31]

The key decision the Association had to make was selecting the most qualified of the teachers to petition for the writ. Edith Williams, Anna M. Vessup, and Eulalie Stevens were chosen because these women could show beyond doubt that they were eligible to vote within the restricted requirements.[32] The petition spoke truthfully of these mature women, who were highly respected in their communities.

By December 27, Judge Levitt had ruled in the women's favor. Consequently, the electoral board was forced to accept the women's applications for voter registration. Virgin Islanders responded to the decision favorably. Shortly after the St. Thomas teachers won their woman suffrage victory, teachers on St. John and St. Croix mobilized and registered to vote.[33]

Several political trends can be observed from this woman suffrage victory and the political consequences. First, women's politicization supported the social welfare arguments that both St. Thomian and African-American woman suffragists included in their rationale for women obtaining the right to vote. For the St. Thomas Teachers Association, progressive education and more tax support for public schools were major reforms they sought from the pending June 1936 Home Rule Act. Similarly, African American women had looked to the ballot to bring educational reforms to their communities. In St. Thomas, additional political reform resulted when, in less than a year, the property and income restrictions that had disfranchised English-speaking Virgin Islanders were lifted.

In analyzing the strategies and motives of the woman suffragists who led the St. Thomas movement, we must return to the issue of class and status and its effect on the politics of women's enfranchisement. Though the suffragists held elite status in their Black communities, they had not called for restricted woman suffrage, as the Puerto Rican elite women had done. The call had been for universal woman suffrage. Only when the Board of Elections refused to act upon Judge Levitt's first court ruling were the women forced to argue their case within the parameters of the existing restricted suffrage limits to the St. Thomas electorate. As in the United States, it appeared that color issues often obscured class and status issues, enabling elite Black women to argue for reforms that would benefit Black working-class and impoverished women as well as themselves. The strategy was enabled further by the persistent struggle of Black woman suffragists and their assistance from a sympathetic court, which, however, represented imperialist agency. Elsie Hill had persuaded the well-known New York lawyer Robert Claiborne to represent the women in court, pro bono.[34] In reality, Hill spoke for herself, but also for the colonized suffragists, and in so doing, assured her own enfranchisement in this alien land, an example of imperialist agency no matter how good the consequences.

Nonetheless, the U.S. connection was a significant factor in the success of the St. Thomas suffragist strategy, as it had been for the Puerto Rican suffragists. Opportunities provided by access to Washington and New York opened heretofore closed doors. Puerto Rican feminists used the opportunity to lobby the U.S. Senate when they met for a conference in Washington. Hispanic women living in New York City organized to promote the idea for enfranchising their sisters in Puerto Rico. Of the St. Thomas suffrage leaders, at least half of them had visited the United States, where the woman suffrage ideology among African American women had been operative. In addition, the influence of a disfranchised New York suffragist, who was close to the source of imperialist empowerment, provided the final opportunity for the St. Thomas woman suffrage victory.

In closing let me return to comparative history as a methodology for examining woman suffrage movements cross-culturally. Different cultural meanings for race, color, and class impede the research process even when gender and political empowerment goals are constant variables in the constructed equation. As a result, sorting through the various meanings, often hindered further by the construction of language, reveals barriers to comparative analysis. Yet each level of interpretation provides a foundation for another, which may revise the first and stimulate continued reanalysis. I find comparative women's history to be an exciting tool with which to ferret out imperialist agency.

NOTES

1. Nupur Chaudhuri and Margaret Strobel, eds., *Western Women and Imperialism: Complicity and Resistance* (Bloomington: Indiana University Press, 1992), 2.

2. Latin American and Caribbean Women's Collective, trans. Michael Pallis, *Slaves of Slaves: The Challenge of Latin American Women* (London: Zed Press, 1980), 26.

3. See Maria Barcello Miller, "Voto, colonialismo y clase: La Lucha por el sufragio femenino en Puerto Rico, 1896–1935" (Unpublished dissertation, Universidad de Puerto Rico, 1993); Magali Roy-Fequiere, "Race, Gender, and the 'Generacion del Treinta': Toward a Diciphering of Puerto Rican National Identity Discourse" (Unpublished dissertation, Stanford University, 1993); Gladys Jimenez-Munoz, "Deconstructing Colonialist Discourse: Links between the Women's Suffrage Movement in the United States and Puerto Rico," *Phoebe* 5, no. 1 (Spring 1993).

4. United States Department of Labor, Women's Bureau, *Political Status of Women in Other American Republics*, September 1956: Notes for Reference (Washington: U.S. Government Printing Office, 1957), 1–2, 7, 10, 15; John Mordecai, *The West Indies: The Federal Negotiations* (London: Allen and Unwin, 1968), 30; William Boyer, *America's Virgin Islands* (Durham: Carolina Academic Press, 1983), 182, 226.

5. Yamila Azize, *La Mujer en la Lucha* (Rio Piedras: Editorial Cultural, 1985); K. Lynn Stoner, *From the House to the Streets: The Cuban Woman's Movement for Legal Reform, 1898–1940* (Durham: Duke University Press, 1991).

6. Latin American and Caribbean Women's Collective, *Slaves of Slaves*, 26.

7. Stoner, *From the House to the Streets*, 113.

8. *The Suffragist*, 7 September 1917.

9. Jimenez-Munoz, "Deconstructing Colonialist Discourse," 9.

10. Ibid.

11. Ibid., 12, 13, 17.

12. See, for example, Linda G. Ford, "Alice Paul and the Triumph of Militancy," in Marjorie Spruill Wheeler, ed., *One Woman, One Vote* (Troutdale, OR: New Sage Press, 1995), 277–94; and Nancy Cott, "Feminist Politics in the 1920s: The National Woman's Party," *Journal of American History* 71, no. 1 (June 1984): 43–68.

13. Jimenz-Munoz, "Deconstructing Colonialist Discourse," 16.

14. Ibid., 19.

15. Stoner, *From the House to the Street*, 113.

16. Rosalyn Terborg-Penn, "Discrimination against Afro- American Women in the Woman's Movement," in *The Afro-American Woman: Struggles and Images* (Port Washington, NY: Kennikat Press, 1978).

17. Patricia Symmonds, "Women in Politics and Public Life," in *National Commission on the Status of Women in Barbados*, vol. 3 (St. Michael, Barbados: Government Printing Office, 1978), 694–99; Jane Jacquette, "Political Science," in K. Lynn Stoner, ed., *Latinas of the Americas: A Source Book* (New York: Garland Publishing, 1989).

18. Boyer, *American's Virgin Islands*, 109–10.

19. Ibid., 113, 121, 140.

20. *New York Times*, 28 February 1917, 10.

21. Yamila Azize, "The Struggle for the Vote in the Decade of the Twenties in Puerto Rico," unpublished translation of a chapter taken from her book *La Mujer en la Lucha*, 4–6, 10–11.

22. *The San Juan Star Sunday Magazine*, 1 September 1991, H–1.

23. Azize, "The Struggle for the Vote . . .," 16–18, 21.

24. Azize, "The Struggle for the Vote," 29–38; Frank Martinez, *The Tragedy of the Puerto Ricans and the Colored Americans* (New York: Frank Martinez, 1935), 43.

25. Azize, "The Struggle for the Vote," 16–18, 21.

26. June Lindquist, interview with the author, Virgin Islands Bureau of Libraries and Museums, Charlotte Amalie, St. Thomas, U.S. V.I., January 1983; Edith Williams, interview with the author, Charlotte Amalie, St. Thomas, U.S. V.I., April 1984; *Virgin Islands Education Review* 1 (December 1981): 25.

27. Ibid.; Bertha Boschulte, interview with the author, Charlotte Amalie, St. Thomas, U.S. V. I., December 1984.

28. Edith Williams, interview with author; *St. Thomas Daily News*, 18 March 1931.

29. *Virgin Islands Educational Review*, 25; Department of Education, U.S. Virgin Islands, *Profiles of Outstanding Virgin Islanders* (St. Thomas: Government of the U.S. Virgin Islands, 1976), 4.

30. Boyer, *America's Virgin Islands,* 170, 186; *St. Thomas Daily News*, 11, 14 December 1935; Bertha Boschulte, interview with the author, June 1984.

31. *St. Thomas Daily News*, 19, 23, 24 December 1935; *Equal Rights*, 14 January 1936, 368.

32. *St. Thomas Daily News*, 28 December 1935.

33. Ibid.

34. *Equal Rights*, 14 January 1936, 368.

3

Gendered Colonialism
The "Woman Question" in Settler Society

DOLORES E. JANIEWSKI

Writing about European women's participation in the empires acquired by their nations, Margaret Strobel discussed white women's participation in "various forms of cultural imperialism, such as missionary work, anthropological study, and 'reform' of indigenous practices that were viewed as harmful by western standards." She added, "European women sometimes identified with the oppressed" and "sought to ameliorate" some of the worst effects of imperialism. As for the women themselves, she concluded, they "often gained opportunities lacking at home and played a central role in shaping the social relations of imperialism" because of the contradictory experiences of being "members of the inferior sex within the superior race" in a colonial setting. Confining her view largely to women subordinated to a "male-centered" colonial system that administered the empire, Strobel's analysis can be usefully applied to white women in the expansion of the continental American empire, so long as it is recognized that women played still more crucial roles in the kind of imperialism, that is "settler capitalism," or "settler colonization," that characterized the parts of North America that became the United States. Although white women served as missionaries, anthropologists, reformers, and the wives of colonial administrators in the English colonies that became the United States, they more crucially contributed their productive and reproductive capacities to the construction of a settler society that displaced the indigenous inhabitants.[1]

Each part of what would become the United States, in turn, experienced the successive waves of colonization that often began as a white European male encounter with indigenous peoples in the initial stages of exploration, trading, and establishing plantations, as was the case in the Virginia colony. At this stage, called "market making" by some scholars, gender relations primarily included European men and indigenous women whose knowledge, prestige, skills, and sexual services benefited the men. The men could make use of these "cultural mediators" in developing ties with the local peoples, exploiting local resources, and becoming informed about local practices that could be useful in an expanding commercial market in colonial commodities. Those involved in the exchange needed to "accommodate each other's cultural universe so that the market between them might thrive."[2]

The arrival of white women was one of the chief indications of the transition from the initial phase of exploration and commercial exploitation to settler colonization, because it usually involved "land taking" as land itself became a commodity. The "common ground" between the settlers and the indigenous people contracted, and profound conflicts, "involving survival itself," emerged. A growing body of scholarship analyzes white women's lives on the successive frontiers that stretched northward out of Mexico and westward from the initial English settlements of coastal North America in the 1600s to the consolidation of Euramerican control over the continent by the end of the nineteenth century. Organized in various subfields of American history—colonial, midwestern, southern, southwestern, Chicano, Native American, ethnohistoric, and western—the literature discusses Anglo- or Euramerican women's interaction with the indigenous peoples, their participation in the domestic, sexual, and market-based economies of their regions, and their contributions to "civilizing" the regions through the establishment of schools, voluntary associations, and churches. A few scholars have studied the work of women employed in the sex industry that exploited the sexuality of women in frontier regions where men often outnumbered women. Defined ideologically as the opposite of the "gentle tamer" image of the settler woman, white prostitutes were featured as the "public" woman, the "sexualized" female in a sexual market that valued women according to a "combination of race, ethnicity, education, sociability, sexual skill, and age" and gave the greatest rewards to "attractive women, usually white, who dressed well, acted like ladies, and played the parts of companions as well as sexual partners." The majority, who lacked the most desirable attributes and who worked in shabby brothels, small cottages, or cribs, were often defined legally as something other than women, that is, as "lewd and dissolute female persons." As female outlaws, despite their "whiteness," these women came dangerously close to occupying the discursive position reserved for "Black" or "indigenous" women in many colonial societies. As the debased vehicles who absorbed the "excess lust" of unattached or frustrated men, prostitutes may have marked a transition between a pattern of marital and sexual relationships with indigenous women and the establishment of Euramerican settler households headed by a male patriarch and a domesticated female partner, a predominantly "male" frontier that persisted in male industries such as mining and logging and in cattle towns. Once "civilized" white women arrived in sufficient numbers, the status of both the indigenous woman and the prostitute became devalued. The issues of miscegenation, immorality, and respectability came to shape sexual relationships and influence marital choices in the context of the formation of a settler society, and "sexual alliance" between European men and indigenous women "gave way to (sexual) conquest." Debating whether to emphasize white women's subordination or their ability to maximize their opportunities and their control over resources in the context of new, and relatively undeveloped, frontier societies, this scholarship tends to a relatively optimistic vision of white women's possibilities, as Strobel has also suggested, when compared to the more settled patriarchal societies they had left behind.[3]

In succession, each of the three kinds of settler colonies identified by scholars—mixed settlement, plantation, and pure settlement—appeared as the colonizers shifted from mixed settlement, a colonial structure including European settlers and a relatively large indigenous population, toward a plantation system based upon coerced, imported labor and a pure settlement colony as the indigenous peoples were dispossessed. Carolyn Merchant discussed "the colonial ecological revolution" that involved an agricultural shift from indigenous patterns of female horticulture and male hunting to patriarchal, male-dominated family farms. As elsewhere, gendered colonialism tended to remove resources and power from indigenous women and transfer them to men, whose authority was apparently enhanced by the increased emphasis on warfare, diplomacy, and trading in articles acquired by hunting, but whose power was fleeting as control over land, other resources, and sovereignty shifted toward white male settlers, military and economic interests, and government authorities. Like other settler colonies, the United States and its ancestral colonies developed forms of racial domination and distinct racialized communities through the interaction of its settlers with indigenous peoples and imported slaves. New institutions of state power began to exert power over the frontier as it became incorporated into regions of the expanding United States. As expressed by Benjamin Ringer, a "'colonist society' [which had imposed] a network of coercive legal, political, and economic constraints and a harness of racial subordination and segmentation on nonwhite minorities" was transformed into "a nation-state rooted in the rights and sovereignty of the people." Its founders simultaneously "legitimated and perpetuated . . . the plural society of a racially bifurcated colonist America regulated by the normative code of a racial creed." Unmentioned by Ringer, the definition of "people" in its political sense applied only to white, property-owning males who headed productive enterprises. As was the case in the individual household, based on common law, white women's presence, labor, and reproductive capacities were assumed to be the property of the white male heads of their respective domestic economies. White women's activities, rights, and duties were allocated within a patriarchal settler society that was separated into "a woman's realm of domesticity and nurture and a man's world of politics and intellect." Propertyless men, African Americans of both sexes, and Native Americans were excluded from the masculine prerogatives of power and often from the "respect" accorded white women as segregation, antimiscegenation laws, and discriminatory land-owning patterns "institutionalized racial-sexual frontiers."[4]

The Anglo frontier metamorphosed into the pure settlement pattern in the northern region, while the plantation replaced it in the southern region, where racially based slavery was essential to the organization of the economy and the social order. In the North, family, indentured, slave, and wage labor coexisted in a complicated and dynamic interaction that formed an elaborate class and racial hierarchy and dynamic economy. In the southern colonies, a shift from indentured servants to slaves completed the establishment of a plantation settlement system. In the decades between 1680 and 1750, slavery provided the basis for the rise of a gentry composed primarily of planters and a few merchants. Patriarchal families gradually replaced more sexually egalitarian families among this class. Another major class developed among the English settlers: yeoman farmers. These included indentured servants, who had lived through their indenture, and new arrivals. Men managed the plantation and usually worked the land, while women took responsibility for domestic labor. In such households, it was assumed that "wives owed their husbands obedience and smooth operation of the household in return for the financial support needed to purchase the necessities of life." In the middle and northern colonies, merchant elites, prospering in the trade of the late 1600s including the slave trade, became the economic center of coastal cities.

Greater social differentiation accompanied the accumulation of wealth. In rural areas, the sexual division of labor assigned to men the work of agriculture and the control of the family's economic resources while women concentrated on the domestic realm. Generally, economic power remained firmly in white male control, as did political power, while women increasingly became defined as the emotional and religious centers of the household as well as unpaid domestic workers.[5]

The American Revolution resulted in the formation of a politically independent ruling class composed primarily of planters, merchants, and master artisans who could use their political power against the other classes, including slaves and wage laborers. That victory simultaneously removed the restraining hand of Great Britain that had slowed the westward movement of settlers across the Appalachians and, hence, resulted in greater coercion directed against Native Americans who occupied the territory into which the settlers began to pour. The "class" of yeomen farmers and planters thus benefited at the expense of the communal occupiers of the land they seized. At the same time, shifts from artisanal to wage labor represented declining opportunities for the economic independence to be obtained by the eventual rise of journeymen to master artisans. This left the hope of westward mobility to become one of the major escapes from an increasingly class-stratified urban economy.[6]

In the newly independent United States, a "slaveholding mentality" became "the wellspring of white supremacist thought and action," giving all whites a stake in racial domination, which persisted even after revolutionary ideals gave impetus to the end of slavery in the northern states. Gender, of course, marked a form of "difference" and "inequality" within Euramerican society. Women did not receive equal citizenship or economic opportunities within colonial or revolutionary America. Yet, the contradiction between claims of equality and the reality of women's lives even among the elite did stimulate the development of an "ideology of citizenship that merged the domestic domain of the preindustrial woman with the new public ideology of individual responsibility and civic virtue."[7] Likewise, racial domination coexisted uneasily with revolutionary pretensions to equality and liberty. Newly empowered national elites began to build a nation out of a population stratified by race and gender, restricting full citizenship to white, property-owning men.

Forced to cede territory by treaty, Native Americans became subject to the efforts of missionaries and governmental agents to transform their economic, political, and sexual relationships. As the United States extended direct control over western areas, federal agents, military officers, railroad and mining interests, and settlers sought to confine the original inhabitants to smaller and smaller territories while "opening" the rest of the land to white settlement and exploitation. Under the so-called "peace" policy of the late 1860s and 1870s, the government assigned reservations to different missionary groups, expecting them to keep up the pressure for assimilation. Like other colonizing societies, the expansionist republic promoted gender transformation to create possessive, patriarchal households in which self-sufficient Christian male farmers would live in nuclear family households while women, excluded from treaty negotiations and leadership positions, would occupy themselves with domestic duties. The exceptions were those women who became missionaries or otherwise participated in the colonizing project outside of the patriarchal household, exerting "moral authority," criticizing male vice, and creating societies, schools, and other institutions under the control of virtuous white women.[8]

In the last phase of settler colonization, a group of eastern reformers, including missionaries, government officials, and educators, combined with a political coalition of western settlers to secure the passage of the Land in Severalty Act in 1887. The Act divided all Native American land into small individual plots and opened the remaining land to sale and settlement. The "Indian" was to disappear into the white citizenry. But the reformers' advocacy of the doctrine of assimilation or cultural annihilation met determined resistance. Unable to maintain economic or political autonomy, Native Americans found that survival lay in maintaining cultural practices, values, and identity. Gender patterns, however circumscribed by governmental and missionary activities, provided a core around which a distinctive culture could survive. Such resistance was aided by the reluctance of Euramerican settlements or states to incorporate Native Americans as full and equal citizens. Neither the "Indian" nor the reservation vanished, despite the hopes of the reformers and the hostility of the settlers. The "closing of the frontier" coincided with the last of the "Indian" wars. The period from the 1890s to the 1930s witnessed the use of the Indian Allotment Act to dispossess Native Americans of much of their remaining land. The granting of citizenship to Native Americans in 1924 represented only another of the mechanisms by which "to extend absolute U.S. control over jurisdiction, land tenure, national allegiance, and governance over even the residues of indigenous territoriality." The Indian Reorganization Act of 1934 created "tribal regimes, ostensibly operated by indigenous peoples" but "ultimately influenced by non-indigenous decision makers," thus concealing the reality of "colonial self-administration" under the "appearance of self-determination."[9] Thus the United States remained tied to its origins as a settler colony into the twentieth century; internal colonies continued to contain the remnants of the indigenous peoples and other racialized peoples unacceptable for complete assimilation into a white-dominated nation-state.

Throughout the four centuries of settler colonization, white women primarily contributed their domestic, reproductive, and economic services to male-headed patriarchal households while benefiting from the colonizing enterprise at the expense of the indigenous people and the coerced labor supply brought from Africa. There were, however, exceptions to this pattern. Rather than discussing settler women, whose activities have been extensively analyzed, or the "sexualized" women who operated as prostitutes on the male frontiers, the remainder of this chapter focuses on activities that correspond to two of Strobel's categories—women as agents of cultural imperialism and as critics of the imperialist project. For these purposes, I examine the career of Alice Fletcher and, to a lesser extent, those of her female associates and successors. Fletcher's activities as anthropologist, government agent, and feminist critic took her to the Omaha in Nebraska in the early 1880s and into the Pacific Northwest, accompanied by E. Jane Gay, from 1889 to 1892. Forty years later, in 1930, Margaret Mead retraced a part of Fletcher's journey by going to Nebraska to observe, research, and write about the Omaha. Both Fletcher's activities and the discursive currents to which she contributed, as Strobel has suggested, simultaneously supported, ameliorated, and criticized the colonizing project in which she played a significant part.

Fletcher's work as an agent of cultural imperialism took place in the context of a drive by reformers, the military, the government, and missionaries to eliminate the "Indian," by the process called "assimilation." Reformist discourse advocated the "disappearance" of the "Indian" into the American citizenry in accompaniment with the opening of Native American territory to the American nation. This vision was supported by women in the Women's National Indian Association (who established missionary stations on reservations), by the Indian Reform Association, and by the Lake Mohonk Conference of Friends of the Indian, all of which were formed in the late 1870s and early 1880s. Native American men, except for those who continued to resist militarily, would become individual, property-owning yeoman farmers. The women would become domesticated housewives enclosed within the family home. The people who were called "Indian" would be saved from extinction by the elimination of their culture, ways of living, and other markers that set them apart as different or "other." In particular, as described by Strobel, Native American women were to be saved from a fate as "unfortunate drudges or subordinates" in line with "reform" of indigenous practices that were viewed as harmful by western standards.[10]

At the same time, the belief in the inexorable necessity of disappearance gave rise to another discourse: the emerging anthropological discourse that intermingled science with the exoticism of the travelers' tales that stressed the value, uniqueness, and picturesque interest of the culture that would soon vanish. Fletcher, in her professional identity as a pioneer ethnographer, shared in the effort to record the "vanishing race" just as, in her reformist guise, she helped to cause the disappearance.[11]

Gender politics of the period generated yet another discourse that differentiated Native Americans into male and female, something the original image had rarely done. Feminists saw in the Native American tradition a golden age of matriarchy that could inspire them. Fletcher's analysis of women's place in Native American society offered a way to criticize the patriarchal character of Euramerican society. By the beginning of the twentieth century, yet another discourse had begun to emerge as Native Americans began to reappear through their own writings, to which Fletcher also contributed by her adoption of and collaboration with Francis La Flesche, her Omaha son. Thus the colonizing project began to produce its own internal opposition as some of its practitioners subverted the assumptions of their own disciplines.

Alice Fletcher first ventured west in 1881 to "study the life of Indian women" in the hope that she could learn about the "historical evolution of the 'woman question.'" On the Omaha reservation, she moved in the circle surrounding Chief Joseph La Flesche whose members described themselves as the "citizens' party." Responding to their concern about insecure land titles, she drew up a petition to Congress signed by a minority of the Omaha men, whom she declared to be "the true leaders among the people." Journeying to Washington, she became involved in a coordinated effort to secure a law allotting the Omaha land. Soon she was meeting with prominent women from the Washington chapter of the Women's National Indian Association, government officials, and Indian reformers, and becoming involved with the circle of reformers, missionaries, and government officials who met at Lake Mohonk, New York, as the "Friends of the Indian."[12]

Fletcher, perhaps the most famous woman participant at the annual meetings of the Lake Mohonk conference, often spoke the language of the reformers. In 1882 she had discussed the need to make Native American men "manly" and to teach them "the power which has made the white race the dominant people," the power of "new and higher wants" that would bring them into brotherhood "in the thought and in the market, in the field and in the home." Due to her testimony, lobbying, lectures, and publications concerning the Omaha, Sioux, and Winnebago, Fletcher acquired a reputation as a scientific expert on Native Americans. In 1883 she received an unpaid appointment as a special agent of the Bureau of Indian Affairs to allot the Omaha lands in order to implement the law whose passage she had secured. At the end of the decade, she would be paid for performing the same duties among the Winnebago and the Nez Perce. Forming a close relationship with Electra and Anna Dawes, Fletcher became an important part of the group of reformers who won congressional support for the division of all Native American lands into individual homesteads in a piece of legislation that would become known as the Dawes Act, after its senatorial champion Henry L. Dawes.[13]

As a result of her practical experience, Fletcher was often a featured speaker at meetings of the reformist/missionary/governmental alliance in which women played an influential part as symbolized by the women in the Dawes family and the wives of other politicians active in "Indian reform." Seeking a future for Native American women, she had developed a place for herself as an expert and honored reformer in a group whose beliefs reinforced "laissez-faire" and anti-statist assumptions. She shared the organization's determination to "save the Indians from themselves" and from their "fatal tendency . . . to fixed tribal life." Like other participants, she saw her mission as instilling "manliness" and encouraging "good order and individual enterprise" amidst the "disintegrating process" that made "the incoming of new life possible" by teaching men to become possessive, property-owning yeoman farmers and women to become domestic helpmates. After her active career as an allotting agent had ended, she summed up her labors as "taking by the hand the people of an alien race and helping them to step across the deep chasm that lies between their past and our present" in an 1895 letter to the members of the Women's National Indian Association with whom she had cooperated in her reform activities.[14]

When Fletcher spoke to feminist audiences, her language shifted from celebrations of the project of cultural imperialism to criticism of its effect on Native American women, and involved at least a partial critique of the assumptions of white supremacy. Speaking to female audiences about her quest and her discoveries, she appealed to a sense of common sisterhood that could traverse racial boundaries and pleaded for help to enable Native American women to adjust to the "new civilization" that was eroding their old way of life. Linguistically, she linked together her female audience in eastern cities and her Native

American sisters huddled in the Trans-Mississippi West by using the language of "sisterhood" rather than reformist maternalism when she spoke to audiences of women instead of reformers. In such circumstances, she specifically acknowledged the existence of "women" among the group to which she always referred in the masculine singular as "the Indian" when she spoke to reformers.[15]

Fletcher's special interest in the situation of Native American women found a warm hearing among feminists. A founding member of the Association for the Advancement of Women in the 1870s, Fletcher contributed a paper on "The Education and Training of Indian Women" at its 1884 convention. Introduced at the 1888 International Council of Women by Susan B. Anthony to speak on the "Legal Status of Indian Women," Fletcher contributed to the feminist awareness of Native American women's situation and provided a way to contextualize and historicize women's situation within Euramerican society. She told her audience about the deterioration of women's status as they came under U.S. law. She referred to the "edge of our laws" under which Native American women had lost their accustomed freedom. "It has been my task," she told her audience at the 1888 International Council of Women, "to explain to Indian women their legal conditions under the law. In bringing these lines down upon their independent lives I have been led to realise how much woman has given of her own freedom to make strong the foundations of the family and to preserve the accumulations and descent of property" and to make possible "the development of civilization." In asking her audience to "take pity on the Indian woman," she was implicitly asking them to think about their own situation.

> They must lose much they hold dear and suffer wrongs at the hands of those, whose added legal powers, when untempered by an unselfish, cultured spirit, makes the legal conditions of woman akin to slavery. I crave for my Indian sisters, your help, your patience, and your unfailing labors, to hasten the day when the laws of all the land shall know neither male nor female, but grant to all equal rights and equal justice.[16]

Clearly Fletcher regretted the necessity that caused these difficulties for Native American women.

According to Fletcher, women among the Omaha had told her, "As an Indian woman I was free. I owned my home, my person, the work of my hands; and my children could never forget me. I was better as an Indian woman than under white law." Following Fletcher's remarks, leading feminists Matilda Joslyn Gage and Lucy Stone commented that Fletcher had shown that Native American law was "more just" than "the family laws of the white men for women." Fletcher's feminist discourse built upon contributions made by earlier feminists who had also studied "the woman question" by observing Native American women.[17]

Fletcher, Matilda Joslyn Gage, and leading suffragist Elizabeth Cady Stanton developed an understanding of women's position, and in the case of Gage and Stanton, a conviction of the potential for emancipating women from gender inequality, by studying gender relations among Native Americans, principally among the Iroquois in the pioneering studies by Lewis Morgan, which also influenced Frederick Engels. Unknowingly, these feminists universalized the matrilineal Iroquian culture to other Native American groups, as their Marxian contemporary would also do. Stanton's address, "The Matriarchate or Mother-Age," for the 1891 National Women's Council used the works of Johann Bachofen and Lewis Morgan to demonstrate the "period of woman's supremacy." She urged "every woman present" to "have a new sense of dignity and self-respect feeling that our mothers during some periods in the past have been the ruling power," which sustained her in the belief that "our turn will come again."[18] Following the example of Stanton and Gage, American feminists used the example of Native American women to criticize the patriarchal nature of their own society, to construct an interpretation of the origins of women's subordination, and to demonstrate the contingent, historical, and man-made creation of patriarchy through law and social custom as would one of Fletcher's anthropological "daughters," Margaret Mead.

Occasionally feminist concerns intruded into Fletcher's communications with reformers and with federal officials despite the usual segregation between her feminist and her reformist selves. Attending the annual conference of the Board of Indian Commissioners in 1889, Fletcher told her audience,

> Three years ago I thought that it was sufficient that the Indian woman should be united to her husband in property matters. . . . [Now] I think it would be much better for the wife to be independent in a property point, of the husband. She would fare better and her children would fare better. But I found when I came here that I ran into the woman question, and, if the Indian woman were given rights that were peculiar to her, it might give some rights to the white women that are not quite ready yet and so I must withdraw. I am told it is quite enough to give the Indian woman what the white woman have. While I am sorry that the Indian woman can not hold her own property, yet I submit that she ought to.

Despite her claims that she had refrained from arguing for rights for "Indian" women that white women (or perhaps white men) were not yet prepared to extend to women in settler societies, Fletcher pushed for the protection of indigenous women's property rights. Privately, as her letters to the Indian Commissioners and the Commissioner of Indian Affairs concerning the Dawes Act's effect on women revealed, she was quite ready to run into and through the "woman question." As she wrote to E. Whittlesey, "In the law as it was written, women are losers. They own nothing in their own right and yet they are as truly heirs to the tribal heritage as the men."[19] It was only publicly that she denied her feminist inclinations, perhaps in deference to the sensibilities of conservative men rather than out of concern for white women's reluctance to have equal property rights.

Fletcher used reformist language when speaking to the Native Americans in her official position as an allotment agent for the Omaha, the Winnebago, and, in her last assignment, to the Nez Perce, whose lands she was assigned to divide into individual plots to which they would receive title and eventually the right to buy, sell, and cultivate them. Her language and her position as the representation of the law and the "Great Father" involved a linguistic assertion of power over men who must disappear as "the Indian" and be reborn as American men and citizens. Despite her inferior gender status in the eastern United States, Fletcher acquired the same manhood that she benevolently wished to bestow upon Native American men. Hearing such language, a listener fluent in the gendered discourse of the period might have noticed the paradoxical contrast between the speaker's gender and her masculinist language, an irony that did not go unnoticed in the acute observations of her close companion, E. Jane Gay.[20] The additional irony that Gay and Fletcher escaped domestic confinement as single, self-supporting career women even as they, and their missionary associates among the Nez Perce, preached domestication to the women among the Omaha, Winnebago, and Nez Perce, whom they sought to assimilate to the American way of life, was one too paradoxical for even the iconoclastic Gay to articulate.

Fletcher's reformist language expressed enthusiastic support for the "voluntary burial of the tribal past" so that the "people may be freer to enter into the new life of civilization." This "reformist Fletcher" celebrated the assimilationist process, writing in 1887 that "men whom . . . I feared would live and die Indians . . . [are] now pushing out into better modes of living and thinking." Fletcher's assignment as an allotting agent to the Nez Perce in northern Idaho, which occupied her summers from 1889 to 1892, supported her reformist inclinations. She became a part of another network—a group of female missionaries who had been involved with the process of attempting to transform the culture of the local Native American groups since the mid-1830s by teaching men that their "proper place" was at the "head" of their family and instructing women in "wifely duties and civilized ways." At the same time, her companion, E. Jane Gay, compared the situation of women in the settler society surrounding the reservation and that of "an Indian woman." Describing the "hopelessness" on the faces of the settler women, and insisting that the Indian woman was "as free as her husband; freer, indeed, for she owns her children, her horses, her home and all its belongings," Gay quoted Fletcher to the effect that "civilization has been built up largely" at women's expense, "at the cost of her independence; and is still an expensive luxury to her." Gay's doubts occasionally extended to the entire project. "It is not difficult," she wrote, "to conceive of the suffering which will follow this sort of opening up of the Reservation." Even in the midst of women committed to the imperialist and reformist project, a skepticism might intrude only to be submerged by a determined refusal to allow "pessimism" to detract from a commitment to the inculcation of "Christian civilization." The "tribal bonds" must be "broken away and the individual man" left "standing more and more responsible for his own future," whatever the costs to women.[21]

But Fletcher's paradoxical career as a pioneering anthropologist revealed an admiration for the culture her reformist activities were seeking to bury. Anything but the detached scientific observer, she wrote about her ethnographic encounters with Native Americans in a deeply personal way. Involved in the transition of anthropology from the domain of the "accidental 'men [and women] on the spot,'" the "armchair anthropologists," and "museum men" to science conducted by professionally trained scholars, Fletcher merged travelers' tales and ethnography in a discursive blend that would lead to a debate as to whether her more famous contemporary Franz Boas, some twenty years her junior, was an impressionist or a scientist as he trained a new generation of scholars who would include Margaret Mead, Ruth Benedict, and an obscure Nez Perce named Archie Phinney, who would be encouraged, as Francis La Flesche had been before him, to write about his people.[22]

Fletcher published a brief account of her personal "journey into Indian country" in *Century* in 1896, which transferred the encounter into a love affair rather than placing it in a feminist or maternalist context. Referring to the desolation of the Great Plains, she wrote,

> I could find nothing to connect myself with nature so unaltered by man. . . .
> [T]here was nothing here on my own plane of life; and thus, alone and self-
> centered, a sense of loneliness began to oppress me, when a sound fell upon

my ear—a strange sound but with a human tone in it . . . an Indian on horseback. The easy figure, the wayward song . . . the absence of all concern with time, of all knowledge of the teeming life out of which I had come, and which was even now surging toward him . . . touched a new thought-center and awoke a new interest. . . . I had crossed the line, another race had welcomed with a song.

Her language conveyed a critical assessment of the "teeming life out of which I had come" even as it turned a meeting between two races along a colonial frontier into a romantic encounter between a lonely woman and a "wayward" denizen of the Plains. Stressing the "human" quality of the song, Fletcher once again challenged the white supremacist assumptions of her period and the taboo on interracial relationships between men and women that was being so ardently espoused at the time she was writing.[23]

Three years later Fletcher published an article entitled "The Indian Woman and Her Problems," asking men and women to work together to help Indian women adjust to the effect of assimilation. Referring to the Native American woman, Fletcher wrote,

There is now no public reward for her work; there are now no tribal ceremonies at the time of planting. . . . The picturesque has gone out of her life. The black cooking stove, the wash-tub, the glinting needle are her silent and inexorable companions. . . . There are also new laws to distress her.

The article closed by asking men and women to work together to help Indian women because it was "impossible to bisect the body politic along the line of sex" and any solution demanded "mutual respect, mutual regard, mutual help, both in thought and in action." Two years later Fletcher told the readers of the *Woman's Tribune* about the Indian woman who "finds herself under a domination that did not exist in the olden times" and with whom she expected them to sympathize.[24] Seemingly, the "feminist" Fletcher had come to regret the effect of the "civilization" and the domestication project upon Native American women.

In between the publication of the two articles, however, Fletcher addressed another gathering at Lake Mohonk in a language that conveyed a maternalist, rather than a mutually respectful attitude toward "dependent peoples." Infusing anthropological theory with her maternalist metaphor, Fletcher told the 1900 conference of reformers at Lake Mohonk,

In the suggestive words of one of the speakers last evening we were cautioned to think of the native Hawaiians as children among the family of races. That is a very good thought in dealing with the so-called dependent races. The life of the nations and of the people of the world is like the life of the human being; it has the childhood period, the adolescent period and the mature period. . . . so we speak of savagery, barbarism, and civilization.

Her professional and personal involvement in "Indian emancipation" that gave "every individual Indian . . . a home and a wife and children just as white men do" expressed an identification with the reformist agenda and its patriarchal assumptions. Fletcher could not always speak the feminist or reformist tongue consistently. Like the satirical writings of E. Jane Gay, Fletcher sometimes enacted the story of allotment in which she played a leading role as a comedy "which cheerfully reconciles and unites its characters," but occasionally she spoke or wrote a tragic or an ironic commentary on the results of the process to which she contributed.[25]

From near the beginning of her encounter with the Omaha to her final pronouncement on the issue in *The Omaha Tribe*, Fletcher wrote about "cultural imperialism" with a contradictory voice that simultaneously applauded and criticized its results, especially when women were concerned. Doubtless influenced by the prevailing belief in evolutionary necessity, she wrote about the need to journey to "a future unknown and inevitable where the Indian must be merged in the American." As an inevitable corollary the "Indian" past must be placed for "safekeeping" in sympathetic hands like her own. Once again, a conflict emerged between her reformist insistence that freedom was "the product of civilization" and her recognition that civilization was a costly blessing. When she spoke with a "maternal" voice, she celebrated her children as "men whom . . . I feared would live and die Indians . . . now pushing out into better modes of living and thinking."[26] But her feminist recognition of gender would not allow her to speak the celebratory voice without interruption.

Her major ethnographic work, *The Omaha Tribe*, written in collaboration with her adopted Omaha son, Francis La Flesche, expressed all the discordant voices and plots that Fletcher's narrative career had utilized. Writing as a reformer, Fletcher introduced the work, declaring, "The past is overlaid by a thriving present. The old Omaha men and women sleep peacefully on the hills while their grandchildren farm beside their white neighbours, send their children to school, speak English, and keep bank accounts." But the joint ethnography shifted toward an ironic and tragic tone as it paid tribute to the gender relations that had placed women "on a moral equality" with men and raised questions about the cost of progress. The authors referred to the Omaha as becoming "less strong to resist the inroad and adverse influences which came with his closer contact with the white race" and expressed sympathy for the person "slow to change his native point of view of justice and of truth."[27] Fletcher and La Flesche conveyed ambivalence about a future that had been constructed over the bones of the culture they so lovingly and respectfully detailed in a collaboration that gossips conceived to be a sexual rather than a parental relationship.

In 1930, shortly after Fletcher's death, an anthropological "daughter" retraced Fletcher's journey to the Omaha. Margaret Mead, trained by Franz Boas, and dispatched by Ruth Benedict and Benedict's husband, New Zealander Reo Fortune, to study the Omaha, sought to answer the same question that had brought Fletcher a half century earlier. She, however, was a generation removed from Fletcher's immersion in the reformist assumptions that had championed assimilation. Mead wrote, "My task was to look at the women, and I had the unrewarding task of discussing a long history of mistakes in American policy toward the Indians and of prophesying a still more disastrous fate for them in the future." Unconsciously echoing E. Jane Gay's moment of despair, Mead described the future that Gay had fearfully predicted. Mead saw "a culture so shrunk from its earlier style . . . that [there] was very little out of the past that was recognizable and still less in the present that was aesthetically satisfying. They had met anthropologists before whom they had come to regard primarily as a source of revenue." Referring to her assignment as "watching the sorrows of fading culture," she noted that Fletcher's memory lingered only in a tale of cultural retribution. Chief Joseph La Flesche's death was described as a punishment for his having divulged "the sacred White Buffalo" to Alice Fletcher, who had sent it eastward to be housed in a museum. Mead's evaluation of Fletcher's reformist legacy offered only one deviation from a tragic plot. The Omaha woman had fared better than the man because "it is impossible to strip her life of meaning as completely as the life of the man was stripped."[28] Free from Fletcher's commitment to the discourse of assimilation and reform, Mead judged the culture by categories from an anthropological discourse that prized aesthetics and exotic appeal, that is, "difference" from her own society rather than its ability to mimic the encroaching "civilization." Speaking from an evolving discourse of "cultural relativism," Mead pronounced the modernist verdict upon her predecessor's contradictory efforts to impose an alien culture on a people while contributing to a critical discourse that undermined the project of "cultural imperialism." Fletcher had bequeathed the discursive tools her successors, including her adopted son, would use to demolish her reformist legacy.

Her career matched the description supplied by Margaret Strobel with two crucial differences: Fletcher represented in herself the anthropologist, the government agent, and the reformer who sought to "ameliorate," promote, and record cultural imperialism at work in the interior United States. She was one of the beneficiaries of the colonizing enterprise that provided her with a career, financial support, and a platform upon which to create for herself a political role at a time when women were disfranchised from the formal political process. But Fletcher was also a feminist and a relatively egalitarian racialist in a white supremacist age. Her developmental approach to Native American society would give birth to the antiracist anthropology of Franz Boas. Her feminist insights would moderate the law for the benefit of Native American women and would give feminists support for their claims that gender was historically and culturally constructed rather than natural, universal, and unchanging. A cultural imperialist Fletcher undoubtedly was, but she was also an agent in the formation of an intellectual resistance movement to colonization. By collaborating with an Omaha scholar, Fletcher contributed to a scholarly enterprise that would transcend "whiteness," interrogate patriarchy, and reverse the earlier patterns of gendered interaction in which the paradigmatic couple had been the European man and the Native American woman. It was no small achievement for a woman who had ventured west to study "the woman question."

NOTES

1. Margaret Strobel, "Gender and Race in the Nineteenth- and Twentieth-Century British Empire," in Renate Bridenthal, Claudia Koonz, and Susan Stuard, eds., *Becoming Visible: Women in European History* (Boston: Houghton Mifflin, 1987), 375–95, 375, 376; as used, for example, by Donald Deoon, *Settler Capitalism: The Dynamics of Dependent Development in the Southern Hemisphere* (Oxford: Clarendon Press, 1983); and Dolores E. Janiewski, "Gendering, Racializing, and Classifying: Settler Colonization in North America, 1590–1990," in Nira Yuval-Davis and Daiva Stasiullis, eds., *Gender, Race, Ethnicity and Class in Settler Societies* (London: Sage, 1995).

2. William Cronon, George Miles, and Jay Gitlin, "Becoming West: Toward a New Meaning for Western History," in W. Cronon, G. Miles, and J. Gitlin, eds., *Under an Open Sky: Rethinking America's Western Past* (New York: Norton, 1992), 13; Richard White, *It's Your Misfortune and None of My Own: A History of the American West* (Norman: University of Oklahoma Press, 1991), 46–47; see also Sylvia Van Kirk, *Many Tender Ties: Women in the Fur Trade Society, 1670–1870* (Norman: University of Oklahoma Press, 1980).

3. Cronon, Miles, and Gitlin, "Becoming West," 14; Sarah Deutsch, "Landscape of Enclaves: Race Relations in the West, 1865–1990," in Cronon, Miles, Gitlin, *Under an Open Sky*, 110–31, 117; Katherine G. Morrissey, "Engendering the West," in Cronon, Miles, and Gitlin, *Under an Open Sky*, 132–44, 138–39;

Marion S. Goldman, *Gold Diggers and Silver Miners: Prostitution and Social Life on the Comstock Lode* (Ann Arbor: University of Michigan Press, 1981); Mary Murphy, "The Private Lives of Public Women: Prostitution in Butte, Montana, 1878–1917," in Susan Armitage and and Elizabeth Jameson, eds., *The Women's West* (Norman: University of Oklahoma Press, 1987), 193–205, 194; Sylvia Van Kirk, "The Role of Native Women in the Creation of Fur Trade Society in Western Canada, 1670–1830," in Armitage and Jameson, *The Women's West*, 53–62; Sherry L. Smith, "Beyond Princess and Squaw: Army Officers' Perceptions of Indian Women," in Armitage and Jameson, *The Women's West*, 63–75; Van Kirk, *Many Tender Ties*; on settler women, see Laurel Thatcher Ulrich, *Good Wives: Image and Reality in the Lives of Women in Northern New England 1650–1750* (New York: Oxford University Press, 1982); John Faragher, *Women and Men on the Overland Trail* (New Haven: Yale University Press, 1979); Lillian Schlissel, *Women's Diaries of the Westward Journey* (New York: Schocken Books, 1982); Glenda Riley, *Women and Indians on the Frontier* (Albuquerque: University of New Mexico Press, 1984); Armitage and Jameson, *The Women's West*; Julie Roy Jeffrey, *Frontier Women: The Trans-Mississippi West, 1840–1880* (New York: Hill and Wang, 1979); Sandra L. Myres, *Westering Women and the Frontier Experience, 1880–1915* (Albuquerque: University of New Mexico Press, 1982).

4. Carolyn Merchant, *Ecological Revolutions: Nature, Gender, and Science in New England* (Chapel Hill: University of North Carolina Press, 1989). The analysis that follows is a summary of the argument made in Janiewski, "Gendering, Racializing, and Classifying"; Cronon, Miles, and Gitlin, "Becoming West," 16–17; 21–22; Patricia Nelson Limerick, *The Legacy of Conquest: The Unbroken Past of the American West* (New York: Norton, 1987); Benjamin B. Ringer, *We the People and Others: Duality and America's Treatment of Its Racial Minorities* (New York: Tavistock, 1983), 16, 8; Linda K. Kerber, *Women of the Republic: Intellect and Ideology in Revolutionary America* (New York: Norton, 1980), 287; Deutsch, "Landscape of Enclaves," 117.

5. Allan Kulikoff, *Tobacco and Slaves: The Development of Southern Cultures in the Chesapeake, 1680–1800* (Chapel Hill: University of North Carolina Press, 1986), 183; Gary Nash, *The Urban Crucible: Social Change, Political Consciousness and the Origins of the American Revolution* (Cambridge: Harvard University Press, 1979), 262; Sara M. Evans, *Born for Liberty: A History of Women in America* (New York: Free Press, 1989).

6. Christine Bolt, "White Power Grows, Reformer Hopes Fluctuate: The 1770s to the 1850s," in Christine Bolt, *American Indian Policy and Indian Reform* (Hempstead: Allen and Unwin, 1987).

7. George Fredrickson, *White Supremacy: A Comparative Study in American and South African History* (New York: Oxford University Press, 1988), 91; Kerber, *Women of the Republic*, 269.

8. White, *It's Your Misfortune*, 311–20.

9. Leonard Carlson, *Indians, Bureaucrats and Land: The Dawes Act and the Decline in Indian Farming* (Westport, CT: Greenwood, 1981); White, *It's Your Misfortune*; M. Annette Jaimes, ed., *The State of Native America: Genocide, Colonization and Resistance* (Boston: South End Press, 1992); Dolores Janiewski, "Learning to Live 'Just Like White Folks': Gender, Ethnicity and the State in the Inland Northwest," in Dorothy O. Helly and Susan M. Reverby, eds., *Gendered Domains: Rethinking Public and Private in Women's History* (Ithaca: Cornell University Press, 1992); Joan Jensen, "Native American Women and Agriculture: A Seneca Case Study," *Sex Roles* 3, no. 5 (1977); Patricia Albers and Beatrice Medicine, *The Hidden Half: Studies of Plains Indian Women* (Washington, DC: University Press of America, 1983); Jaimes, *The State of Native America*, 69;

White, *It's Your Misfortune*; Carlson, *Indians, Bureaucrats and Land*; Frederick Hoxie, *A Final Promise: The Campaign to Assimilate the Indians, 1880–1920* (Lincoln: University of Nebraska Press, 1984).

10. See also Christine Bolt, "Assimilationist Pressures Mount: The 1860s to 1920," in Bolt, *American Indian Policy and Indian Reform.*

11. Dolores Janiewski, "Giving Women a Future: Alice Fletcher, the 'Woman Question,' and 'Indian Reform,'" in Nancy A. Hewitt and Suzanne Lebsock, eds., *Visible Women: New Essays on American Activism* (Urbana: University of Illinois Press, 1993), 325–44; Alice C. Fletcher to Frederick Putnam; Alice Fletcher to Frederick Putnam, 3 August 1889; Alice C. Fletcher to Frederick Putnam, 28 September 1890, Peabody Museum papers, Harvard University Archives, Pusey Library, Harvard University, Cambridge, MA (hereafter PM/HU); Joan Mark, *A Stranger in Her Native Land: Alice Fletcher and the American Indians* (Lincoln: University of Nebraska Press, 1988).

12. Alice C. Fletcher to Lucian Cass, Peabody Museum, Cambridge, MA, 3 August 1881, Peabody Museum papers, Harvard University Archives, Pusey Library, Harvard University, Cambridge, MA (hereafter PM/HU); Alice C. Fletcher to John Morgan, 31 December 1881, Alice C. Fletcher Francis La Flesche papers, National Anthropological Archives, Smithsonian Museum of Natural History, Washington, DC (hereafter Fletcher/NAA).

13. *Woman's Journal*, 11 February 1882; Hiram Price, Commissioner of Indian Affairs, to Honorable Secretary of the Interior, 20 April 1883, Fletcher/NAA; see Hoxie, *A Final Promise*; Carlson, *Indians, Bureaucrats and Land*; Francis Paul Prucha, *Americanizing the American Indians: Writings by the "Friends of the Indian," 1880–1900* (Lincoln: University of Nebraska Press, 1973).

14. Women's National Indian Association, "In Memoriam: Harriet W. Foote Hawley" (Washington, DC: National Indian Association, Washington Auxiliary, 1886); Alice C. Fletcher to Dr. J. E. Rhoads, President, Indian Rights Association, 7 April 1887, Fletcher/NAA; Alice C. Fletcher to Carolina S. Dall, October 1884, Caroline S. Dall papers, microfilm edition, University of Massachusetts, Amherst, MA; U.S. House of Representatives, "Report of the Commissioner of Indian Affairs," Executive Documents, 48th Congress, 2nd Session, 1884–85, 722; *Southern Workman* 13, no. 11 (November 1884); Alice Fletcher to Dr. J. E. Rhoads, Indian Rights Association, 7 April 1887, Fletcher/NAA; *The Indian's Friend*, c. 1895–1896, Fletcher/NAA.

15. Alice C. Fletcher, quoted in the *Women's Tribune*, 31 March 1888.

16. Alice C. Fletcher, quoted in *Report of the International Council of Women Assembled by the National Woman Suffrage Association*, 25 March to 1 April 1888 (Washington, DC: Rufus H. Darby, 1888), 241.

17. *Women's Tribune*, 31 March 1888; Lydia Maria Child, *Hobomok and Other Writings on Indians*, Carolyn L. Karcher, ed. (New Brunswick, N.J.: Rutgers University Press, 1986), xi–xxiv.

18. Elizabeth Cady Stanton, "The Matriarchate or Mother-Age," read at the Women's National Council, Washington, DC, February 1891, by Susan B. Anthony, Stanton-Anthony papers, University of Massachusetts, Amherst.

19. U.S. House of Representatives, Executive Documents, "18th Annual Conference with Representatives of Missionary Boards and Indian Rights Association," 50th Congress, 2nd Session, 17 January 1889, 840; Alice C. Fletcher to E. Whittlesey, 30 October 1889, Fletcher/NAA; Alice C. Fletcher to Commissioner of Indian Affairs, 4 April 1889, Special Cases, Bureau of Indian Affairs, Record Group 75, National Archives, Washington, DC (hereafter RG75/DC).

20. E. Jane Gay, "Choup-nit-ki: With the Nez Perces," unpublished manu-

script in Jane Gay Dodge papers, Schlesinger Library, Radcliffe College, Cambridge, MA. See also E. Jane Gay, *With the Nez Perces: Alice Fletcher in the Field, 1889–92*, Frederick E. Hoxie and Joan T. Mark, eds. (Lincoln: University of Nebraska Press, 1981).

21. Michael Coleman, *Presbyterian Missionary Attitudes toward American Indians, 1837–1893* (Jackson: University Press of Mississippi, 1985) 124, 84, 94; Gay, *With the Nez Perces*, 34–35, 129, 174, 133, 174.

22. Alice C. Fletcher, "Tribal Life among the Omahas: Personal Stories of Indian Life," *Century Magazine*, new series, 29 (1896), 450–61; Alice C. Fletcher to J. E. Rhoads, President, Indian Rights Association, 7 April 1887, Fletcher/NAA; Arnold Krupat, *Ethnocriticism: Ethnography, History, Literature* (Berkeley: University of California Press, 1992), 84, 89.

23. Alice C. Fletcher, "Tribal Life among the Omahas"; George M. Frederickson, *White Supremacy: A Comparative Study in American and South African History* (New York: Oxford University Press, 1981).

24. Alice C. Fletcher, "The Indian Woman and Her Problems," *Southern Workman* 28 (1899), 172–76; Alice C. Fletcher, "The Indian Woman Problems," *Woman's Tribune*, 31 August 1901.

25. *Proceedings of the Eighteenth Annual Meeting of the Lake Mohonk Conference of Friends of the Indian* (1900), reported and edited by Isabel C. Barrows, 1901, 73; Krupat, *Ethnocriticism*, 135.

26. Alice C. Fletcher to Frederick Putnam, 7 June 1884; Alice C. Fletcher to J. E. Rhoads, President, Indian Rights Association, 7 April 1887 (Fletcher/NAA).

27. Alice C. Fletcher and Francis La Flesche, *The Omaha Tribe, Twenty-Seventh Annual Report of the Bureau of American Ethnology* (Washington, DC: U.S. Government Printing Office, 1911), 30, 615, 628, 629.

28. Margaret Mead, *Blackberry Winter: My Earlier Years* (New York: Morrow, 1972), 191, 190; Margaret Mead, *Letters from the Field: 1925–1975* (New York: Harper & Row, 1977), 95, 96; Margaret Mead, *The Changing Culture of an Indian Tribe* (New York: Columbia University Press, 1932), 134.

4

Actions Louder than Words
The Historical Task of Defining Feminist
Consciousness in Colonial West Africa

CHERYL JOHNSON-ODIM

The term "feminism" is layered with multiple meanings, inter-pretations, and perspectives. In recent years, primarily due to research and writing emanating from and being conducted in the non-western world, and to the contribution of women of color in the western world, some scholars have begun to speak of feminism in the plural, as femi-nisms. Others have elected not to use the term feminism at all, but to coin other terms, such as womanist.[1] Still others, as I have done else-where, have attempted to redefine feminist philosophy in a way in which women remain integral to it but that includes activity and thought aimed at eliminating structural inequalities (racism, imperial-ism) that oppress both women and men.[2]

As a result, in recent years much of feminist theory originating in the West has reached out to include analyses of nonwhite, non-western women of varying classes and in various places. Some feminist theory has begun to embrace what historian Joan Wallach Scott has termed "an historicizing approach [that] stresses differences among women and even within the concept of 'women.'"[3] Yet, Scott acknowledges two things. First, that women of color, in both national and international fora, have been responsible for, in her words, "exposing the implicit whiteness of [western] feminism" as well as its essentializing and ahis-torical tendencies.[4] And two, that the historicizing and acknowledg-ment of the salience of difference is still working its way into western feminist theory and is seen as divisive by some western feminist theoreticians.

The tremendous growth (at least if we judge by publications) in post-1960s theories of feminism mostly took place in the United States and western Europe. In part due to the fact that they proliferated as fast as or even faster than specific research, theories of feminism often proceeded from the theoretical to the concrete; hypotheses went in search of examples. Moreover, much of the specific research on which theories were based was undertaken in western, Christian, industrialized, capitalist societies. This sometimes engendered a reductionist reasoning that resulted in two equally unsatisfactory conclusions vis-à-vis the study of the lives of women outside the West. First, it defined feminism in a cultural context and along a historical continuum that were western. Secondly, it looked to the "Third World" with a western eye in search of examples of western feminism, or anthropological antecedents of women's preindustrial, precapitalist power that could fit someplace along a western historical continuum that could be defined as universal. Nancy Hewitt telescopes the point in observing that

> Without intending to, Western women's historians may become mere raiders of a lost ark—seeking out the telling anecdote, the apparent parallel, the seeming sisterhood; exploring the primitive, the pre-capitalist, the pre-patriarchal; searching for either the pre-modern and traditional or the mythic and matriarchal, with which or against which to define ourselves, still at the center. . . .[5]

There were problems with this logic even among some women resident in the West. Among women of color long resident in the West, African American women for example, debate has often ensued over whether race or sex took precedence in African American women's struggles—as if African American women could separate the two, given that they are indivisibly nonwhite and female in a society that locates nonwhites and females at its lowest rungs.[6] For instance, the debate over whether African American women were doing "race work" or "feminist work" in their anti-lynching campaigns seems a false dichotomy, even granted that most victims of lynching were men. The popular perception of the justification for lynching was that Black men had sexually assaulted white women. But the construction of Black men as sexually uncontrolled and savage was linked to the construction of Black women as promiscuous and lascivious.[7] If the struggle of African American women against lynching was "race work," given that it focused on a concern particular to African Americans, was the struggle of white women to pass a white-woman-only suffrage bill also "race work" rather than feminist struggle?

African American and African women share common terrain in relating women's struggle against oppression to the struggles of their communities against oppression. African women who opposed colonialism, for instance, opposed it on the dual grounds of its oppression of their *people* (both male and female) and its rendering of women, to use Fran Beale's phrase of over twenty years ago, as "slaves of slaves."[8] Interestingly enough, when the Nigerian woman's rights and anticolonial activist Funmilayo Ransome-Kuti took her message to London in the 1940s, she accused colonialism of making women slaves.[9]

The historicizing and contextualizing of women's actions allow us to locate "difference" in a useful way—such that it can be understood in relation to conditions. Thus we can make meaningful comparisons about those things that seem to oppress or liberate women and delineate connections between women's different statuses in different places. We can also investigate other models and agendas of feminism beyond those located in the activities of European and Euroamerican women.

In my dissertation, written over fifteen years ago, I went in search of Yoruba women's roles in the anticolonial struggle in Nigeria.[10] I believe I did important work in uncovering women's activity on behalf of women and in elucidating the important and powerful role of the "community of women" in the lives of Yoruba women and girls. Among the precolonial Yoruba (and actually far beyond for most women), it was the community of women that would make as many decisions affecting the lives of girls and women as men. This was primarily a result of the sexual divison of labor, women's important roles in the productive and distributive sectors of the economy, the proliferation of dual male and female societies and offices, and a cultural ethos that placed the group above the individual. Still, I paid less attention to the complexity of the web in which women's identities and actions were constructed—including the extent to which women operated (and often continue to operate) in a dialectic of oppression and power.

Africanist scholars have long resisted (and I believe rightly so) the extension to Africa of the public/private dichotomous analysis of women's productivity.[11] Women were (most still are) employed directly in production that crossed such boundaries, and they derived a certain autonomy and status from their roles as cultivators, traders, artisans, and providers of other marketplace services. Yet there is a discrepancy, a contradiction, in the autonomous ways women behaved collectively and in women's obeisance as daughters-in-law and especially as wives. Women are far more subordinated to men privately than publicly, and even to other women such as mothers-in-law or senior wives (wives entering a polygamous marriage before other wives).

More and more I realize the difficulty of describing women's statuses in West Africa in cultures that sometimes simultaneously oppressed, venerated, and feared women, in whose economies women were integrally productive workers in both the home and the marketplace, in whose philosophical/spiritual cosmologies women were often centered, and that provided space in which even nonelite women exercised power. Thus, it is no wonder that we so often have contradictory pictures of women in "traditional" West African societies. Whether it is the legendary market women, the women's "wars," or the anticolonial activists, we are presented with ample evidence that ordinary, nonelite women exercised autonomy and planned massive grass-roots responses aimed at directing and controlling their collective and shared destinies.

This contradiction, combined with the historical juncture at which much of West African women's history begins to be produced, affects the way that history is written. In fact, the "modern" (post-1960s) historiography of West African women doesn't seem to have passed through any real "women as victims" stage of development, with the possible exception of some of the recent historiography on the continental enslavement and pawnship of women.[12]

In fact, the idea that writing women's history proceeds along a linear trajectory of development, one defined by the methodological, conceptual, and theoretical models of the development of women's history in Europe and the United States, is often assumed by western scholars. Nancy Hewitt has observed:

> By rendering Western women's history more cohesive and complete in retrospect than it has been in its making we will find it easy to "add 'n stir" ... other "marginal" women into existing frameworks and will resist their transformative power the way men's history resisted ours.[13]

The writing of the histories of women in West Africa has the opportunity to shape and to gender the writing of West African history at an earlier juncture in the development of that historiography than did that of European or American women's history in the development of those historiographies.

The construction of gender in much of West Africa depended as much on lifecycle as it did on sex, wealth, or status. A woman's order as wife in a polygamous marriage (for example, as first or second wife), her ability to bear children, her status as mother and as mother-in-law, or her being postmenopausal resulted in often radically different constructions of "gender privilege" or "gender oppression."

The need for historians of women in West Africa to generate theory and construct paradigms that are rooted in African historical developments, modes of production, and cultures (surely related to the first two) is clear. Given differences in West African settings, this will not essentialize African women's history but rather provide us with the interpretive data to inform gender theories in Africa and elsewhere.

In some arenas, the colonial period in Africa can provide us with a window on the commingling of gender constructions and consciousness. That is, in urban areas where the colonized and the colonizers (both women and men) intermingled regularly and were drawn into one another's world views, we can see mutually transformative processes at work. It is useful in such settings to locate "difference" and "sameness" and "hybridity" to aid in our understanding of how gender is constructed and to allow "difference" to inform our theory and paradigms relating to the construction of gender and to models of feminism.

One way of doing this lies in examining West African women's anticolonial protest movements. In these movements a partnership often existed between "traditional" women and "westernized" women.[14] These protests took place under circumstances where colonialism was much in evidence but not *more* so than "traditional" culture and "traditional" socioeconomic and political organization.

There are a number of well-documented studies of such movements, including their leadership.[15] Though arguments are sometimes made that westernized women activists were taking their cue from the West and even from the nationalist men of their cohort group, and that they supplied the real "leadership" to many of these activities, I think this is of limited significance and a false dichotomy. Such an argument ignores the fact that the base of support for most of these movements was among nonwesternized, non-elite women; that these women used "traditional" women's protest tactics such as ridiculing men (both the colonizers and indigenous men whom they considered to be in sympathy with the colonizers) in song and dance, camping en masse in vigils outside the homes and offices of men and refusing to let them pass; that they referred to the "good old days" when they considered that some "traditional" power or right of theirs was being trespassed upon; and that they *assumed*, in a time when political activity by women was disparaged and considered unnatural by the colonizers and their supporters, that they had a right as women to engage in public, political activity. Much of West African women's anticolonial protest arose from a philosophical point of departure that was not anything they learned from the colonizers, and they employed tactics that were historically their own.

My own work has been biographical studies of women leaders.

Information uncovered in these studies has led me to rethink interpretations of their evidence and to speculate about uses of biographical evidence, particularly in the colonial West African setting. Doing biographical studies of feminist women in colonial Nigeria identified the extent to which women's leadership revolved around actual interaction with, and empowerment by, other women. I am using the term feminist here based on at least *two* of its most universally agreed upon components: women who seek to challenge both the restriction of women's rights, and women's marginalization from centers of power and decision making.

What I am suggesting is that we reexamine the biographical approach for things it can tell us about the creation of feminist theory, and moreover, about what *counts* as theory. The relationship between sociopolitical theory and praxis ought to be organic. That is, theory is not only *writing* that emerges from careful observation and analysis of action, but *action* itself is a kind of theory. It is through action that theory is both created and realized. The anticolonial actions of West African women made a theoretical statement about their gender consciousness, about their definition of feminism. And, it was a theoretical statement rooted in their own traditions rather than being imported from the West.

Even if we examine the "leadership" (where it is identifiable) of women's anticolonial protests, we see that it is tied to a historically indigenous mode of action. That "leadership" is characterized by being at the forefront of all-women's protest movements as much, or more, than by any individual interactions with anticolonial organizations led by men, or by individual interaction with foreign and indigenous members of the colonial hierarchy. Women, especially urban women in direct contact with colonialism, despite their increasing class, ethnic, and religious differences, continued to identify gender qua gender as an important organizing base, as they had done historically. It was not *new* to them to see their collective destiny embodied in gender solidarity, it was *old*. Though not monolithic in their aims, they *assumed* gender as a primary bond and organizing base as they most certainly had for centuries.

The class development, and the ethnic and religious diversity created by the colonial experience provided new challenges to an old way of organizing, but the West had nothing to teach African women about organizing as women. Whether "traditional" or members of the newly emerging westernized elite, women activists looked primarily to their *past* modes of protest to help remake their future. But, looking to the future, they appropriated those aspects of external ideologies that seemed most likely to benefit women. They sought to align themselves closely with ideas that were the most consonant with their own cos-mologies—the struggle for women's right to vote, for instance, reso-nated with the "traditional" notion that women had a role to play in the political sphere.

The struggle against women's taxation separately from their hus-bands was both a reaction to the transgression of this policy against the family-based taxation of the formerly independent African societies and states, and the desire of women to couple their taxation with the right to vote. The struggle against the power of the colonial bureauc-racy to decide the placement of markets and the prices of commodities traded therein was intended to maintain women's power in their roles in production and distribution. Even among the westernizing elite, the struggle for equal pay for equal work, and for access to all grades of the civil service, was an extension of women's historical role of working outside the home, which was as much an obligation of adulthood as a right for most of the women of West Africa.

I will examine, in brief, two women's protest groups of the colonial era in Nigeria. These groups are illustrative of the points I have made above, and they are different from one another.

The first, the Lagos Market Women's Association (LMWA), was an organization of at least ten thousand market women in Lagos, Nigeria. Lagos was the center of the colonial bureaucracy in Nigeria after 1914, when the protectorates of Northern and Southern Nigeria were joined to be the British colony of Nigeria. Though the exact date for the formation of the LMWA is not clear, by the 1920s it was active and a powerful organization that represented the market women before both the "traditional" African authorities such as the various chiefs, and the colonial hierarchy. Guilds predated the organization of the LMWA, which represented a collectivity of markets. In addition, at least as early as 1908, ad hoc groups of market women's guilds had united to protest the imposition of taxes on the selling and use of water in the city. The formation of associations of women representing various markets, and of women's guilds representing various occupations (such as hairdress-ers, sellers of cooked food, shea-butter producers), predated colonial-ism by centuries.

The most well-known head of the LMWA during the colonial peri-od was Madam Alimotu Pelewura. A fish trader in Ereko market at least as early as 1900, Pelewura shared several other characteristics of the market women: she was unlettered, a Muslim, and poor. Pelewura was the elected *Alaga* (head) of Ereko market, which in a 1932 colonial government study was reported as one of the most efficiently run markets in Lagos.[16] Shortly after the study, the Commissioner of the Colony publicly lamented the power of market women's guilds such as those at Ereko and advocated that market women's associations should be more "social" in nature. He stated that the degree of power women exercised within certain markets should be "nipped in the bud."[17]

In the 1920s, the LMWA provided a base of power for one of the first nationalist political parties in Nigeria, the Nigerian National Democratic Party (NNDP), founded in 1923. Though some historians have posited that the NNDP founder Herbert Macaulay inspired the formation of the LMWA and was a shadow leader of the Association, several elderly market women informants (in 1975) told this author that Macaulay and Pelewura walked hand in hand, that is to say, as equals. In a speech to a gathering of NNDP members in Abeokuta in 1942, Pelewura opened with the powerful declaration, "I am she who is called Pelewura," and, in noticing an audience of mostly men, added, "We wonder why your womenfolk did not show up here today. Tell me of that thing which men can undertake alone without the help of the womenfolk?"[18] Furthermore, though the LMWA would solicit Macaulay's help in hiring those with skills LMWA members did not possess, such as lawyers and accountants to aid them in their interactions with colonial authorities, the LMWA long outlasted the NNDP and allied itself with a number of other nationalist political organizations. There is no evidence to support the idea that Macaulay either inspired the founding of the LMWA or was a shadow authority figure in the Association.

By 1932 Pelewura was appointed a member of the *Ilu* committee by the traditional African (Yoruba) authorities of Lagos. The *Ilu* committee was a component of traditional government, a body of chiefs and others who advised the *Oba* (king). With their policy of indirect rule for Lagos (and other parts of Nigeria), the British did not dismantle indigenous political institutions but rather sought to undermine and manipulate them in ways which rendered them primarily titular and consultative when it came to decision making, as well as helpful when it came to implementation of colonial directives. A representative of the market women had historically sat on the *Ilu* to ensure that women's concerns were voiced and considered. At the time of her appointment, Pelewura was a spokeswoman for eighty-four market women's organizations. As will be seen, the *Ilu* would deeply disappoint the colonial authorities when, in a confrontation with the market women, the *Oba* would make it plain that there was no historical precedent for his (or the *Ilu*'s) contravening a decision that the women made about their spheres of power.

Between 1932 and 1951, there were several major confrontations between the market women and the colonial authorities. These had to do with the taxation of women, the location of markets, the price of commodities, and women's right to vote.

In 1932 rumors spread that the colonial government intended to tax women in Lagos. Though a limited tax on women had been inaugurated in the nearby town of Abeokuta in 1918, the market women of Lagos were prepared to resist such taxation. They sent a delegation to see the Administrator of the Colony, C. T. Lawrence, who assured them the government had no intention of taxing women in Lagos. Despite that assurance, in 1940 the colonial government enacted an Income Tax Ordinance which proposed to tax women whose incomes exceeded fifty pounds per annum. Immediately the market women began to organize, and on December 16, 1940, within days of the enactment of the Ordinance, over a hundred women assembled outside the office of the Commissioner of the Colony. The women were adamant that the tax be repealed and, receiving no assurance to that effect, left to report to the *Oba* Falolu. In a petition formulated by the women (drawn up by a hired clerk) and "signed" with over two hundred of their thumbprints, they stated that female taxation had to be repealed because it violated "native law and custom" and was untimely due to the hardship created by World War II. The petition further reported that the *Oba* Falolu and his chiefs agreed with them that female taxation was not only contrary to custom but undesirable.

On December 18, the markets of Lagos were nearly deserted as the women marched in the thousands. They first went to the Office of the Commissioner of the Colony. Receiving no satisfaction there, they then marched to Government House, where soldiers barred the door. Eventually two women, one of whom was Pelewura, were admitted by Governor Bourdillon. Pelewura later reported in an interview with the *Daily Times* newspaper that Bourdillon apologized that Lady Bourdillon was out that day and could not receive them. She said she replied they were not particular about reception that day. They delivered their petition and later in the evening held a mass meeting at Glover Memorial Hall. Both Pelewura and the Commissioner addressed the crowd, which ranged in estimates from one thousand to seven thousand women. When the Commissioner, in his address, stated that women in England paid tax, it was reported that Pelewura responded that she was not surprised, since England was where the money was made and that Africans were poor "owing to many factors over which they had no control." She went on to state that "Europeans should not interfere with native custom and impose taxation on women" and, according to official reports, wound up with a Yoruba version of "votes for women or alternatively no taxation without representation."[19]

Within two days, the government raised the ceiling for women's taxation from fifty pounds income per annum to two hundred pounds. Clearly, this meant that almost no market woman would be taxed. A letter was dispatched to the market women and delivered to Pelewura, advising her of the new policy. Pelewura reportedly responded that once the principle of female taxation was conceded, it was only a matter of time before all women had to pay tax. History proved her prophetic.

During the World War II years, the Nigerian colonial government instituted a system of price controls on food that came to be known as the Pullen Marketing Scheme, named after Captain A. P. Pullen, who was appointed as its director in 1941. The Pullen scheme had expanded by 1943 to such an extent that the government not only sought to cap the prices of food sold in the markets but wanted to send agents to buy food outside of Lagos and bring it to Lagos to sell in the market at designated centers at government-set prices.

The Lagos market women had several objections to the Pullen scheme. As the primary distributors and retailers of food, they had historically exercised control over its pricing. Moreover, most of the market women were petty traders operating on the smallest profit margin and were unable to sustain even short-term losses. Government prices for foodstuffs were unrealistic, often amounting to less than retailers had to pay to purchase them for resale. A vigorous black market developed, and by 1944 the official estimate of the number of Lagosians fed by the black market was as high as two-thirds. When arrests were made for black market profiteering, employees of European firms received lesser sentences than market women arrested for the same offense.

The market women were determined to resist the price controls. The women proposed that, rather than prices being set by the government, a committee composed of twelve experienced market women of the LMWA should regulate prices. When the women farina sellers of Ijebu-Ode (a town near Lagos that supplied much of Lagosians' supply of farina) stationed themselves on the main road between Ijebu-Ode and Lagos and refused to allow any lorries carrying farina to pass, the LMWA supported their actions. Early in 1944, Pelewura was summoned to several meetings with the Deputy Controller of Native Foodstuffs and the Commissioner of the Colony to discuss the possibility of finding a way for the market women to support the price controls. At one such meeting, Captain Pullen proposed that Pelewura assist him and offered to pay her to do so. According to official reports, Pelewura refused and accused Pullen of "seeking to break and starve the country where she was born."[20]

A meeting of the market women (reportedly three thousand of them) with the *Oba* and chiefs was also unhelpful to the colonial authorities. At that meeting, Chief Oluwa informed Pullen that no market woman would go against the LMWA prohibition on abiding by the price controls. The LMWA achieved a limited success in August 1945, when the government agreed to decontrol the price of gari, a staple food of the population of Lagos and the one in greatest scarcity. By September 1945, the government decontrolled food prices. The war was over, the protest was mounting, and there seemed to be no logic to keeping them in place.

Most interestingly, when a widespread general strike occurred in Nigeria in 1945, the marketwomen supported the striking workers and voluntarily suppressed the price of market commodities to demonstrate their solidarity. The LMWA also made generous contributions to the Worker's Relief Fund.[21]

This brief description of some of the activities of the LMWA is indicative of the market women's awareness of the acute frustrations of the colonial period. More importantly, it is evidence that they had in place conceptual formulations and practical mechanisms to represent themselves, and that they drew on their history as much as their present reality of colonialism/westernization to promote their interests in being active agents in decision making about their lives. The assumptions they made about the proper spheres for women's activity were solidly rooted in their history and in fact contravened colonial notions of "woman's sphere."

The second major women's organization in colonial Lagos that I will discuss is the Nigerian Women's Party (NWP). The NWP was founded by a group of women who were members of the newly emerging Christianized, westernized elite. Its most prominent member, and its president from its inception until its demise around 1956, was Lady Oyinkan Ajasa Abayomi. Abayomi's father was the first Nigerian knight (Sir Kitoye Ajasa), and her mother (Oyinkan Bartholomew) was the daughter of first treasurer to the Egba United Government.[22] Abayomi was sent to Britain for postsecondary education. Though both of her parents were relatively conservative, after the death of her first husband, Abayomi married Dr. (later Sir) Kofoworola Abayomi, who was a leader of the Nigerian Youth Movement (NYM), an early nationalist organization founded in 1935. Even before this marriage in 1934, Abayomi had distinguished herself as a freethinker and a political

activist who was more radical than her parents, albeit less revolutionary than some other Nigerian women activists.[23] She was among the
first women in Lagos to drive a car, and in 1927 had founded the British
West African Educated Girls' Club (later the Ladies' Progressive Club)
to raise funds for African girls' secondary education. In 1935 Abayomi
joined the women's wing of the NYM and became increasingly aware of
the problems common among African women of all classes, ethnicities,
and religions. She began to exhort elite women to take a more active role
in improving the conditions of unlettered, poor women. In an article
published in the NYM journal in 1935, she warned that "The uppishness
among the few privileged women who have been educated abroad
must be killed. Unless the so-called highly educated make themselves
open and approachable they will have no one to lead...." She ended the
article by sounding a note for women's equality: "women also should
be given free chances to develop their faculties for the benefit of the
race."[24]

On May 10, 1944, Abayomi held a meeting in her Lagos home to
discuss women's political situation. The twelve women gathered there
decided to form the Nigerian Women's Party. In an interview the following day in the African-run *Daily Service* newspaper, Abayomi, and
another NWP founder, Tinuola Dedeke, addressed the reasons for the
founding of the NWP. Abayomi decried the fact that, though women
owned property and paid taxes, they had no political representation
because they could not vote. She specifically criticized the lack of any
women on the Lagos Town Council or the Legislative Council, the two
bodies on which the colonial government had allowed some African
representation. She also pointed out the lack of government scholarships for girls to study in Britain, comparing the Nigerian situation to
that of the British colony of Sierra Leone, where such scholarships
existed. Dedeke implored women to "cast away all feelings of religious
and tribal differences and present a united front for the sake of their
motherland."[25]

Within a short time, the NWP had drawn up its Constitution that set
forth its goals:

> The Women's Party makes its strongest appeal to the women of Nigeria
> irrespective of class or any other distinction, reminding them of their back-
> ward and unenviable position among the women of other races and calling
> them to action. It appeals to those who may be outside the ranks of the
> Women's Party for sympathy and cooperation:
>   1. To shape the whole future is not our problem, but only to shape
> faithfully a small part of it according to rules laid down.
>   2. To seek by constitutional means the rights of British citizenship in its
> full measure on the people.

3. To work assiduously for the educational, agricultural and industrial development of Nigeria with a view to improve the moral, intellectual and economic condition of the country.

4. To work for the amelioration of the condition of the women of Nigeria not merely by sympathy for their aspirations but by recognition of their equal status with men.[26]

Though patrons could be adults of any nationality at home or abroad who agreed with the objectives of the Party, membership was open only to women of African descent. An executive committee was formed consisting of a president, vice president, two secretaries, a legal adviser, two treasurers, and seven ex officio members elected from the general membership. One of the duties of the legal adviser was "To study closely all government bills and other measures affecting the people, irrespective of class or any other designation. . . ."[27] There were also three committees established: Health and Education, Market and Native Industry, and Political and Social.

Though its intentions were to establish branches throughout Nigeria, for a variety of reasons, the NWP's activities were effectively confined to Lagos. One reason was that the party had limited resources. Though estimates of its numerical strength ranged from five hundred to two thousand, the number of truly active members, as opposed to those who aligned themselves with the Party on an ad hoc basis over special issues, was apparently quite small. In addition, though the Party sought to solicit membership among the market women, it was not nearly as successful in recruiting them as members as were the market women's own associations, particularly the LMWA. One prominent market woman, Rabiatu Alaso Oke, who was unlettered and Muslim, did serve on the executive committee of the NWP. Though Pelewura had a working relationship with the NWP and shortly after its founding announced her personal willingness to cooperate with the Party, she never appears to have held any official status and it is not even clear if she was actually a member. There was at least one major disagreement between the NWP and the market women over remarks made by Funmilayo Ransome-Kuti, a leftist and leader of the Abeokuta Women's Union.[28] Still, the NWP cooperated with the market women during the resistance to the Pullen price controls and conducted free literacy classes in the evening for market women at the CMS Grammar School.

The NWP took up four major issues during its most active phase: (1) girls' education and literacy classes for adult women; (2) the employment of women in the civil service; (3) the right of female minors to trade freely in Lagos; and (4) the securing of women's rights in general, but particularly the right to vote.

Many in the NWP leadership were schoolteachers and were seriously concerned by the lack of educational facilities for girls' education, particularly at the secondary level. Moreover, the NWP fought to have the curriculum offered to girls expanded; they wanted science and foreign languages added to the curriculum. The Party advocated the provision of government scholarships for Muslim girls, who were at a particular disadvantage since both primary and secondary education was dominated by various Christian church denominations. Last but not least, the Party sought to have the government provide adult literacy education, particularly for women.

The second issue, employment of women in the colonial civil service, had been a major concern since the 1930s, when Charlotte Olajumoke Obasa and her Lagos Women's League (defunct by the 1940s) had battled for African women's employment. The NWP argued not only for women's employment but for equal pay with men in the same grade of the service. Female teachers, for instance, were paid 33 percent less than men employed in the same rank. There was other discrimination. Particularly rankling was the apparent preference by the government for hiring European women, usually wives of administrative officers, as nurses and secretaries.

In 1946 the legislature passed the Children and Young Persons Ordinance, which struck at the heart of African traditions. The Ordinance prohibited children under fourteen from engaging in street trading, required parental permission for girls between fourteen and sixteen to trade, and limited to daylight the hours in which young girls were allowed to trade. Though this legislation may have had as its intention the protection of child labor, it was crafted without consultation with the African community and contravened local customs, in which girls were apprenticed to trade for their mothers and other relatives as a kind of vocational training in preparation for economic independence as adult women. The police force exceeded acceptable behavior when it began meeting trains entering Lagos and removing all girl traders who seemed below age, and arresting young girls, including young married women with babies on their backs. In a letter to the *Daily Service*, the NWP expressed the fear that the authorities intended to introduce a pass system similar to that in effect in South Africa. The NWP worked with the market women's associations in succeeding in having the ordinance suspended.

The NWP constantly agitated for the right of women to vote. In 1950 southern Nigerian women were finally enfranchised. That year, the NWP ran four candidates in the Lagos Town Council election. All four NWP candidates lost. After this election, the NWP began its gradual demise. The Party continued to advocate for girls' education and health care reforms, but by 1956 it effectively disappeared when it joined other Nigerian women's groups to establish the National Council of Women's Societies, a decidedly less politically oriented group.

Most of the active membership of the NWP straddled the "traditional" and the "new," the indigenous and the foreign. Though often much acculturated in western ways, these women also maintained an allegiance to their own culture. They were that middle strand who sometimes opted for slower and less radical change by exhorting colonialism to improve itself rather than end immediately. It was particularly in their advocacy of women's rights that they were a thorn in the side of the colonizers, and often in the side of African men as well. The NWP was clearly a champion of women's rights, especially those of poor women. While there may have been some noblesse oblige in their actions, they were sincere in their desire to see all women treated as equals with men. Their notion of the political sphere as a proper arena for women's activity was certainly nothing they learned from the West.

These two organizations, the Lagos Market Women's Association and the Nigerian Women's Party, are examples of feminist activity in the colonial setting in the capital city of the most populous British colony in Africa. The feminist activity they represent was inspired not by western models, but by their own models. Though their activity may have gone unnamed as feminism, and unarticulated in ideological terms, their modes of organization and their language of protest are transparent in their advocacy of women's equal status with men and women's right to power over their own lives and participation in the general political sphere. In actions louder than words, they created theory.

NOTES

1. Alice Walker appears to be among the first to use this term. In her book *In Search of Our Mother's Gardens* (New York: Harcourt, Brace, Jovanovich, 1983) she describes a womanist as a Black feminist or feminist of color and says, "womanist is to feminist as purple is to lavender."

2. Cheryl Johnson-Odim, "Common Themes, Different Contexts," in Chandra T. Mohanty, Ann Russo, and Lourdes Torres, eds., *Third World Women and the Politics of Feminism* (Bloomington: Indiana University Press, 1991).

3. Joan Wallach Scott, "Introduction," in Joan Wallach Scott, ed., *Feminism and History* (New York: Oxford University Press, 1996), 1.

4. Ibid., 6.

5. Nancy Hewitt, "Uneven Developments: Women's History Reaches Puberty," unpublished paper delivered at the Social Science History Association Conference, Minneapolis, 1990. A version of this paper has been published as "Reflections from a Departing Editor: Recasting Issues of Marginality," *Gender and History* 4, no. 1 (Spring 1992): 3–9.

6. Joan Wallach Scott writes, "Some kind of analysis is needed of a complicated and highly specific relationship of power. . . . Does race take priority over class and class over gender, or are there inseparable connections among them?" See Scott, "Introduction," 8.

7. For a brilliant discussion of this connection, see Angela Davis, "Rape, Racism and the Myth of the Black Rapist," in Angela Davis, *Women, Race and Class* (New York: Random House, 1981). See also Cheryl Johnson-Odim, "Common Themes, Different Contexts."

8. Fran Beale, "Slave of a Slave No More: Black Women in Struggle," *Black Scholar* 6, no. 6 (March 1975): 2–10.

9. See the quotation in the British newspaper the *Daily Worker*, 10 August 1947. Funmilayo Ransome-Kuti is among the most important women leaders in Nigeria's history. She was the most radical Nigerian woman of the colonial period. For more on her, see Cheryl Johnson-Odim, "On Behalf of Women and the Nation: Funmilayo Ransome-Kuti and the Struggles for Nigerian Independence and Women's Equality," in C. Johnson-Odim and M. Strobel, eds., *Expanding the Boundaries of Women's History* (Bloomington: Indiana University Press, 1992); and Cheryl Johnson-Odim and Nina Mba, *For Women and the Nation: A Biography of Funmilayo Ransome-Kuti of Nigeria* (Urbana: University of Illinois Press, 1997).

10. Cheryl Johnson, "Nigerian Women and British Colonialism: The Yoruba Example with Selected Biographies" (Ph.D. dissertation, Northwestern University, Evanston, IL, 1978).

11. See, for example, Ife Amadiume, *Male Daughters, Female Husbands* (London: Zed Press, 1987); Niara Sudarkassa, *Where Women Work: A Study of Yoruba Women in the Marketplace and in the Home* (Ann Arbor: University of Michigan Press, 1973); Kamene Okonjo, "The Dual-Sex Political System in Operation: Igbo Women and Community Politics in Midwestern Nigeria," in N. Hafkin and E. Bay, eds., *Women in Africa* (Stanford: Stanford University Press, 1976), 45–58; Karen Sacks, *Sisters and Wives* (Westport, CT: Greenwood Press, 1979); Simi Afonja, "Land Control, A Critical Factor in Yoruba Gender Stratification," in C. Robertson and I. Berger, eds., *Women and Class in Africa* (New York: Holmes and Meier, 1986), 78–91; Leith Mullings, "Women and Economic Change in Africa," in Nancy J. Hafkin and Edna G. Bay, eds., *Women in Africa* (Stanford: Stanford University Press, 1976), 239–64; and Nancy J. Hafkin and Edna G. Bay, "Introduction" to *Women in Africa*, 1–18.

12. I do not include in this discussion the explosive literature on female circumcision/genital mutilation since this is a literature not primarily written by historians and frequently not even historicized.

13. Hewitt, "Uneven Developments."

14. By "traditional," I mean the way people did things before the arrival of colonialists external to the region who brought western culture. For an important discussion of false dichotomies between "traditional" and "modern," see Cheryl Johnson-Odim and Margaret Strobel, "Conceptualizing the History of Women in Africa, Asia, Latin America and the Caribbean, and the Middle East," *Journal of Women's History* 1, no. 1 (Spring 1989): 36–37.

15. See, for example, Nina Mba, *Nigerian Women Mobilized: Women in Southern Nigerian Political History 1900–1965* (Berkeley, CA: Institute of International Studies, 1982); Cora Ann Presley, "Labor Unrest among Kikuyu Women in Colonial Kenya," in Robertson and Berger, eds., *Women and Class in Africa*, 255–73; Cora Ann Presley, *Kikuyu Women, the Mau Mau Rebellion and Social Change in Kenya* (Denver, CO: Westview Press, 1993); Jean O'Barr, "Making the

Invisible Visible: African Women in Politics and Policy," *African Studies Review* 18, no. 3 (1975): 19–27; Judith Van Allen, "Sitting on a Man: Colonialism and the Lost Political Institutions of Igbo Women," *Canadian Journal of African Studies 6*, no. 2 (1972): 168–81; and Cheryl Johnson-Odim, "Madam Alimotu Pelewura and the Lagos Marketwomen," *Tarikh 7*, no. 1 (1981): 1–10.

16. For more information on Pelewura, see Johnson-Odim, "Madam Alimotu Pelewura and the Lagos Marketwomen," in *Tarikh*, 7, no. 1 (1981): 1–10.

17. Colonial Secretary's Office Files #248/24 at the National Archives, Ibadan, Nigeria.

18. Pelewura's speech is in the file "Political Parties in Abeokuta," at the Abeokuta Archives, Abeokuta, Nigeria.

19. *Daily Times*, 18 December 1940, cited in Johnson-Odim, "Madam Alimotu Pelewura."

20. Macaulay Papers Collection, University of Ibadan Manuscripts Collection, Box 13, File 5, Ibadan, Nigeria. For further discussion of the struggle between Pelewura and Pullen, see *Daily Service* newspaper for 23 September 1942, National Archives, Ibadan, and Colonial Secretary's Office Files #2516 and #2686, National Archives, Ibadan.

21. For more information on the strike and the market women, see Wale Oyemakinde, "The Nigerian General Strike of 1945," *Journal of the Historical Society of Nigeria* (December 1974): 693–710.

22. For more information on Abayomi, see Cheryl Johnson-Odim,"Lady Oyinkan Abayomi: A Profile," in Bolanle Awe, ed., *Nigerian Women in Historical Perspective*" (Lagos, Nigeria: Sankore Publishers, 1992).

23. The most radical Nigerian woman of the colonial period was certainly Funmilayo Ransome-Kuti. For her story and that of the Abeokuta Women's Union that she founded see Johnson-Odim, "On Behalf of Women and the Nation"; Johnson-Odim and Mba, *For Women and the Nation*.

24. Lady Oyinkan Ajasa Abayomi, "Modern Womanhood," *NYM [Nigerian Youth Movement] Journal*, the Macaulay Papers Collection, University of Ibadan Manuscripts Collection, Box 73, File 7, Ibadan, Nigeria.

25. *Daily Service* newspaper, 11 May 1944, National Archives, Ibadan, Nigeria.

26. The NWP's Constitution was among the private papers of Tinuola Dedeke in Lagos, Nigeria. I am uncertain as to what happened to this collection following her death in the 1990s. The Constitution is also cited in Johnson-Odim, "Nigerian Women and British Colonialism," and in Mba, *Nigerian Women Mobilized*.

27. Cited in the NWP's Constitution; see note 26.

28. For details, see Johnson-Odim, "Lady Oyinkan Abayomi." The bulk of the research on which this chapter is based was done in Lagos, Ibadan, and Abeokuta, Nigeria, in 1975–76 and in 1989. I used several Nigerian newspapers, particularly the *Daily Service, Daily Times*, and *West African Pilot*; the Colonial Secretary's Office Files and the Commissioner of the Colony Files at the National Archives, Ibadan; the Macaulay Papers Collection at the University of Ibadan Manuscripts Collection; the private papers of Tinuola Dedeke and Funmilayo Ransome-Kuti (the Ransome-Kuti papers are available at the University of Ibadan Library); and interviews with Oyinkan Abayomi, Tinuola Dedeke, and Funmilayo Ransome-Kuti. For additional references, please refer to Johnson-Odim, "Nigerian Women and British Colonialism."

5

Frontier Feminism and the Marauding White Man

Australia, 1890s to 1940s

MARILYN LAKE

"Here in Australia," Louisa Lawson observed in 1891, with characteristic matter-of-factness, "it is considered more a crime to steal a horse than ruin a girl."[1] On the Darling Downs, at the turn of the century, another pioneering wife explained, "Women in the farming districts don't occupy a very high place in the masculine community—being classed usually according to their degree of usefulness with the other animals."[2] (And, thanks to Anne Maree Collins's work on bestiality, the extent of the usefulness of the other animals is only now beginning to be fully appreciated.)[3] Yet a third female pioneer, some twenty years later, had reason to return to the comparison of women to the "other animals." Millicent Preston Stanley, the first woman to enter the New South Wales Parliament, when campaigning for the establishment of a chair in obstetrics at the University of Sydney, noted that several new positions had recently been granted in veterinary science: "if the university is able to grant the means in the case of the horse, it should be equally able to grant 'horse-rights' for women."[4]

Frontier societies, as women have long observed, enshrined masculine values and interests. In frontier societies white men roamed free, but men's mobility seemed to spell women's misfortune. In 1926, the British Commonwealth League, a London-based feminist organization formed to promote women's citizenship rights, resolved that it was felt necessary to stress responsibility to the wandering member of the British race, who may be without ties in a new country. For such members may work great damage to their own and to other races if they have not means of recreation or of fellowship, but live in dangerous loneliness."[5]

In feminist discourse, mobile men were dangerous men, and the wandering members of the British race—the nomad tribe, the swagmen, the men on the track—became a bunch of marauding white men. The mobility of men, that condition said to characterize the frontier and to be definitive of freedom, was assumed, by men and women alike, to be inherently threatening to women. The discursive emphasis on the freedom of men in frontier societies resulted in turn in a heightened perception of women's situation as one of "isolation," "vulnerability," and "defenselessness."

In this chapter I explore the ways in which the outlook of feminism in Australia, from the 1880s to the 1940s, was crucially shaped by the historical context of the frontier and suggest that the frontier, as a conceptual and geographical space, acquires its meaning within an imperial as well as a national context. I argue the importance of gender relations and the family to the imperial project in Australia and conversely the centrality of colonialism to gender politics and feminism in the settler colonies.

Nationalist writers and many historians of Australia have tended to represent the frontier experience as emblematic of the national experience. On these "outskirts of civilisation" the essential meaning of what it was to be Australian was somehow distilled or laid bare—the truth of Australian life exposed. For Russel Ward it was the birthplace and forcing ground of the legendary Australian—the practical man, rough and ready, independent and antiauthoritarian, a man given to few words, but resourceful and supportive of his mates.[6] For historians of Aboriginal dispossession, such as Henry Reynolds, it was on the frontier that the criminality, brutality, and violence that characterized the settlement of Australia were most fully exposed.[7] Feminists, too, have shared this tendency to represent the frontier experience as paradigmatic. From the 1920s, especially, the marauding frontiersman began to figure in many feminist representations as the true representative of Australian masculinity, his systematic abuse of Aboriginal women suggestive of the inherent degradation that characterized free sexual relations. These otherwise divergent depictions of the frontier—the nationalist, the postcolonial, and the feminist—share this assumption: that "on the border," white men could "do as they liked," as residents of the Port Philip district informed George Augustus Robinson.[8] For white men, the frontier was a fantasy of freedom; for white feminists it was a focus of fear and anxiety, a place beyond their ken, where undomesticated men turned feral.

Writing of the genesis of modern feminism, Maggie Humm reminds us that, although distinctive as a movement, feminism has been variously shaped by the "cultural, legal and economic policies of particular societies" in which it was formed. "Feminist campaigns are inevitably shaped by national priorities and national politics."[9] I wish to suggest that the outlook of Australian feminism in the late nineteenth and early twentieth centuries was shaped by the context of an imperial frontier in four main ways. First, in the context of a British colonial settlement, white women assumed a special authority as the agents of civilization and custodians of the race. Second, a pioneering society was a masculine society. In these male-dominated colonies, there was a particular feminist emphasis on the need to reform characteristically masculine behaviors (drinking, gambling, and a predatory sexuality), which seemed to flourish on the frontier, but which increasingly came to be seen as antithetical to civilization and women's and children's welfare. Third, in response to perceptions of women's special vulnerability in a masculinist society, there was a heavy emphasis in Australian feminist campaigns on the need to provide "protection," rather than, say, "emancipation" for women and girls. Writing about leading New South Wales feminist Rose Scott, Judith Allen has suggested that, "although overseas suffragists also pursued the vote as a principal means to the end of challenging men's sexual behaviour and power," Scott articulated this connection fully, clearly "influenced by late nineteenth century conditions in Australia."[10] Building on this, I would suggest, fourth, that it was the spectacle of white men's systematic sexual abuse of Aboriginal women and of "unprotected" white women and girls in a male-dominated and homosocial society that confirmed twentieth-century Australian feminists in their view of sexuality as inherently degrading for women. Unlike some of their peers in the United Kingdom and the United States, it was not until the 1960s (at precisely the moment when, coincidentally, Aboriginal women had disappeared from feminist view) that Australian feminists began to claim rights as sexual subjects.

In characterizing the distinctiveness of the Australian version of frontier feminism, I want to suggest that the crucial conceptual dynamic underpinning the Australian feminist project in the early twentieth century was what I have elsewhere called feminists' sense of "double difference"—their construction of a New World identity and

politics marked by difference from, and temporal advancement beyond, both the feudal oppressions of the European Old World and
the "primitivism" of the Stone Age culture of Aboriginal Australians.[11]
Australian feminists saw themselves as nation builders, consciously
engaged in the project of fashioning a new order of protectionist state.

Nineteenth-century colonial discourses that drew distinctions between primitive/barbarous societies and civilized/Christian ones allocated a special place to white women as the bearers of culture, morality, and order. Adele Perry, the Canadian historian of the backwoods of
British Columbia, has observed that in such a world quite ordinary
white women were assigned an awesome responsibility as the most
civilized representatives of the civilized race.[12] They were also agents
of the "governing race," as delegates to the British Commonwealth
League noted.[13] This positioning was the source of their authority as
activist reformers and feminists, authorized and enjoined to take their
mission of purity out into the world. The imposition of "purity" could
be seen as especially important in the Australian colonies, given the
possibilities of contamination from the convict legacy and from the
existence and close proximity, in some parts of Australia, of indigenous
societies.

This meant that white women had a special responsibility as exemplars of civilized standards: drinking and sexual promiscuity were
regarded as especially heinous offenses in women. Thus it was decreed
that "sexual lapses of women must ever be held more deplorable than
those of a man simply because the offence in the woman's case causes
more harm within her environment and more rapid and permanent injury to her own more delicate moral and intellectual fibre."[14] This
tyrannical double standard was enshrined in law and became a major
focus of feminist reform—not in the direction of claiming increased sexual liberties for women, as would be the case in the 1960s, but in demanding that men, too, discipline and control themselves, that they
literally live up to the "civilized" standards that they invoked to justify
their political power.

In this colonial, nation-building context, women saw a particular
responsibility to reform men's behaviors to bring them into line with
more "civilized" standards. As New South Wales feminist Rose Scott
explained, "licensed or unlicensed vice can only mean evil, and . . . a
really great nation can only be built by inculcating the virtues of self-
control and purity."[15] This was an urgent task in frontier societies,
where the predominance of single, mobile men fostered a strong homosocial national culture, sustained by bonds of mateship between men;
casual sex with animals, other men, indigenous and other "unpro-

tected" women and girls; and the dissolute practices of gambling and drinking. As I noted in 1986, in a masculinist context such as Australia's that saw the elevation of these practices to the status of a national culture, women's mission of respectability could acquire a particularly subversive, threatening dimension.[16] It was one thing for women to attempt to work changes on men in private, wooing them from public house to private home with their own good housekeeping, as envisaged by the *Queenslander*, for instance:

> Bright, educated, companionable, capable women will make cheerful, economical homes, keep the men from gambling and other bad habits, render embezzlement and speculation unnecessary and generally purify life. That is provided they are thoroughly good. This crowns all.[17]

The exercise of private influence was woman's prerogative. It was quite another matter for women to attempt to lay down the law, but feminists embarked on public campaigns to do just that, seeking to outlaw drinking and to restrict men's sexual access to women and girls. Temperance reform assumed a particularly important place in the politics of frontier feminism. The preoccupation with men's behavior also led to a particular concern to protect Australian boys from the models of manhood around them. Whereas the difficult position of daughters attracted the attention of English feminists, as Barbara Caine has noted, Australian feminists worried about the vulnerability of their sons.[18] "Is it not a painful fact to contemplate," asked Louisa Lawson,

> that according to present conditions it can be looked upon as a miracle should a boy reach man's estate and escape the contaminations of vice which daily example makes him familiar with from boyhood? To be able to smoke, swear, drink and gamble like a man is the Alpha and Omega of his infantile dreams."[19]

In 1898, Rose Scott also deplored the fact that "boys are taught by public opinion that it is manly to know life! To drink, to gamble and to be immoral. . . ."[20] Australian boys had "as great a right to be safeguarded for purity and self-control" as did girls, declared "Irven" in *Labor Call*, over twenty years later in 1919.[21]

Immorality was thought to accompany the nomadic lifestyle of frontiersmen. Unsettled men posed a particular sexual threat to the women and girls who shared their terrain. Cases such as the following were widely reported in colonial newspapers. In 1871, twelve-year-old Ammelie Weise was sent to the head station at Hirst Vale near Dalby to collect food supplies. When she returned some hours later, her dress was torn and she was crying. The girl explained to her mother that a shearer temporarily in the area had followed her from the station and demanded a kiss. She refused; the man told her that he would "see about that" and forced her to the ground and assaulted her.[22] Feminist campaigns aimed to curb this freedom of men to do as they pleased, a condition that was seen as definitive of life on the frontier.

In this scenario, the key to the consolidation of colonies into nations was the settlement and domestication of a mobile and dangerous manhood. Feminists were emboldened to attempt a transformation of the freewheeling, independent Lone Hand into a responsible, caring, temperate, chaste, self-controlled, considerate, selfless Domestic Man. Needless to say, their intentions met with considerable resistance. "Am I likely to get married?" wrote George Underwood, a young selector in southwest Queensland to his family. "Yes, just as I am to produce a pair of wings and fly. I am a real bachelor just now. . . . I cook for myself, wash my own clothes, in short am my own housekeeper."[23] Or, in the words of Randolph Bedford's father, who encouraged him to "go bush":

> You're me all over again, lad. There's only one thing that will tie you down, and that's responsibility. A wife and children will put the hobbles on you. You'll look over the fence at the horses who are going somewhere; but you'll have to stay in the paddock.[24]

(Note again the colonial tendency to identify with the horses.)

In the metropolis of England in the nineteenth century, surplus women—also called redundant women—were deemed to constitute a major social problem. The difficulty of their existence—their lack of opportunity—became a major preoccupation of English feminists, who put much time and energy into reforms such as promoting access to education, which would enable single women to live independent lives. As Barbara Caine has written, for Victorian feminists in England, "the plight of single women was of the utmost importance."[25] In frontier societies such as Australia, there was a surplus of men, but they were not, of course, conceived of as redundant or superfluous. They were for feminists, however, a problem. The situation in Queensland, deemed by commentators to be "the most Australian" of all the colonies, was especially marked: at the turn of the century there were 171 males for every 100 females. The preponderance of men had important social consequences, notably a very high marriage rate for women. In all the Australian colonies, marriage was the common condition of women over a certain age, and the nature of marriage and the condition of married women became major concerns of Australian feminists. Frontier feminism tended to be more concerned with the condition of mothers and wives than the tribulations of spinsters. For several decades, feminists in Australia focused on attempts to elevate the marriage relationship—lifting it from being a species of prostitution to a "sweet companionship" and, by the twentieth century, attempting to end the "sex slavery" of the wife through the introduction of motherhood endowment, which was envisaged as an ongoing payment of an income by the State to all mothers. It was campaigned for but never won.[26]

Because of the perceived vulnerability of women and girls on the frontier, feminist campaigns concentrated on providing "protection." Colonial settlements were, in effect, extensive white men's protectorates, purporting to provide protection to those groups most vulnerable to white men's own depredations—Aborigines, Chinese, women, and girls. But who would protect these groups from their protectors? Men were allegedly women's natural protectors. Thus one Queensland politician was moved to remark of his colony in the 1860s, "Women are in a more defenceless position than at home, from our limited population and scattered habitations and consequently they are very liable to violence in the absence of their natural protectors."[27] In such a construction of the problem, the subjects actually perpetrating the violence were rendered anonymous, but as the American feminist Charlotte Perkins Gilman was moved to comment, "As a matter of fact, the thing a woman is most afraid to meet on a dark street is her natural protector."[28]

Nineteenth-century feminist activism in Australia was animated by the conviction that men had failed in their ordained role as protectors. Women themselves would henceforth take responsibility for this task, authorized by their status as mothers. As Louisa Lawson argued, "If we are responsible for our children, give us the power and sacredness of the ballot and we will lift ourselves and our brothers to a higher civilization."[29] This political mobilization of the identity of mother to promote a form of maternal government was a crucial dimension of the concomitant decline in the importance in the role of the helpmeet / wife, who was increasingly conceptualized as a mere creature of sex.

The protection of women and girls demanded a number of reforms: temperance, raising the age of consent, opposition to contagious diseases legislation (which oppressed women working as prostitutes by targeting and searching them), custody rights over children for white and Aboriginal mothers, and the appointment of women to a range of public offices—as jail wardens, doctors, factory inspectors, police officers—so that women need never fall into men's hands. By the 1920s and 1930s, feminist activists attempting to reform the conditions of indigenous women and children in Western Australia and the Northern Territory demanded the appointment of women protectors to Aboriginal administration, because they would better defend their "less favoured sisters" from the marauding white man.[30] Returning from a trip to northern Australia in the early 1930s, Mary Bennett reported, "the worst thing I have seen is the attitude of the average white man to native women—the attitude not of the mean whites but of the overwhelming majority of white men. . . . Wherever there is a white man's camp there is a need for protection for these girls," said Bennett. "It is the average ordinary white man who is to blame for this trouble."[31] On the frontier, the true nature of the average, ordinary white man was laid bare.

The consequences of white men's uncontrolled behavior on the frontier were seen to be most destructive in the area of sexual relations—for both Aboriginal and non-Aboriginal women. Louisa Lawson wrote about the degrading position of white women forced to endure their husbands' sexual relations with Aboriginal women. In a preface to her poem "The Squatter's Wife," Lawson referred to the actual case of a "beautiful and gifted girl," who had married a squatter only to find on her arrival at his property that there were two bark huts—one for herself and the other for "her husband's black mistress and family." For the white woman, men's lusts rendered the frontier a place of loneliness and debasement. Lawson addressed the squatter's wife, Alice Gertler, in these terms:

Lonely hut on barren creek,
Where the rotting sheep-yards reek,
Far away from kith and kin,
None save thee and native gin
Many a weary mile within—
    Alice Gertler.

The legendary freedom of the frontiersman was reconceptualized by Lawson, in racist terms, as an especially base form of licentiousness:

Bound to one who loves thee not,
Drunken off-spring of a sot;
Even now at wayside inn
Riots he in drink and sin,
Mating with a half-caste gin—
    Alice Gertler.[32]

Whereas Lawson's depiction of the white man's sexual relations with Aboriginal women focused on the degradation visited on the white woman, twentieth-century feminists increasingly expressed outrage at the abuse of Aboriginal women themselves.

By the 1920s, a number of feminists came to see white men's sexual abuse of indigenous women as paradigmatic of uncontrolled masculin-

ity. To these feminists, the large increase in the mixed-descent population between the wars—the "half-caste problem"—provided dramatic
evidence of the extent of white men's depredations. Feminists such as
Mary Bennett, Edith Jones, Bessie Rischbieth, Ruby Rich, and Constance
Cooke organized national and international campaigns to draw attention to the trafficking in Aboriginal women and girls.[33] They also
argued that men's uncontrollable lusts were undermining the moral
authority of white Australia, of the new nation in the Pacific. "I cannot
see how white supremacy can last out this decade even," despaired
Bennett in the 1930s. "We, I mean white supremacy is in the most
imminent danger and everybody is blind. In my view, our only chance
of survival is to put our 'spiritual' house in order and to do it mighty
quick."[34] In losing sexual control, the white man would lose political
control.

What was to be done? Mary Bennett was clear and insistent in
language that echoed Rose Scott's claims of some forty years before.
She spoke of "the loving protection needed by these girls and women,
native and half-caste, in the state of transition from native culture to
white civilisation and the shielding from the terrible crop of evils that
have sprung up in this borderland of transition."[35] This space—the
borderlands, emblematic of Australia at large—was an anarchic and
unstable space of transition where the freedom of the white man had
led to the systematic degradation of women and girls.

Feminism on the frontier was authorized by colonial discourses
that positioned white women as the moral guardians of civilization. But
I would want to emphasize that feminism was not contained by colonial discourses: feminism was complicit in the paternalism of the imperial project, but feminism also challenged some of that paternalism's
most fundamental assumptions, notably that women should occupy a
familial dependent status in the colonies and new nation and that "unprotected" women were fair game. By the 1920s and 1930s, major feminist organizations such as the Australian Federation of Women Voters,
the Women's Services Guilds in Western Australia, and the Women's
Non-Party Association of South Australia were demanding a place in
the new nation for both Black and white women as independent citizens.

In place of the controlled interbreeding between "half-castes" and
whites—"the absorption of the blacks by the whites," that is, the union
of white men and "half-caste" women—envisaged by government
officials, Mary Bennett embarked on schemes to render Aboriginal
women independent and self-supporting in their own communities.
She personally taught them weaving and craft skills with this aim.
Bennett described her work to Bessie Rischbieth in these terms:

The money thus earned goes back to the workers. It is enough that the women and the girls can be self-supporting and are self-supporting. Economic dependence is the root of all evil. The half-caste problem also results very largely from the same cause—their dependence. The evils of the patriarchal system have become commercialised, the unfortunate women having acquired value as merchandise from white settlement. . . . And so, though all the hunting grounds have been taken up as sheep stations, and the native culture has been completely destroyed, there has been an extraordinary recrudescence of polygamy for prostitution. . . . But the women intrinsically are fine and ready for a position of respect and independence. This is why I have asked that they shall be permitted to invoke and obtain the protection of the law of the land. . . .[36]

Bennett's appeal for "the protection of the law of the land" is important here. It speaks to a historic convergence of forces that came to shape and define the Australian feminist investment in a protectionist nation-state. The stress on the necessity of women's protection in a frontier masculinist society coincided with a nationalist commitment to building a new order of nation-state, which would produce, in the words of Bessie Rischbieth, "the sort of civilisation women of all countries dream about."[37] The defining elements of this new order were nicely captured in Lilian Locke-Burns's celebration of the Labor government's introduction of a maternity allowance in 1912:

In no other part of the civilised world as far as one can ascertain, is so much being done by the State in the way of providing for mothers and children as in the Australian Commonwealth. And yet how far we are still from a proper realisation of the value of a child as an asset of the State, and how little we realise the true position the mothers of the community would occupy in a properly organised social system, where the economic independence of women was fully recognised and assured. In Great Britain and some other countries which lay claim to some share in democratic reforms, the mothers are only protected (if protection it may be called) under some form of social insurance. In the American states also very little has been done so far in this direction beyond some attention to delinquent children and the usual institutional efforts that we find in most countries which have evolved beyond the barbaric stage. Neither in England nor America do we hear of any such humanitarian provision as the Australian maternity allowance. . . .[38]

This tribute is interesting both in its identification of the New World civilized nation's mission as the protection of women and its definition of that mission as the responsibility of the State. For Australian women citizens, the state was envisaged as a powerful beneficial force, enabling them to resolve the seeming contradiction posed by their twin ideals of "protection" and "independence." Feminists enlisted the state as a crucial ally, able to provide the protection that would make possible women's independence from men. Arguing that their sex was more nurturing, loving, and peace-loving than men, feminists endorsed the idea of a separate maternal citizenship for women, who were excused and excluded from the work of national self-defense abroad and enjoined to seek the protection and support of male relatives at home. Paradoxically, then, feminists contributed to the processes whereby women in the new nation were locked into the status of the protected sex and arguably into a psychology of helplessness and defenselessness that continues to pose a major dilemma for feminists today. The protected ones could not know real freedom. Moreover, as the inheritors of frontier feminism, Australian women still confront the contradictions posed by living in a strongly masculinist culture (which has just proclaimed Anzac Day to be *the* national day of remembrance), which has yet institutionalized the power of a protectionist femocracy.

NOTES

1. Louisa Lawson, "First Public Speech," 13 June 1891. Lawson Family Papers, Mitchell Library A1898, Sydney, Australia.

2. Quoted in Katie Spearitt, "The Poverty of Protection: Women and Marriage in Colonial Queensland, 1870–1900" (Honours thesis, History Department, University of Queensland, 1988), 58.

3. Anne Maree Collins, "Woman or Beast? Bestiality in Queensland, 1870–1949," *Hecate* 17, no. 1 (1991). Men charged with bestiality said they had made "use of the (animal) as if it were a woman," 38.

4. Quoted in Gail Griffin, "The Feminist Club of New South Wales, 1914–1970: A History of Feminist Politics in Decline," *Hecate* 14, no. 1 (1988).

5. "Women and Oversea Settlement and Some Problems of Government," British Commonwealth League Conference, 22–23 June 1926, Report. Fawcett Library, London, England.

6. Russell Ward, *The Australian Legend* (Melbourne: Oxford University Press, 1966).

7. Henry Reynolds, *Frontier Aborigines, Settlers and Land* (Sydney: Allen and Unwin, 1987).

8. Ibid., 52.

9. Maggie Humm, ed., *Modern Feminisms: Political, Literary, Cultural* (New York: Columbia University Press, 1992), 2, 7.

10. Judith Allen, *Rose Scott* (Melbourne: Oxford University Press, 1994), 96.

11. Marilyn Lake, "Between Old World 'Barbarism' and Stone Age 'Primitivism': The Double Difference of the White Australian Feminist," *Australian Women: Contemporary Feminist Thought* (Melbourne: Oxford University Press, 1994).

12. Adele Perry, "'How Influential a Few Men and a Few Families Become': White Women, Sexuality, Family and Colonialism in Nineteenth-Century British Columbia," paper presented at the 18th International Congress of Historical Sciences, Montreal, August 1995. On white women's assumed authority as civilizers, see also Vron Ware, *Beyond the Pale White Women, Racism and History*

(London: Verso, 1992), and Nupur Chaudhuri and Margaret Strobel, eds., *Western Women and Imperialism: Complicity and Resistance* (Bloomington: Indiana University Press, 1992).

13. British Commonwealth League Report, "Women and Oversea Settlement."

14. Quoted in Spearitt, "The Poverty of Protection," 26.

15. Quoted in Allen, *Rose Scott*, 134.

16. Marilyn Lake, "The Politics of Respectability: Identifying the Masculinist Context," *Historical Studies* 86 (1986).

17. Quoted in Spearitt, "The Poverty of Protection," 39.

18. Barbara Caine, *Victorian Feminists* (Melbourne: Oxford University Press, 1993), 36.

19. Lawson, "First Public Speech."

20. Rose Scott, "Womanhood Suffrage," speech notes, March 1898. Rose Scott Papers, ML MS 38/38, Mitchell Library, Sydney, Australia.

21. "Irven," "Sex Hygiene," *Labor Call*, 19 June 1919.

22. Quoted in Spearitt, "The Poverty of Protection," 31.

23. Ibid., 25.

24. Lake, "The Politics of Respectability," 118.

25. Caine, *Victorian Feminists*, 36.

26. On the reform of marriage, see, for example, Patricia Grimshaw, "Bessie Harrison Lee," in Marilyn Lake and Farley Kelly, eds., *Double Time Women in Victoria, 150 Years* (Ringwood: Penguin, 1995); and on motherhood endowment, Marilyn Lake, "A Revolution in the Family: The Challenge and Contradictions of Maternal Citizenship," in Seth Koven and Sonya Michel, eds., *Mothers of a New World: Maternalist Politics and the Origin of Welfare States* (New York: Routledge, 1993). Motherhood endowment was different from the maternity allowance introduced in 1912.

27. Spearitt, "The Poverty of Protection," 30.

28. Quoted in Judith Hicks Stiehm, "The Protected, The Protector, The Defender," *Women's Studies International Forum* 4, nos. 3–4 (1982): 373.

29. Lawson, "First Public Speech."

30. Fiona Paisley, "Ideas Have Wings: White Women Challenge Aboriginal Policy, 1920–37" (Doctoral thesis, Women's Studies, LaTrobe University, Melbourne, Australia; 1995), ch. 4.

31. Mary Bennett, reported in *West Australian* and *Daily Mail*, Rischbieth Papers, 2004/12/351.

32. Louisa Lawson, "Scrapbook," vol. 1, Lawson Papers, Mitchell Library, MS A 1895.

33. Fiona Paisley, "'Don't Tell England!' Women of Empire Campaign to Change Aboriginal Policy in Australia between the Wars," *Lilith* 8 (Summer 1993).

34. Mary Bennett to Bessie Rischbieth, 6 November 1934. Rischbieth Papers, NLA 2004/12/64.

35. Mary Bennett to Bessie Rischbieth, April 1932. Rischbieth Papers, NLA 2004/12/23.

36. Ibid.

37. Bessie Rischbieth to Carrie Chapman Catt, 24 November 1924. Rischbieth Papers, NLA 2004/7/62.

38. Lilian Locke-Burns, "State Provision for Mother and Child," *Labor Call*, 26 June 1919.

6

The *Porfiriato* and the Mexican Revolution

Constructions of Feminism and Nationalism

GABRIELA CANO

A debate on feminism and the role of women in society evolved among the Mexican literate sectors from the 1880s to 1910 and 1911.[1] An element that permeated the positions in the debate was the representation of the Mexican identity. The way the Mexican nation was conceived played a crucial part in the definition of the feminine ideal and in the discussion on feminism.

The feminine ideal—the "Mexican woman"—was defined with elements of the liberal representation of the Mexican nationality developed during the nineteenth century. *Criollo*[2] patriotism, neo-Aztec tendencies, and the search for human types and sceneries, as well as those artistic and literary expressions that were identified with Mexico, converged in the making of this representation. Thus, the "Mexican woman" was defined with concepts that conveyed the sense of national belonging and that noted the differences between the sexes.

A reconstruction of the Indian past was a central component in the liberal view of the nation. On one hand, it provided a sense of exoticism, and on the other hand, it contributed to creating an organic and homogeneous view of the past.[3] Both elements were characteristic of modern representations of nationhood; exoticism was directed to international consumption, whereas the idea of a unified heritage served the purposes of the liberal version of Mexican history that tended to reconcile opposing political factions and diverse social groups and to present an integrated view of the historical process. It must be stressed, however, that the recognition of Indian legacy did not imply an acceptance of present-day Indians. On the contrary, the liberal republican political project did not have a space for indigenous groups, their traditional forms of social organization, or their strong cultural heritage, which kept them apart from what liberals considered the mainstream *mestizo* or mixed Mexican Republic. Indians were seen by liberals as an obstacle to progress, an obstacle that would eventually be effaced. In time, Indians would be assimilated into democratic and egalitarian culture and would, therefore, disappear as a segment of society with a specific culture and with traditional forms of sociability. Indian culture was valued, exceptionally, as a symbol of a past heritage.

Feminism was perceived as a double threat to the "Mexican woman." A masculinizing effect was feared, and at the same time feminism was attacked on the grounds that it was a foreign influence—Saxon and Protestant—alien to the ways of the Mexican woman. The enemies of feminism conferred on it a destructive power—some even said it had genocidal effects—and this seemed convincing because they argued that it threatened not only national identity but also women's identity, both concepts being closely linked.

At the turn of the century, the representation of the "Mexican woman" became, without a doubt, a battlefield. Both feminists (who, from an egalitarian and differentiating perspective, fought for a larger sphere of action and for women's right to independent decisions) and conservatives (who held that submissiveness was the national quality of women) claimed they were entitled to define "the genuine Mexican woman."

With the Revolution, fears about the foreign nature of feminism seemed to vanish, at least in some radical political circles. In 1915, after five years of civil war and at the peak of political and military strain, feminism gained some ground among the constitutional forces, the revolutionary faction from the North of the country that eventually defeated the peasant armies and modernized the State. From a liberal standpoint that stressed the non-religious nature of the State, the Northern revolutionaries discovered in feminism a useful weapon to fight the Catholic Church, a powerful enemy of the revolutionary government. Not that they were particularly interested in supporting women's rights, but feminism could be an ally when fighting the Church's influence within the family and society at large.

Nineteenth-century liberals emphasized over and over that traditional feminine traits were identified with Catholicism, a notion that was reinforced after the Revolution. On the other extreme, masculine traits were linked to the Revolution—to social transformation—just as the dictatorship of Porfirio Díaz had identified masculinity with progress and patriotism. This representation of political attitudes was consistent with the revolutionaries' determination to exclude women from citizenship in 1917, when the armed period of the Revolution ended.

Nevertheless, feminism had a political place in the postrevolutionary administrations during the twenties because, to a certain degree, it played a role in the difficult relations between Mexico and the United States, since it was used by the Mexican government as a diplomatic approach. In 1924, President Alvaro Obregón had a diplomatic interest in sending an official delegation to the Pan-American Conference of Women in Baltimore. Although the Mexican Revolution developed a strong political nationalism to oppose the North American attempts to intervene politically and economically, a diplomatic relationship with the United States was essential in order to achieve the capitalistic modernization pursued by the Mexican postrevolutionary administrations.

The political struggle of feminism during the Revolution and the twenties was also a struggle for the representation of national and gender identities, and it was closely related to the Porfirian debate on the "Mexican woman."

The Revolution, on the other hand, did not alter in any significant way the liberal conception of Indians as an obstacle to progress. As in the nineteenth century, the tendency of revolutionary reforms was to integrate Indians for national republican use, not to recognize them as groups with any sort of autonomous rights. In terms of representation of nationhood, the Revolution strengthened the symbolic importance of Indian heritage.

NATIONAL OBSTACLES TO FEMINISM

At the turn of the century, the argument used by enemies of feminism was that it had a foreign nature and that its goal was to impose radical egalitarianism. For example, in 1909, Horacio Barreda, an old-fashioned Comtian[4] from the orthodox wing who was promoted by Pierre Laffite, said that the feminists wanted to make men and women equal in all aspects of their lives, in their social functions as well as in their personal characteristics.[5] Such egalitarianism would cause women to set aside their domestic role as mothers and wives and would make them masculine and, as another author pointed out, "[they] will become tribunes in skirts who will defend their rights with violent invectives against their oppressors."[6] With masculinization, domestic disorder would emerge—"men [will] rock cradles and women will make dissections and pronounce judicial allegations"[7]—followed by a social chaos that eventually would give way to genocide: "the extermination of the human race."[8]

At the same time, another antifeminist claim was that masculinization was nothing but a harmless specter since feminism was a foreign influence with no possibilities of being adopted in Mexico. Thus, after sounding the alarm about the serious risk of feminism, Barreda concluded that "the Americanization of the Mexican woman,"[9] which, according to him, was an ideal pursued by feminists, should not worry anyone, since, fortunately

> The influence of our social background, our ethnic heritage and Latin education, as well as the less powerful influence of the biological disposition of women will become a formidable obstacle to feminism which will protect the Mexican woman. . . .[10]

According to this perspective, neither college education, paid work, nor feminist claims were attractive to Mexican women since these goals were opposed to their biological nature and their national identity. This view was also defended by Andrés Ortega, a writer and follower of Spencerian ideas who, in order to be more convincing and perhaps in order to convince himself that Mexicans would reject feminism, introduced a female voice in his arguments to address feminists:

> Mercy! Unlike you, I was not born a man; I was not born for the turbulent arguments in the Parliament . . . neither was I born for the shameless explanations at the school of Medicine, nor for the brilliant arguments in front of a jury.
>
> I was born to wait for you at home, with open arms and modest kisses, in order to be your loving and simple wife, the mother of your children. . . . Educate me according to my nature, to my feminine mind [to my nature as a] woman, a Mexican woman.[11]

If this was a general conception, if Mexicans rejected feminism spontaneously because of its alien nature, one is prompted to ask the question, Why such great efforts to attack it? If the consequences of feminism were so insignificant as Barreda sustained, why did he dedicate to it an extended and dense essay published in six parts?

The "Mexican woman" in Barreda, Ortega, and other writers, more than a social reality, was a strategy designed to attack feminism. The qualities attributed to the "Mexican woman" were exactly the opposite of what, according to the enemies of feminism, was the feminist ideal. Domesticity, modesty—"woman's most precious treasure," in Ortega's words[12]—sentimentalism, and submissiveness were identified as feminine traits. Julio Sesto, Spanish-born novelist and journalist, summarized these opinions in 1908: "Mexican women are the most balanced women I have ever met. They are good daughters, good wives, good mothers, hard-working, intelligent, sentimental, discreet, elegant and fertile. One can find virtue in everything they do."[13] Sesto implied that the "Mexican woman" is *mestiza*, that is, a mixture of Spanish and Indian blood in which European physical traits, such as whiteness, have predominated and diluted Indian ones.

This representation of the properly feminine gained credibility and an appearance of stability when proposed as an expression of the Mexican identity which, at that time, was seeking its own traits in nature as well as in cultural expressions. The "Mexican woman," said Sesto, is a "national gift," words that were also used to describe the land, the diversity of the scenery, or any artistic work of some value.

OTHER "MEXICAN WOMEN"

In spite of their differences, other representations of the "Mexican woman" shared the notion of domesticity and upheld the importance of being a mother and a wife. No one—not even those who supported intellectual and educational equality between the sexes—attempted to invalidate the differences in social roles between men and women, as feared by those haunted by the specter of masculinization.

At the beginning of the 1890s, literature became for some a legitimate activity for the "Mexican woman." An example was the book of *Poetisas mexicanas. Siglos XVII, XVIII y XIX (Mexican Women Poets. 17th, 18th, and 19th Centuries)*, published under the auspices of the Porfirian government and edited by the liberal thinker José María Vigil.[14] As well, there were two other collections of female poetry published in the states of Puebla and Zacatecas.[15]

Representative of *criollo* patriotism, Vigil envisioned the Mexican nationality more as a peculiar sensitivity and culture that emerged with the Spanish Conquest and developed with no significant ruptures in subsequent centuries, than as a political entity found in a specific moment. According to this writer, the *"criollo* spirit"—that is, the Spanish soul that took root in Mexico—was the main character of culture, whereas the Indian soul vanished until it disappeared almost completely. In Vigil's view the *criollo* spirit was masculine; however, he recognized the fact that women writers—themselves *criollas*—contributed to the creation of the "Mexican woman" with their delicate feelings and fertile imagination.

Colonial nuns, winners of secular literary competitions, and collaborators in women's magazines from the second half of the nineteenth century were all grouped under the label of "Mexican women writers." Ignoring the diversity of historical circumstances and the differences in literary value, the editor of *Poetisas mexicanas* considers that Mexican women writers are characterized by sweetness, submission and domesticity: "they are above all, women, and women in Mexico—no metaphor implied—are the Angel of the House. . . ."[16] Thus, the writer becomes a trait of national identity since she expresses the subjective pecularities of the "Mexican woman": "[she] unconsciously embellishes the ideas and feelings of her sex with words."[17]

Vigil's representation of the "Mexican woman" did not emerge spontaneously; it was created for international consumption as part of the making of a nation that, at the same time, attempted to praise what was genuinely Mexican and advertise the progress achieved by the country. *Poetisas mexicanas* and the Pueblan and Zacatecan poetry books mentioned above were published for the Chicago World's Fair that took place in 1893 in order to celebrate the four hundred years since the discovery of America. The fair featured a Woman's Pavilion, specially built to exhibit women's works from different countries and races.[18] Mexico was represented with a poetry book display and a crafts exhibit, which showed handkerchiefs handcrafted in the city of Toluca, Indian woven pieces from Tehuantepec, gold- and silver-embroidered military uniforms, oil paintings, and china decorated with watercolors.

The poetry books as well as the crafts were considered typical national products and, at the same time, examples of the devotion and sensitivity of the "Mexican woman." The Indian woven works were displayed as an element of exoticism and a symbol of a heritage destined to disappear, not as a vigorous part of the modern nation. But the poetic works, in Vigil's words, also proved that "creativity was not exclusive to the stronger sex."[19] The image of the woman writer, as opposed to the manual labor of Indian women, contributed to the notion that intellectual capability, understood as literary creativity, could become a legitimate quality of the "Mexican woman."

Intellectual activity was the main element in the making of the "Mexican woman" that was promoted by the feminist magazine called *La mujer mexicana* (*The Mexican Woman*).[20] Published by a female team of writers, two physicians, and a lawyer (themselves pioneers of professional education for women), the magazine appeared monthly for three years, from 1904 to 1906. Through its pages, declared one of its founders, "we wanted to leave forever the imprint of our sprit on every field of human knowledge." *La mujer mexicana*, she added, wished to have a "feminist character in order to be distinguished from the merely literary magazines, which, until then, had been published by women."[21]

For *The Mexican Woman*, the population of the nation was uniform: ethnicity was nonexistent. Indians were a cultural heritage but not a social component of a modern nation. Therefore, the expression of Indian women as a distinct group with specific characteristics was not even considered by the feminists of *The Mexican Woman*.

"Nation, Home and Science"[22] was the motto of this representation of the "Mexican woman," and it certainly summarized the meaning of the feminist affiliation of the magazine.[23] Feminism, in this context, was not considered masculinizing, nor was it a threat to national identity; on the contrary, it could lead to patriotic attitudes. According to *La mujer mexicana*, feminine patriotism was not only expressed through the procreation and the upbringing of children; it arose in civic participation and professional activities.

The identification of patriotism with female intellectual enterprises was strongly put forward by the Mexican-born writer Laureana Wright de Kleinhans,[24] who was, in her time, the most brilliant and radical defender of women's emancipation. She supported equal individual rights for men and women, but believed the most important task for women was to work for an intellectual education and moral strength, since these were the only tools with which they could achieve independence and leave behind the narrowness of the domestic sphere. In Wright de Kleinhans's view, motherhood was an essential and privileged area of women's life; however, she believed that "maternity was not the only human representation [for women]."[25]

According to Wright de Kleinhans, intellectual achievements—everyday tasks such as teaching or writing—were as heroic and worthy of national praise as civic or military enterprises. Speaking of Matilde Montoya, the first woman physician in the country, Wright de Kleinhans stressed that, when Montoya "first decided to become a doctor, she considered travelling to the US, but for the benefit of our national honor, she was unable to do so."[26] After describing with an epic tone the problems confronted by Montoya, Wright de Kleinhans concluded, "The day this heroic woman graduated, obtaining the first professional scientific degree, is engraved in gold letters in the history of patriotic progress."[27]

Appreciating the importance conferred on national history as a key element of national identity and of patriotism, Wright de Kleinhans understood that the legitimization of the civic and intellectual achievements of the "Mexican woman" had to be incorporated into the historical narrative of the nation. The official chronicles, she wrote, do not offer anything to "ennoble our sex through our works."[28] And, she added, "unfortunately, our patriotic history sometimes omits and sometimes forgets; [it is] usually superficial and abridged, specially when it refers to civic enterprises of women."[29] Wright de Kleinhans wanted to correct those omissions with her own writings; therefore, she wrote several biographies of "distinguished women" who lived from pre-Hispanic times to the nineteenth century. In the lives of pre-Columbian Indians, colonial nuns, and nineteenth-century teachers, writers and pioneers of the professions, Wright de Kleinhans discovered that the women's civil, military, and intellectual activities were compatible with their domestic chores and family obligations as mothers, wives, daughters, and sisters, and she declared that both activities were equally worthy contributions of the "Mexican woman." Following the dominating liberal view of history, Wright de Kleinhans included the biographies of several women of the pre-Hispanic past—for example, the señoras of Tula, Malinalxóchitl, Tecuiloatzin, Tlillacaptzin, Malinal, Coacuelle, Itzaxilotzin, Atozquetzin, and Matalzihuatzin among others—but she did not refer to any of her Indian contemporaries. Moreover, she mentioned no Indian woman from colonial times or from the nineteenth century, as if Indians had disappeared after the Spanish Conquest.[30]

Originally published in different magazines, the dozens of biographies written by Laureana Wright de Kleinhans appeared in the volume *Mujeres notables mexicanas*, published ten years after her death, under the auspices of the Festivities of the Centennial of Independence, celebrated in 1910. The main purpose of these festivities was diplomatic, the goal being to present Mexico's modern image to the Western world, just as had been done at the 1893 Chicago World's Fair. A "Mexican woman" who was equally capable of scientific and educational achievements and of devotion to home and children was an adequate image to represent progressive Mexico.

The First Lady, Carmen Romero Rubio de Díaz, was the main feminine figure in the political and diplomatic protocol during the Centennial. Her image was the portrait of the balanced type of "Mexican woman" as defined by Julio Sesto: modest and sentimental and, at the same time, soberly elegant and intelligent in an unobtrusive way. "Carmelita" relativized the importance of the challenging qualities underlying "Mexican Woman," which were constructed by Wright de Kleinhans and by *La mujer mexicana*: personal strength and autonomous views.

THE INSIDE ENEMY

Although it did not disappear completely, the notion of feminism as a masculinizing and foreign influence lost ground with the Mexican Revolution.

The differences between both conceptions are evident if one compares the revival of feminism in the state of Yucatán as seen by the two writers Francisco Bulnes, a Porfirian and Catholic opponent of the Revolution, and Julio Hernández, an anticlerical professor. Both were born in the first half of the nineteenth century; both had negative views on feminism. To Bulnes, feminism was the absolute denial of the "Mexican woman"; it could only attract "homely women, desperate widows and poor seamstresses, all inclined to hysterical emotions." He considered it a destructive influence that nurtured "a hatred against society that was more theatening than a Barcelonian anarchist."[31] On the other hand, Julio Hernández declared that feminism "guided by an 'equalitarian frenzy' was an endemic illness turned epidemic but, nevertheless, unharmful."[32]

Bulnes maintained that it was dangerous to have women dedicated to social causes that were neither charitable nor pious. Julio Hernández proclaimed that the positive aspects of feminism lay in its potential to keep women away from pious work.

Anticlericals considered feminism an ally in the struggle against the influence of the Church on society, since women's emancipation claimed rational education for women. In their defense of feminism, anticlericals represented the "Mexican woman" as a supporter of conservative ideologies, an ally of the Church, and therefore, an obstacle to progress and to the Revolution.[33] Hernández called feminism a "formidable enemy to our republican institutions."[34]

Anticlericalism envisioned the "Mexican woman" as an ally of the Vatican, a domestic enemy of the nation. Due to her weak soul and her eternal infancy, wrote Julio Hernández, she was "in the hands of error" and "at the mercy of the declared enemies of Liberty and Nation, perpetrators of the interventionist crimes that we have suffered because of their admiration to all that is foreign." He added that the "Mexican woman" sent large sums of money to Rome, and opened the door of her home to the priests' influence who, by these means, "rule over the national government."[35]

In its most extreme version, anticlerical misogyny placed the "Mexican woman" beyond nationality. She is "Roman," declared Julio Hernández, "therefore, one cannot accept her as a fellow compatriot or as an element of progress."[36] Thus, the Mexican nation was conceived as a masculine community with no place for women. A less radical position admitted the possibility that women might have access to nationality if they were educated on a nonreligious and scientific basis and if they freed themselves from the guardianship of priests.

The feminist congresses that took place in January and December of

1916 in Yucatán can be undersood as efforts of the constitutional Revolution to weaken the alliance between women and the ecclesiastical power, and to integrate women within a project of economical modernization. Organized and financed by the military government of Yucatán, these congresses were not spontaneous encounters, nor did they have political independence. According to the constitutional governor Salvador Alvarado, the political mobilization of women was an adequate tool if it was meant to support laicism in society.[37] "The most efficient procedure to achieve these goals, that is, to emancipate and educate women," read the invitation to the First Feminist Congress in Yucatán, "is to have the presence of women, with their energy and initiatives, in order to fight for their rights, to claim the education they need and to demand their incorporation to State affairs. . . ."[38] Despite the political control to which these congresses were subjected, a great variety of views on the role of women in society were expressed openly. The differences among the delegates were so great in the First Congress that the event became a public scandal.[39]

The Yucatecan constitutionalists, as well as the other factions at war in the Mexican Revolution, inherited liberal views about Indians. Thus, revolutionary policies concerning the Indian population were assimilationist. The objective was to eliminate specific components of Indian culture and social organization, which were considered backward and an obstacle to progress.

Women were not recognized as subjects by the Yucatecan constitutionalists; they were considered useful political instruments. However, the Yucatecan constitutionalism, influenced by socialist ideologies, promoted an egalitarian image of men's and women's contributions to society. This perspective also understood feminism as a phenomenon with a specific profile that distinguished it from "the various forms of feminism around the world which are celibate feminism, suffragism, bourgeois feminism and radical feminism."[40]

An association between egalitarian claims and national traits characterized this conception of feminism: "we demand women's rights and activities similar to those of men, in education, life and democracy, and in accordance to the Mexican social revolution." This position generated a representation of the "Mexican woman" that was defined by the right "to build the Mexican Fatherland on unequivocal bases of equality."[41] Such an image influenced the constitutionalist policies toward women—on both the local and national levels—but gender equality was not its main purpose.

In the feminist congresses held in Yucatán, the image of the "Mexican woman" with equal rights was mentioned many times, but the political agreements referred to the procedures to fight the influence of the Church. They also proposed a different vocational training for women and men. In spite of the fact that the First Congress acknowledged the same abilities for men and women for public service, and that it stressed the unfairness that laws were made only by men, it never demanded women's suffrage.[42]

The Constitution issued in 1917 by the victorious faction in the Revolution granted many social and labor rights to women, but it denied women's suffrage. Among the liberal congressmen, the conservative image of the "Mexican woman" prevailed over the principle of individual equality. According to this peculiar conception of republican democracy, the revolutionary laws should guarantee above all the triumph of liberal governments and the protection of the Revolution from the inside enemy called the "Mexican woman." Therefore, ignoring the demand for women's suffrage was not considered incoherent with the principles of individual equality nor with the "Against re-election, effective suffrage" formula that had guided the revolutionary movement and that was acknowledged by the constitutionalists as their cornerstone.[43]

The Revolution validated the representation of the "Mexican woman" as an agent of reactionary positions and thus valorized the link between conservative trends and femininity. At the same time, as other authors have argued, revolutionary discourse identified virility with social transformation.[44]

PERMANENCE OF THE "MEXICAN WOMAN"

Nevertheless, at the beginning of the twenties, the revolutionary administrations granted a political space to feminism, since it was a tool that could help ease the diplomatic relations with the United States—then severely damaged as a result of the legislation over foreign ownership of natural resources issued by the Constitution of 1917. In order to gain strength to confront domestic opposition and to project a positive international image, the Mexican government needed the United States' diplomatic recognition without having to give up nationalist economic policies.

The opportunity to strengthen diplomatic relations arose in 1922, when the U.S. State Department invited the Mexican government to participate in the Pan-American Conference of Women to be held in Baltimore, Maryland, in conjunction with the Annual Convention of the League of Women Voters. The Mexican delegation acted as a diplomatic mission whose aim was to help secure the relationship between both countries. Thus, in order to promote goodwill between the Mexican and the American people, the delegates organized social and cultural events in the cities they visited on their way to Maryland.[45] One of the most significant events was held at Liberty Hall, in Philadelphia. There, heading the delegation, and in the name of the Mexican president, Elena Torres presented a Mexican flag to the mayor's wife.[46] This was interpreted by some of the Mexican press as a symbolic act that represented an intention of the Mexican government to renounce the nationalistic economic policies established in the Constitution. In fact, the following year, Alvaro Obregón's administration partially yielded to the American demands on the rights over oil.

On the other hand, the presence of the Mexican delegation in Baltimore had favorable consequences for the development of feminism in Mexico. The First Pan-American Feminist Congress held in 1923, in Mexico City, legitimized feminism as a political force, even if women's citizenship rights did not have legal recognition.

The Mexican flag presented in Philadelphia had been embroidered by Mexican women. Years before, in 1893, at the Chicago World's Fair, Mexico had also been represented by embroideries, symbols of women's industriousness and delicacy. The analogy in the gifts suggests that, in spite of the political status achieved by feminism during the twenties and the intensity with which the problem of women's identities surfaced at the time,[47] the domesticity implied in the image of the "Mexican woman" was still valid. On the other hand, the increasing conflict between the State and the Church reinforced the representation of the "Mexican woman" as an ally of the Church and the conservative wing.

NOTES

1. Porfirio Díaz's administration, also called the Porfirian dictatorship or *Porfiriato*, began in 1876 and ended in 1911; the civil war was known as the Mexican Revolution.

2. The concept of *criollo* patriotism comes from David Brading. It refers to the pride in New Spanish culture developed in late colonial times. It usually involves devotion to Our Lady of Guadalupe, xenophobic resentment against the Spaniards, and disparagement of the Conquest. David Brading, *The Origins of Mexican Nationalism* (Cambridge: Cambridge University Press, 1984).

3. See Mauricio Tenorio, "Crafting the Modern Mexicos: Mexico's Presence at the World Fairs, 1880s–1920s" (Ph.D. dissertation, Stanford University, 1993).

4. For late Comtianism, see W. Dirk Raat, "Augustín Aragón and Mexico's Religion of Humanity," in W. Dirk Raat, ed., *Mexico: From Independence to Revolution* (Lincoln: University of Nebraska Press, 1982), 241–69.

118 | GABRIELA CANO

5. Horacio Barreda, "Estudio sobre el feminismo," *Revista positiva*, IX, 1909, reprinted in Lourdes Alvarado, *El siglo XIX ante el feminismo. Una interpretación positivista*, Mexico City: UNAM, CESU, 1991, p. 38.

6. Andrés Ortega, "El feminismo. Discurso pronunciado por el señor licenciado Andrés Ortega en el acto de ser recibo como miembro de la Sociedad Mexicana de Geografía y Estadística," *Revista de la Sociedad Mexicana de Geografía y Estadística*, 5a. época, vol. II (1907): 326–27, reprinted in Ana Lau and Carmen Ramos, eds., *Mujeres y revolución (1900–1917)* (Mexico City: INEHRM, 1993), 98.

7. Manuel Flores, "La mujer y las profesiones liberales," *El mundo ilustrado*, 5 de mayo de 1901, in Mílada Bazant, ed., *Debate pedagógico durante el porfiriato* (Mexico City: SEP/El Caballito, 1985, Biblioteca pedagógica), 144.

8. Ibid.

9. Barreda, "Estudio sobre el feminismo," 136.

10. Ibid.

11. Ortega, "El feminismo," 95.

12. Ibid.

13. Julio Sesto, "El Mexico de Porfirio Díaz" (Valencia, Venezuela: F. Sempere y Cía, 1908), reprinted in Lau and Ramos, *Mujeres y revolución*, 107.

14. José María Vigil, *Poetisas mexicanas. Siglos XVII, XVIII, XIX* (facsimile of the 1893 edition; reprinted, Mexico City: UNAM, 1977, Nueva Biblioteca Mexicana 43).This facsimile uses different numeration systems: the reproduction of the text is paginated with Arabic numerals, and the prologue and introductory study with Roman numerals.

15. *La lira poblana. Poesías de las señoritas Rosa Carreto, Severa Aróstegui, Leonor Cravioto, María Trinidad Ponce y Carreón, María de los Angeles Otero y Luz Trillanes y Arrillaga* (Imprenta de Francisco Díaz de León Sucs., 1893); and *Colección de varias composiciones poéticas de señoras zacatecanas* (Zacatecas, Mexico: Tipografía económica, 1893).

16. José María Vigil, "La mujer mexicana. (Estudio dedicado a la distinguidísima señora Carmen Romero Rubio de Díaz)," Mexico City: Tipografía de la Secretaría de Fomento, 1893, reprinted in José María Vigil, *Poetisas mexicanas*.

17. Ibid.

18. María Elena Díaz Alejo and Ernesto Prado Velázquez, "Estudio preliminar," in Vigil, *Poetisas mexicanas*, ix–xxxv.

19. Vigil, "Prólogo," *Poetisas mexicanas*, vii–viii.

20. *La mujer mexicana. Revista mensual científico-literaria consagrada a la evolución, progreso y perfeccionamiento de la mujer mexicana* was consecutively directed by Dolores Correa Zapata, Laura Méndez de Cuenca, and Mateana Murguía de Aveleyra. The editorial board included, among others, the writers Dolores Roa Bárcena de Camarillo, María Enriqueta Camarillo de Pereyra, Dolores Jiménez y Muro; the physicians Columba Rivera and Antonia Ursúa; and the lawyer Victoria Sandoval de Zarco. Luz Fernández vda. de Herrera was in charge of the administration.

21. Letter from Luz Fernández vda. de Herrera to Julia Nava de Ruizsánchez, 29 July, 1921, "Historia del feminismo," *La vida. Revista mensual ilustrada* 1, no. 1 (February 1923): 10.

22. This is a verse from Severa Aróstegui, "A la sociedad protectora de la mujer en su velada inaugural," *La mujer mexicana* 2, no. 3 (March 1905): 3.

23. See Manuela Contreras, "El feminismo," *La mujer mexicana* 1, no. 1 (January 1904): 6; Camila Vera de Azorey, "Feminismo," *La mujer mexicana* 2,

no. 4 (April 1905): 5; Guadalupe G. de Joseph, "El feminismo en México," *La mujer mexicana* 2, no. 11 (November 1905): 12.

24. Born in 1846 in Taxco, Guerrero, to a Mexican mother and an American father, Laureana Wright González wrote extensively on women's emancipation and on political and historical topics. Her articles, biographical essays, and poems appeared in several newspapers and literary magazines. In 1887 she founded *Violetas del Anáhuac. Periódico literario redactado por señoras,* which she edited until her death in 1896. She also wrote two short books, *Educación errónea de la mujer y medios prácticos para corregirla* (1891) and *La emancipación de la mujer por medio del estudio* (1892), which summarize her views on women's education. Her best-known work is the posthumous volume, *Mujeres notables mexicanas* (Mexico City: Tipografía económica, 1910).

At twenty-three she married the Alsacian Santiago Kleinhans and gave birth to a daughter, Margarita.

25. Laureana Wright de Kleinhans, "La mujer perfecta," in *El correo de las señoras* 12, no. 1 (1893): 1.

26. Laureana Wright de Kleinhans, *Mujeres notables mexicanas,* 534.

27. Ibid., 541.

28. Ibid., 370.

29. Ibid.

30. Ibid., 1–74.

31. Francisco Bulnes, *Toda la verdad acerca de la revolución mexicana. La responsabilidad criminal del presidente Wilson en el desastre mexicano* [1916] (Mexico City: Libro-mex., 1977), 114.

32. Julio Hernández, *La nueva sociología mexicana y la educación nacional* (México, Librería de la vda. Ch. Bouret, 1916), in Lau and Ramos, *Mujeres y revolución,* 144.

33. Manuel Delgado interprets anticlericalism as an aggression against what is viewed as feminine power in a revealing essay on contemporary Spain, *Las palabras del otro hombre. Anticlericalismo y misoginia* (Barcelona: Muchnik Editores, 1993).

34. Hernández, *La nueva sociología,* 147.

35. Ibid.

36. Ibid., 148.

37. The topics discussed at the First Feminist Congress of Yucatán were the social means "to liberate women from the yoke of tradition"; the role of primary education in women's emancipation; the occupations and arts to be provided by the state in order "to prepare women for a life of intense progress"; the public functions to be performed by the Mexican woman so that she is "a leading element in society and not only a follower." "Convocatoria al Congreso Feminista de Yucatán emitida por el gobernador y comandante militar Salvador Alvarado," 28 October 1915, in *El Primer Congreso Feminista de Yucatán. Anales de esa memorable asamblea* (Mérida, Mexico, 1916, facsimile edition Mexico City: INFONAVIT, 1975), 32. A very similar agenda was discussed at the Second Congress. See *Dictamen de la primera comisión absolviendo el primer tema del segundo congreso feminista local* (Mérida, Mexico: Imprenta del gobierno constitucionalista, 1916), 32.

38. "Convocatoria al congreso Feminista."

39. The inaugural address to the First Congress, *"La mujer del porvenir,"* written by Hermila Galindo, hurt the sensibility of several delegates because it argued that sexual drive was equally intense in men and women. For the

reactions to Galindo's intervention, see *El Primer Congreso Feminista de Yucatán*, 71. Galindo did not attend the January congress; however, in December she traveled to Yucatán and personally explained her views and refuted the accusations of immorality. See *"La mujer del porvenir,"* 195–202, and *Estudio de la Srita. Hermila Galindo con motivo de los temas que han de absolverse en el Segundo Congreso Feminista de Yucatán* (Mérida, Yucatán: Imprenta del Gobierno Constitucionalista, 1916).

40. "La evolución del feminismo," in *El Primer Congreso*, 16.

41. Ibid.

42. "Informe enviado al Ejecutivo por la Junta Directiva" and reports presented by the acting committees, *El Primer Congreso*, 129–79.

43. An analysis of the debate on women's suffrage in the Constitutional Congress can be found in Gabriela Cano, *"Las feministas en campaña," Debate feminista*, vol. 4 (1991): 269–92.

44. Jean Franco, *Las conspiradoras. La representación de la mujer en México* (Versión actualizada) (Mexico City: El Colegio de México-FCE, 1994, Colección Tierra Firme), 140; and Ilene V. O'Malley, *The Myth of the Revolution: Hero Cults and the Institutionalization of the Mexican State* (Westport, CT: Greenwood Press, 1986), 133–34.

45. One of the members of the delegation wrote a chronicle of the trip; see Julia Nava de Ruizsánchez, *Informe que rinde la Secretaría de la Delegación Feminista al Congreso de Baltimore ante el Centro Feminista Mexicano* (Mexico City: n.p., 1923).

46. Ibid., 64.

47. Franco, *Las conspiradoras*, 144.

7

The Politics of Irish Identity and the Interconnections between Feminism, Nationhood, and Colonialism

BREDA GRAY AND LOUISE RYAN

Feminism[1] is inextricably linked with the growth of "secular nation-states, industrial capitalism and war and peace among nations."[2] Kumari Jayawardena links the rise of feminist movements with antico-lonial and nationalist struggles, both of which herald moves toward secularism and social reform.[3] As Carol Coulter points out,

> Not only in Ireland, but throughout the colonised world, women came onto the public stage in large numbers through the great nationalist movements of the beginning of this century. . . . However, their involvement in the revolutionary movements was not matched by their place in the newly created states.[4]

Other writers see nationalist ideologies and politics as mobilizing women in the interests of the nation-state, which is an expression of men's interests.[5] Nationalisms, according to Cynthia Enloe, "typically spring from masculinized memory, masculinized humiliation and masculinized hope."[6] Deniz Kandiyoti points out that these different perspectives share the view that women have a different relationship to national identity than do men.[7]

This chapter explores the complex relationships between feminism and nationalism from the beginning of the twentieth century in Ireland, examining in particular the twenty-six-county state and the gendered development of national identity from just before the establishment of that state in the 1920s. It is not possible here to address adequately all aspects of feminist engagement with nationalism and colonialism. Instead, the discussion is selective and focuses on some key sites of contestation, tracing the continuities and changes in feminist protest over the past one hundred years.

Nationalisms are a modern phenomenon[8] and take many forms, changing focus and direction in different times and places. They are, as Anne McClintock suggests, "invented, performed and consumed in ways that do not follow a universal blueprint."[9] Nationalisms can be revolutionary ideologies concerned with resisting domination, or dominant ideologies legitimizing the interests of established elites.[10] Both forms can be identified in Ireland over this century. Both of these forms of nationalism look simultaneously backward and forward in time, drawing on "tradition" and modernization as sources of legitimation and as foci for the maintenance of unity.[11]

Nationalism in its different forms in Ireland over this century has variously emphasized either tradition and the past, or the future and modernization. Anne McClintock sees nationalism's simultaneous concern with the past and the future as involving the negotiation of a path "between nostalgia for the past, and the impatient, progressive sloughing off of the past."[12] This temporal anomaly is, in her view, resolved by representing the contradiction as a "'natural' division of *gender*."[13] She characterizes this split in the following way:

> Women are represented as the atavistic and authentic "body" of national tradition (inert, backward-looking, and natural), embodying nationalism's conservative principle of continuity. Men, by contrast, represent the progressive agent of national modernity (forward-thrusting, potent, and historic), embodying nationalism's progressive or revolutionary principle of discontinuity.[14]

We suggest that the relationship between women and nationalism is more complex than McClintock suggests. Her complete association of women with tradition, nature, and the past is certainly true in particular times and contexts in Ireland; however, Irish feminist activism has contested these associations, and women can be seen as being incorporated within signifiers of modernization and progress in more recent national iconography. For example, in the 1980s, Irish women were included in the Irish Industrial Development Authority's poster campaign, "the young Europeans,"[15] as modern, educated, European citizens who could take their place at high levels within a European economy.[16]

THE GENDERED NATURE OF NATIONAL IDENTITY

The lack of attention to gender relations in the formation of collective identity and the development of cultural cohesion has led to large gaps in the theorization of nationalisms.[17] Nira Yuval-Davis asks why women are "hidden" in the various theorizations of the nation when women play such a central role in the biological, social, cultural, and symbolic reproduction of nations.[18] One reason for the exclusion of women, according to Yuval-Davis, may be the relegation of women to the private domain by classical social contract theorists. Women are, therefore, not seen as contributing to the public, political sphere in which discourses of nation and nationalism take place. The public/private dichotomy is reinforced by the nature/reason dichotomy, within which women are identified with nature rather than with the more masculine attributes of reason and aggression that are seen as essential to nation and nationalisms.[19] A further explanation for the continuing exclusion of women from theories of national identity is the close identification of women with family rather than with paid "productive" work that contributes to the gross national product. Patriarchal nationalist uses of "woman" as a symbol of nation serve to contain the political potential of women by reinforcing public/private, nature/culture, and productive work/nonproductive work dualisms.

R. Radhakrishnan examines the strategic use within nationalism of the insider/outsider dichotomy.[20] He sees this dichotomy as a line of exclusion between the native insider culture and the foreign outsider culture. The latter is deemed negative and seen as a threat to the native culture. The alien culture is frequently presented as immoral, evil, and dangerous.[21] George Mosse makes the point that nationalism not only idealizes men but also represents women as the "guardian of the traditional order."[22] He goes on to say that "woman as a national symbol was the guardian of the continuity and immutability of the nation, the embodiment of its respectability."[23] The portrayal of women as symbols of the nation renders invisible their everyday work as reproducers and maintainers of the nation's culture. While this is true of nationalist attempts to develop a "core" Irish national identity in the early decades of this century, the reliance on woman as symbol of tradition is less stable toward the end of this century in the Republic of Ireland.

It is important to note here that symbols can be, and are, interpreted differently and deployed in many ways in different interests. It is not possible within the confines of this chapter to address fully how symbols are received, challenged, and resisted; however, we pay some attention to this in our discussion of feminist resistance to Irish national symbols. Like Floya Anthias and Nira Yuval-Davis,[24] we want to emphasize that roles are not merely imposed on women; women also participate actively in processes of reproducing, maintaining, and modifying their roles in the production of national identities.

FEMINIST CHALLENGES TO NATIONALIST ATTEMPTS TO CONSTRUCT "CORE" NATIONAL IDENTITY

The woman as symbol of Ireland identified both woman and Ireland with nature, and was used by colonist and nationalist alike, as "Irish nationalism internalised elements of the very colonial culture it struggled to free itself from."[25] Sabina Sharkey argues that the gendering of symbols of the Irish nation must be understood within the context of colonialism. "Ireland," she suggests, "like other sites of colonization, was gendered female and this rhetorical act engendered a range of further possibilities and strategies within the register of colonial discourse."[26] Catherine Nash highlights the ways in which the bitter animosity between the Celtic Spiritual revivalists (Anglo-Irish, mainly aristocracy) and the Gaelic Irish-Irelanders (nationalist Irish middle classes) in the late nineteenth and early twentieth centuries was underscored by a contestation of Irish tradition and a redefinition of women's roles.[27] Two opposing constructions of Irish women emerged that reflected a dichotomy between the Celtic spiritual world on the one hand and the Gaelic Catholic world on the other.

Constructions of femininity by cultural nationalists in the early 1900s and later, by the church and new state, according to Nash,

> denied women an autonomous sexuality in their idealization of asexual motherhood. The young woman was replaced by the depiction of the old peasant woman who could represent the successful outcome of a life lived in accordance with the demands of motherhood . . . and way of life extolled in the state.[28]

It would be wrong to give the impression that the nationalists' constructions of Irish national identity went unchallenged and uncontested. One of the most significant critiques of nationalist rhetoric and symbols, in the early twentieth century, came from within the Irish suffrage movement. Although the suffragists were far from being united on the issue of nationalism,[29] they had, nevertheless, to engage with the Home Rule and Unionist movements as well as with the more militant nationalist groups. Perhaps it was their lack of unity on this contentious issue that gave rise to their interesting and multifaceted critique of nationalism. In their pursuit of the vote, the suffragists were repeatedly hampered by the policies of the Home Rule Party, which refused to include a female enfranchisement clause in the Home Rule Bill.[30] Some suffragists came to the conclusion that Irish politics were too influenced by the priorities of men, so that while men campaigned for Irish independence, women continued to live and work in appalling conditions.[31]

The Irish suffragists attempted to broaden the definition of politics in Irish society by calling into question the public/private dichotomy. They argued that such issues as child abuse, domestic violence, and rape needed to be brought to public attention. The suffrage paper *The Irish Citizen* was a very useful vehicle in challenging the privacy of the domestic sphere and in demanding a wider public role for women.[32] Although a number of suffrage organizations expressed their reluctance to damage the Home Rule movement in any way,[33] this in no way meant a passive acceptance of the nationalist definition of Irish womanhood. In fact, the issue of tradition was especially interesting to the suffragists. There was no sense in which the nationalist men had a monopoly on how this was interpreted. A number of suffragists used tradition in a very clever way to legitimate their feminist campaigns. Some argued, for example, that Ireland had traditionally been a feminist country in which the rights of women had been safeguarded, and they looked to Sinn Fein and other nationalist groups to honor and respect these ancient Irish traditions. This can be seen not so much as a challenge to nationalist symbols as an attempt to reinterpret and redefine those symbols for a feminist agenda.

THE ESTABLISHMENT OF A NATION-STATE IN THE 1920s AND 1930s

The establishment of the Free State in the 1920s makes this an extremely significant decade. The Free State was brought about by the partitioning of the island of Ireland into the twenty-six-county state and the six counties of Northern Ireland, which remained within the United Kingdom. While the suffragists and other women's groups had been vocal prior to this period, it is important to examine the processes through which such critical voices were silenced during the period of nation building in the 1920s and 1930s.

Following independence, the Free State was faced with establishing a sense of shared community within the twenty-six-county state. Drawing on Benedict Anderson's theory of the nation as an imagined political community,[34] we can understand the activities of the state and church in the 1920s as efforts to legitimize the existence of a divided country and create a new imagined community within the boundaries of the twenty-six-county state. This complicated the process of developing a satisfactory national identity because the state had to contain nationalist aspirations for an independent thirty-two-county Ireland. Such a nationalist aspiration could only be retained in spirit as it was not a reality. As the twenty-six-county Irish state had not yet come to terms with itself as a state, it was difficult to develop a relationship to Northern Ireland, a relationship that is central to current discussions of Irish national identity. The immanent business of the 1920s state was the creation of its own national identity.

The 1920s represented a period when national identity was debated and discussed in the twenty-six counties, with the state playing a key role in constructing an appropriate Irish national identity. These debates were a reaction against colonial constructions of Irishness and focused on identity as shared but also as exclusive of "outsiders." Identity was seen, therefore, as representing difference and sameness, inclusion and exclusion simultaneously. The state, concerned primarily with the task of nation building, emphasized the common characteristics and traits of all Irish people as a "race." This assumed that the sameness of Irish people was defined in relation to the assumed uniqueness of Irish culture, language, sports, and lifestyle that made Irish people different from all other "races." Irish people were all similar to one another but were, in their uniqueness, different from all other people who lived outside of the national boundaries. This insider/outsider dichotomy had the effect of underestimating the heterogeneity of Irish people in the 1920s and overestimating the uniqueness of the Irish "race."

The emphasis on the insider/outsider dichotomy and the "sameness" of Irish people in the 1920s could be explained in terms of a postcolonial search for a satisfactory national identity.[35] The family, as the locus of traditional Irish culture and morality, was deemed by the state, the church, and pressure groups to be in need of protection from foreign corrupting influences.[36] In the new Irish Free State, censorship laws were passed to ensure protection from foreign influence. The Censorship of Films Act was passed in 1923, followed by the Censorship of Publications Act in 1929, which banned all literature on birth control. Censorship in Ireland was different from censorship throughout Europe in this period, as it was not just censorship of pornography or a censorship based on literary aesthetic codes, but a censorship based on purely Catholic values.[37] Censorship was seen by moral protection groups as "an heroic effort to revive our national language, national values, national culture."[38] By placing the family at the center of Irish culture, the nation came to be symbolized more and more by Irish motherhood and the sanctity of the Irish Catholic family.

The portrayal of a traditional and pure Irish race rendered invisible the sexual violence and abuse that were part and parcel of Irish society. The new state and the Catholic Church worked in unison in the 1920s to make Irish culture exclusive and closed to outside influence and to represent Irish culture as pure and untainted by external corruption. Irish culture was delicate and had to be protected.

Terrence Brown claims that there was little or no opposition to the processes by which "Irishness" was being constructed in the 1920s except from writers like Yeats and Joyce, who were labeled un-Irish and pagan.[39] However, research by Mary Clancy[40] suggests that other groups of Irish people were protesting against legislation that restricted lifestyles and definitions of "Irishness." In particular, feminist groups and women who had been active in the earlier suffrage movement continued to demand rights for Irish women and remained a voice of opposition against many government policies. But such voices carried little weight in Irish society. They were, in most cases, outside of Parliament, and in any case received little or no support from politicians who were virtually unanimous in their support for Catholic morality. Catholic morality had become the hallmark of Irish national identity and part of what made Irish people unique and different from English people.

The exclusiveness and male-defined nature of the Irish national character that developed after independence is explored in Mary Clancy's research on the Dail (House of Representatives) and Seanad (Senate) debates during the 1920s and 1930s. Her research illustrates the extent to which sexist legislation was institutionalized despite protest by feminists in the Seanad and by women's groups. With reference to the ban on all information on birth control, Clancy suggests that "[u]nderlying the censorship debate was a significant desire to extend control over aspects of women's lives in general."[41] Throughout this period there was a subtle attempt to exclude women from public life.[42] Women's roles as wives and mothers were portrayed by the state and the media as primary and private functions that had no public dimension. This attitude toward women was reflected in the proposal to ban all newspaper reporting of rape and sexual assaults.[43] In this way, the reality of the sexual violence that existed in Ireland could be kept hidden and private. A decade earlier, the suffragists had fought against precisely this attitude to sexual violence.

In 1925, the government attempted to prohibit women from entering certain areas of the civil service just on the basis of sex. Women in the Seanad, the Irish Women Citizens and Local Government Association (former suffrage group), and the Irish Women Workers Union (IWWU) all voiced their opposition to such an attack on women's rights.[44] The bill was eventually defeated by the Seanad. This is a rare example of the government being defeated by the voices of dissent in the 1920s.

Clancy's work is useful not only because it highlights women's political activism and challenges dominant constructions of Irish identity but also because it sheds some light on the people who made up the Irish Free State government. The state was mostly made up of middle-class Catholic men. These men employed an official national identity not only to legitimate the existence of the Free State but also to obscure their own existence. The national stereotype of the rural peasant, the humble Irishman and his even humbler wife, masked the rise to power of the urban middle classes. The national identity and traditions were presented as fragile and in need of protection from outside influences. The bitter experiences of colonialism were drawn on to reinforce the view that all foreign influences were negative and corrupting. As a small island on the edge of Europe, Ireland was represented by the government as fighting hard to maintain its uniqueness and independence from Britain. The definition of insiders and outsiders, and the emphasis on exclusion of difference and on sameness within, characterize the ways in which Irish national identity was constructed in the 1920s.

The 1930s were marked by the rise to power of Eamon de Valera and the Fianna Fail Party[45] after spending several years in the political wilderness following the civil war.[46] According to Carol Coulter, Fianna Fail set about putting their mark on the twenty-six-county state by rewriting the country's Constitution.[47] Underpinning this new Constitution was a deep-rooted conservatism that is clearly represented by those articles of the Constitution that applied to women. The document defined women as mothers and enshrined the special "duties" of women within the home. Mounting feminist protest to the proposed Constitution provided the impetus for the mobilization of many women both as individuals and in groups. A number of veteran suffragists, including Hanna Sheehy Skeffington, joined nationalist women such as Kathleen Clarke, among others, in contesting the narrow and conservative image of Irish womanhood that was being set down in the Constitution.

The provisions that caused particular offense to the IWWU were

Articles 40, 41, and 45. Articles 40 and 45 both implied a natural inequality between men and women, by referring to the "inadequate strength of women." The Irish Women's Working Union, for example, feared that this could be used to bar them from certain types of employment. Article 41 dealt with the special duties of women within the home and expressed the hope that women would not be forced to neglect these duties. A number of feminists feared that this would be used to limit the opportunities for women in public life.[48]

After meeting with a delegation from the IWWU, de Valera agreed to alter the wording of Articles 40 and 45 so that they no longer referred to the inadequate strength of women. Having extracted this promise from de Valera, the union agreed to drop its protest campaign, much to the frustration of other feminists.[49] It could be argued that this decision on the part of the IWWU severely weakened the feminist campaign against the Constitution. In summarizing the effect of the Constitution, Carol Coulter suggests that "the letter of the Constitution, the accompanying legislation and the spirit it embodied, militated heavily against the involvement of women in public life."[50]

It could be argued that the conservatism of the new state in the 1920s and especially in the 1930s stifled feminist critique and protest, while the earlier years of political unrest and the struggle against colonialism had facilitated feminist mobilization and campaigning. De Valera's St. Patrick's Day speech in 1941 highlights the extent to which Irish national identity in the 1940s still relied on the location of women within the family and in rural Ireland. De Valera spoke of his ideal Ireland as

a land whose countryside would be bright with cosy homesteads, . . . with the romping of sturdy children, the contests of athletic youths and the laughter of comely maidens, whose firesides would be forums for the wisdom of serene old age.[51]

NATIONALISM-FEMINISM, MODERNIZATION, AND TRADITION IN THE LATTER HALF OF THE TWENTIETH CENTURY

The 1950s represented a turning point in the Republic of Ireland.[52] Chronic economic depression and high levels of emigration forced the state to shift from protectionist economic policies to free trade and the promotion of multinational investment in Ireland. As a result, the postindependence search for a "core" national identity was replaced with a politics of economics,[53] which represented a shift away from concern with the unresolved "national question" toward modernization and development.[54] The emphasis on modernization was reinforced when the Republic of Ireland became a member of the European Economic Community in the 1970s.

Making economic well-being a central national goal in the 1950s led to developments in Irish society that were reflected in the changing socioeconomic situation of women.[55] Ursula Barry points to the "fivefold increase in the labour force participation rate of married women between 1961 and 1991."[56] Despite this rate of increase, "the participation of Irish women on the labour market remains low, averaging at 30 percent rather than the 40 percent average common to other parts of Europe."[57]

Changes have also taken place in family composition and size since the 1960s. The total fertility rate has fallen from 3.9[58] in 1971 to an alltime low of 1.9 in 1993.[59] The 1993 figures, according to Anne Taylor (former director of the Council for the Status of Women), "show a different lifestyle amongst women now compared to that of their grandmothers."[60] Although processes of modernization and a shift away from a nationalist search for a "core" national identity may have benefited women in some respects, there is evidence that the more traditional aspects of national identity are still easily invoked when women demand their reproductive, property, employment, and other rights.

The interdependence of sexual and Irish national identity is seen by many feminist writers in Ireland as "a major cause of women's subordinate position."[61] Clair Wills suggests that,

> in the discourse of the Right in Ireland, as in Britain and America, the family, and in particular the mother, becomes the guarantor of a particular conservative view of the polity which identifies family with national stability.[62]

The clearest example of this in the Republic of Ireland in recent years, Wills suggests, is the battle still raging over women's reproductive rights and the place of the family in Irish society. Public debate about gender politics in Ireland has received greatest attention during the abortion and divorce referenda in the 1980s and 1990s.

In the early 1980s, a group of right-wing organizations, including the newly established Irish version of the Society for the Protection of the Unborn Child (SPUC),[63] formed the Pro-Life Amendment Campaign. They were successful in forcing the government of the day to hold a referendum to amend the Constitution in order to protect the right to life of the unborn child. The referendum, held in 1983, was passed by a 70:30 majority,[64] thereby placing a constitutional ban on abortion in the Republic of Ireland. Although the dominant discourses during the abortion referendum campaign linked women with mother-hood, and the family with the "Irish Catholic nation,"[65] feminist cam-paigners forced womanhood and Irishness onto new ground. The ref-erendum campaign facilitated the development of "a form of public language" in which to discuss abortion.[66] This new public language enabled Irishness and Irish women's actual lives to be discussed more openly. The 1920s constructions of woman and nation invoked by the Pro-Life Amendment Campaign were seen by many to be irrelevant to many women's lives in the Ireland of the 1980s.

The full implications of this constitutional ban on abortion came to light in early 1992 when a fourteen-year-old girl, who was raped by a friend of the family, was prevented by the Attorney General and the High Court from going to England for an abortion. According to Anne Speed, "The travel ban was portrayed locally and internationally as a 'rapist's charter' and a form of 'state rape.'"[67] After the pregnant girl threatened suicide, the Supreme Court reversed the ban on her right to travel outside the state for an abortion on the basis of the equal right to life of the mother. This was followed by a further referendum in 1992, which passed amendments to the Constitution to allow travel for an abortion and the provision of information on abortion.

In 1986, the proposal to remove the constitutional ban on divorce in certain circumstances was rejected in referendum by 63.5 percent of those who voted.[68] It is interesting that the prodivorce literature not only appealed to new pluralist conceptions of Ireland and Irishness but also clung on to the 1920s and 1930s rhetoric of the Irish family. The need to appeal to both progressive and traditional constituencies high-lighted the continuing significance of the Catholic Irish family within Irish society. The defeat of the divorce referendum represented, accord-ing to Patricia Prendiville, "the continued allegiance of a large number of people to the notion of the family and its centrality to the social fabric, as well as the overriding considerations of wealth and succession to wealth."[69] One of the 1986 antidivorce slogans read, "Divorce Impover-ishes Women and Children—Vote No." It is difficult, however, to see how the prevention of divorce might preserve the Irish family, and prevent women's poverty, when the 1991 census shows an increase of nearly 50 percent in separated couples since the referendum in 1986.[70]

A further referendum on divorce took place in November 1995, in which 50.3 percent voted for the introduction of divorce[71] and 49.7 percent voted against it. While many felt that this referendum would provide the opportunity to face up to the reality of Irish family life in the late twentieth century and to legislate accordingly, the campaign was a closely fought one. Again, the ideal Irish family formed a central focus of both the pro- and antidivorce campaigns. Both sides were keen to demonstrate their support for the Irish family. However, Dick Walsh in the *Irish Times* noted a link being made by the antidivorce campaigners between the family and traditional Irishness. He labeled those taking this view as "cultural defenders who would have us believe that marital breakdown is not in the Irish tradition."[72]

The No-Divorce campaign[73] poster slogan, "Hello Divorce . . . Bye Bye Daddy, Vote No," represented women and children as the innocent victims whose positions would be weakened by the threat to the institutions of marriage and the family. While women were still represented in terms of dependence on the family, it was noted by many commentators that the antidivorce position, when stated by representatives of the Catholic Church, had little effect on voters. The Catholic Church in Ireland had, during 1994–95, suffered a succession of scandals relating to child abuse that undermined the authority of the Church. Yet, some commentators suggest that the high level of uncertainty that prevailed in Irish society in November 1995, even with regard to the Catholic Church (which had previously remained a solid reference point), meant that voters took a more conservative position in relation to the introduction of divorce. The continuing power of the family as an important icon of Irishness and women's role as reproducing the nation is evident from the experiences of the divorce and the abortion referenda. These debates represent a process by which tradition and modernization are being negotiated and renegotiated in Irish society, with women's lives and their reproductive and individual rights becoming pawns in the process. What has been described as the "conservative backlash" or return to "traditional values of family, faith and fatherland" in the 1980s is seen by Luke Gibbons as "a logical extension of the modernisation policies pursued by successive governments and development agencies since the 1950s."[74] Drawing on examples of Margaret Thatcher's Great Britain and Ronald Reagan's United States, Gibbons points to the development of fundamentalism within the West in the 1980s. Fundamentalism of a similar nature reemerged in the Republic of Ireland in the 1980s and 1990s in the context of debates about abortion and divorce. In the case of Ireland, traditional constructions of Irishness and the "Catholic Irish family" are invoked to give fundamentalist discourses an authentic Irish gloss.

Writers like John Waters and Bill Rolston[75] allude to the continuing effects of colonialism on the Republic of Ireland in the 1990s and the difficulties that a postcolonial nation encounters in gaining a confident sense of identity. This continuing insecurity in relation to identity often means that feminist activism is perceived as threatening and as aligned totally on the side of modernization. Yet Irish feminists this century have had to and continue to engage with forces of tradition and modernization simultaneously.

TRACING SOME OF THE CONTINUITIES AND CHANGES IN THE TWENTIETH CENTURY

Despite the many changes in Irish society since the beginning of this century, the Irish women's liberation movement, since the 1970s, has had to fight battles similar to those of the suffragists, in forcing public debate on issues such as sexual assault, rape, domestic violence, reproductive rights, and sexual harassment. Women's health centers, rape crisis centers, and other such organizations were formed in the 1970s and 1980s and provided services to women, lobbied government for change, and exploited the Irish media network to make these issues a public concern. In these ways, feminists have been successful in shifting political debate in the Republic away from the ongoing concern with economic success and traditional versions of national identity to wider social issues. It is also noteworthy that the dominant institutions influencing Irish life and values are changing with the weakening of the position of the Catholic Church and the ever-increasing power of the national and international media networks to influence representations of Irishness and Irish womanhood.

Like the suffragists at the beginning of the century, Irish feminists in the final decades of the twentieth century have drawn support from outside Ireland when necessary. The European context has been a valuable asset to Irish feminism in the 1980s and 1990s[76] in areas of equality in employment, social welfare, and speeding up the legalization of homosexuality. In contrast to the almost total exclusion of women from the first Dail, women's representation at the state level has increased in the 1990s. Mary Robinson's election as president for Ireland is seen as symbolizing a triumph of "modernising, liberal agenda for Ireland, and as a defeat for those associated with nationalism and Catholic traditionalism."[77] The election in 1992 of twenty women to Dail Eireann (that is, 12 percent of the Dail) and the widespread public involvement of women in academia, the professions, and at local community levels, although still curtailed by patriarchal structures and sexism, are a signal of some change in relation to the representation of women in the public sphere in the Republic of Ireland.

The development of the civil rights movement in Northern Ireland in the 1960s and the subsequent conflict there made it difficult for the government in the Republic to ignore the "national question," yet economic issues continued to dominate political agendas in the south.

Although many feminists in the Republic wanted to support their counterparts in the north, the issue of Northern Ireland was to be a cause of much division within the women's movement in the south and between north and south. Gerardine Meaney suggests that feminists in the Republic of Ireland since the 1970s have tended to see nationalism and republicanism as "contagious diseases" and refuse to engage with them.[78] In response to Edna Longely's assertion that it is not possible to be both feminist and republican, Gerardine Meaney suggests that a feminism that does not engage with nationalism, "with the hard realities of Ireland," runs the risk of becoming no more than "a middle-class movement directed towards equal participation by privileged women in the status quo."[79] By engaging with nationalist women, feminists must also address the ways in which nationalist movements have disparaged and oppressed women.[80]

CONCLUSION

This chapter discusses the process of nation building in the twenty-six-county Ireland early in this century, and its development since then. Now in the 1990s, with the coming of the peace process, a framework for a new Ireland is being negotiated. As Margaret Ward suggests, it is likely that this new Ireland may be negotiated without reference to women's and feminists' concerns. Irish feminist historians have retraced the process of nation building in the twenty-six counties of the 1920s and 1930s and highlighted the ways in which women were silenced and excluded within processes of nation building. Irish feminists in the 1990s have the advantage of this knowledge and so can reflect on their role in determining Ireland's political and cultural future. However, Irish feminists continue to struggle with finding ways of overcoming women's exclusion. While women may be more self-conscious of their exclusion, they continue to struggle with the question of how to put this awareness into action. The need for action is evident when one looks at those involved in the current peace negotiations and the marginalization of women in the process.

Clar nam Ban was recently established as a coalition of nationalist women from north and south who recognized that the presence of women at a community level was not reflected at a national or public level. They have put forward proposals in a document entitled "Women's Agenda for Peace," which was submitted to the Forum for Peace and Reconciliation (set up by the Irish government to forward the peace process). They point to the need for a new Constitution, self-determination for women, choice about fertility and sexuality, child care, and the means to be independent in "a new Ireland."

Toward the end of this century, Irish feminists are faced with challenges at many levels in Irish society. While seen as a progressive, modernizing force in modern Ireland, Irish feminism (theory and activism) has much to contribute to a critique of modernizing trends such as post-Fordist production processes and growing consumerism, which have widespread implications for Irish women's everyday lives. Irish feminists' critical engagement with traditional constructions of Irishness also continues on many fronts, including the struggle against the institutionalization of the "Irish Catholic family" with its marital bias in the Constitution. The Northern Irish peace process and its possible outcomes mean that feminists north and south, from nationalist and unionist traditions, will have to find ways of forging links across political divides in the future interests of all Irish women. Irish feminists have contributed by their activism and cultural production to the ongoing process of rectifying the distortions in Irish national identity wrought by centuries of colonialism and by patriarchal nationalism. It is on the many foundations established by Irish feminists in the early twentieth century that their sisters in the late twentieth century can build.

NOTES

1. Feminisms comprise various social theories and practical politics that attempt to explain and transform patriarchies. Caroline Ramazanoglu, *Feminism and the Contradictions of Oppression* (London: Routledge, 1989).

2. Karen Offen, "Defining Feminism: A Comparative Historical Approach," in Gisela Bock and Susan James, eds., *Beyond Equality and Difference: Citizenship, Feminist Politics and Female Subjectivity* (London: Routledge, 1992), 78.

3. Kumari Jayawardena, *Feminism Nationalism in the Third World* (London: Zed Books, 1986).

4. Carol Coulter, *The Hidden Tradition: Feminism, Women and Nationalism in Ireland* (Cork: Cork University Press, 1993), 3.

5. Cynthia Enloe, *Bananas, Beaches and Bases: Making Feminist Sense of International Politics* (Berkeley and Los Angeles: University of California Press, 1989); Nira Yuval-Davis, "Gender and Nation," *Ethnic and Racial Studies* 16, no. 3 (1993): 621–32; Nira Yuval-Davis and Floya Anthias, *Women-Nation-State* (London: Macmillan, 1989).

6. Enloe, *Bananas, Beaches and Bases*, 44.

7. Deniz Kandiyoti, "Identity and Its Discontents: Women and the Nation," *Millennium: Journal of International Studies* 20, no. 3 (1991): 429–43.

8. Ernest Gellner, *Nations and Nationalism* (Oxford and Cambridge: Blackwell, 1983).

9. Anne McClintock, "Family Feuds: Gender, Nationalism and the Family," *Feminist Review* 44 (1993): 67.

10. Peter Jackson and Jan Penrose, eds., *Construction of Race, Place and Nation* (London: UCL Press, 1993).

11. Tom Nairn, *The Break-up of Britain* (London: Verso, 1981).

12. McClintock, "Family Feuds," 66.

13. Ibid.

14. Ibid.

15. The Industrial Development Authority's poster and slogan, "The Republic of Ireland: We're the Young Europeans," is an ironic one as many of those who posed for the photo/poster accompanying the slogan were forced to emigrate due to the failure of Irish government economic policy to create work in Ireland. Joseph O'Connor, "Introduction," in Dermot Bolger, ed., *Ireland in Exile* (Dublin: New Island Books, 1993), 12.

16. The contradictions and tensions in state policies between modernization and traditional views of the family as the building block of the nation with women firmly placed within it are evident on the one hand, in the government's reluctance to introduce legislation on abortion and divorce and, on the other hand, in its representation of Irish women as modern, educated Europeans.

17. Jill Vickers, "Notes toward a Political Theory of Sex and Power," in H. Lorraine Radtke and Henderikus J. Stam, eds., *Power/Gender: Social Relations in Theory and Practice* (London: Sage Publications, 1994).

18. Yuval-Davis, "Gender and Nation," 622.

19. Rebecca Grant, "The Sources of Gender Bias in International Relations Theory," in Rebecca Grant and Kathleen Newland, eds., *Gender and International Relations* (Bloomington: Indiana University Press, 1991), cited in Yuval-Davis, "Gender and Nation," 622.

20. R. Radhakrishnan, "Nationalism, Gender and the Narrative of Identity," in Andrew Parker, Mary Russo, Doris Somer, and Patricia Yaeger, eds., *Nationalisms and Sexualities* (New York: Routledge, 1992), 77–95.

21. George L. Mosse, *Nationalism and Sexuality* (Madison: University of Wisconsin Press, 1985).

22. Ibid., 17.

23. Ibid., 18.

24. Yuval-Davis and Anthias, *Women-Nation-State*.

25. Desmond Bell, "Framing Nature: First Steps into the Wilderness for a Sociology of the Landscape," *Irish Journal of Sociology* 3 (1993): 19.

26. Sabina Sharkey, *Ireland and the Iconography of Rape* (London: University of North London Press, 1994), 5.

27. Catherine Nash, "Remapping and Renaming: New Cartographies of Identity, Gender and Landscape in Ireland," *Feminist Review* 44 (Summer 1993): 39–57.

28. Ibid., 47.

29. Rosemary Cullen Owens, *Smashing Times* (Dublin: Attic Press, 1984); Cliona Murphy, *The Women's Suffrage Movement and Irish Society in the Early Twentieth Century* (Philadelphia: Temple University Press, 1989).

30. Leah Levenson and Jerry Natterstad, *Hanna Sheehy Skeffington: Irish Feminist* (New York: Syracuse University Press, 1986); Margaret Ward, "Votes First above All Else," *Feminist Review* 10 (1982): 21–36.

31. Louise Ryan, "Traditions and Double Moral Standards: The Irish Suffragists' Critique of Nationalism," *Feminist Review* 10 (1996): 21–36.

32. Louise Ryan, "The Irish Citizen Newspaper 1912–1920: A Document Study," *Saothar* 17 (1992): 105–111; Louise Ryan, "Women without Votes: The Political Strategies of the Irish Suffrage Movement," *Irish Political Studies* 9 (1994): 119–39.

33. *The Irish Citizen*, February 1913.

34. Benedict Anderson, *Imagined Communities* (London: Verso, 1991).

35. Margaret O'Callaghan, "Language, Nationality and Cultural Identity

in the Irish Free State, 1922–1927: The Irish Statesman and the Catholic Bulletin Reappraised," *Irish Historical Studies* 24, no. 94 (1984): 226–45.

36. Mosse, *Nationalism and Sexuality.*

37. Terrence Brown, *A Social and Cultural History* (London: Fontana, 1987).

38. Censorship campaigner Father Devane, quoted in Brown, ibid., 70.

39. Brown, ibid.

40. Mary Clancy, "Aspects of Women's Contribution to the Oireachtas Debates in the Irish Free State," in Maria Luddy and Cliona Murphy, eds., *Women Surviving* (Dublin: Poolbeg, 1990).

41. Ibid., 211.

42. Nash, "Remapping and Renaming."

43. Clancy, "Aspects of Women's Contribution."

44. Ibid.

45. The Fianna Fail Party, founded in 1927 by Eamon de Valera, was made up largely of those politicians who opposed the 1922 Treaty with Britain. The party was, therefore, linked with the more Republican side of Irish politics. It remains the largest single party in Dail Eireann today.

46. The civil war, which began in 1922, was sparked by the Treaty with Britain that had the effect of partitioning the island of Ireland into the Free State and those counties (as yet undetermined) that remained in the Union with Britain. The civil war involved those who supported this Treaty against those who saw it as a sellout to Britain. The war ended in 1923 with the victory of the pro-Treaty side.

47. Coulter, *The Hidden Tradition.*

48. Ibid.

49. Mary Jones, *These Obstreperous Lassies* (Dublin: Gill and Macmillan, 1989), 142.

50. Coulter, *The Hidden Tradition,* 27.

51. Quoted in Dermot Keogh, *Twentieth-Century Ireland: Nation and State* (Dublin: Gill and Macmillan, 1994), 133–34.

52. The new Taoiseach, John A. Costello, declared Ireland a republic at a press conference in Ottawa on 7 September 1948. The Republic of Ireland was formally inaugurated on Easter Monday 1949. Keogh, *Twentieth-Century Ireland.*

53. Richard Breen, Damien F. Hannon, David B. Rottman, and Christopher T. Whelan, eds., *Understanding Contemporary Ireland: State, Class, and Development in the Republic of Ireland* (Dublin: Gill and Macmillan, 1990).

54. Paul Bew, Ellen Hazelkorn, and Henry Patterson, *The Dynamics of Irish Politics* (London: Lawrence and Wishart, 1989).

55. Ailbhe Smyth, "The Women's Movement in the Republic of Ireland 1970–1990," in Ailbhe Smyth, ed., *Irish Women Studies — A Reader* (Dublin: Attic Press, 1992), 245–69.

56. Ursula Barry, "A Changing Picture: Women on the Irish Labour Market," *Irish Reporter* 7 (First Quarter 1995): 15.

57. Ibid.

58. This rate represents the average number of children a woman bore during her reproductive years.

59. T. S. O'Rourke, "Fall in Irish Birth Rates Welcomed," *The Big Issues,* Issue 12 (16 February–1 March 1995): 11.

60. Ibid.

61. Clair Wills, "Review Essay: Rocking the Cradle? Women's Studies and the Family in Twentieth-Century Ireland," *Bullan* 1, no. 2 (1994): 97–106.

62. Ibid., 99.

63. SPUC demanded that the then Taoiseach, Dr. Garret FitzGerald, agree to a constitutional ban on abortion. Although abortion was already illegal, SPUC wanted that illegality enshrined in the Constitution.

64. Anne Speed, "The Struggle for Reproductive Rights: A Brief History in its Political Context," in Ailbhe Smyth, ed., *The Abortion Papers* (Dublin: Attic Press, 1992).

65. Mary Kelly, "Censorship and the Media," in Alpha Connelly, ed., *Gender and the Law in Ireland* (Dublin: Oak Tree Press, 1993).

66. Pauline Jackson, "States of Emergence," *Trouble and Strife* 14 (Autumn 1988): 46–52.

67. Speed, "The Struggle for Reproductive Rights," 96.

68. The ban on divorce in Ireland is to be found in Article 41.3.2 of the Constitution, which provides that "[no] law shall be enacted providing for the grant of a dissolution of marriage." Peter Ward, "The Second Time Around," *Irish Reporter* 15 (Third Quarter 1994): 23–25. The issue of the financial consequences of divorce was central to the debate prior to the referendum. The antidivorce lobby argued that the introduction of divorce would have the effect of impoverishing women and children based on the maintenance awards made by courts in other European countries that allow divorce. Ward, "The Second Time Around."

69. Patricia Prendiville, "Divorce in Ireland: An Analysis of the Referendum on the Constitution," *Women's Studies International Forum* 11, no. 4 (1988): 363.

70. Fintan O'Toole, "Mammy, Daddy and Kids in One House," *Irish Reporter* 15 (Third Quarter 1994): 13–15.

71. The provisions being voted for included the condition that the couple be separated for four years before divorce can be granted.

72. Dick Walsh, "Divorce Defeat Would Spur the Cultural Defenders to Intervene Again," *Irish Times*, 18 November 1995, 14.

73. There were two campaigns against the introduction of divorce—the antidivorce campaign and the no-divorce campaign.

74. Luke Gibbons, "Coming out of Hibernation? The Myth of Modernity in Irish Culture," in Richard Kearney, ed., *Across the Frontiers: Ireland in the 1980s* (Dublin: Wolfhound, 1988), 217.

75. John Waters, *Jiving at the Crossroads* (Dublin: Blackstaff Press, 1991); John Waters, *Race of Angels: Ireland and the Genesis of U2* (Dublin: Blackstaff Press, 1994); John Waters, *Everyday Like Sunday* (Dublin: Poolbeg Press, 1995); Bill Rolston, "The Training Ground: Ireland Conquest and Decolonisation," *Race and Class* 34, no. 4 (1993): 13–34.

76. Gerardine Meaney, *Sex and Nation: Women in Irish Culture and Politics* (Dublin: Attic Press, 1991).

77. Coulter, *The Hidden Tradition*, 1.

78. Meaney, *Sex and Nation*, 13.

79. Ibid., 12.

80. Ibid.

8

Coexisting and Conflicting Identities

Women and Nationalisms in
Twentieth-Century Iran

JOANNA DE GROOT

In recent years historians of women and of nationalisms have
been making considerable use of the notion of "identity." In the case of
nationalisms, Benedict Anderson's development of the concept of the
"imagined community" has been the source of significant argument
over differences, convergences, and interactions of cultural and political elements in their histories.[1] Historians of women have found the
concept useful for their explorations into the constructions and operations of "femaleness" or "femininity" in past thought and action. This
chapter draws on these debates and explorations, showing how studies
of nationalism can benefit from a cultural approach, and how scholars
can benefit from considering the *personal* dimensions of *political* life and
the *political* dimensions of personal lives, along lines developed by
feminist theory and scholarship. The intention here is not to endorse
any ethnocentric concept of identity as a fixed or "normal" category,
since I agree with critiques that challenge such views.[2] Rather, I use
the term to indicate a whole range of diverse practices (actions, feelings, thoughts) whereby people position and understand themselves in
their particular historical setting, and are likewise positioned and understood by others.

This strategy is particularly appropriate and effective for historical
exploration of relationships between women and their gender-specific
interests on the one hand, and the pursuit of national or ethnic interests

on the other. Much can be gained from examination of women's recruitment to and activities in nationalist movements, or the treatment of women and their gender-specific interests in campaigning organizations, state policies, and nationalist discourses. Nonetheless, alongside such practical, ideological, and institutional themes, historians need to investigate and analyze the processes and resources used to create people's views of their place or membership in a "gender" or "nation," views that shape and are shaped by political thought and action. The sense of belonging to a group designated "women" or "Iranians," and of the defining characteristics, interests, and behavior associated with those who belong to such groups, is not merely a topic worth study in its own right, but also an influential component of political thought and action. Understanding histories of this sense of belonging involves addressing a complex range of customary and innovative practices, and of popular and elite creative/imaginative activity in scientific, religious, cultural, educational, and everyday settings. It calls for a clear grasp of those difficult questions about the interactions between political, material, and cultural elements in histories of gender and of ethnic nationalism. Challenging though all this may be, a focus on the issue of identity offers the possibility of illuminating both the role of nationalism in the political experience of Iranian women, and the constitutive place of women and gender in the history of Iranian nationalism.

My exploration of gender and national identities in Iran begins with the "moment" of modernity constituted from the mid-nineteenth century by the dynamics of the changing relationships of people in Iran with one another and with those outside Iran. Within Iran at that time, the Qajar dynastic state was renegotiating relationships both with the powerful sectional and regional elites with whom it shared power and authority, and with a wider range of subject groups ranging from aspiring merchants to overburdened producers and articulate intelligentsias, religious and secular. This renegotiation created varied frustrations, hopes, and grievances among all these groups as they dealt with new fiscal, political, or administrative initiatives by the regime. The second area of change flowed from the involvement of different groups of Iranians in extended, intensified, and challenging dealings with European governments, entrepreneurial interests, and cultural influences. Whereas previously Iranian mercantile, diplomatic, and strategic links and concerns had been predominantly with regions of the Ottoman Empire and with dynasties or communities in Central Asia, Northern India, and Afghanistan, during the nineteenth century their prime focus shifted toward the Russians, the British, and to a lesser extent other Europeans. Trade and production (both agricultural and manufacturing) were recomposed in relation to European demands, investment, and imports; diplomatic and military pressures created by the expanding empires of the British in India and the Russians in Central Asia occupied the energies and attention of Iranian rulers and government officials; political, cultural, and technological developments in Europe were a new point of reference, resource, or challenge for Iranians promoting or resisting social and political change.[3]

It was these changing internal and external dynamics that formed the context in which ideas and identities focusing on nation and on gender developed. The discourses that emerged were preoccupied with *modernity* in the sense of being very much a set of debates, anxieties, and aspirations concerned with the *current* circumstances in which Iranians found themselves. Standard accounts of this process emphasize Iranian views of European legal, educational, economic, and political institutions and ideas (whether favorable or hostile) and their sense of confrontation between Iranian cultural (especially religious) assumptions, practices, and values and European alternatives. Such accounts also give prominence to the influence and intervention of European governments and European commercial interests in Iran, and link Iranian concern with these external forces to growing Iranian interest in social and political change involving the state. They argue that the connections made by Iranians between perceived threats of foreign and/or non-Muslim interference in Iran and the inability of the rulers of Iran to protect or support Iranians in resisting, adapting, or benefiting in that situation gave creative impetus to *nationalist* responses by Iranians speaking as Iranians. The terms *mellat* and *melli* (nation and national) were used to designate both an Iranian "nation" (as opposed to outsiders and foreigners) and an Iranian "people" (as opposed to government). Studies of religiously inspired clerics or laypersons depicting "Islam in danger," of merchants and entrepreneurs frustrated by foreign competition and government policies, or of administrators, idealists, and reformers drawing on European models to reshape Iranian law, education, or bureaucracy all touch on these themes.[4]

What has been less emphasized is the close association of modernist and nationalist discourses with gender and sexual themes, and with discussion on the role and status of women. From the mid-nineteenth century onward, a set of cultural tropes were established in which "progress," "nation," "freedom" were constituted in terms of gender roles, relations, and characteristics as well as in ethnoreligious and anti-imperialist terms. These tropes are a powerful cultural legacy that has shaped (and still shapes) Iranians' engagement with issues concerning women, gender, and sexuality, and women's engagement with the politics of nationalism and reform. Although the "woman question" element in this legacy is easier to see and analyze than the element of gender imagery and vocabulary, both have played a significant part in the history of women and politics in twentieth-century Iran, and each element has influenced the other. One important feature of this history is the passage of certain political concerns and cultural constructions from the politico-social thought of Iranians in the later nineteenth century to the cultural nationalist politics of the 1960s and 1970s, a phenomenon that should encourage historians to give these concerns and constructions due attention.

The web of connections between ideas of gender, the sense of nationhood, the "woman question," and debates on social and political change can be approached through historical exploration of two crucial sets of meanings and arguments. One set constituted the perceptions of Iranian intellectuals about European societies and about European critiques of Iran by reference to women's role, rights, and status. The other constituted understanding of the politics of national emancipation and improvement through gendered and sexual images. The first set of meanings drew on readings of European writing and visits to Europe by those Iranians who by virtue of status, education, or occupation had means to study or travel. They included members of the intelligentsia and the official classes and clerics concerned about European influences on religion and knowledge as well as growing numbers of merchants and migrant workers. Time spent in Russia, France, England, or central Europe, meetings with Europeans in Iran or the Ottoman Empire and in Europe, and study of European writings in translation or in their original languages all involved encounters both with contemporary European social, political, and commercial practices and with European views of their own and Iranian society. On the one hand Iranians observed for themselves the social interactions of European men and women and their conduct of courtship, marriage, and family life, and became aware of European forms of girls' education and the legal regulation of women's rights. On the other hand, they encountered European perceptions and analyses of Iran, in which critical and unfavorable comparison with European societies and governments loomed large. Among the complex range of ideas, information, and images that constructed European notions of "the Orient" (as Asian countries were termed by nineteenth-century Europeans), gender and sexual themes and comment on the condition, status, and treatment of women had significant place. This might be expressed in Christian indictment of

Islam, in secular reforming projects and arguments for the export of progress and civilization from Europe to Asia, and in the language of expansion and expertise deployed by politicians and officials.[5]

However, our concern is not with the elaboration of European "Orientalism," but with its significance for Iranians' creation of a gendered nationalist politics. Three important elements emerge. First, Iranians dealt with the condition of European women in their debates about the routes to progress and/or virtue in their own society, whether they saw European examples as useful models or dangerous threats. Travelers' accounts, projects for reform, and defenses of existing Iranian practice included descriptive discussions of the education and social control of women and their legal rights in marriage, family, and society constituted as empirical evidence for particular arguments. Second, Iranians opened up a political debate about the universal validity, utility, and morality of current Iranian and European treatment of women. Some argued that established Iranian practices were the expression of cherished Islamic tradition and precept, some that they were evidence of Iranian failure to reach European levels of progress and civilization, some that they were the legacy of Arab corruption of indigenous "Iranian" traditions. Similarly, European practices might be presented as shining examples to follow, as threats to the security and integrity of Islamic religion, or as comparable to equally valuable, if lost, ancient Iranian practices. Third, those male Iranians who came to debate and contend over the future of their government and society deployed cultural constructions of women and gender in European societies in the process of shaping their own identities as male patriots, Muslims, reformers, or "authentic" Iranians, just as Europeans shaped themselves with reference to exotic "Orientals."

Iranian visitors in Europe or observers of Europeans produced reactions and descriptions that placed gender issues alongside technology, government, and religion as key markers of difference between Iranian and European societies, thus bonding gender to ethnic/national characteristics or identities in their cultural discourse. From the early nineteenth century onward, male Iranian observers (diplomats, intellectuals, officials, the Shah himself) drew on their (limited) contacts with mainly upper- and middle-class Europeans to describe and comment on the presence of women in mixed social gatherings, female dress codes, and the conventions shaping marriage and sexual conduct. Their accounts vary in length, detail, and explicitness but consistently focus on the "otherness" of European as opposed to Iranian gender rules and relationships. While restricted to a small number of literate and curious commentators alongside a wider range of ideas and information transmitted by merchants, travelers, and migrant workers linked to the Russian-ruled Caucasus and Baku oil industry, such accounts became a resource for growing social and political debates from the 1870s.[6] The effect of these debates was not just to illustrate sociocultural difference in regard to gender and women, but to bring it into arguments about the problems, objectives, and policies most relevant for Iranian government and society. Advocates of change and progress, who in the later nineteenth century often linked such aspirations to the adoption or adaptation of European legal, commercial, political, or social practice, gave their arguments a significantly gendered spin. Whether, like Mirza Malkom Khan or Mirza Aqa Khan Kermani, they advocated education for women as mothers of future citizens and patriots (male!) or, like Kermani and Mirza Fath Ali Akhundzadeh, they focused on the veiling of women and arranged polygamous marriage, reform for women was made an indicator or even a condition of general social or political improvement. Conversely, those who saw Iran's problems as stemming not from lack of "progress," but from foreign threats to Islamic/Iranian cultural and political practice, argued that such threats might well be realized through alteration in the hallowed codes of women's marital, social, or sexual conduct. Clerics writing on politics, such as Muhammad Karim Khan Kermani or Shaikh Fazlullah Nuri, linked the defense of Islamic custom with the maintenance of moral and political stability and virtue. In this they shared a paradoxical common ground with the "modernizers" they opposed, since both groups made women and gender issues key signifiers of the "best" outcomes for Iranian social and political life in general. The distinctions between "religious" or "secular" views were less important from the point of view of women and politics than the power of discourses, which, as I have argued elsewhere, simultaneously entwined gender at the core of political language *and* marginalized the expression of women's autonomous interests.[7]

The development of political arguments over gender, women, and the well-being of Iranians, whether identified as a national/ethnic group or as a religious community, involved the construction of cultural meanings whereby notions of "the nation" were gendered and notions of "women/womanhood" were ethnicized. Malkom Khan's exhortations to fellow Iranians to take up the cause of national political and legal reform were couched as encouragement to find or learn *manliness*, just as he identified the political role of women as promotion of that cause and as inspiration *for men*, the "angels of the advancement of humanity." Both Mirza Malkom Khan and Mirza Aqa Khan Kermani represented foreign domination or influence through the image of

Iranian women raped, enslaved, or abused, making the "nation" itself a gendered/feminized entity and women the signifiers of national integrity and security. Beyond that Mirza Malkom Khan spoke of Iranian subjugation or backwardness as *loss of manliness* among Iranian males.[8] These points carried force not just as political argument for particular reforms or policies but as influential elements in the creative imaging of "nation," "government," "progress," "backwardness" constructed by Iranian writers in the 1880s and 1890s, and became a powerful legacy for later generations of thinkers and activists. In their efforts to define and advocate the needs and interests of Iranians of their time, these writers also sought to establish an Iranian *identity*, in which elements of gender and sexuality had a significant part. The construction of this identity involved critiques and comparisons with other identities (Arab, European, Japanese, Turkish) and a significant discussion of Iran's dominant religious tradition (Shi'a Islam) as a constituent of Iranian identity. The complex and nuanced positions taken in this discussion ranged from celebration of "Iranianness" independent of religious content (drawing on an imagined pre-Islamic Iranian culture) through various positive views of the place of Shi'a Islam in Iranian culture, whether in some reformed/purified/modernized form or as a cultural core needing defense and protection, not change.[9]

In the cultural construction of Iranian identity, gender and sexual references make regular appearances. Just as observers of European sex/gender practices came to shape not just a set of male/female distinctions but also a set of Iranian/European distinctions, so those with political objectives of reform and/or defense of Iranian interests deployed images of women and sexual practice for that purpose. When the Azeri-Iranian Talibov/Talibzadeh linked the threat of "our pure Shari'a" (i.e., Iranian Islamic tradition) to the dominance of foreigners over Iranians, and Iranian lack of legal rights and protection, he chose the image of suppression of religious practice to please foreign women and of the unveiling of Iranian women for this purpose. Mirza Aqa Khan Kermani's posing of Iranian national culture, history, and identity against the pernicious influences of the "Arab invasion" and obscurantist practitioners of Islamic "superstitions" similarly made use of images of marriage, sexual violation or immorality, and the seclusion or veiling of women in his own racialized anticlerical nationalism. Images of progress and enlightenment were constructed with reference to female education and free-choice marriage as *symbolic elements* as much as substantive policies, just as notions of cultural authenticity and tradition based in religion were constructed in terms of female modesty and religiously sanctioned sex/gender rules.[10]

These cultural strategies give a sense of the development of specific political discourses focused on questions of legal, social, and political reform and on the position of Iranians vis-à-vis Europeans, for which questions *about* women and images *of* women were an important cultural resource. Not only did these strategies shape the notions of "nation," "progress," or "womanhood," which so exercised moderate reformers, or defenders or radical opponents of existing social and political institutions, but it also came to color political language generally, building on existing meanings to create a powerful incorporation of gender within that language. One of the oldest terms for political disorder and social subversion—*fitna*—simultaneously indicated female sexual excess and deviance, just as the notion of *namus* (honor) named a sexual, familial, publicly monitored phenomenon. In both instances, constructions of morality and propriety (whether communal, individual, legal, or religious) had a sexual and gendered spin involving the control of female social / sexual conduct by men and the protection of male vested interest expressed through family honor, religious prescription, and, by the early twentieth century, national self-esteem and integrity. Terms like "honor," "corruption," "modesty," or "respectability," one of whose purposes was to delineate rules for male-female relations and marital and sexual conduct, came to be deployed in the political arena to address concerns with law, social reform, constitutional politics, and the nature of foreign influence and dynastic government. Even where specific issues of the treatment, role, or status of women were not under explicit political discussion, political language included gender coloring that touched powerful cultural concerns and imaginings around women and sexuality. In doing so, this language offered a potentially significant link between the ideas and arguments of the intelligentsia and a much broader range of values, discourses, traditions, and opinions among other groups of Iranians, a link whose importance has persisted throughout the twentieth century.

Indeed the reason for dwelling on this formative phase of modern Iranian political culture is precisely the persistence and potency of its legacy for relationships between women, politics, and nationalism. We are speaking here not about a single linear development, but about the creation of a body of ideas, images, arguments, and beliefs that Iranians continued to use in many varied ways as one of the resources for *different* and even opposed political practices. Discussion about the position and rights of women contributed to the growth of the politics of secular modernizing development, of cultural nationalism and the defense of religion as a core component of national identity, and of anti-imperialist xenophobic opposition of "Iranians" to (European) foreigners. Within the reformist and materialist political traditions created by Iranians between the 1890s and the 1940s, women's education and sociolegal position was a prominent signifier of escape from "backward," "feudal" institutions and practices, a signifier deployed by authoritarian modernizing rulers and their liberal and leftist opponents. In the continuing political concern to assert and strengthen Iranian autonomy from European, and later American, intervention and influence, women were symbolic figures of cultural authenticity and self-esteem and the test of Iranian (men's) ability to resist such external threats. In the debates over the alteration and defense of religious tradition and practice, regulation of gender difference and of female conduct was central. Women's employment and education, their dress codes, marital and legal rights, and their spatial separation from men have been topics not only for decision on appropriate political action but also for debate as contested sites of cultural meaning. Above all, Iranian understandings of the gendered identity of women (contrasted with men) evolved in conjunction with their grasp of new identities as Iranians (as against foreigners and regional/ethnic diversity) and as Muslims (confronting infidels and heretics/apostates). The *distinctive* elements in each of these identities existed in tension with their *interactive interdependence* on one another in the complex totality of overlapping cultures created by Iranians in modern times, shaping Iranian modernity itself.

The complexity of this situation is well shown by the engagement of Iranian women in this creative process. Quite apart from initiating or joining protests over heavy taxation and food shortages and political pressures and supporting a range of sectional and religious causes, as many urban women did in the nineteenth century, a minority of women privileged by status and family connections used education and opportunity to articulate their contribution to political culture. In doing so, they sought to express both gender-specific elements associated with gender-specific demands for change and justice for women, and also those religious, ethnonational and ideological elements which in their view identified them as patriots, Muslims, and agents of general social progress and national integrity. In the case of Qurrat-al-'Ayn, a woman leader in the Babi movement in the 1840s and 1850s, this meant using intellectual and religious skill, talent, and conviction to play an influential role as this important dissenting group transformed itself into a defiantly alternative religious movement. She made use of the cultural resources of her time and society (confrontational traditions of millenarianism and martyrdom, images of holy women), claiming female spiritual agency and autonomy rather than modernist forms of "women's rights." However, this in itself necessitated challenges to the religiously based restrictions on Iranian women's freedom to learn, teach, or write, their dress code, and their associations with men outside the family/household domain, and in this sense Qurrat-al-'Ayn staked her claims as a woman as well as an effective radical religious and political leader. The interaction of gender/sexual controversy with ideological and political challenge in her career is revealed in Babi debates on her unveiling and its relation to her authority in their movement, her need to challenge any connection between her views and actions and sexual conduct, and portrayals of her by anti-Babis in an explicitly sexual light.[11]

As Iranian political cultures engaged with European influences, pressures, and ideas in the last decades of the nineteenth century, so Iranian women's contribution to that culture also evolved. Their established cultural resources (poetry, religion, popular anecdote, and precept, including shrewd explicit treatments of sexual and gender themes) were supplemented and sometimes supplanted by new emphasis on rights, progress, and reason, and on the confrontation between indigenous and foreign cultural and moral values. Alongside discourses of modesty and propriety, which challenged masculine self-interest and engaged with their own religious traditions, women made claims to patriotic participation in the progress and protection of the "nation," and to the education and social recognition that would aid such participation. In identifying themselves and their interests as women, they also entered the arena of political debate on the question of what it was to be "Iranian," "Muslim," "progressive," "moral," or "just." Albeit in restricted contexts, women writers like Bibi Khanom Astarabadi and Taj-as-Saltaneh addressed the dominant male Iranian categories of religious morality and prescription (in the case of the former writer) and rational/national progress (in the case of the latter) from the distinctive perspective of women. They combined assertions of distinctive gender concerns (women's mistreatment and debasement by men, for male solidarities, women's claims to legal, cultural, and social recognition) with debate on other aspects of Iranian life in which they expressed themselves as intellectuals and social commentators concerned with human conduct and the well-being of society.[12]

The first three decades of the twentieth century, a time of political upheaval and innovation surrounding the transformation and ultimate abolition of the ruling dynasty, the creation of forms of constitutional government, party politics, and a political press, and the imposition of an autocratic modernizing regime, were the historic moment for the expansion of these trends. Political culture, mainly, but not solely, in Iranian towns, was transformed by the dynamic growth of opportunities for organization and debate in the fields of social reform, ideological argument, and political activism by a host of protesters, journalists, interest groups, and intellectuals (religious and secular). The creation of "Fundamental Laws" (the Constitution) and an elected national assembly (*Majles*), which for their supporters and participants were to be the means and guarantors of justice, government reform, and social progress, brought these issues, hitherto discussed in restricted clandestine settings, into a larger public domain. British and Russian strategic, diplomatic, and military interference in this rapidly changing political world kept the issue of Iranian "national" integrity and autonomy at the center of street politics, ideological debate, and government concern. The dynamics of growing numbers of active interest groups and their shifting alliances and conflicts fueled organization and argument and raised issues of democracy, accountability, and political participation. Group activism, pamphlet and newspaper writing, street demonstrations, and sermons at religio-political gatherings, were all deployed in pursuit of the many objectives thrown up in this new political world, involving growing numbers of participants.[13]

It was in this context that both the cohabitation and the confrontation of the political identities that had been evolving in the late nineteenth century were more fully elaborated and expressed. Engagement with the important issues of the period developed significant gendered political discourses, and placed the "woman question" on various political agendas (pro- and anticonstitutionalist), while stimulating women's own political initiatives. Consideration of each of these political areas reveals how the growth of different versions of "national" identity and interest drew on but also challenged the concept, status, and roles of women, gender, and sexuality. The most visible manifestation of this process was the presence of women in key episodes or moments of the constitutional struggles of 1905–12, and as social activists during the second and third decades of the twentieth century. Women's activism encompassed the expression of particular loyalties and grievances by lower-class urban women in protests against the Shah or in support of particular leaders and factions, the formation of female political societies, and privileged women's contributions to the press in their own and other journals. Crucially these activities and initiatives were used by the women involved to manifest their sense of themselves both as women/gendered subjects and as participants in other categories that they identified as "the people," "the faithful," "patriots," or "freedom lovers." Women of all classes explained their participation and commitment in religio-political conflicts in Kerman in 1905–6 and in antiautocracy protests in Tehran and Tabriz at the same period in terms of support for true religion and the best interests of Iran and desire for social justice and constitutional reform. Their activities and explorations also embodied (implicitly or explicitly) their claims to pursue such aims in (gendered) person.

As political problems unfolded following the initial grant of a constitution (1906), the anticonstitutional coup and constitutionalist countercoup (1908–9), and growing British and Russian intervention, so women's political involvement also developed further. As "patriots" they came to the *Majles* and the streets to oppose threats to the constitutional regime and Iranian independence and to urge male Iranians to resist such threats, and involved themselves in boycotts of European goods along the line of the *Swadeshi* movement in contemporary India, as well as giving financial support to these causes. Granted the conventions of segregation and seclusion that shaped the everyday life of Iranian women and the lack of support for women's education and self-expression, women found themselves addressing the question of their own rights, role, and freedoms while pursuing these nationalist/constitutionalist goals. As they founded schools and female political associations, corresponded with and developed the political press, and took to the streets and mosques, women experienced contradictory relations between the two aspects of their political lives. On the one hand, they could develop demands for female emancipation in terms of their contribution to the cause of the nation, constitution, progress, or justice; on the other hand, such demands, once made, themselves became contentious, even divisive, items in the political arena where these causes were pursued. The outcome of this contradiction was the subordination of female *political* claims on the nation, and the commitment of some groups of women to the pursuit of *social* goals for themselves as gendered subjects, with long-lasting consequences for feminist thought and politics.[14]

The presence of women in political protests, their self-representation in print and self-assertion on behalf of their gender interests, and their organizational and educational initiatives were not isolated phenomena. Male political activists, heirs to two decades of discussion on female education, polygamy, and veiling, continued to debate those issues and embed them in their projects for political change, for defense of the nation and its religion, and for social progress and/or stability. When information about women's societies came before the *Majles*, these societies were debated in terms of whether they were "anti-Islamic" or "corrupt," and defended as being consonant with conventional activity (learning dressmaking) and national solidarity (organizing boycotts of foreign goods), but also because, as one leading liberal said, "When the Constitution grants freedom to assemble it meant . . . both men and women."[15] Experiments with schools for girls attracted both support and condemnation, not on grounds of any intrinsic merit for those involved, but in comparable terms of whether they were a contribution or a threat to general morality or progress. Formal religious condemnation of the new schools and attacks by lower-class opponents on the privileged women who established and supported them suggest the opening up of divides along religious/secular and popular/elite lines, which were becoming a feature of politics as a whole. Although the "woman question" did not dominate the political agendas of those involved in the new, and limited, political arena, preoccupied as they were with the problems of European intervention and building a new system of government, responses to the woman question indicated trends that were to be part of future developments.

More pervasive was the gendered and sexual coloring of the language used in the new political arena. While the *Majles* discussion of women's political associations was very limited, the supporters of the new political order and of the nationalist cause regularly signaled the gravity of the threats to both, and of the struggle to maintain them, in gender/sexual terms. Attacks on the autocracy and on foreign intervention used the discourse of violated family/sexual honor and of the oppression of women. Protection of women defined as the wives/responsibility/possessions of men from such abuse was a key indicator of patriotic, progressive *manliness*, a term frequently used by both men and women in their exhortations to (male) Iranians to be active in the national/constitutional cause. Those women who mobilized for this cause often presented their actions as a challenge to men to be *manly*, calling on *masculine* pride and self-respect as a constituent of national self-esteem and self-defense and commitment to domestic justice and progress. As the struggle to maintain and extend constitutional government and national independence became part of the foundation myth of Iranian nationalism, those constructing it gave it a significantly gendered form. They recast old discourses of honor, religion, and male dominance in the new context of patriotism, and placed women's activism within the narrative of national regeneration as evidence of a historic episode of such gravity that "even" women were drawn to participate in it. Thus, in recounting the dramatic deeds of particular women (as individuals or groups), Kermani, Kasravi, and Shuster included them in the national/constitutional movement as patriotic heroines rather than as gendered subjects ("women") or partners with equal agency to men (citizens, constitutionalists). As Najmabadi has argued, the linguistic ambivalence of the term *zanha-yi-melli*, which can mean either the autonomous women or the subordinate wives of the nation/ people, is a vivid representation of the simultaneous presence and subordination of Iranian women in the national narrative.[16]

More generally the language of sexual morality, corruption, and chastity developed in political writing, poetry, and social comment was a continuing element in the new discourses of politics. The continued use of religion as a marker of "national" identity and authenticity, and the political importance of the religious classes and popular religious culture, were points of reference for all the participants in the new politics whether modernizing constitutionalists, religious dissidents, or defenders of tradition. Thus old-established connections of social and political order with gender and sexual order and the control of women, which had been framed in *religious* terms, also translated into the new political language of national regeneration, stability, independence, and progress. The very women who took on clerical and popular opposition to their founding of modern schools for girls named those schools *Chastity* or *Honor*, as well as *Prosperity* or *Progress*. Both male and female constitutionalists cast programs for the advancement of women in terms of a refashioned modesty or purity, expressed in women's commitment to study to be progressive wives and mothers of patriots and to be asexual associates of male nationalists, rather than in the old practices of veiling and seclusion. Corruption was to be avoided not by adherence to religious conventions of *bodily* control of women, but by new forms of *intellectual* and *moral* self-restraint. Thus the denigration of old practices used not a libertarian critique of control of female sexuality but a *moral displacement* of corruption and sexual hypocrisy onto the traditional order, and stigmatized older female cultures of open sexuality as reactionary, lower-class, and ignorant. The "new chastity" of reforming nationalism was counterposed to the religious and traditional defense of established gender codes in the name of Shi'a morality and orthodoxy, which opposed women's reforms as both unchaste and heretical. As with male politicians of the French Revolution, or late-nineteenth- and twentieth-century Indian nationalists, women's identity and the "woman question" were indeed given key positions in the new projects of republicanism or nationalism, but in terms of conformity and constraint as well as emancipation.[17]

The importance of the period from the first constitutionalist initiatives to the establishment of Reza Shah Pahlavi's autocracy lies in its character as a historic moment in which new political identities and discourses were elaborated in practical activism, ideological debate, and the cultural construction of political life. The prominence rightly given to substantive changes in government, social relations, or material life in the period from 1900 to 1930 should not obscure the broad and lasting *cultural relevance* of the period as the point of reference for the development of modern Iranian political and social ideas and interest of all kinds. This applies particularly to histories of women and gender relations in twentieth-century Iran, where shifts in political culture over this period significantly outweighed material change, not because of the emergence of any particular cultural pattern, but because of the creation of a diverse and complex legacy. Within this legacy, religious and secular nationalisms, reforming secularisms, resistance to and admiration of European influences and examples, imaginings of "tradition" and "progress," female self-assertion, and male-dominated politics were each constituted both as distinct trends and as overlapping interacting elements of modern political culture in Iran. In a very real sense, this period was a seedbed for the various articulations of "women" and their politics in relation to the politics of the "Iranian nation" which had their own historic moments later in the twentieth century. It is to two contrasting subsequent moments when different elements in this cultural legacy were deployed as resources for particular political projects that we now turn.

The divisions among the governing political groupings, the effect of British and Russian interventions, and the 1914–18 World War, with the consequent failure of governments to be very effective, whether implementing reforms, ensuring their own stability, or meeting the various expectations of Iranians, opened the way to a new autocratic ruler. Reza Khan, who became Reza Shah Pahlavi in 1925, pursued his own dynastic ambitions through a program of secularizing, centralizing, and modernizing initiatives that took on the reforming aspirations of the Constitutional Era and recast them in statist repressive forms. Suppression of independent political life from the late 1920s went along with effective attacks on dissident, tribal, regional interests and the power of the religious classes. The regime's rhetoric and practice of nationalism and secular modernity brought allies from among those who shared those ideals, consolidated its own power, and via growing educational, military, and bureaucratic systems, started to normalize such discourses among new white-collar and professional groups who became an identifiable if not influential part of urban society. Both the frustrations of political exclusion and the opportunities created by this sociocultural change fueled the political culture that emerged when Reza Shah was ousted by British and Soviet intervention in Iran in 1941, removing repressive restraints and reawakening old concerns with threats to Iran's national independence.

At one level, this political culture revived the concerns with representative government and national regeneration that had informed the Constitutional Era. At another level, it was shaped by new concerns and dynamics that were the product of the years of Reza Shah's regime. Crucial among these were a much sharper and more structural opposition of secular and religious interests and discourses (unlike the fluid antagonisms and coalitions of earlier times), a more materially based view of social needs and goals, and much greater emphasis on centralized initiatives as the means to good government and social reform. Politically active and articulate Iranians were likely to see much more clearly defined choices between secular and Muslim visions of "the nation" or the good society and to place greater emphasis on which among contending political interests wielded state power since how that power was exercised would determine national well-being. Between 1941 and 1953, they had for the first time the opportunity to support mass-based organizations with programs and ideologies, although as in the past this was an opportunity available primarily to the urban classes, though to more of these than in the past. In consequence, the identities "Iranian," "patriot," "freedom lover" were revived but also transformed, and new identities—"worker," "leftist," "intellectual"—were added to the repertoires of Iranian political culture.[18]

In this context, we can consider it a historic moment when the coexisting and conflicting identities affecting women were reconstituted in two significant respects, and the new elements in the articulation of gender and nationalist politics were joined with established patterns of discourse. The first significant development was the heightened use of programs of reform featuring women as the signifiers of modernity, progress, and *state power*. Already in the 1920s, Iranian reformers like Taqizadeh (who later supported the Pahlavis) and Kazemzadeh were incorporating discussion and advocacy of such programs as part of an increasingly uncompromising secular modernist nationalism. Reforms in marriage, veiling, and women's education were linked to the spread of modern secular knowledge and opposition to the conservative clerical dogmatism that prevented it, to social and moral progress via women's influence as wives and mothers, and to national pride and culture which they also fostered in those capacities. On one hand, such reformists allocated women specific roles in the advancement of a westernized, strong, progressive Iran, and on the other hand they cast their accounts of strength and progress in terms of changing women's roles and status. This ideological shift was emphasized by Reza Shah's use of autocratic executive power to pursue publicly a "reform" program including education for women, compulsory unveiling, and state control of women's organizations which had hitherto flourished as autonomous bodies. Despite the uneven and limited practical effect of these policies, statist endorsement of certain aspects of the "woman question" was culturally significant. It consolidated the use of gender and women's issues as signifiers of modernity and state power; it gave public and official backing to issues previously treated as too contentious for such support, so that whereas the *Majlis* of pre-Pahlavi times wished to erase discussion of women's rights from its records, the unveiling and education campaigns of the 1930s were given high profile and publicity; and it gave a powerful secularist coloring to the relationship of women reform and the national interest, linking all those to the ideals of modernity while stigmatizing their opponents as reactionary and unpatriotic.

The secularization of political discourses on women and the nation also involved a clearer distinction between the "secular" and the "religious" in politics, social life, and culture. The growth of modern education and bureaucracy created a more obviously secular / modern intelligentsia and professional groups who were to play key roles in the political culture and organization of the 1940s. As a result both of changed outlook and values, and the state sponsorship of secularist approaches, these groups developed a distinct culture of debate and activity which, although suppressed or exiled in the 1930s, survived and expanded in the more open political climate of the 1940s. Reformists, dissidents, leftists, and liberals, whose stance toward religious culture and religious specialists (*'ulama, mullas*) in the Constitutional Era had been nuanced and flexible, increasingly positioned themselves as critics and opponents of religious / clerical ideas and influence. Indeed one aspect of Reza Shah's policies that they supported, and of which they were both the agents and beneficiaries, was the removal of the *'ulama* from their roles in the legal and educational systems and the creation of secular alternatives. Although the real dynamics of religion in modern Iranian culture were complex, as were the relations between modern intellectuals and religious ideas or beliefs, there was an increasing trend toward constructing bipolar oppositions between "enlightened" secular positions on social or political questions and the "backward" traditionalism of *mullas* and conventional religion. This bipolarity shaped the discussions of connections between the condition and treatment of women and projects for national progress and independence. In the political writings and organizations of the period, women were identified with such projects, and even in some cases mobilized to work for them, while simultaneously being cast in conventional, patriarchally determined roles. Women's moral, political, and social contribution was seen as being centered on marriage, motherhood, and contributions to the nation made through domestic and family life, while polygamy was criticized and education encouraged so that women could do this in a "modern" and "enlightened" manner.

In taking this stance, male activists paralleled the efforts of women activists, who came mainly from educated and privileged groups. Following the suppression of their independent groups and publications, such women pursued education and welfare work under state patronage in the 1930s, and campaigned more independently for women's interests both inside and outside other groupings in the 1940s. They too used the language of secular progress, nationalism, and enlightenment to define and pursue their interests as "women" and as "Iranians" or "reformers." They also took on some of the language of the language of "natural" female qualities and occupations, although they engaged in both explicit and implicit criticisms of the more restrictive or masculinist applications of that language. The complexity of such women's situation is well expressed in Bamdad's account of their activities in the 1930s and 1940s, in which she herself participated, which shows both the persistence of self-expression, autonomous agency, and claims to gender equality, and their difficult relations with other agendas, whether those of the authoritarian state or independent male politics. Women engaged with a complex political culture in which their gender aspirations coexisted (as with education) or conflicted (as over civil and political rights) with the nationalist, statist, or reformist agendas created by men. Self-assertion by women, whether in the Pahlavi-sponsored Ladies Centre of the 1930s, or in the women's organizations and political movements of the 1940s, combined uneasily with acceptance of conventional (male dominance) and their own subordinate positions in the organization and agendas of those movements.

Some of the complexities of this historic moment can be glimpsed through the representational and political deployment of the issue of women's veiling by Iranian women and men. The older reformist discourse of Kermani and Akhundzadeh, which connected the veiling of women to social backwardness and lack of freedom or equality, was reworked by the advocates of reform and democracy in the 1930s and 1940s. The reworked discourse was also taken up by the authoritarian state as a signifier of the modernity that it represented and claimed to implement, upholding the credibility of that autocracy with some of its domestic and European allies on the basis of its "progressive" stance on the issue. However, Reza Shah's compulsory unveiling decree of 1936 *also* represented the undemocratic imposition of a policy to which Iranians' responses included religious and popular opposition to what was seen as intervention in approved moral/religious practice, and debate over legitimate versus unacceptable versions of national culture. Women's responses ranged from optimistic support for an emancipatory initiative, to a sense of exclusion from debates and decisions on that initiative, and awkwardness and embarrassment at pursuing it without appropriate social or cultural support.

Male discussions of veiling and marriage also involved complex and ambivalent reconstructions of sexuality and femininity. Changes in codes of dress, or criticisms of polygamy and temporary marriage (*sigheh*) were developed not so much as emancipatory moves but as means to consolidate "proper" sexual conduct and marital relations in modern secular forms, which were contrasted with the tokenist, dishonest provisions of religious convention. Women in modernized dress, without veils, could express "real" modesty by personal restraint and nonexotic behavior with men, using new educational opportunities (though we should note the persistence of male literary fantasies of sexually available women!). Reformed marriage would provide appropriate foundations for women's "natural" role in family and household, which was to be the location for their contribution to social well-being and morality, foundations that justified opposition to women's entry into other spheres by the authors of reformist discourse. Commentators on these issues focused less on the needs and rights of women or men than on modernist anticlericalism, celebration of interventionist reform, and patriotic opposition of valued Iranian practices to undesirable western alternatives (a concern stimulated by Iranian confrontation with the British, Russian, and American presence in Iran in the 1940s).

This "moment" of engagement by politically active Iranians with gender issues and the "woman question" during the 1930s and 1940s involved continued appropriation and subordination of these concerns within the politics of nationalism and state formation. Mobilization around government projects in the 1930s and within reformist and nationalist politics in the 1940s was the dynamic focus of political cultures and political organizations. While such cultures and organizations were gendered in significant ways, gender issues and language tended to confirm existing gender structures rather than criticize or change them, and to deploy women as signifiers or objects rather than as agents within the political domain. Dominant versions of national, social, and gender interest developed in that domain emphasized practical reform and rational knowledge (however rhetorically) and in that sense became secular. Reza Shah's own private comment to his wife on unveiling/seclusion in 1936 serves to encapsulate the male authority, statism, and ambivalence involved in linking "women" and "the nation," and modernization: "It is easier for me to die than to take my wife unveiled among strangers, but I have no choice. The country's progress requires that women must be set free, and I must be the person to do this."[19]

The return of an autocratic monarchical regime in 1953, with the overthrow of the nationalist coalition led by Muhammad Mussadeq, fostered both the revival of statist modernization and the development of a spectrum of opposition to the regime that was as diverse as the nationalist coalition had been. It was the secularist and leftist elements of both that confronted the most explicit and thorough repression, as the apparently most credible rival claimants to the power and legitimacy of the Shah. Other religious and moderate elements could be absorbed and placated partly because there had been no reversal of the weakening of religious institutions and religious specialists within formal politics, and partly because social changes in Iran during the 1950s and 1960s created opportunities as well as grievances. Economic development funded by oil revenues and foreign investment, the growth of a large white-collar service sector (state and private) and of modern education and media, were key sociocultural features of that period, fostered by the state but acquiring their own dynamic. Whereas those whom modernity affected had been a minority, although influential, in the social mosaic of Iran up to the 1950s, thereafter modernity came to shape the lives of the majority of Iranians from urban wage workers to rural communities, and from university graduates to slum dwellers. A new historic moment was in the making.[20]

In the realm of political culture, this new moment can best be understood as a renegotiation of secularist nationalism and the growing influence of modernized religious versions of political opposition and national identity. The divisions and failures of the old nationalist opposition left its participants fragmented, exiled, and ineffective, and much of their program of reform appropriated by the state in authoritarian repressive form. With much of the material content of the nationalist project now being undertaken by the regime, it would be the cultural and idealistic elements of that project that were the main resource of opposition groups. Among a younger generation of students and secular intellectuals, this took the form of various leftist movements which could base opposition on ideals of revolution and social justice cast in the internationalist and often European mold of various Marxist and socialist ideologies. For many others, it was the tradition of defending cultural authenticity as the signifier of national well-being and integrity that was developed to underpin opposition to the American influence, which was seen to be penetrating state policy and social life alike. Cultural nationalism could be fostered by the reconstruction of religious opposition, which moved from a stance of resistance or withdrawal within the arena of modern politics to creative engagement with it. The old equation of Iranian culture/identity with Islamic traditions, and the presentation of those traditions as the source of moral stability and political energy were key elements in this process.

There were a number of different contributors to the process. Some members of the *'ulama* (Taleqani, Khomeini) began to recast their religious critique of the regime in such a way as to emphasize morality and antidespotism in a *modern* setting, an approach with increasing relevance to Iranians experiencing all the cultural disruptions of social change in the 1960s and 1970s. Lay religious activists explored areas of convergence between their views and the radical hopes and fears of Iranians. Most notable of these was the preacher/writer Ali Shari'ati, whose recasting of a radical Shi'a Islam that inspired people to struggle for social justice in a culturally "authentic," morally forceful framework proved to be relevant and popular. His writing and lectures synthesized an image of Iranian cultural tradition, a populist reclaiming of religion by ordinary believers from the hierarchy, and modern activism represented as a historic Iranian legacy. These initiatives linked up with earlier initiatives like those of the populist cleric Kashani and the reformist Muslim Bazargan who had been involved in nationalist politics with secularist allies, and most particularly the tradition of cultural opposition to European threats to Iranian culture. This opposition was most famously expressed in Jalal Al-i Ahmad's essay "West-toxication," a powerful polemic against the corruption of Iranian culture by crass mimicry and importation of western ideas and practices. Al-i Ahmad wrote in a tradition going back to writers of the Constitutional Era but with a force and relevance much more directly related to the situation of Iranians in the 1960s, when such ideas and practices were indeed visible in every milieu.[21]

In this reformed cultural nationalism, gender and sexual themes played a significant role not merely for a limited number of intellectuals and activists but in a wider cultural setting. The images that associated western corruption with the collapse of sexual morality in the face of permissiveness and frivolity were directly relevant to many Iranians newly migrated to the rapidly growing modern urban sector, who dealt precisely with a clash of mores and loss of conventional tradition or control. The stereotype of the "European painted dolls" spoke to the anger and anxieties generated among the urban popular classes by social change, by reforms that offered some women greater opportunity, and by the difficulty of choices among old and new practices. The turn to "Islamic morality" was a means to express both patriotism and resentment at the inequities and failures of the Shah's "Great Civilization," or indeed the old nationalist/leftist coalition, to deliver justice, prosperity, or opportunity for many Iranians. Images of the Shi'a heroine Fatima embodied in representation the acceptable female activism of the devoted daughter, wife, and mother, dependent and asexual in ways ironically paralleled by the "chaste comrade" supporting the male activists of the left revolutionary groups.[22]

Thus the coexisting and confrontation of gendered and national identities in Iranian political culture took another turn around the spiral on which they had been launched at the onset of modernity. Veiling and Islamic values were signifiers of womanly and Iranian propriety in the 1890s and were to be so again in the 1970s, with a new resonance in a society that had been radically transformed in the intervening decades. The "western" cultural threat that was an imagined future at the start of the century had become a part of complex daily realities by the time the second Pahlavi Shah was overthrown. The behavior of women in the home and on the streets, and their rights and roles in law and daily life had been announced by a few reformists to be the markers of national well-being in the Constitutional Era. By the 1970s, such views were the staple of mass-circulation materials. Women activists at the start of the century forged a cautious relationship between their claims as women and their desire to link them to other national and reformist causes. Their experiences during the century illustrate both Iranian women's capacity for self-assertion and the fragility of any attempt to pursue women's autonomous interests within antidespotic, anti-imperialist, and reformist political coalitions whose gendered cultures marginalized women as well as including them. It is *both* the benefits of women's coexisting with such movements and the constraints that this has imposed that the historian of women and politics in Iran needs to appreciate.

NOTES

This is a revised version of a paper presented at the International Women's History Section of the International Congress of Historical Sciences in Montréal, Canada, in August 1995. I thank Ruth Pierson, Nupur Chaudhuri, and Beth McAuley for their helpful advice and extreme patience with me during the recasting of this piece.

1. Benedict Anderson, *Imagined Communities: Reflections on the Origins and Spread of Nationalism* (London: Verso, 1983).

2. Gayatri Spivak, *In Other Worlds* (London: Routledge, 1987); Elizabeth Spelman, *Inessential Woman* (London: Women's Press, 1988); Chandra Mohanty, "Under Western Eyes," *Feminist Review* 39 (1988): 61–88; C. Mohanty, "Intro-

duction" and "Cartographies of Difference," in Chandra Mohanty et al., eds., *Third World Women and the Politics of Feminism* (Bloomington: Indiana University Press, 1991).

3. Ervand Abrahamian, *Iran between Two Revolutions* (Princeton: Princeton University Press, 1982), chs. 1 and 2; John Foran, *Fragile Resistance: Social Transformation in Iran from 1500 to the Revolution* (Boulder, CO: Westview, 1993), part 2; Guity Nashat, "From Bazaar to Market: Foreign Trade and Economic Development in Nineteenth-Century Iran," *Iranian Studies* 14, nos. 1–2 (Winter–Spring 1981): 53–85; Ahmad Seyf, "Silk Production and Trade in Iran in the Nineteenth Century," *Iranian Studies* 16, nos. 1–2 (Winter–Spring 1983): 51–71; A. Seyf, "Commercialisation of Agriculture: Opium in Persia 1850–1906," *International Journal of Middle East Studies* 16, no. 2 (May 1984): 233–50; Gad Gilbar, "The Persian Economy in the Mid-Nineteenth Century," *Die Welt des Islams* 19, nos. 1–4 (1979): 177–211; G. Gilbar, "Persian Agriculture in the Late Qajar Period," *Asian and African Studies* 12 (1978): 312–65; G. Gilbar, "The Big Merchants (*tujjar*) and the Persian Constitutional Revolution," *Asian and African Studies* 11, no. 3 (1977): 275–303; Shaul Bakhash, *Iran: Monarchy, Bureaucracy and Reform under the Qajars* (London: Ithaca, 1978); Guity Nashat, *The Origins of Modern Reform in Iran 1870–1880* (Urbana: University of Illinois Press, 1982); Hamid Algar, *Religion and the State in Iran 1785–1906* (Berkeley and Los Angeles: University of California Press, 1969); H. Algar, *Mirza Malkom Khan* (Berkeley and Los Angeles: University of California Press, 1973); Mangol Bayat, *Mysticism and Dissent: Socio-Religious Thought in Qajar Iran* (Syracuse: Syracuse University Press, 1982); Said Amir Arjomand, *The Shadow of God and the Hidden Imam: Religion, Political Order and Societal Changes in Shi'ite Iran from the Beginning to 1890* (Chicago: University of Chicago Press, 1984); Nikki Keddie, *Religion and Rebellion in Iran: The Tobacco Protest of 1891–92* (London: Cass, 1966); N. Keddie, *Roots of Revolution* (New Haven: Yale University Press, 1980); N. Keddie, *Sayyid Jamal-ad-Din "Afghani": A Political Biography* (Berkeley and Los Angeles: University of California Press, 1972); David Gillard, *The Struggle for Asia 1828–1914: A Study in British and Russian Imperialism* (London: Methuen, 1977).

4. Algar, *Religion and the State* and *Mirza Malkom Khan*; Bakhash, *Iran*; Bayat, *Mysticism and Dissent*; M. Bayat, *Iran's First Revolution: Shi'ism in the Constitutional Revolution of 1905–9* (Oxford: Oxford University Press, 1991); Keddie, *Religion and Rebellion* and *Sayid Jamal-ad-Din "al-Afghani"*; G. Nashat, "From Bazaar to Market"; Mansur Moaddel, "Shi'ite Political Discourse and Class Mobilisation in the Tobacco Rebellion," *Sociological Forum* (1992).

5. Victor Kiernan, *The Lords of Humankind* (London: Penguin, 1969); Edward Said, *Orientalism* (London: Routledge, 1978); Sarah Graham-Brown, *Images of Women* (London: Quartet Books, 1988); Maxime Rodinson, *Europe and the Mystique of Islam* (London: I. B. Tauris, 1988); Joanna de Groot, 'Sex' and 'Race': The Construction of Image and Language in the Nineteenth Century," in Susan Mendos and Jane Rendall, eds., *Sexuality and Subordination* (London: Routledge, 1989); J. de Groot, "Conceptions and Misconceptions: The Historical and Cultural Context of Discussion on Women and Development," in Haleh Afshar, ed., *Women, Development and Survival in the Third World* (London: Longmans, 1991); Billie Melman, *Women's Orients: English Women and the Middle East* (London: Macmillan, 1992).

6. Muhammad Tavakoli-Targhi, "Imagining Western Women: Occidentalism and Euro-eroticism," *Radical America* 24, no. 3 (July–September 1990, published 1993): 73–87; M. Tavakoli-Targhi, *Women of the West Imagined: Occi-*

dentalism and Exotic Europeans (Berkeley and Los Angeles: University of California Press, 1992); Denis Wright, *The Persians among the English* (London: I. B. Tauris, 1985); Ibrahim Sahafbashi Tehrani, in Muhammad Moshiri, ed., *Travels (1880s)* (Tehran, 1968), in Persian; Nasir-ad-Din Shah, *Diary of H.M. The Shah of Persia*, trans. J-S. Redhouse (London, 1874).

7. Mirza Malkom Khan, *Qanun* (newspaper in Persian), 1889–90, fascimile edition Tehran, 1977, nos. 4, 7, 15, 19; Mirza Aqa Kermani, *One Hundred Letters* (1880s and 1890s), in Persian, text printed in *Nimeh-yi-digar*, no. 9 (1990); Sholeh Abadi, "Mirza Fath 'Ali Akhundzadeh and the Question of Women," in Persian, *Nimeh-yi-digar*, no. 17 (Winter 1993): 29–37; Mangol Bayat, "Mirza Aqa Khan Kermani," in Elie Kedourie and Sylvia Haim, eds., *Towards a Modern Iran* (London: Cass and Co., 1980); Feridun Adamiyat and Homa Nategh, *Social, Political and Economic Thought of the Qajar Period in Unpublished Documents* (Tehran, 1978), in Persian; Joanna de Groot, "The Dialectics of Gender: Women, Men and Political Discourse in Iran c. 1890–1930," *Gender and History* 5, no. 2 (1993): 256–268; Muhammad Karim Khan Kermani, *Commentariso* (Tehran, 1967), in Persian, 388–391; Shaikh Fazlullah Nuri, *Collected Works*, Muhammad Turkoman, ed. (Tehran, 1983), in Persian; Roshanak Mansur, "Women's Image in Constitutional Literature," in Persian, *Nimeh-yi-digar*, no. 1 (1984): 12–30.

8. Malkom Khan, *Qanun*, no. 7 (August 1890); Mirza Aqa Kermani quoted in Bayat, "Mirza Aqa Khan Kermani," in Kedourie and Haim, eds., *Towards a Modern Iran*, 79, 81.

9. Bayat, "Mirza Aqa Khan Kermani" and *Mysticism and Dissent*; Bakhash, *Iran*; Keddie, *Religion and Rebellion*; Parvin Paidar, *Women and the Political Process in Twentieth-Century Iran* (Cambridge: Cambridge University Press, 1995), chs. 1 and 2.

10. Fath 'Ali Akhundzadeh, *Comedies* (UNESCO, n.d.), in Persian/ Azeri; Akhundzadeh, *Collected Articles* (Tehran, 1985), in Persian; Talibov/Talibzadeh, *The Book of Ahmad* (1893), in Persian, ed. Muhammad Mashiri (Tehran, 1967/ 68); Kermani, *One Hundred Letters* in *Nimeh-yi-digar*; Tavokoli-Targhi, *Women of the West Imagined* and "Imagining Women"; Tavokoli-Targhi, "There Was a Woman, There Was Not a Woman," *Nimeh-yi-digar*, no. 14 (1991): 77–110.

11. Abbas Amanat, *Resurrection and Renewal: The Making of the Babi Movement in Iran, 1844–1850* (Ithaca: Cornell University Press, 1989), ch. 7; Farzaneh Milani, *Veils and Words: The Emerging Voices of Iranian Women* (Syracuse: Syracuse University Press, 1992), ch. 4; Mirza Muhammad Taqi Shiphr, *The Abrogation of Histories (History of the Qajars)*, ed. Muhammad Bihbudi, Vol. 3 (Tehran, 1965), in Persian, 200, 219, 241; Comte Joseph de Gobineau, *Religions et philosophies dans l'Asie Centrale* (Paris, 1865; 2nd ed. 1990), 180–184.

12. Taj-as-Saltaneh, *Memoirs* (c. 1914–15), in Persian, eds. Mansureh Eteradeh and Cyrus Sa'daqndian (Tehran, 1992); Bibi Khanom Astarabadi, *The Vices of Men* (1894, in Persian), ed. Afsareh Najmabadi (Chicago, 1992); A. Najmabadi, "Hazards of Morality and Modernity," in Deniz Kardiydi, ed., *Women, Islam and the State* (London: Macmillan, 1991); A. Najmabadi, "Veiled Discourse, Unveiled Bodies," *Feminist Studies* 19, no. 3 (1993): 4–87.

13. Ervand Abrahmian, "The Crowd in the Persian Revolution," *Iranian Studies* 2, no. 4 (Autumn 1969): 128–150; E. Abrahmian, "The Causes of the Constitutional Revolution," *International Journal of Middle East Studies* 10 (1979): 381–414; E. Abrahmian, *Iran between Two Revolutions*, ch. 2; Bayat, *Iran's First Revolution*; Vanessa Martin, *Islam and Modernism: The Iranian Revolution of 1906* (London: I. B. Tauris, 1989); Robert McDaniel, *The Shuster Mission and the Per-*

sian *Constitutional Revolution* (Minneapolis: University of Minnesota Press, 1974); Asghar Fathi, "The Role of the *Lutis* in the Constitutional Revolution," *International Journal of Middle East Studies* 11 (1979); Said Amir Arjomand, "The 'ulama's Traditionalist Opposition to Islam," *International Journal of Middle East Studies* 17 (April 1981): 171–190; Nazimal-Islam Kermani, *History of the Awakening of the Iranians* (1910–18), in Persian, 2 vols. (Tehran, 1978); Ahmad Kasravi, *History of the Constitution of Iran*, in Persian, 2 vols. (Tehran, 1978); Edward Browne, *The Persian Revolution* (1910; revised, London: Cass and Co., 1966); Morgan Shuster, *The Strangling of Persia* (London: Unwin, 1912).

14. Kosravi, *History of the Constitution*, Vol. I, 97, 180–82; Vol. II, 610, 646; Nazim al-Islam Kermani, *Awakening*, Vol. I, 361–539; Vol. II, 92–93; Badr-al-Moluk Bamdad, *From Darkness into Light*, trans. and ed. F. R. C. Bagley (New York: Exposition Press, 1977), ch. 3; Jaret Afary, "On the Origins of Feminism in Twentieth Century Iran," *Journal of Women's History* 1, no. 2 (1989): 75–87; J. Afary, "The Social and Political Thought of Iranian Women," in Persian, *Nimeh-yi-digar*, 17 (1993): 7–28; J. Afary, "Steering between Scylla and Charybdis: Shifting Gender Roles in Twentieth-Century Iran," *NWSA Journal* 8 (1996); Paidar, *Women and the Political Process*, ch. 2; Homa Nategh, "Some Writings and Movements of Women in the Constitutional Period" (in Persian), *Ketab Jomen* 30 (1980); H. Nategh, "Factional Battles in the Constitutional Revolution" (in Persian), *Alefba* 3 (1983): 30–52; H. Nategh, "The Woman Question in Some Left Publications from the Constitutional Period in the Reza Shah Era" (in Persian), *Zaman-i-no* 1 (November 1983): 8–14; Mangol Bayat, "Women and Revolution in Iran," in Lois Beck and Nikki Keddie, eds., *Women in the Muslim World* (Cambridge: Harvard University Press, 1978); Mahdokht San'ah, "Account of the life of Sedigheh Doulatabadi," *Nimeh-yi-dagar*, no. 17 (1993): 64; Eliz Sanasarian, *The Women's Movement in Iran* (New York: Praeger, 1982); Shuster, *The Strangling of Persia*, 183–89; Joanna de Groot, "Kerman in the Later Nineteenth Century: A Regional Study of Society and Social Change" (Ph.D. dissertation, Oxford University, 1978), pp. 444, 451, using British Foreign Office records, series F0248 (consular records), Vol. 846 for 1905 (reports on events in Kerman, 5–12 November and 12–19 November), Vol. 878 for 1906 (similarly for 10–24 March and 8–18 May), vol. 938 for 1908 (similarly for 12–20 February).

15. *Majles* (National Assembly of Iran) *Proceedings* (Tehran, 1946), in Persian, Vol. I, 255, also pp. 217, 266, 483–85.

16. Nazem al Islam Kermani, *Awakening*, Vol. I, 295–96, 446–47, 453, 610–11; Vol. II, 222–24; Shuster, *The Strangling of Persia*; *Majlis Proceedings*, Vol. II, 1528–35; Bayat, "Women and Revolution in Iran"; Bamdad, *From Darkness into Light*; Paidar, *Women and the Political Process*, ch. 2; A. Najmabadi, "Zanha-ye-millat: Women or Wives of the Nation," *Iranian Studies* 26 (1994): 51–71.

17. French and Indian comparisons can be pursued via Lynne Hunt, *Politics, Culture and Class in the French Revolution* (Berkeley and Los Angeles: University of California Press, 1984); L. Hunt, *The Family Romance of the French Revolution* (London: Routledge, 1992); Dorinda Outram, "Le langage mâle de la vertu: Women and the Discovery of the French Revolution," in Peter Burke and Roy Porter, eds., *The Social History of Language* (Cambridge: Cambridge University Press, 1987); Olwen Hufton, "The Reconstruction of the Church," in Gwynne Lewis and Colin Lucas, eds., *Beyond the Terror* (Cambridge: Cambridge University Press, 1983); Sabine Melzer and Lesley Rabine, eds., *Rebel Daughters: Women and the French Revolution* (Oxford: Oxford University Press, 1992); Partha Chatterjee, *Nationalist Thought and the Colonial World* (London: Zed Press, 1986); Kunkum Sangari and Sudesh Vaid, eds., *Recasting Women:*

Essays in Indian Colonial History (New Brunswick, NJ: Rutgers University Press, 1990), ch. by Mani, Chakravarty, Banerjee, Chatterjee, Tharu; Mrinalina Sinha, *Colonial Masculinity* (Manchester: Manchester University Press, 1995); John Alter, "Celibacy, Sexuality and the Transformation of Gender into Nationalism," *Journal of Asian Studies* 53, no. 1 (1994): 45–66; Tanika Sarkar, "The Hindu Wife and the Hindu Nation: Domesticity and Nationalism in Nineteenth-Century Bengal," *Studies in History* 8, no. 2 (1992): 213–35.

18. Abrahamian, *Iran between Two Revolutions*, chs. 3–5; Foran, *Fragile Resistance*, chs. 6, 7; Shahrough Akhavi, *Religion and Politics in Contemporary Iran: Clergy-State Relations in the Pahlavi Period* (New York: State University of New York Press, 1980); Amin Banani, *The Modernisation of Iran 1921–1941* (Stanford: Stanford University Press, 1961; reprint 1977); Julian Bharier, *Economic Development in Iran, 1900–1970* (Oxford: Oxford University Press, 1971); Donald Wilber, *Riza Shah Pahlavi* (New York: Exposition Press, 1975); Richard Cottam, *Nationalism in Iran*, rev. ed. (Pittsburgh: Pittsburgh University Press, 1979); Fakhreddin Azimi, *Iran, the Crisis of Democracy, 1941–53* (London: I. B. Tauris, 1989); Farhad Diba, *Mohammad Mossadegh: A Political Biography* (London: Croom Helm, 1986); Mohammed Faghfoory, "'Ulama-State Relations in Iran, 1921–1941," *International Journal of Middle East Studies* 19, no. 4 (1987): 413–32; Siphir Zabih, *The Mossadegh Era: Roots of the Iranian Revolution* (Chicago: Lake View Press, 1982).

19. Paidar, *Women and the Political Process*, 78–134; Bamdad, *From Darkness into Light*, chs. 4, 5; Muhammad Taqizadeh, *Collected Articles*, ed. Iraj Afhsar (Tehran, 1972), in Persian; M. Taqizadeh, *Kaveh* (newspaper in Persian, 1920s, facsimile edition Tehran, 1977); Ahmad Kasravi, *Our Sisters and Daughters* (in Persian, 1944), (Tehran, 1974); Ruth Woodsmall, *Moslem Women Enter a New World* (London: Unwin, 1936); Clara Colliver Rice, *Persian Women and Their Ways* (London: Seeley Service, 1923); Homa Nategh, "The Woman Question"; Najmabadi, "Hazards of Morality and Modernity" and "Veiled Discourse"; Sanasarian, *The Women's Movement in Iran*, chs. 3, 4; Tavakoli-Targhi, "There Was a Woman."

20. Foran, *Fragile Resistance*, chs. 8–10; Abrahamian, *Iran between Two Revolutions*, chs. 10–11; Fred Halliday, *Iran: Dictatorship and Development* (London: Penguin, 1979); Joanna de Groot, "The Formation and Re-formation of Popular Protest in Iran," in Kenneth Brown, Sami Zubaida et al., eds., *Urban Crisis and Social Movements in the Middle East* (Paris: Harmattan, 1989/90); Bharier, *Economic Development in Iran*.

21. Said Amir Arjomand, *From Nationalism to Revolutionary Islam* (New York: State University of New York Press, 1984); Afsaneh Najmabadi, "The De-Politicisation of a Rentier State," in Hazem Beblawi and Giacomo Luciqni, eds., *The Rentier State*, Vol. II (London: Croom Helm, 1987); A. Najmabadi, "Iran's Turn to Islam," *The Middle East Journal* 41, no. 2 (1987): 202–217; de Groot, "Formation and Re-formation"; Akhavi, *Religion and Politics in Contemporary Iran*; Paidar, *Women and the Political Process*, chs. 5–7; Hamid Algar, "Imam Khomeini 1902–62," in Ira Lapidus and Edmund Burke, eds., *Islam, Politics and Social Movements* (Berkeley and Los Angeles: University of California Press, 1988); Michael Fischer, *Iran: From Religious Dispute to Revolution* (Cambridge: Harvard University Press, 1980); Sami Zubaida, *Islam, the People and the State* (London: Routledge, 1989); Ervand Abrahmaian, *Revolutionary Islam: The Mojahdin* (London: I. B. Tauris, 1989).

22. Paidar, *Women and the Political Process*; Sanasarian, *The Women's Movement in Iran*; Afsameh Najmabadi, "Hazards of Morality and Modernity"; Ali

Shan'ati, *Woman in the Heart and Eye of Muhammad* (Tehran, 1976), in Persian; Najmabadi, *Fatima Is Fatima* (Tehran, 1980), in Persian; Anne Betteridge, "To Veil or Not to Veil" and Janet Bauer, "Poor Women and Social Consciousness in Revolutionary Iran," in Guity Nashat, ed., *Women and Revolution in Iran* (Boulder, CO: Westview Press, 1983); Afary, "Steering between Scylla and Charybdis."

9

Orthodoxy, Cultural Nationalism, and Hindutva Violence

*An Overview of the Gender
Ideology of the Hindu Right*

TANIKA SARKAR

Right-wing politics in India has had a long and stable history, even if its most important work had taken place, for the most part, in unspectacular daily training sessions in contrast to later violent activities. Only in the past decade has right-wing politics burst onto the center stage of parliamentary politics, bringing along with it a mass movement of great violence and a political agenda that threatens to alter the self-definition of the Indian nation as a secular democracy.[1]

This new phase is often dominated by women's faces and women's voices.[2] This is a major departure, indeed, for even though a women's wing of the Rashtriya Swayamsevak Sangh—the key and apex body that holds together the heterogeneous organizational structure of the Right—has existed since 1936, it has had a remarkably low-key, quiet, almost obscure existence. The women of the Right were presumed to live homebound, conservative lives, away from public spaces and concerns.[3] The leap taken by the women's wing of the Rashtriya Swayamsevak Sangh (RSS) from a routinized, slow-growing, low-key organizational phase to a strident, dazzling, public identity, with equal participation in campaigns of great violence against Indian Muslims, has been one of the greatest surprises sprung upon Indian politics by the Right. The breakthrough coincides with certain rapid and fundamental transformations in the economic, social, and cultural world of the urban middle classes from which most of the right-wing women activists come.

This chapter is a tentative exploration into this moment in the history of right-wing women's politics. To understand the moment more fully, however, it is necessary to reinsert this history into the earlier processes of middle-class formation and into the development of a militant Hindu supremacism that has aspired to form a Hindu nation since the late nineteenth century. At the same time, it helps to counterpose to this an overview of other political formations—those of liberal, nationalist, and left-wing politics. The incorporation of the history of the Hindu Right and its women within a broader history of political movements and thinking helps to illuminate, through contrasts and comparisons, the distinctive aspects of the gender ideology of the Right. It gives a sense of what it was that Hindu revivalism and supremacism reacted to and contested.

COLONIAL RULE AND THE FORMATION OF THE HINDU MIDDLE CLASSES

At first, colonial rule fashioned the Hindu middle classes largely out of the traditional upper and literate castes of the Bengal, Bombay, and Madras Presidencies. It drew on these classes in other regions somewhat later and to varying degrees. Although the castes from each region had specific and distinct motivations for joining in experiences of the process, on the whole they formed the new intelligentsia that made its living out of tenurial income from landholding, jobs in the lower rungs of the colonial administrative machinery, and the new liberal professions of law and journalism, and teaching at the new educational centers. In concrete terms, the formation of the new Hindu middle classes did not upset the Hindu caste and gender profile of the precolonial ruling groups that had monopolized higher learning, property, and administrative power in upper-caste male hands.[4]

Throughout the colonial period, the sphere of domestic practices, ritual, and belief—the domain of personal laws—was legally exempted from State intervention, unless Indians could justify proposed changes on the basis of scriptural and customary sanction. As a result, both Hindu caste and gender norms were largely allowed to remain mired in precolonial upper-caste male domination. Again, with the growth of a variant of Hindu supremacist cultural nationalism from the late nineteenth century, the domestic-religious sphere was conceptualized as one of relative autonomy, as the last bastion of a vanished freedom, the site of a possible, emergent nation. Between the 1870s and 1890s, certain kinds of Hindu anticolonial agitations grew out of resistance to the colonial State's proposed changes to the age of consent, the introduction of divorce, and the reform of Hindu marriage laws.[5]

At the same time, the experience of colonialism itself led to grave introspection and reflections among the new Hindu intelligentsia on the historical flaws within Hindu society that had enabled this surrender to a more successful and aggressive power. As a result, a whole range of distinct, mutually opposed diagnoses were made and resolutions suggested that provided the basis of the nineteenth-century social and religious reform movements. Some of them—the supporters of the liberal reforms of the earlier part of the century—came to develop arguments against the absolute power of upper-caste male domination. Their new acquaintance with contemporary European philosophies enabled them to formulate an autonomous and creative self-critique in the language of universal rights, though often it was a highly modified and tempered notion of rights.[6]

At another level, colonial rule had unleashed social and economic transformations that were based on calculations of administrative and political expediency and economic profits for the colonial ruling classes. These would occasionally disturb and overturn the precolonial modes of power. Christian missionary work had brought a limited degree of education to some categories of low castes who could now have access to new professions and who could demand more. Commercialization of agriculture or new revenue arrangements could destabilize the caste basis of rural landholding and property structures. In western India, a small segment of low castes had acquired education and found urban jobs. From the midcentury, their leaders demanded from the State a larger share of resources. They also built up movements among broader sections of their castes, defying the rule of Brahmins.[7] Hindu women, educated at first by liberal husbands or fathers, began to write about the need for more institutionalized education, reform in Hindu marriage practices, and transformations in domestic norms and values.[8]

There were, then, simultaneous reinforcement of precolonial power structures as well as the emergence of crucial centers of opposition. Hindu orthodoxy that had expressed itself as simple status quo–ism at the beginning of the social reform movements now needed to think beyond the old parameters of scriptural or customary citations—particularly since its Hindu reformist rivals proved to be equally adept at the game. It needed to prepare itself for a recreated hegemonic role rather than depend upon the stability of inherited social power and controls. If the old hierarchies were primarily grounded in carefully regulated distances and exclusions among castes and sexes, the new revisions needed to work out strategies of carefully regulated domains of shared enterprises and aspirations, while equally carefully leaving the essential bases of social power and domination undisturbed. Toward the turn of the century, the Hindu revivalist imaginary came to depend more and more on the figure of an enemy that the community must fight in order to see itself as a community at all.

A word about the relationship of reform and cultural nationalism with the colonial state: Cultural nationalism, down to its present-day Hindutva incarnation, has tried hard to cloak itself in an anticolonial mantle, claiming that reformists were a colonial creation, fathered by western power and knowledge systems. In particular, the language of universal rights within an Indian context, toward which liberals were tentatively and hesitatingly groping, was seen as the most disturbing, and represented the most blatant, sign of surrender to the West. Its own indigenousness, on the other hand, was identified as the authentic and meaningful move to retain a noncolonized identity, the truly anticolonial gesture. From this premise could flow a larger argument that comfortably associates reform with loyalty and complicity with colonial rule. Cultural nationalism, then, has sought to appropriate obliquely the space of political anticolonialism as well. It is important to remember, therefore, that barring a brief moment of opposition during the agitation over age of consent, cultural nationalism has not taken up an overtly anticolonial political stand. More importantly, the colonial State did not consider liberal reformers as its progeny, nor was it unduly worried by or opposed to the gender perspectives of revivalists or cultural nationalists.

HINDU REFORMS AND THE FIGURE OF WOMEN

From the late nineteenth century, nationalist organizations formally extended the language of rights to the right to self-government, which, in this phase, recruited their cadres largely from educated professional middle classes. Indian business, that had now acquired a nascent capitalistic-industrial wing, added its demands for at least a modicum of self-determination in commercial, monetary, and fiscal matters, often in conjunction with the demands and protests of political nationalism. These demands disturbed and overturned the erstwhile colonial enthusiasm for the middle classes that had stayed loyal to the State during the military and popular anti-British rebellions of 1857. These demands also made the State review Hindu patriarchal norms and traditional ruling classes in a more favorable light. Indian princes with

their feudal pageantry, social conservatism, and exploitative administrations became the preferred field of colonial political investment,
legal reforms became a suspect area, and the growing combativeness of
bourgeois feminism at home created something of an alliance between
the Hindu orthodoxy and the colonial rulers. The colonial project of a
guided and controlled modernization lost its credibility in the eyes of
the State. The new middle class could no longer be seen as clones of the
liberal English gentlemen, as Thomas Babington Macaulay who between 1833 and 1838 served on the British Supreme Council that gov-
erned India had promised, but seemed to attain considerable nuisance
value as discontented and demanding potential rivals. The conflicts
and debates over gender issues in nineteenth-century India need to be
reviewed against this political backdrop.

From the early decades of the nineteenth century, proposed legal
changes within the Hindu conjugal order were deeply problematic
with respect to the foundations of Hindu domestic norms, often developing in ways that were unforeseen even by the reformists themselves.
Brahmanical prescriptions for upper-caste women, on the whole, had
left them with few rights of property inheritance, either paternal or
matrimonial. Widow remarriage was forbidden; marriages were indis-
soluble under almost all circumstances; women were ideally to be
married in their infancy; and extremely severe injunctions about absolute monogamous chastity were imposed upon them. Men, on the other
hand, were exempted from compulsory infant marriage, they were
allowed polygamy, and chastity was not required of them. While low
castes were not bound by these injunctions, it had long been the practice
that upwardly mobile segments of low castes would seek ritual improvement of caste status by emulating Brahmanical domestic practices as closely as possible.[9] The Hindu reformist projects of banning
widow immolation, legalizing widow remarriage, abolishing cohabitation in a girl's infancy, and vesting the woman with the right to seek
dissolution of marriage, therefore, put at risk a larger structure of hegemonic Brahmanical prescriptions that transcended strict upper-caste
boundaries.

The nineteenth century was the century par excellence for the
review of Hindu conjugality. In the first decades, the debates around the
widow-immolation issue split Hindu society right down the middle. In
mid-century, the agitation around widow remarriage strengthened the
cleavage. In the 1870s, a proposed package of reformed marriage practices by the reformist Brhmo Samaj sect recommended raising the age of
marriage, the abolition of polygamy, the woman's right to seek divorce,
and the notion of the woman's consent to marriage that could cut across

caste and community boundaries. The century ended on the bitter differences over raising the age of consent. In and through these arguments, a new status quo–ist, a cultural nationalist, and a reformist political nationalism emerged.[10]

In an ironical twist, while Hindu reformists managed to get quite a few of their proposed conjugal laws passed, they were unable to vest the new laws with the hegemonic power that older patriarchal norms possessed. Nor were the new laws grounded in a particularly strong or coherent vision of individual rights, let alone in gender justice. Their most significant historical function, then, was not so much to create a full-fledged alternative order—contestative, destabilizing, problematizing—as to loosen up a hard patriarchal discipline through a softer counternorm of "companionate marriage" with equal disciplinary prescriptions for both partners.

The new discipline of companionate marriage, however, allowed also for a shared spiritual and ritual domain unlike the highly differentiated spheres under unreformed patriarchy. Equal access to spiritual resources meant much higher educational expectations for and from the woman. Envisioned was a greater degree of real affect between husband and wife, based on shared devotional activities and intellectual exchanges, albeit initiated under the husband's mentorship. The liberal domestic ideal was also animated by an implicit recognition that the marriage tie required an active and continuous sexual relationship: in their demand for widow remarriage, the liberals contested the orthodox notion that widows remained married to their dead husbands and, hence, any other relationship would amount to adultery. They also recognized the right of widows to possess sexual desires. Such ideas, by the later decades of the century, began to find a resonance from the writings of Hindu women. Tarabai Shinde, in fact, accused liberal reformers of timidity, moderation, and double standards.[11] An independent and radical critique of Brahmanical prescription began to emerge from a small but strong political group arising from educated, middle-class, low-caste activists who equated the gender discrimination of Brahmanism with its caste discrimination, thereby threatening to open up fault lines and create fractures within the Brahmanical stronghold itself on gender issues.

There were two responses to the predicament from the old patriarchal leadership and authority structures. Both contributed to revivalist cultural nationalism among Hindus. The first may be termed a status quo–ist patriarchalism that, unlike the old orthodoxy and its inherited social authority, aimed to secure hegemony by anchoring its gender norms not in prescription but in a strident, even militant, cultural nationalism. It sought not a displacement of colonial power nor even a diminution of it, but absolute power for itself so that it could dictate the terms of Hindu patriarchy. The different meanings attached to an ideal or typical Hindu womanhood converged, not just to create the image of a pure and authentic Hindu domesticity, uncontaminated by any thoughts western or colonial, but also to locate the sites of the existent and hidden freedom and the future, hidden nation within the feminine body, unmarked by western education or laws, molded entirely by Hindu scriptural discipline, and, therefore, truly noncolonized. The line of argument was articulated and sharpened over the age-of-consent controversy. Since the debate took place over the violent death of a little girl from marital rape, an aporia was opened up within the logic of Hindu supremacism that simultaneously wanted to project Hinduism as nurturant and loving and to place it as superior to Christianity, Islam, and liberal reformism.

Faced with this crisis of choice—Hindu domesticity as love and nurture or as pain and discipline—Hindu cultural nationalists, at the turn of the century, moved away from the domain of domesticity and conjugality altogether, and initiated a new project for the salvation of Hindus. Swami Vivekananda shifted the patriotic agenda onto an exclusively male group of ascetics who would rejuvenate Hindu society through full-time social service. Through constructive charity, they would try to incorporate the lower castes. Through social work among lower orders, Hindu social leadership would also acquire training in and capacity for hegemonic control over the Hindu world.[12]

The second response was the Arya Dharm and Arya Samaj organized by Swami Dayananda that struck deep and strong roots among the trading and service castes of Punjab and Western United Provinces. They had affluence, some education, and ambitions for administrative power, and their aspirations had been thwarted and threatened by the work of Christian and Brahman missionaries and the entrenched cultural domination of an Urdu-speaking Muslim elite. Hindu supremacism took on a more aggressive edge in this context, but Dayananda also imparted to it a more comprehensively transformative social agenda.[13]

Dayananda envisaged not an exclusively male vanguardism but an energized Hindu community whose nucleus was going to be the family, remodeled on differently interpreted Vedic laws. The domain of the domestic was neither given up nor frozen, but was going to be the pivot around which a unified and aggressive community identity would compose itself to combat Islam, Christianity, and the liberal reformers.

The designs for change looked suspiciously like what reformers had advocated all along: widow remarriage, an end to child marriage, marriage across caste barriers, and education for women. The overall design and the desired effects, however, spelled out a very different agenda. Companionate marriage, which would stretch out the intellectual and spiritual possibilities of the woman and which might endow women eventually with a sharper notion of selfhood, did not enter into the scheme at all. Widow remarriage was meant to lead to a more economic use of childbearing Hindu wombs. Child marriage was discouraged as unconducive to healthy and numerous progeny. The woman was to be educated in the interests of better child management and an improved child-rearing regimen. Each change was stripped of any possibilities of individual benefit; rather each one enthroned totalitarian and authoritarian community surveillance. Widows could only marry widowers, and the relationship could be terminated after the required number of sons had been born. The mother was advised to turn away from breast-feeding her newborn infant so that her body could be prepared for bearing and feeding the next baby as soon as possible.[14]

The crucial difference between liberal reform and this new revivalist reform basically hinged on deeply opposed perspectives on laws for domestic reforms and on their implications for the new Hindu community. Liberal reformers' reliance on legislation as an instrument for social change was rife with problems in a colonial situation. Yet, the legal rights granted to the woman cleared a space for an individuated legal identity that could, at least notionally, be pitted against the family and the community. Hindu revivalists made the community the exclusive source for all change and reform, to be mediated through the family. The woman was, therefore, absolutely enmeshed and integrated with both. Bypassing the path toward embourgeoisement through liberal individualism, the rising, yet educationally and culturally lagging and conservative, trader castes were given the alternative mode of self-modernization and empowerment through the agency of a unified and totalitarian community discipline.

Yet, the agenda was dangerously alien to a lot of the orthodox Hindus or Sanatanists of the times, and Dayananda's deeply revisionist patriarchy made the Arya Dharm and the Arya Samaj look like a surrender to liberal reformism in a different guise. The cleavages could only be overcome through the construction of a common enemy of the Hindus—the Muslim, who were supposedly endlessly breeding, abducting Hindu women and forcing them to bear Muslim children, and conspiring to convert and thereby nullify the Hindu majority. From the turn of the century, revivalist Hindu supremacist self-reform would survive by reinventing this enemy figure over and over.

HINDU SUPREMACISM VERSUS DEMOCRATICALLY ORIENTED MASS MOVEMENTS

The 1920s, especially with the advent of Gandhian leadership, saw a revolutionized political horizon, with the growth of a series of mass movements—some of them among the largest in the world—that drew in movements of peasants, low castes, tribal peoples, and women from all social groups, as well as educated middle classes and segments of the Indian bourgeoisie. Anticolonial movements, even with their deep internal contradictions, were most often the axis around which mobilization and self-mobilization would be organized; yet, the anticolonial agenda would inevitably carry very different and conflicting meanings for these people, depending on their social location. Also, within and often outside the orbit of mainstream nationalist consensus, there would be autonomous movements among peasants, tribal peoples, low castes, and the working classes, as well as among women, who organized against their social subordination within Indian society. At the constitutional level, the Congress was committed to an electoral democratic system with growing women's representation.

It was also in the stormy decades of the 1920s that the Hindu Right separated itself definitively as a distinct political formation and founded a delicately calibrated organizational structure in the shape of the Rashtriya Swayamsevak Sangh (RSS). (Its women's organization developed a decade later, in the mid-1930s.) It is important to place the RSS among the new political currents, for its founding and its subsequent modes of action clearly reveal that the colonial condition was not what it opposed: it opposed the new political formations within India, the development of democratically oriented mass movements.

Also in the mid-1920s, a vibrant working-class militancy led by the Left began to mobilize itself. Class politics often neatly coincided with anticolonial imperatives, since, more often than not, mill owners and capitalists were European and were tenderly protected by the colonial State against strikes and protests by workers. Women, on several occasions, were extremely prominent as union organizers.[15] Around working-class action, a distinct tradition of left-wing politics began to manifest itself, powerful enough by the late 1920s to call forth waves of industrial general strikes and force the colonial State to put together conspiracy cases that would pull in all leftist labor leaders and place them in prison. The strand of radical class militancy repeated itself in a number of peasant and tribal movements. Among somewhat more elite, urban liberal feminists, demands for franchise and better educational provisions began to be systematically formulated.[16] In western India, which was about to become the origin and headquarters of Hindutva politics, the nineteenth-century tradition of low-caste protest reasserted itself with the organizational moves of a brilliant leader of untouchables, B. R. Ambedkar, who began to demand separate electoral representation for untouchables.[17] To all these developments, the tradition of Hindu supremacism and caste power could not have an adequate or coherent response.

The most disturbing and serious challenge, however, came from the consolidation of Gandhian mass politics at the time of the Non-Cooperation-Khilafat movement. The Congress, now thoroughly revamped by Gandhi, was ready for building bases among peasants, tribals, and rural people, bestowing upon them the iconic privilege of being the true subjects of the patriotic struggle. Gandhi as a leader played delicately and skillfully on a difficult point of equilibrium—balancing mass politics with Indian bourgeois requirements, detaching the mass anticolonial struggles, as far as possible, from class conflicts. Yet, on the whole, the incorporation of subordinated social groups into the heart of mainstream nationalism was significantly empowering to the former. It also forced a radical rhetoric and self-definition on the Congress as a movement, dominantly, of the Indian poor, imparting to the Congress a new responsibility that a number of radical leaders and autonomous peasant movements would seek to stretch out in future.

While Gandhi upheld traditional religious prescriptions for women's ideal roles and spoke about separate but equal spheres, he also demanded full participation from them in the struggles. He made it possible for them to do so by feminizing the movement in significant ways: promoting nonviolence, promoting the notion of patriotism as a religious duty, and including womanly activities such as working at the spinning wheel. What happened in practice was something far removed from the invocation of separate spheres. Gandhian movements actually made no distinctions between women's work and men's work within the political realm, whatever Gandhi might pronounce as an ideal division of work within the household.[18]

The other disturbing development for the Right was the successful knitting together of Muslim politics with the nationalist mainstream through highly militant anticolonial agitations. The possibility of united struggles on shared issues and with an alternative stream of leadership was a specter that alarmed the established conservative leaders of both communities, who, after the withdrawal of the movement, lost no time in driving the communities apart through a series of organized communal conflicts.

All these developments made redundant the communal politics of Urdu-Hindi controversy or anti-cow-slaughter violence of earlier decades. The Hindu Mahasabha, an electoral organization of the Hindu Right, was patently unable to cope with them, or to make its presence felt on the political scene. The RSS, however, had in place a plan of self-mobilization and self-strengthening of the upper-caste, anti-Muslim urban middle classes through an extraordinarily comprehensive and disciplined regime of daily ideological and physical training centers. It was founded to provide a long-term strategy for survival and growth at this critical juncture and began by training middle-class Brahman youths of Nagpur in a political program that did not concern itself with issues of colonial power or resistance to it, nor with gender, caste, or class justice. Its pedagogy taught a sense of a single Hindu community that would realize and actualize itself through anti-Muslim violence. The RSS hoped this single and focused program would both train the upper castes in leadership qualities and render irrelevant the issues of class, caste, and gender.[19]

The RSS was founded in 1925. It was, and still is, an all-male organization. From the beginning, however, women from RSS families repeatedly asked it to open its doors to them or to allow them to develop a women's front. It is important to ask why the consent to a women's front, so often sought and so adamantly withheld, was finally granted in 1936, when Lakshmibai Kelkar was allowed to set up the Rashtra-sevika Samiti on the same lines as the RSS daily training centers.[20]

For the kind of caste-class perspective that the Hindu Right possessed, the 1930s were another period of profound crisis. The decade saw a rapid and dynamic advance of the Left in Indian politics, the consolidation of peasant and trade union fronts, and the unity among socialistic elements both inside and outside the Congress. After becoming a very major force in the working-class belts in Calcutta and Bombay, the Communists were launched on breaking into rural poor peasant politics, helped by the United Front line of the Communist International, which permitted tactical alliances with national bourgeois political organizations.

The Government of India Act of 1935 had, for the first time, enfranchised 10 percent of the Indian population, a trend that was obviously going to continue.[21] In view of the extension of the mass electoral base, both the emergence of militant untouchable politics and Ambedkar's demand for separate electorates for untouchables gained a new and disturbing significance for the Right, since they would reduce the numerical majority of Hindus. The demand for further extensions of the franchise also revealed the fragility of upper-caste claims to social authority.

The Rashtrasevika Samiti, then, was developed as a response to the crisis. It is extremely significant that both the Sangh and the Samiti were meant to train and develop a given body of cadres, coming each time from a narrow class-caste cluster. The same strategy was repeated at the time of a later crisis when, coming out of a ban and seriously discredited after Gandhi's assassination, the Sangh concentrated on building a chain of schools for children of its own families. It seems that every crisis is transcended by the Hindu Right by reinforcing and bringing under a more thorough control its own social base and cadre group. Enlargement of the base is a secondary consideration, undertaken only after adequate self-mobilization and self-consolidation. The function of ideology is then, initially and crucially, to interpolate the entire range of the Right's actual and potential cadre base as fully developed class and caste subjects; only then is hegemony sought over the others.

Up until the 1980s, the major function of the Rashtrasevikas was to train the mothers and wives of RSS families in Sangh values and disciplines and, through the agency of Samiti-trained women, reach other families through the neighborhood and matrimonial ties, who would then transmit the Sangh lessons to other members of the same class-caste cluster (since neighborhoods and matrimonial ties are structured on caste and class lines). Informal contacts, then, have been a major part of Samiti activity, through which long-term ideological work could be undertaken.

Physical training programs were meant to improve the stock of Hindu leaders whose initial training could now be entrusted to mothers who would transform the home into a preparation room before the child joined the daily training program and the schools of the Sangh. According to the instructions of the supreme ideological guru of the RSS, mothers were to instill habits of deference, obedience, and respect for Sangh leaders. Through stories and parables, they were to transmit messages of the Sangh and teach the children the meaning of Hinduism and patriotism as interpreted by the Sangh. They would scramble selected fragments from history, myths, and stories about "tirthas and temples," and transform them into a single coherent moral ideology about "faith in our Dharma and pride in our history."[22] The importance of growing up with a continuously transmitted unitary worldview is enormous, as is the mechanism of the mother's storytelling in the child's earliest infancy, a time when the critical faculties are not fully developed and a critical knowledge of the world is not yet acquired. The format of storytelling necessarily demands a suspension of questioning.

Mothers, then, were political agents. The early function of the Samiti gives us a privileged entry into the distinctive dimensions of the strategies of the Hindu Right. Our understanding of the Hindu Right needs to be informed by a clear idea about the political significance of everyday relations, of personal dispositions and habit formation, and of domestic ritual and devotional practice in the RSS scheme for hegemony.

WOMEN'S PLACE IN THE HINDU RIGHT

In the last decade or so, with the Ramjanambhoomi campaigns which, in the name of reclaiming the presumed birthplace of Ram, have led to enormous violence against Indian Muslims and to the demolition of the historic Babri Mosque, the location of women within the Hindu Right has gone through striking changes. Women have incited, led, and participated on equal terms in pogroms; they have come to occupy leading positions among the various fronts of the Sangh organization; and the organization has spawned a large number of women's wings that are active, militant, and extremely strident. At the same time, this public visibility of violent women unfolds through a paradox. As they assume a powerful public identity, they increasingly hark back to and insistently invoke a hard form of old patriarchal controls: valorization of widow immolation, male polygamy, demands for withdrawal of women from the workforce, and the abolition of divorce.[23]

Elsewhere, I have, with some care and hope, tried to locate fractures within the Hindutva discourses, to point to possible contestations of patriarchal controls by women that might generate intolerable tensions within the movement.[24] One can, perhaps, seek a resolution of the current paradox by interpreting the invocation of the old order as the effort to overcome such tensions. I feel, however, that this would be, at best, a very partial explanation.

I prefer to read the two trends as mutually reinforcing, rather than as contradictory processes. It is true that the older Samiti training did equip women from conservative, upper-caste, urban, middle-class families with skills to negotiate the new educational and employment opportunities that have recently been opened up for them in northern Indian cities and small towns. At the same time, the more they take up their place in the public domain, the more integrated they become in their class and caste privileges. As part of an affluent circle, drawing the bulk of their familial income from business or the service sector, they might become actively opposed to trade union movements in their workplaces. They could—and indeed they did—vociferously oppose lower-caste demands for extended reservation of government sector jobs. This new identity, then, will go a long way to countermand their relative lack of rights within the domestic sphere—inferior property or inheritance rights or the system of patrilocality, which render them an incomplete class-caste subject in other respects. The integration into a patriarchal familial order would, in fact, be ironically strengthened rather than undercut by the new public roles of middle-class women.

The larger access to public spaces works in yet another way to achieve the same result. The new phase coincides with the onset of a tidal wave in the growth of urban consumerism, powered recently by the new liberalization policies of the State. They open India's doors to the commodities of the world, and that necessitates an unprecedented growth in the advertising culture and in new media sales techniques. Far from forbidding such consumption, the social base of the Sangh organization will be complicit with it as well as be dependent upon it. Within the service sector, such consumption will be an unavoidable mark of social status. Also, the small industrial/manufacturing/trading classes will be actively engaged in the production and dissemination of the household gadgets and fashion items that constitute the bulk of the country's manufactures.[25] Since women decide on such purchases most of the time, they will be solicited to purchase more.

The new educational and employment opportunities improve a woman's bargaining power within the family. They also extend her claims to a larger share of the family budget. As women begin to seek out more and more things that are meant specifically for themselves and not for the family as a whole, the new consumerism becomes the site of an individuation beyond the family, a claim to a sort of an individualism that, however, is nonconflictual. This is not an individualism based on notions of gender rights or social justice that might have led to women's painful isolation within the familial domain, but one based on consumerist preoccupations endlessly circulating around a new self-image, created entirely out of a ceaseless flow of consumer nondurables.

As the consumer culture makes women aware of their power and the possibilities of remaking their body, it also divides them from other women, who are projected as competitors in the new workplace and rivals in the more mixed social circles. Above all, it commits women to an endless and doomed battle with the aging process. Aging, in the older culture, was coveted as a mellow time of grace, accumulated wisdom, and some power. Now it has become the sign of loss and decay, from which women's purchases will not buy a final escape.

The old order, then, might appear to women not as prison but as a sanctuary, with warm solidarities and shared concerns. That mythicized lost golden age could seem recoverable within a new political community of Hindus. That is why the televised Ramayana serial of 1986 could bring together an eroticization of Sita's docile devotion with a political rallying cry around the centrality of Ram for all Hindus. Ultimately, then, the Hindutva version of Hindu community grants women a consumerist selfhood. The anxieties of that acquisition are simultaneously managed with the projection of the imagined community as actualized and embodied within a violent organization.

NOTES

1. For this phase, see Tapan Basu, Pradip Dutta, Sumit and Tanika Sarkar, and Sambuddha Sen, *Khaki Shorts and Saffron Flags: A Critique of the Hindu Right, Tracts for the Times* (New Delhi: Longman, 1993).

2. For a description of this phenomenon across the country, see Tanika Sarkar and Urvashi Butalia, eds., *Women and the Hindu Right* (London: Zed Press, 1995).

3. See Tanika Sarkar, "Heroic Wives, Mother Goddesses: Family and Organisation in Hindutva Politics," in Sarkar and Butalia, *Women and the Hindu Right*.

4. For the social profile of the new intelligentsia, see Anil Seal, *The Emergence of Indian Nationalism: Competition and Collaboration in the Later Nineteenth Century* (Cambridge: Cambridge University Press, 1968), chs. 1–3.

5. See Tanika Sarkar, "Rhetoric against the Age of Consent: Resisting Colonial Reason and the Death of a Child Wife," *Economic and Political Weekly,* 4 September 1993.

6. See Charles Heimsath, *Indian Nationalism and Hindu Social Reform* (Princeton: Princeton University Press, 1964).

7. For an account of these movements, see Rosalind O'Hanlon, *Caste Conflict and Ideology: Mahatma Jotirao Phule and Low Caste Protest in Nineteenth Century Western India* (Cambridge: Cambridge University Press, 1985).

8. For a survey of the material from Bengal, see Ghulam Murshid, *Reluctant Debutantes: Response of Bengali Women to Modernisation* (Rayshahi: Sahitya Sam-sad, Rayshahi University, 1983).

9. Shekhar Bandyopadhyaya, "Caste, Widow Remarriage and the Reform of Popular Culture in Colonial Bengal," in Bharati Ray, ed., *From the Seams of History: Essays on Indian Women* (New Delhi: Oxford University Press, 1995).

10. Tanika Sarkar, "The Hindu Wife and the Hindu Nation: Domesticity and Nationalism in Nineteenth-Century Bengal," *Studies in History* 8, no. 2 (1992).

11. As discussed in O'Hanlon, *A Comparison between Women and Men*.

12. Sarkar, "The Hindu Wife and the Hindu Nation."

13. See Kenneth W. Jones, *Arya Dharm, Hindu Consciousness in Nineteenth Century Punjab* (Columbia, MO: South Asia Books, 1989). See also T. F. Jordens,

Dayananda Sarsvati: His Life and Ideas (New Delhi: Oxford University Press, 1978).

14. Uma Chakravarti, "What Happened to the Vedic Dasi? Orientalism, Nationalism and a Script for the Past," in Kumkum Sangari and Sadesh Vaid, eds., *Recasting Women: Essays in Colonial History* (New Delhi: Kali for Women, 1990), 56.

15. Tanika Sarkar, "Politics and Women in Bengal: The Conditions and Meaning of Participation," in J. Krishnamurty, ed., *Women in Colonial India: Essays on Survival, Work and the State* (New Delhi: Oxford University Press, 1989).

16. Gail Pearson, "Reserved Seats: Women and the Vote in Bombay," in Krishnamurty, *Women in Colonial India*. Also, Geraldine Forbes, "The Indian Women's Movement: A Struggle for Women's Rights or National Liberation?" in Gail Minault, ed., *The Extended Family: Women and Political Participation in Indian and Pakistan* (Columbia, MO: South Asia Books, 1981).

17. Gail Omvedt, *Dalit Visions: Tracts for the Times* (New Delhi: Orient Longman, 1995).

18. Aparna Basu, "The Role of Women in the Indian Struggle for Freedom," in B. R. Nanda, ed., *Indian Women: From Purdah to Modernity* (New Delhi: Vikas, 1976). See also Forbes, "The Indian Women's Movement"; Sarkar, "Politics and Women in Bengal"; Radha Kumar, *The History of Doing: An Illustrated Account of Movements for Women's Rights and Feminism in India, 1800–1990* (New Delhi: Kali for Women, 1993), chs. 4 and 5.

19. Basu et al., *Khaki Shorts and Saffron Flags*.

20. Sarkar, "Heroic Wives, Mother Goddesses."

21. Sumit Sarkar, *Modern India: 1885–1947* (London: Macmillan Press, Cambridge Commonwealth Series, 1989), ch. 6.

22. M. S. Golwalkar, *Bunch of Thoughts* (Bangalore: Prakashn Vibhag, Rashtriya Swayam Sevak Singh, 1966), 30.

23. S. Anitha, Manisha, Vasudha, Kavitha, "Interviews," in Sarkar and Butalia, eds., *Women and the Hindu Right*.

24. Tanika Sarkar, "The Woman as Communal Subject: Rashtrasevika Samiti and the Ramjanambhoomi Movement," *Economic Political Weekly*, 31 August 1991.

25. C. T. Kurien, *Global Capitalism and the Indian Economy, Tracts for the Times* (New Delhi: Orient Longman, 1994).

10

Surviving Absence

Jewishness and Femininity in Liberation France, 1944–45

KAREN H. ADLER

The last week of 1944 in France—Christmas and New Year—was devoted to "the week of the absent," when the hundreds of thousands of French nationals who had been taken away as a result of Nazi and Vichy policies were put to the forefront of public consciousness. These included about 60,000 political deportees to concentration camps, the 940,000 remaining prisoners of war taken during the six weeks of fighting in 1940 before the humiliating defeat and armistice with Germany, 650,000 laborers forced to work in Germany and, rather less explicitly, deported Jews. Most of this last group had been killed in Auschwitz, and only 2,190 of the almost 76,000 deportees were to return.[1] "The week of the absent" had practical as well as ideological aspects. Political and welfare organizations across the political spectrum mobilized women to pack thousands of parcels for French soldiers who were being held in Germany, while performers mounted fundraising shows.[2] At the same time the provisional government launched its cinematic, poster, and press propaganda efforts to restore the French home, with women back in the kitchen ready to welcome the *chef de famille* (head of the family).[3] In a sentimental article published the day after Christmas, "The Presence of the Absent," one newspaper reminded readers that "there are those who will be absent forever on the battlefields, in the Resistance Maquis and German camps: we will feel their absence while we live. We know that they would wish us to replace them in the hard labor of this country's restoration."[4] The textual umbrella of the *absent* unified a set of people whose experiences, motivations, and even nationality separated them. At the same time, various ideological fronts espoused a fervent politics of unity. In certain ways, while politically opposed to each other, Communist Party efforts to form a politically cohesive National Front mirrored a Gaullist rhetoric of true French unity to reignite French republican universalist ideals.[5] In addition, they counteracted Nazi politics of separation and hierarchy, which had been used to such catastrophic ends across Nazi-occupied Europe.

It is not silence, that notion made familiar (even cliché!) by feminist history, that pervades this history of Jewish women in France after the German Occupation, but absence. Annette Wieviorka's ground-breaking work on the history and memory of the Jewish deportations from France repudiates the idea that Jews themselves were unable to articulate their experiences, and identifies instead a historiographically manufactured silence that ignored the relatively large number of testimonies published immediately after the war, and again in a second flurry of publishing activity later on.[6] As she unpicks the processes by which survivor testimony in the public domain became forgotten, she pinpoints a projection of French history's own shame and terror onto an inability of survivors themselves to "express the inexpressible," and locates its abstention from consideration of either the enormity or the particularities of the French case. But if Holocaust historians are "guardians of an absent meaning,"[7] then French historiography's suppressive efforts have helped create a distorted meaning of "absence." Few are still more absent than the Jewish women, even among those writers whose main concern is to extract, not meaning from the incomprehensible, but the workings of the detail amid the terrible mass. As a historical undertaking, then, this exploration of Jewish women's reinsertion into French society after Liberation is curious and not a little frustrating. Sources are scattered, sparse, and, given French State secrecy, sometimes forbidden. Absences—material, discursive, and philosophical—proliferate: the tantamount absence from primary material of these subjects as anything other than distorted referents; the physical absence of about 78,000 Jews living in France before the Occupation;[8] the centralization in official texts of a group that had become known as "the absent"; and, for many of those who lived through it, the absence of meaning of the whole murderous project.[9]

The sheer quantity of people moving across France from the time the Liberation began in the summer of 1944,[10] to the return of prisoners of war, deportees, and forced laborers a year later, cannot be underestimated.[11] Not only those who had been taken from France and had survived on their way back, but the hundreds of thousands of internal refugees who had fled the north to the south and from cities to the country, and those whose homes had been bombed were trying to return home. Among these were the three-quarters of the prewar Jewish population of France who had evaded arrest and deportation. It was a restoration that combined a renewed sense of republican national pride and liberty with frustrations over governmental disorganization and fears that Vichy administrators would slip seamlessly from working for one regime to the next. The winter of 1944–45 was harsh, rail transport and industrial production were at a virtual standstill, and the privations, daily power cuts, and severe food shortages made life, especially for women, arduous.[12] The exultant promises of Liberation were very much tempered by its stark and sometimes violent realization.

The return of the deportees was much heralded—but precisely who was signified by the term needs clarification. In English, fifty years after the events, "deportee" tends to refer first to Jews who had been taken to killing centers in eastern Europe and, second, to resisters taken to concentration camps located mainly in Germany.[13] During the Occupation of France, the term "déporté-e" referred overwhelmingly to those forced to work in Germany under the compulsory labor scheme, the Service du Travail Obligatoire.[14] Resistance and Jewish deportees were categorized as "political" and "racial" and, early on in the repatriation process, returning Jews were subjected to a humiliating echo of the racialization that had removed them in the first place, as their new identity cards were stamped, no longer with a "J," but with a large red "R."[15] The arrival of the first trainload of 280 non-Jewish women inmates from Ravensbrück in Paris on April 12, 1945, to an official welcome at the Gare de Lyon from General de Gaulle was widely reported (although President Roosevelt's death the same day rather eclipsed its journalistic weight). Suzanne Birnbaum, who had been deported to Auschwitz, disembarked from a plane to the sound of the Marseillaise,[16] yet such a welcome was rare for most Jewish women. The 740 weak and sick women survivors returned in ones and twos, via circuitous journeys often lasting for months, such as the two Sonderkommandos (Jews whose job it was to sort through and burn the corpses after gassing) interviewed in Cairo.[17] The enormous if conflicted efforts to repatriate French nationals from Germany made by the Ministry of Prisoners, Deportees and Refugees, headed by Resistance hero Henri Frenay— flying them home, providing printed and broadcast information, and so forth—simply did not apply to the Jewish deportees; once in France, they had to rely on contacts within the Jewish community.[18] Anecdotal evidence seems to suggest that just as it was immigrant, as opposed to French, Jews who tended to join Jewish Resistance organizations, so it was "foreign" Jews who responded to calls for housing and short-term care on the return of foreign deportees.[19]

At this point, the historiographical and cultural absence of the Jewish deportee, started during clandestine times,[20] gains cultural value, irresistibly tied to unificatory impulses in which difference is sidelined in favor of an imagined national unity. After Liberation, those who had died bravely for their country were memorialized, as opposed to those Jews who had been removed for a less worthy reason, which was described either as racial or religious. The particularities of post-Holocaust history in France are dependent on the fact that three-quarters of the prewar Jewish population of France had survived. However, two-thirds of the deportees had been of non-French origin, not including those who had had their French nationality stripped under the Vichy statute of July 22, 1940. Thus, more Polish than French nationals were deported.[21] Differences of class and national origin between the so-called "foreign" and *vieille souche* Jews (those whose families had been in France for a number of generations), while challenged by resisters,[22] endured both during and after the Occupation. The roots that had helped *vieille souche* Jews find, and pay for, hiding places persisted. Nonetheless, this relationship underwent certain adjustments after the shock of discovery of the Holocaust, about six months after the Liberation of Paris.

LIBERATION AS PROPITIATION

> That day, for the first time in four years, we were finally like other people, we could taunt the police with our false papers, burn our stars or tidy them away in a drawer, we could shout our names, say who we were over the telephone, in restaurants, we were no longer those "foreigners," those tourists, those clandestines who tiptoed through the city of our birth, or those escapees from prison, tracked from shelter to shelter, from attic to attic. We were returned to our deepest identity, to society, to France... to the war. . . . Everything was simple like before, intoxicating with ease, with dangers reconquered, with a common destiny. We plunged into a deep and divine sameness. We were *reconciled*.[23]

Jacqueline Mesnil-Amar's celebration of Liberation offers an image of uncompromised reinsertion into French society, with "France" becoming a virtual synonym for "life." Born into a wealthy Paris banking family, she spent the Occupation in hiding in Paris and, toward the end, began to write a diary.[24] Her book, published a decade later, is in two parts: the first contains the diary, while the second reprints a number of articles published between 1944 and 1946 in the monthly newsletter of the Central Service of Israelite Deportees, a Jewish deportees' tracing service that she helped set up. The need for secrecy gives the diary more space for reflection since accounts of resistance activism which she shared with her husband André Amar, leader of the Paris section of the Zionist resistance organization, the Armée Juive, would have been dangerous.[25] Thus, details of the time spent finding safe addresses for her daughter, her parents, and herself, all housed separately, adjoin musings on her firm identity as a French Jewish woman.[26] However, this textual presentation of herself as inactive in a recognizably resistance sense connives with the preponderant vision at the time of women, and also Jews, as passive nonresisters.[27] Clues to her class allegiance are legion; it remains apparently unpunctured by her changed circumstances. Her greatest admiration, apart from that for Nana in whose house she lives, is for the effortless combination of activism and chic on the part of Suzanne S. On 23 August 1944, Jacqueline finds Suzanne S. getting ready to participate in the Paris uprising (August 19 through 25):

> Suzanne wants to come down to the street with me and calls her young maid. . . . "Get out that nasty little suit for me," she shouts. A tailor-made suit for insurrection! The lovely ladies have put away their good clothes. No more hats. It's the time of the *sans-culottes* and the *tricoteuses*.[28]

A fortnight earlier, Mesnil-Amar had been sitting in the Tuileries gardens with her friend Mme L., a prisoner-of-war wife, from whom she has kept secret her Jewishness. They share the pain of an absent husband, since André has now been arrested with other members of his network. The layering of separation and connections is nonetheless grounded in a sureness represented by Mesnil-Amar's love of France:

> My city Paris, such a show, such a vision of France so subtle and secret. Surely in the thick shadows of your prison, dear absent, wherever you are, wherever your heart beats, surely certain faces of those you have loved return around you, and certain features of your Paris haunt and reassure you. This tapestry of stones and foliage which is France . . . soil charged with faith and scepticism, with defeats and victories, with blood and freedom, crossroads of so many ideas, struggles, and these houses, these streets, these woods, deepening through the centuries. . . . And I look at this woman sitting, estranged and familiar to me, rooted so deeply in this soil through the past and the future, and beside her I feel shifting and transitory, coming from far yonder through the centuries, with another secret face which is also

me, and I come from "elsewhere," I don't know where, from nowhere, and despite myself I am also sister to all these children of Israel whom I don't know, the foreigners, the unknown, the hunted, the lost, my companions in misery, pursued and targeted like me by our Fate, our misunderstood God.

And yet, in this torment which shakes Europe, in this corner of Paris, in this garden, this evening like so many other evenings, like thousands of other women without news, Mme L and I wait, we wait.[29]

France is envisaged as a living dialectic, its whole a sum of its contrasts. The femininity shared with Mme L. as waiting wives is allied to a mythic and tenuous connection to a mysterious Jewishness. Her "othering" of the Jewish people, including herself, who are not from "nowhere" but mainly from eastern and central Europe, is typical of the *vieille souche* Jew and can be recognized in the reactions of German Jews to the so-called *Ostjuden* (Jews from eastern Europe), of Ashkenazim (Jews of European origin) to Maghrebian Jews, of the economically stable to the poor newcomer. In Mesnil-Amar's case, a romanticized distancing adjoins the longing she feels for her reentrance into a life that is currently hidden from her. For all the nostalgia, she appears not severed from her beloved country—indeed, she stresses its enduring antiquity in the material aspects of Paris she sees around her; she is not lost, but in attendance for change.

But "we were *reconciled*"? Scarcely. The most striking aspect of the book's second section in comparison with the first is its profound *lack* of reconciliation. The diary's yearning and loss, with its hymns to Paris and high French culture, are replaced by a deep sense of betrayal by her adored France. This dislocation has multiple roots: first, a difference in genre, in the change from writing a secret diary to purposeful journalism; second, a widening of the audience since that for a diary might be conceived far from that for the articles; and third, knowledge of the Holocaust itself, news of which broke a few months after the launch of her newsletter, the *Bulletin du Service Central des Déportés Israélites*. But perhaps the most crucial difference is in her discursive transformation from onlooker and passerby to political engagement she can claim as her own. While inextricably bound up in the terror of the Occupation, she nonetheless had the economic and social resources to survive, knowing the right people and having the wherewithal to pay them. Even the notion of tourism, expressed in her liberationist celebration, implies that her absence is temporary and will be reversed by an eventual return home. This vision is in contrast to the one she provides of immigrant Jews, her sympathy for their fate and admiration for their combatants who made up the majority of the Jewish Resistance[30] tempered by a residual superiority:

These people even more alone than us, and poorer too! Sometimes, such easy victims, innocent and pathetic prey, offered up to the torturers, sometimes combative in the extreme, like these young Jews, the OJC comrades. Young heroes . . . whom no-one helped apart from chance neighbors or the concierge who had no contacts with state representatives or ministers or mayors—nor anyone in the world! And, let's admit, scarcely even with French Jews! Sometimes they were bitter toward a certain France which they loved, to which they had come with their parents and which abandoned them. I like them just as they are, even badly brought up, quibbling, difficult, quick-tempered and fanciful, but often kind-hearted, generous, intelligent and who threw themselves completely into the clandestine war . . . with their dark eyes, their fiery complexion, their foreign accents, their imprudent words, their over-French "noms de guerre" and their vengeance.[31]

No such disdainful typology is present in the journalistic pieces which, on the contrary, are fueled by an anger that Jewish unity remain fractured and splintered and that Jewish losses be smothered by French victoriousness. Here, despite her activism in the Jewish Resistance, and despite the threat posed to those dear to her, the crucial division between French and foreign Jew remains real and enduring. National, class, and cultural differences of resisters in the Organisation Juive de Combat (OJC) are perhaps more marked than any unifactory notions of their cohesion by Jewishness or politics.

UNIVERSALISM OF SUFFERING

Such a vision is in contrast to the pervading force in national liberationist politics by which the rediscovery of patriotic fervor would underlie a solid coalition. One of the instruments of this tendency was the suffering that, allegedly, all French had felt equally and that allowed a cleansed and purified citizen to emerge:

> In the German [prisoner of war] camps, beyond all social horizons, beyond all political opinion and religious quarrels, united by misery and suffering we had rediscovered unity, we had discovered struggle and resistance for ourselves, and rediscovered patriotism.[32]

Despite the absence of prisoners of war from the resistance theater of war and hence from the activism to which so much value accrued in these months of liberation, the delegate Jean Dechartre claims the development of resistance via the universal suffering of each man in the camp. The Christian urge to find redemptive meaning in tragic suffering is particularly strong at this time. The restoration of the Republic—and with it, its incorporationist tendencies of enlightenment universalism—is characterized by the merging of the republican figurehead

Marianne into the Catholic Mary. As the suffering of Jesus on the cross gives essential meaning to Christianity, so the suffering of the French under Nazism translated to give new impetus to the renewal and rebirth of their nation, and reworkings of traditional Catholic imagery proliferate at this time, from the sacred heart of Raymond Gid's red, white, and blue poster to welcome the absent, "Return to France, Return to Life,"[33] to Georges Rouault's sombre antiwar series, the *Miserere*.[34]

This pandemic of universal suffering gave place to a liberal humanist pretension against the existence of discrimination, as those who had been bombed out gained discursive equivalence to the prisoner-of-war wives who had waited for their husbands' return or the Jewish orphans who had lost their parents. The logical consequences of this view found reflection in policy formulation, as efforts were made to ensure that differentiation was not made between one set of sufferers and another. In discussions on legislation to safeguard the future of war orphans, for example, emphasis was laid on not making a special case of the children of foreign deportees, the vast majority of whom would have been Jewish, although they also included a number of Spanish Republicans. During debate on a new law outlining their entitlements, it was decided that children who had had one parent deported "cannot be treated better than prisoners' children whom no organization has taken in charge," and the law would apply therefore only to those deprived of both parents by deportation or one parent deported and the other deceased for other reasons.[35] It would seem from this proposition that a sort of penalty was attached to the achievement of one of the Jewish Resistance's initial tasks, the saving of children. The relative success of this project and the concomitant tragedy of their parents' deportation take place in the establishment of a value-laden notion of suffering whereby greater worth accrued for greater resistance effort. And yet it was precisely among those who might be expected to lay greater claim to suffering, immigrant resistance Jews, that we find a relinquishment of their position in the hierarchy of suffering. Jeanne Pakin was a regular contributor to *Droit et Liberté*, the antiracist Jewish weekly that was the official voice of the Communist-affiliated Jewish Resistance and Welfare Union (UJRE), whose readership was largely the politicized, often immigrant Jew. She had fought in the Jewish Communist Resistance in Paris throughout the Occupation,[36] and was a member of the executive committee of the Union of Jewish Women. She wrote:

> In comparison to other central and eastern European countries, the Jewish community in France escaped the large Nazi massacres relatively lightly. Consequently, it will be called upon to play an important role in the

renaissance of Jewish life in Europe. Certainly, we have suffered cruelly with our 120,000 deportees. But, thanks to the active solidarity of the French people, we were able to save a great number of our children, destined for destruction by the Hitlerites.[37]

In posing the inverse of "worth through suffering," Jeanne Pakin argues for a certain predominance in a Jewish European future, and yet her reflections point up with clarity the overladen sense of pain elsewhere by its refusal in a Jewish context.

Jeanne Pakin was not the only one to oppose the dominance of suffering and redemption. General de Gaulle's V-E Day victory speech stressed the utterly worthwhile sacrifice toward the universal national good that had been made by all the French: "Not a single effort by her [France's] soldiers, her sailors, her aviators, not an act of courage or self-effacement by her sons and daughters, no suffering by her men and women prisoners, no mourning, no sacrifice, not a tear will have been lost!"[38] Under Mesnil-Amar's pen, her repeated (if misquoted) "no mourning, not a tear in vain" becomes a dissident response to de Gaulle's victorious litany. By incorporating unremarked the mass of lost Jewish life, the fact of this awkward waste becomes overridden and removed from national glory. Her emphatic, and certainly sentimental, connection to a France she sees as entirely hers is now accompanied by a feeling of attachment to foreign Jews, united by virtue of their fatal connection under Nazi policy.

I have to say that on this fabulous night we Jews of France march in France's joy, with more ghosts at our side than anyone else. . . . they arrived on the platform at Auschwitz station where the SS, helped by their doctors, screamed so methodically the call to death. . . . *All the children* in lorries, so many children, massacred because they could not work, thrown in the ovens with their mothers because they wouldn't leave them. . . . All this was not in vain? There was some sense in such suffering? Do I understand this evening, General de Gaulle, that France claims as its own not only the misfortune of these French Jews that it can't deny because they belong to it, these French Jews bursting with love for their one and only homeland, of whom we know exactly which hymn they sang as they left, with which shout they died, but the misfortunes of the *others*, of those who weren't French? These people to whom France gave asylum and took to its land, whom they rounded up via "summonses" and "passport checks" and held for months in Vichy camps, then knowingly handed them over to the Germans for a fate they knew precisely, these foreigners of whom so many had lost their sons for France, and these poor foreign prisoners in the French army who return now and find no one, neither wife nor children, taken alas by our French policemen? General de Gaulle, your speech goes far tonight. Do I take it that none of this suffering will be disowned, even the most repellent, the most distant, the most foreign, and must I believe that your "Vive la France" includes all these dead?[39]

These are hardly the words of someone who feels reconciled; the less-than-conscious "othering" within the diary is now exposed by her newfound necessity to act on behalf of those who had lost out on help to save them during the deportations. Mesnil-Amar's angry mobilization of these absent dead, figuratively waving them under de Gaulle's nose as she had joyfully proposed doing with the false papers of the living at Liberation, repositions them back into territory from which they would physically be forever gone.

MOTHERHOOD: THE AMBIVALENT PRESENCE

If the absent dead were either mourned or effaced from national memory, their inheritors were the children, and by extension, the mothers. Within the atmosphere of maternity and enthusiastic natalism, which characterized Liberation France, the unease provoked by the Jewish orphan is worthy of exploration. Motherhood, argues Claire Duchen, was the salient feature of all public discourse on women after Liberation. Regardless of her actual social position, "woman-as-mother was . . . the image that the new provisional government wanted to promote in the new France";[40] this discourse extended way beyond the government, and things were no different where the Jewish woman was concerned. But whereas the "French" mother could trace her valorization from before the Occupation, via Vichy's slogan, "Work, Family, Fatherland," to the dutiful reproducer of the nation's future in the postwar period, the Jewish mother had been vilified in antisemitic literature as the producer of monsters, an oversexualized figure in the great Jewish conspiracy.[41]

At the moment of Liberation, France was scarcely haunted by what it had done to the Jews, responsibility being attached (if mentioned) to the occupying forces. The one exception to this might be a sense of indignant shame for the "Vel d'Hiv" round-up of July 16–17, 1942, largely contingent on the fact that, for the first time, women and children had been arrested, and children separated from their mothers.[42] Now, postwar, children became literally incorporated into the national drive for rebirth and were claimed as much by the nation as by the individual mother. But with the loss of so many children and parents, the restoration of the family after Liberation took on a very different aspect for Jewish families.

In order to solve the problem of the orphaned children of deported parents, legislation was drafted to ease the adoption process—and, to convince waverers, the proposition buttressed its arguments with moral suggestions, that adoption could also help in the "fight against abortion" and "to transform those homes without children into complete and normal families."[43] Mindful of prevailing psychological belief, it was explicitly drafted to avoid future "unpredictable consequences" that would result from adopted children finding that their new parents were not their biological ones, and so demanded that information regarding their biological parentage never be given to such children. The relative unimportance placed on the original, probably Jewish, mother clarifies for us the image of the child as national, rather than personal, bounty and the Jewish mother as discursively dispensable. The resolution was undoubtedly proposed in the progressive interests of children, and the urgent need for suitable homes for so many even made it feasible to consider single and divorced people as suitable adoptive parents, though during the parliamentary debate, Lucie Aubrac, the proposition's main mover, underlined that virtually all Jewish and Spanish Republican children had been hidden in families that had children and were thus already "complete and normal."[44] Many of the children in question were old enough to remember their mothers, as Alexis Danan brought home to readers of the formerly clandestine newspaper *Libération* in "The War against Children," a series carried daily for two and one-half weeks between December 18, 1944, and January 3, 1945. It was by no means common for the press to devote itself to a single subject over such a considerable period; like much of the press, *Libération* was a single sheet, although it was still broadsheet before even tighter paper restrictions in the spring of 1945 forced almost all newspapers, amid much protest, to reduce their size still further.[45]

The condemnation of the removal and murder of little Jewish children is self-evident and often moving in "The War against Children," written by a socialist journalist and novelist who had launched a major campaign in the 1930s to improve conditions affecting underprivileged children.[46] Equally, he exposed French culpability in carrying out such acts of brutality.[47] And yet the terms in which the relationship of Jewish victim to the French—either resister or collaborator—is framed are not a matter of mere dichotomy. Danan explores the French aspect of the European Jewish catastrophe in a lengthy, populist series, at a time when other writers concentrated exclusively on the suffering of French political deportees and prisoners of war. At the same time, he presents his case in familiar narratives of passivity and hopelessness. The early and continual resistance efforts of the caring professions—and by implication, women—is the subject of the eighth article in the series.

Danan's inclusive definition of resistance is noteworthy at a time when few commentators acknowledged that the types of oppositional effort open to the majority of women, such as hiding children, were indeed resistance. (Such efforts were seen more in terms of duty, in opposition to the value given to the armed struggle, in which far fewer women participated.)[48] Yet, for all his empathy with the dreadful fate of these children, his seeming failure to underline the fact that the hiding of Jewish children was organized largely by Jews operates within an established tension between the good French (female) carer and the passive Jewish mother.

The series is colored by the enduring social expectation that the mother keeps continual and all-knowing watch over her home and children, even in the face of power difficult for her to counteract or predict. These mothers are essentially passive (that is, not resistant), who watched in agony as their children were torn from them, or were sought out by caring doctors, social workers, or teachers to allow their children to be hidden. No reference is made to those who actively sought safe places for their children despite the implications of possibly permanent separation. Similarly, the pathos of the story is emphasized by accentuation of one child's passivity and ignorance, who, aged five when taken into hiding, didn't know how many brothers or sisters he had and couldn't even remember his name:

> He was five when a Protestant organization collected him. Impossible to know anything about him. He doesn't even know how many brothers and sisters he had. As far as his name goes, he only had some idea since being sent to school. In any case, the name made him laugh because it sounded foreign. He thought it was a trick. "I'm called Raymond, just Raymond," he said to his classmates.[49]

Compare this with *Droit et Liberté*'s treatment of the same subject. Presented in an active rather than passive mode, this little girl knows, even at the age of two and one-half, that her new, non-Jewish name is the only one to be uttered in public:

> She still knew her real name. Because Micou is her *nom de combat*. Yes, Micou is a draft evader [*réfractaire*]. She doesn't want to let herself be taken by the Huns. Micou defended herself, she changed her name and went to find a refuge at Auntie Julie's, who welcomed her with wide open arms. And once when her mummy called her real name by mistake, Micou, with her plump little finger against her lips, told her mysteriously with big round eyes, "Don't say that any more, Mummy. I'm called Micou." Yes, at two and a half, Micou understood conspiracy, applied the laws of vigilance and even taught her mother.[50]

Real-life cases could probably be found for both examples. The two narratives, however, show *Droit et Liberté*'s exposition of consciousness, the individual's ability to resist and the deliberate, careful, and even, perhaps, in the face of impossible circumstances, chosen separation of mother from her child, set against Danan's applause for an organized Resistance that found itself faced with individual ignorance and stubbornness. Just as a valorization of resistance, increasingly desperate formulations of unity, and the association of France and Frenchness with the Resistance are the universalizing banners flown during the Liberation, so passivity becomes a form of almost voluntaristic exclusion from the true French body.

Danan's conclusions in one article provoked outrage, and angry ripostes appeared in the *Bulletin du Service Central des Déportés Israélites* and the Zionist journal *La Terre Retrouvée*. In an open letter published three days before the death marches were to start from Auschwitz, and less than a fortnight before the liberation of that camp, the *Bulletin* condemned his call that the hidden children of deported parents remain with their hiders even in the event of their parents' return.[51] As we have seen, the future of hidden children was a subject of considerable discussion, and Danan was not alone in suggesting that the reunification of child and parent would not necessarily be automatic. For example, in government discussion on what to do with the "semiassimilated" children of foreign deportees, it was felt that to squander their talents and potential would be a pity, even though their full assimilation might be costly and demanding. Until it was pointed out that perhaps it would be better to wait until the possible return of their parents, it had been suggested that they be sent abroad.[52] Of a four-year-old child who is the only one of a family of ten not to be deported, Danan writes:

> If his mother returns from the dead one day, what will she be to her son? And what will he be to her? It seems that they gave him to some kind country priest. . . . Who would say that this child, if his parents ever return, belongs more to these survivors via some theoretical blood rights or legal status than to the farmers who for over four years nourished him with their bread and their tenderness exactly like their own and with their own? . . . Something cruel must be said . . . these children if they still dream of a mother whom they idealize . . . in reality don't really want to find her, and at the bottom of their hearts the most lucid clearly wish on the contrary never to find her again. The new milieu has absorbed them without return.[53]

In a certain sense, he appears to suggest, by being deported, parents had rescinded their right to overall care of their children. The question of Danan's irony is moot. His suggestions seem so preposterous in this article, apostrophically addressed to deported Jews—"We can count on your wisdom. You won't come back. . . . If you are not dead, your children are dead to you. Everything is consumed,"—that we cannot but read them as hyperbolic incitement to readers' outrage. But the irony was lost in certain quarters. The Central Service of Israelite Deportees' opening complaint was with regard to the severing of links between children and their deported parents, which had "scandalized and disgusted" them and "seemed completely unnatural." Rachel Cheigam, writing in *La Terre Retrouvée*, gave him the benefit of the doubt, fearing that "his words had betrayed his thoughts." However, she responded to his suggestion that Jewish children would not wish to see their parents in such a distressed condition, "ugly, shadowy, dramatically foreign to the world of the living," by asking whether Christian children of those deported as resisters would equally "prefer" to be separated eternally from their parents. Equally, she pointed up the unsocialist element in his piece by refuting the notion that even worker parents would not wish to relinquish their children, even in the case that those currently caring for them could offer them greater financial security.[54] Beneath the complaints, though, there lies a sense that Danan had betrayed their hope, as Jews, of the return of the deportees—a hope that by this time was becoming more and more slim. Danan's brutal honesty, therefore, acted as a profound disturbance of the impossible fantasy of an eventual restoration of prewar life; but it was further colored by his differentiation in value placed on the French non-Jew and the Jew in France, and thereby carried profound implications for women.

COMING HOME

The uncertainty implicit in the demand for Jewish women to mother is further underscored when it comes to their place in the home, and even the very right to a home. The tensions described above are multiplied with the explicit return of the absent body, as Jews came back to Paris to reclaim their homes, now mainly emptied of all their belongings. In his excellent critical deconstruction of the universalism of French republicanism, Max Silverman's insistence on the modern overweening preponderance of national identity above all other forms of identification is perhaps more pertinent to only half the population—the same half encompassed by the so-called universalist tendencies of Enlightenment thought that he describes.[55] For while underlining the racial and national exclusivity of this universalism, so central to the

Declaration of the Rights of Man's right to citizenship, Silverman fails to comment on its gendered element.[56] The relationship of women to the requirement that identification with the national community "supersede all other forms of identification in the modern era"[57] is far more fissured and temporary, and that of Jewish women perhaps even more so, given traditional suspicions regarding Jews' supposed inability to identify with the nation-state. For women, we find an equally strong obligation that they identify with the home and family. There is nothing straightforward about such identificatory tugs. Under Vichy, the requirement that women stay in the home was made in the name of duty both to the nation and to the family. Jewish women were beyond the national body, nonnational—neither really foreign nor French, but Jews, betrayers of the nation by their ability to give birth to Jewish boys.[58] After Liberation, women were once again expected to identify with the home—and yet, newly enfranchised and conscious that citizenship demanded duty as well as conferring rights, also called to honor their nation. The conflicted and multiple identificatory demands placed on them indicate the uncertainty surrounding their place in national reconstruction and ambivalence about their public place.

But the Jewish home—and any easy assumptions about the nuclear family often in tatters—had been the site not of admirable resistance, but of terror, flight, and abandonment. The first law concerning the restoration of property, October 11, 1944, stipulated that the occupier had to have been forcibly removed; fleeing for one's life was not regarded as worthy or as making a recognizable or significant resistance contribution. Even though the law was soon, but only slightly, modified (January 9, 1945) after vociferous protest, its successful passage through the Provisional Consultative Assembly is indicative of the marginal place the Jewish home occupied in the nation's approbation at a time when the home was a site of literal and metaphorical rebuilding and a great deal of attention as the hundreds of thousands who had been bombed out and non-Jewish internal refugees who had moved to other parts of France were trying to go home.[59] The legislation stipulated that an occupier could regain property on condition that "he had been evicted from his apartment without his consent."[60] It was further confined by the fact that, if the dwelling were occupied by "those housed under emergency conditions, evacuees, refugees" or the "spouses, forebears, children, guardians of mobilized soldiers, prisoners of war, political or labor deportees," these could not be evicted—and as about one person in ten fit these criteria, and despite, as Raymond Sarraute and Jacques Rabinovitch rightly noted, the fact that Jews were also descendants, spouses, and so forth, the majority of cases of reclamation of housing by Jews was paralyzed.[61]

Following the passage of this legislation and after the war's end, organized antisemites in Paris took the opportunity of Jewish attempts to reclaim "Aryanized" property to stage a number of violent protests. Demonstrations of up to 600 people outside town halls were frequent during spring 1945, according to newspaper reports, and the police apparently did nothing to stop them.[62] These unrepentant Pétainists went under the names variously of the "Tenants of Good Faith" or the "Renaissance of the French Home," the former taking their title from the clause in the October 11 law that anyone occupying in good faith apartments that had been evacuated under constraint of the German authorities could not be evicted.[63] In addition, a poster campaign in the Marais and Belleville areas of Paris, both with a high density of Jewish population, was accompanied by street demonstrations with the aim of preventing former owners gaining admittance to their homes. In the name of resistance martyrdom and suffering, though roundly and publicly condemned by recognized resistance organizations,[64] calls to rid France once and for all of its Jewish presence helped mobilize angry crowds such as the one outside 184 rue de Belleville (a poor working-class, left-wing, largely immigrant district) at the end of May 1945.[65] The former occupier, Fanny Lustman, who had immigrated from Poland to Paris in 1930, returned in October 1944 from Lyon, where she had fled the previous year to avoid the roundups.[66] Seven months later, at the end of a day during which the police finally served an eviction notice on the current occupant, a Mlle Bruno, who had steadfastly refused to leave (despite still being the tenant of another property elsewhere in Paris), a number of men entered the flat and threw all the original owner's furniture and clothing from the window into the street, where it was burned. Some weeks later, when a report was filed with the pressure group Amitié Judéo-Chrétienne, Mme Lustman had still not dared return.[67] The Antiracist Alliance engaged in combating these demonstrations by mounting an oppositional poster campaign in Paris and the provinces.[68] During the following year, the right-wing Republican Union of the French Family held a number of public meetings in Paris.[69] They continued to complain of foreign Jews taking their property and more particularly their business and were not reticent in their "violent" xenophobia and antisemitism.[70] Among their demands was that the changing of foreign names be outlawed and that shopkeepers be obliged to write their full name on the door to their premises.[71]

The Union of Jewish Women also took up the cases of many women who were unable to reenter their accommodation, pointing out that efforts to reconstruct a dignified life were especially hampered by the economic disruption caused by the death of male heads of households or adult sons who had entered the armed Resistance: "For the Jewish woman," they said, "the problem of reconstruction is a particularly thorny one because of many hostile factors."[72] In order to overcome these factors, many widows of deportees demanded professional training, not only, as they said, in traditionally feminine areas of clothing manufacture, but in electrical work, radio manufacture, and metal work, for which they anticipated a great need in the coming years of reconstruction, but there is little evidence that these plans were realized in any substantial way.[73]

Simultaneous with these antisemitic demonstrations at Liberation and again a year later as prisoners of war and deportees returned, France witnessed massive violence when thousands, and quite possibly tens of thousands, of women who had allegedly collaborated with the Germans were stripped and paraded through the streets, with their heads shaved, insulting placards tied round their necks, their bald heads and arms daubed with swastikas.[74] This violent reassertion of masculinity, which many thousands saw and scarcely any tried to prevent, represented in certain ways a national heave back to a normality in which women and men knew their proper place, and the shame of the defeat in 1940 was viciously transferred onto women. The majority of the targeted women were poor, often living alone or with other women. Tracking them down was often the first task of a liberating column; in one case, the men marching into a town split, half of them taking on the last remaining fascist snipers, the others seeking out women in order to strip, shave, and parade them.[75] The simultaneity of these two violent outbursts begs certain questions. Both were heavily nationalist. That against women was carried out by and large by thirteenth-hour resisters—those who had decided a couple of weeks before Liberation that they were resisters after all and who thus made certain claims on the Left. The other ferment was by a reactionary Right that refused to relinquish its belief in Vichy while reclaiming a certain resistance rhetoric. Both sides attacked the easiest victim to hand and both, in the reassertion of their version of "true" republicanism, fell back on just that Vichy rhetoric that had forced women to assume traditional, domestic roles and attempted to void the country of its foreign elements. These violent, nationalistic responses to the social and physical shift of people in 1944–45 throw into sharp relief how very unliberating Liberation was for many.

When alive, the absent parent (now dead) had been welcomed by

France with uncertainty, often interned even before Vichy statutes demanded it,[76] and then deported. Orphaned children, who not only *could* be welcomed into the French family but, in many cases, were already there, having hidden during the Occupation, then became the substitutive emblem of their parents. Arguments about the children's Christianization and assimilation into rural French homes, which focused on the benefits to France or the loss to Jewish communities, symbolize the replacement value discursively loaded onto the child. More awkward, as we have seen, was the returning adult, and it is particularly noteworthy that the antisemitic protests of 1945–46 were organized in the name of the home and the family, a small, inward-looking, protectionist and, above all, gendered, locution. In the long run, for the adult woman, the act of motherhood itself was a more significant marker than nationality, so fulsome was the perceived need for French children who, regardless of the mother's nationality, could be declared French at their birth on French soil.[77] The parent's physical absence, culpability for which French public national discourse was extremely reluctant to admit, was effectively effaced by this focus on new motherhood. Yet those who did remain haunted this discourse, at least in the very early years after Liberation. Finally, in the historiography, it is no accident that the enormous output that has been published on the memory of this period in the last decade is by this inheritor, rather than the witness, generation itself.

NOTES

A number of people have offered very helpful comments on this chapter at various stages. I would particularly like to thank my doctoral supervisor H. R. Kedward as well as Peter Gordon and Reina Lewis. All translations from French are my own.

1. Of seventy-five transports from France, only six were not to Auschwitz-Birkenau, this being the destination of more than 70,000 of the 75,721 Jews deported from France, about a quarter of the prewar Jewish population of France. Serge Klarsfeld, *Le Mémorial de la Déportation des Juifs de France* (Paris: Serge et Beate Klarsfeld, 1978), no page numbers. Klarsfeld's statistics indicate that 31,157 women (41 percent of the total) had been deported, but it is impossible to verify the gender of an additional 3,277 deportees. Figures for the other groups are those generally accepted today; wide variations were used at the time. See Annette Wieviorka, *Déportation et Génocide. Entre la Mémoire et l'Oublie* (Paris: Plon, 1992); Ministère des prisonniers, déportés et réfugiés, *Bilan d'un effort* (Paris, 1945).

2. Events in Paris ranged from Maurice Chevalier at the Casino de Paris to a church service in memory of colonial soldiers who had died in captivity: *Libération*, 23 December 1944.

3. The male head of the household had legal as well as social status. Government efforts to ensure repatriates were welcomed were lavish, though

not always successful. See propaganda material and plans in Ministry of Prisoners, Deportees and Refugees, Archives Nationales (AN) F9 3169. François Cochet, *Les Exclus de la Victoire: histoire des prisonniers de guerre, déportés et STO (1945–1985)* (Paris: SPM, 1992).

4. *Libération*, 26 December 1944.

5. See especially General de Gaulle's speech at the Hôtel de Ville on the day Paris was liberated, 25 August 1944, when he spoke of a "real France, the whole of France, liberated by itself."

6. Annette Wieviorka, "On Testimony," in Geoffrey H. Hartman, ed., *Holocaust Remembrance: The Shapes of Memory* (Oxford: Blackwell, 1994), 24.

7. Maurice Blanchot, *The Writing of the Disaster* (Lincoln: University of Nebraska Press, 1986), cited in Geoffrey H. Hartman, "Introduction: Darkness Visible," in Hartman, *Holocaust Remembrance*.

8. In addition to the more than 75,000 who had been deported, deaths in captivity in France prior to deportation are estimated in the region of 3,000.

9. For the perpetrators, the meaning was abundantly clear: rid the world of Jews. For the inheritors of the history, the scale of the Holocaust and the losses it forced make it often incomprehensible.

10. It took eight months to liberate all French metropolitan territory, from the Normandy landings on June 6, 1944. The east of the country was finally free of German presence and bombardment by both sides in February 1945.

11. On repatriation of organized French nationals in Germany (soldiers, forced laborers, political deportees), see Cochet, *Les Exclus de la Victoire*. Jewish concentration camp survivors waited in some cases for years in Displaced Persons camps—such as the former concentration camp Bergen-Belsen—in Germany before they were granted permission to migrate. Féla Brajtberg-Fajnzylber, *Le Témoignage ordinaire d'une Juive polonaise* (Paris: La Bruyère, 1991). Brajtberg-Fajnzyiber was at Bergen-Belsen between May 1945 and April 1948, before being permitted entry to France.

12. The daily press carried detailed information on changing entitlements to rations. See also, Claire Duchen, *Women's Rights and Women's Lives in France 1944–1968* (London: Routledge, 1994), ch. 1.

13. The difference between killing centers and concentration camps still needs underlining. The former—Auschwitz-Birkenau, Belzec, Chelmno, Lublin-Majdanek, Sobibor, and Treblinka—were the centers where the murder of Jewish, Roma, and Sinti peoples was carried out on an industrial scale. In the far more numerous concentration camps, deportees of numerous categories were forced into slave labor, starved, executed, and mistreated in horrifying ways; they were not, however, murdered *en masse*. The confusion often arises because Auschwitz-Birkenau was both a concentration camp and a killing center. The term is from Raul Hilberg, *The Destruction of the European Jews*, rev. ed. (New York: Holmes and Meier, 1985).

14. These now form one of the most forgotten groups in the history of this period, and their full history has yet to be written. They formed, at best, a very minor part of public commemoration at the fiftieth anniversary. See Karen Adler, "'Un mythe nécessaire et sacré?' Responses to the 50th Anniversary of Liberation," *Modern and Contemporary France* NS3, no. 1 (1995): 119–26.

15. Sylvie Lalario, "Retours en France et réadaptations à la société française de femmes juives déportées" (Master's thesis, University of Paris VII, 1992–93), 123.

16. Suzanne Birnbaum, *Une Française juive est revenue* (Paris: Editions du Livre Français, 1946), 193.

17. *Front National*, 15 March 1945.

18. See Cochet, *Les Exclus de la Victoire*, for details of internal conflicts, inadequate budgets, quarrels with the Allies, etc.

19. See author's interview with Magda Cohen, 7 March 1995, and call for housing in Bulletin du Service Central des Déportés Israélites, 15 April 1945.

20. In my reading of the resistance press aimed at women, it is only the Jewish press, with very few exceptions, that explicitly protests the roundup and deportation of Jews. See Karen Adler, "No Words to Say It? Women and the Expectation of Liberation," in H. R. Kedward and Nancy Wood, eds., *The Liberation of France: Image and Event* (Oxford: Berg, 1995), 77–89.

21. Klarsfeld, *Le Mémorial*.

22. See, for example, *Notre Voix* (September 1942).

23. Jacqueline Mesnil-Amar, *Ceux qui ne dormaient pas. 1944–1946 (Fragments de journal)* (Paris: Editions de Minuit, 1957), 119. Emphasis in original. Ellipses in original are presented with unspaced dots (...); my ellipses are presented with spaced dots (. . .). Mesnil-Amar's extraordinarily long sentences have been retained in translation.

24. She may have written her diary throughout the period; only that of 1944 was later published.

25. The headquarters of this network was in Toulouse. David Knout, *La Résistance Juive en France, 1940–1944* (Paris: Editions du Centre, 1947), 152.

26. At the book's opening, she has lived in Bordeaux and Marseille and at nine Paris addresses.

27. It was only from the late 1970s onward that women's role in the resistance began to be explored. Among the now-extensive literature, see Union des Femmes Françaises, *Les Femmes dans la Résistance* (Paris: Editions du Rocher, 1977); Paula Schwartz, "Redefining Resistance: Women's Activism in Wartime France," in Margaret T. Higonnet et al., eds., *Behind the Lines: Gender and the Two World Wars* (New Haven: Yale University Press, 1987). As an example of the emphatic marginalization at the time, note that only 6 of the 1,059 *Compagnons de la Libération*, the most prestigious resistance medal, went to women, and as Lucie Aubrac pointed out, four of them posthumously. Cited in Claire Gorrara, "Reviewing Gender and the Resistance: The Case of Lucie Aubrac," in Kedward and Wood, *The Liberation of France*, 152.

28. Mesnil-Amar, *Ceux qui ne dormaient pas*, 103. Her parents' response to the uprising shows even more class disdain, using the distancing technique and demonstration of cultured education of foreign language. Her parents were "slightly defiant towards the FFI [soldiers of the Forces Françaises de l'Intérieur] whose revolutionary allure disconcerted them! My father said to me, 'It's a bit "Frente popular" all this! No officers! No uniforms! What times we live in!' My mother found them rather badly brought up, 'very ill bred' [in English in original], these heroes of Paris." Ibid., 95.

29. Ibid., 60–61.

30. The definition of a "Jewish Resistance" has come under considerable debate. For one summary, see Patrick Binisti, "Identité juive et résistance: deux notions distinctes," *Le Monde Juif*, no. 152 (September–December 1994).

31. Mesnil-Amar, *Ceux qui ne dormaient pas*, 104. The OJC was the Zionist resistance organization. Compare Knout's remark that it was Jews of *French* origin who took the least Jewish-sounding wartime pseudonyms, or what he calls "'Aryan' sounding" names. Knout, *La Résistance Juive en France*, 137.

32. Jean Dechartre, debate on Ministry of Prisoners, Deportees and Refugees Budget, *Journal Officiel (JO)*, 6 December 1944, 37.

33. Reproduced in *La France et les Français de la Libération 1944–1945. Vers*

une France nouvelle? (Paris: Musée des Deux Guerres Mondiales/BDIC, 1984), 131.

34. Unseen until 1948, it had been inspired by the First World War and made in 1927. See also Michael Kelly, "Death at the Liberation: The Cultural Articulation of Death and Suffering in France 1944–47," *French Cultural Studies* 5, part 3, no. 15 (October 1994): 227–40.

35. Report of meeting, Sous-Commission: Protection des enfants, 18 December 1944. AN F⁹ 3184.

36. Jeanne Pakin, interview with the author, 16 August 1995.

37. Jeanne Pakin, "Les enfants de nos déportés," *Droit et Liberté*, 24 March 1945.

38. Radio speech, 8 May 1945, reprinted in Charles de Gaulle, *Discours et Messages, 1940–1946* (Paris: Berger-Levrault, 1946), 591.

39. Mesnil-Amar, *Ceux qui ne dormaient pas*, 139–41. Emphases in original.

40. Duchen, *Women's Rights*, 28–29.

41. See, for example, *Je suis partout*, 27 July 1942. I am grateful to Penelope Hamm for this reference.

42. Over 12,000 foreign and stateless Jews in Paris were rounded up by French police and held for up to five days in the stifling July heat with inadequate food and water in the Vélodrome d'Hiver cycle stadium before being sent to French camps prior to deportation. The fate of the more than 4,000 children rounded up was the subject of Berlin-Vichy discussions, and initial German reluctance to take the children was eventually overcome by French insistence. Not one of the children returned. The outcry caused by this roundup at the time was certainly not confined to Jewish expression. Michael R. Marrus and Robert O. Paxton, *Vichy France and the Jews* (New York: Basic Books, 1981), 263, 270–79.

43. Proposition of Resolution no. 327, 21 February 1945, *JO*, Documents de l'Assemblée Consultative Provisoire, 1944–45, 422–23. (Twelve women delegates presented this proposition. Since this Parliament sat before any elections, its members were delegated by various resistance and official organizations; many of them were to stand to become deputees in the first elected Parliament in October 1945.)

44. *JO*, 31 July 1945, 1669. The proposition was passed into law without amendment or discussion.

45. See "Emergency Parliamentary Debate on Suspected Sabotage of Paper Supplies by Former Collaborators," *JO*, 9 March 1945. *Libération*'s print run at this time was about 180,000. See Henri Amouroux, *La Grande Histoire des Français après l'Occupation*, vol. 9, *Les Reglements des comptes, septembre 1944–janvier 1945* (Paris: Robert Laffont, 1991), 322. As a comparison, the daily with the largest print run, 326,000, was the Communist paper, *l'Humanité*.

46. The campaign was supported by Suzanne Lacore, under secretary of state for children in the Popular Front. Alexis Danan had published a fictional treatment of the social problems facing mothers in poverty, *Maternité* (Paris: Albin Michel, 1936), and would become founding editor of *Les Cahiers d'Enfance* in 1953. Nearly 2,000 deportees were under six years old and more than 6,000 under thirteen (8.5 percent of the total): Klarsfeld, *Le Mémorial*.

47. Alexis Danan, "Escalier C, 5e étage," *Libération*, 18 December 1944.

48. Alexis Danan, "Les Alliés clandestins," *Libération*, 27 December 1944.

49. Alexis Danan, "Les vivants mêmes sont morts," *Libération*, 30 December 1944. Georges Wellers notes that very young children in Drancy sometimes didn't know their own names: *De Drancy à Auschwitz* (Paris 1946) in Marrus and Paxton, *Vichy France and the Jews*, 264.

50. "Comment Micou a eu sa trottinette," *Droit et Liberté*, November 1944. The story ends with the survival of mother and daughter; Micou gets a scooter as a present, which she names "Liberation" and decorates with a tricolor ribbon.

51. *Bulletin du Service Central des Déportés Israélites*, 15 January 1945, 3. The transfer of inmates westward, often on foot, began on 17 and 18 January 1945; Soviet troops entered Auschwitz on 27 January 1945.

52. Commission consultative pour l'étude des questions familiales et de la protection des enfants de prisonniers, déportés et réfugiés, 25 October 1944. AN F⁹ 3184.

53. Alexis Danan, "Les vivants mêmes sont morts."

54. *La Terre Retrouvée*, 1 February 1945.

55. Max Silverman, *Deconstructing the Nation: Immigration, Racism and Citizenship in Modern France* (London: Routledge, 1992).

56. It scarcely needs underlining that the vote was denied women from the Revolution in 1789 to almost the end of the Second World War, April 1944, and exercised for the first time in October 1945. France was one of the last western nations to grant women the franchise.

57. Silverman, *Deconstructing the Nation*, 32.

58. The conspiracies feared by antisemites were regarded as the responsibility of Jewish men more than women; thus, women's role is tangential via her reproductive abilities, and Jewish girl babies become less of an obvious threat. See also note 41.

59. The housing crisis was enormous: 1,229,000 housing buildings had been destroyed or damaged during the war (more than half between June 1944 and June 1945). Danièle Voldman, ed., "Images, Discours et Enjeux de la Reconstruction des Villes françaises après 1945," *Cahiers de l'IHTP*, no. 5 (June 1987): 157.

60. Quoted in Raymond Sarraute and Jacques Rabinovitch, *Examen Succinct de la Situation actuelle juridique des Juifs* (Paris: Centre de Documentation des Déportés et Spoliés Juifs, 1945), 19.

61. Ibid., 17.

62. See *Droit et Liberté*; *Franc-Tireur* and *France-Soir*, April– July 1945.

63. Law quoted in Frédérique Boucher, "Abriter vaille que vaille, se loger coûte que coûte," in Danièle Voldman, ed., *Cahiers de l'IHTP*, no. 5 (June 1987): 129.

64. See copies of posters from the spring and summer of 1945 in AN 72AJ 598. I am grateful to Simon Kitson for drawing this material to my attention.

65. Antisemitic vitriol was equally hurled in the direction of the media and government, supposedly in the grip of Jews. One letter-writing campaign declared itself loyal to de Gaulle and France in the name of "the True French Resistance" and wanted France rid of the "Hun" as much as the Jews. See AN F9 3137.

66. See newspaper report in *L'Aurore*, 1 June 1945, though it gives the house as number 182 and the dispute as between Mme Lundmann and Mlle Brueau.

67. "Enquête sur l'incident," 18 June 1945, in Papiers Vanino: AN 72 AJ 598.

68. Alliance antiraciste, "Congrès national 21–22 juin 1947" (Paris: Alliance Antiraciste, 1947), 3.

69. The public was, however, limited to those who could prove at the door that they were not foreigners, according to a report in the antiracist journal *Au Devant de la Vie*, no. 2 (November 1945).

70. See police report to Ministre de l'Intérieur of the meeting held 10 October 1946 by Union Républicaine des Familles in AN F¹A 3355.

71. See unsigned report, "Union républicaine des familles françaises: compte rendu de la grande réunion d'information . . . , Salle Wagram, 3 October 1945," in Bibliothèque de Documentation Internationale Contemporaine (BDIC). This claims support for the organization from, among others, the deputy Marthe Richard.

72. "Les femmes veulent vivre!" *Droit et Liberté*, 10 April 1945.

73. *Droit et Liberté*, 27 April 1945. On the contrary, the major Jewish training establishment, ORT (Organisation-Reconstruction-Travail) set up special courses for returning women deportees and wives of deportees in the traditionally female and Jewish area of garment manufacture. Eric Schieber, *Un An de Reconstruction Juive en France* (Paris: ORT, 1946), 6.

74. See Alain Brossat, *Les Tondues: Un carnaval moche* (Levallois-Perret: Manya, 1992).

75. Fabrice Virgili, "Les Femmes tondues," unpublished paper, IHTP, Paris, 6 March 1995.

76. The draconian law passed by Daladier's government on 12 November 1938 provided for special "centers" to be established for the surveillance of undesirable foreigners. Quoted in Marrus and Paxton, *Vichy France and the Jews*, 57.

77. See Code de la Nationalité, 19 October and 2 November 1945.

11

Men, Women, and the Community Borders

German-Nationalist and National
Socialist Discourses on Gender,
"Race," and National Identity in
Austria, 1918–1938

JOHANNA GEHMACHER

COMPARISONS AND CONNECTION

As a motto for his book *Nations and Nationalisms,* Ernest Gellner borrows the words of George Santayana alluding to gender relations: "Our nationality is like our relations to women: too implicated in our moral nature to be changed honourably, and too accidental to be worth changing."[1] Such comments are contemptuous. Women are not only treated with disrespect by these words, they are by definition excluded from the chummy "we" having a nationality. And yet there is some irritating plausibility in that sentence that becomes more comprehensible if one considers a similar comparison proposed by Benedict Anderson. More cautiously, he states that "in the modern world everyone can, should, will 'have' a nationality as he or she 'has' a gender."[2] You could, of course, object that, from the viewpoint of recent feminist theories, the certainty of "having" a gender cannot so easily be accepted.[3] This assumption becomes clear, however, if you apply Anderson's extensions concerning nationality to gender as well: In the modern world everyone can, should, will "have" a gender identity, as he or she has a nationality. There is certainly a lot of pressure along these lines.

Another picture: One of the earliest National Socialist propaganda leaflets addressing Austrian youths appealed to girls and young women: "Aryan girls," it reads, "be on your guard against Jewish girls as friends. The Jewish community has ordered them to prepare you for the sin against your blood. They will lead you to dances, bars, etc., that are Jewish contaminated, alien to the Volk, where you will become helpless victims of Jewish playboys and lecherous Jews. You will be lost to your German people from the day you become captivated by those lechers. As women you will only get Jewish children."[4]

The pamphlet not only shows the Austrian National Socialists' aggressive and racist antisemitism, it also curiously relates the German *Volk*, as defined by National Socialists, to regulations concerning the relations between men and women. These quoted sentences are part of a wider discourse that constructs women as targets of aggression against the German people and as that people's weakest point.[5] It is, however, not sufficient to analyze this discourse in the context of male sexist fantasy. Young women also participated in this ideology that brought racist-defined borders of the *Volk* into line with gender differences and female sexuality. According to these women, seduction was Jewish in nature: "More and more insistent and passionate grew the words of Jewish riff-raff whispered into our ears."[6] Resistance to this sexual temptation was defined as a prerequisite of belonging to the *Volk*: "And woe betide us if we become addicted to this fault again, then we will be expelled from the community of our people."[7]

GENDER AND RACE: BACKGROUND TO THE ISSUE

Widely varying as the quoted texts may be, they all nevertheless claim that national and gender identity are interrelated. Ernest Gellner does not go into the gender issue in his book—that is, if you don't take into account the above-mentioned comparisons and some further ones that clearly demonstrate his convictions about a woman's place. Nevertheless, his thesis about nationalism as effect and form of modernization could also be interesting for feminist thought. For instance, his considerations of social genetics in industrial society could be linked to theories about the making of the modern family. More generally, common points and interdependencies between the development of the modern gender system and the nation-state could be put up for discussion. There are striking parallels to be found when considering the limits of the deconstruction of national as well as gender identity. And, of course, it has to be asked how the Nazis' phantasmic linking of the "purity of the people" with women's sexual behavior can be connected to the intermingling histories of gender and nation.

The racist and sexist pictures of these antisemitic discourses symbolize a most critical part of Austrian history: a time when the crisis of national identity after World War I led to the country's occupation by Nazi troops, which were welcomed by a large majority of Austria's population. Having been born a female Austrian, I am "accidentally" "implicated" in the racism and sexism that are part of the country's history. I therefore have a personal and academic interest to come to terms with that past. The backgrounds and the contexts of this special discourse on gender and "race"[8] and what motivated some women to participate in it are the main issues of this chapter.[9]

NATIONAL IDENTITY IN CRISIS

The First Austrian Republic was constructed out of the German-speaking parts of the Habsburg Empire, which broke asunder at the end of the First World War. The shortest definition of the Austrian nation-building process forced on the country by the peace treaties is ascribed to the French Premier Georges Clemenceau, who is quoted as saying, "Austria is what is left." There are reasonable doubts about the authenticity of this statement. The relevance of the phrase, however, lies in the frequency with which it was publicly quoted to characterize the First Austrian Republic—upon which little love and respect were bestowed, at least according to its opinion-forming class. Self-pity and reprimand about not having had any say in their own destiny united those who lamented the decline of the Habsburg Empire's grandeur with those who intended to make Austria a part of a greater Germany. But whereas the prospects for the restoration of the Habsburg Monarchy did not stand a chance, either in domestic or in foreign policy, it was the very demand for the annexation to Germany (the *Anschluß*), which, although denied by the peace treaties, attained wide support and relevance in those years of permanent economic and social crisis. Nearly all of Austria's political parties claimed the country's German identity, most of them even explicitly demanding the *Anschluß*. That meant that almost any expression of national identity by political organizations was connected to the notion of German. This ubiquitous connection made it very difficult to attribute any homogenous political objectives to this general orientation toward the German.

After the Peace Treaty of St. Germain in 1919, the major political parties came to terms with reality and tried to proceed toward the formation of a democratic order despite heavy domestic conflicts. At the same time, a small but constantly growing movement, which called itself national and *völkisch*,[10] came into being; its participants' German-nationalist demands became intertwined with the degradation and rejection of the emerging democratic state. Due to the nationwide bias toward a German-national identity, their influence on public discourses was quite impressive.

A large number of rather dissimilar organizations, such as two rival National Socialist parties, an anticlerical farmers' party (Landbund), and a variety of cultural associations, found common ground in *völkisch* ideology. During the twenties, the Pan-German People's Party (Großdeutsche Volkspartei, GDVP) was the leading force. Being the junior partner in a coalition government with the Catholic and conservative Christian-Social Party (Christlich-Soziale Partei), with whom they shared the fear of a possible socialist government, the GDVP reluctantly participated in the construction of a democratic state. The GDVP voters, however, were largely drawn from the various radical German- nationalist antidemocratic and racist organizations and in this manner put pressure on the GDVP to set a more authoritarian and anti-semitic course. At the beginning of the thirties, Hitler's overtly anti-democratic National Socialist German Workers' Party (NSDAP) gained force and attracted a greater proportion of the GDVP's former followers. An "alliance of struggle" between the GDVP and the NSDAP only set the seal on the GDVP's decline. In the years of the Austro-fascist authoritarian regime (which the Christian-Social Party had violently formed in 1933 as they were not willing to share power with the Social Democrats or with the NSDAP), most of the various *völkisch* organizations became cover-up associations for the National Socialists, whose party had become illegal.[11]

The complete infiltration of all *völkisch* organizations by the Nazis was facilitated by a shared political logic. Since they all presented the *Anschluß* as the solution to every economic, social, political, and cultural problem, an explanation had to be produced for the subordination of all these issues to the question of the nation. They found a way of transforming these problems into questions of nationality by constructing "the Jews" as the interior aliens of the *Volksgemeinschaft* or "*Volk* community." This was precisely the background for the discourses on "race" and gender as cited in the introduction.

GENDER RELATIONS IN CRISIS

During the process of industrialization in Austria, the traditional consensus about the division of labor between women and men disintegrated. Out of this, an active and widely discussed movement for women's equal political rights emerged in the late nineteenth century. From the very beginning, however, this movement's weaknesses could be seen in the division along lines of class and nationality.[12]

Although in 1918, when the Republic was founded, the support for women's suffrage remained unchallenged because of the radical changes in gender relations that took place during the war, both the proletarian and the bourgeois women's movements suffered a crisis due to their own premises. Bourgeois feminists had concentrated their efforts solely on suffrage for women. After having achieved this, they seemed to lack almost any instrument for more extensive social criticism and remained outside the realm of real political power. The Social Democratic women, on the other hand, took part in political power alongside their party; but when, because of the achievement of equal rights, the party's women's organizations were dissolved in 1918, they lost their most important power structure for achieving their own aims within the party.[13]

Legally, gender had ceased to be a criterion for political rights; de facto, however, being a woman continued to be a criterion for exclusion in male-dominated politics. If women wanted to be politically active, they had to find a way to come to terms with this ambivalence. In their efforts to create a specifically female politics, on the one hand, they themselves affirmed gender to be a political category. If, on the other hand, they claimed that gender as a political category had been abrogated by law, then this usually meant denying their virtual exclusion from party politics. Both wings of the women's movement dealt with this dilemma in an ambivalent manner. Bourgeois feminists increasingly concentrated on concepts for professionalizing motherhood, while the Social Democratic model of comradeship in gender relations merely covered up the increase of women's reproductive tasks within the party's reform program.[14]

Within the labor market—where, due to the economic crisis, competition was fierce in any case—women competed with men on an equal level in legal terms, whereas the conditions on which they could ground their efforts had remained unequal. On the one hand, they still did not—and would not for a long time—have equal educational opportunities. On the other hand, the reproductive demands on women of all classes had increased. At the same time as an increasing percentage of working-class women became housewives in the full sense of the word due to the greater importance of family life among Viennese workers,[15] a large part of the middle class became impoverished after 1918. Many middle-class women now had to keep house without servants. They tried to keep up standards by working longer and harder within the household. Quite a few of the younger middle-class women had been the first generation of women in their families who were forced into the labor market. This frequently meant being confronted by fathers, brothers, and husbands for whom clutching at traditional concepts of gender relations seemed to be the last symbolic barrier against their social decline.

THE IDEOLOGY OF THE *VOLKSGEMEINSCHAFT* AS SOCIAL UTOPIA

As previously mentioned, the ideology of the *Volksgemeinschaft* pulled democratic organizations such as the GDVP toward the openly antidemocratic NSDAP. *Volksgemeinschaft* literally means "community of the *Volk*"; but, as discussed more fully later, *Volk* cannot simply be translated as "nation" or "people." The word *völkisch*, as derived from this concept, has no precise English equivalent either. Not only is "community" not the same as "society," but the two are regarded as contradictory.

The concept of *Volksgemeinschaft* inseparably linked domestic and foreign policy objectives. It not only defined the boundaries of the *Volk*, it also defined how the thus-constituted *Volk* was to be structured from the inside: as a community. The importance of this definition can only be understood if the profound social rupture caused by the fierce class struggle during the First Austrian Republic is taken into account. The *völkisch* organizations especially attracted those segments of the middle classes who felt threatened by proletarianization, as well as the almost exclusively German-speaking civil servants of the former empire. A large portion of this latter group had lost their jobs at the beginning of the Republic, with all of them suffering a decline in their social status. These jobless or at least downgraded groups felt trapped between the working class, represented mostly by the Social Democrats, and the largely Catholic bourgeoisie and the farmers, both represented by the Christian Social Party. To these disaffected groups, the concept of the *Volksgemeinschaft* suggested a model of society that seemed to solve all social conflicts "organically."

The GDVP proposed an order it called *ständisch*. This meant that the state should be based on governance by the estates or corporations of the various professions; deputies from precisely defined corporations should form a "Council of Estates" that would partly take the place of the former Parliament and its political parties. The proponents of this model increasingly sought its justification through the concept of the *Volkskörper* (Volk's body); they defined the *Volk* as having a "body" whose limbs were the estates, the total of which had to be healthily maintained. In this ideology, the Jews were the primary "aliens" and "others" who were regarded as a health menace to this "body." It was by this means that the boundaries of the *Volk* could be shifted into the interior of the existing society.

Within the GDVP's quest for an order of estates, the image of the people as a "body" only formed a background for this program. The NSDAP, in contrast, concentrated its efforts on a violent "racial struggle" against Jews. According to their promises, if the "purity" of the people was attained, social justice and prosperity would turn up as a direct consequence. The Jews, in their view, were workers' leaders who were inciting the masses, as well as capitalists exploiting the people. If they were expelled, a *Volksgemeinschaft* of fair German employers and industrious workers, a community without conflicts, would emerge. The *Volksgemeinschaft* as they promised it can thus be interpreted as a harmonization strategy that worked by projecting unsolvable conflicts onto an imagined "counternation."

THE GENDER POLITICS OF THE PAN-GERMAN PEOPLE'S PARTY

It seemed that the "organic" social model of the *Volksgemeinschaft* also offered answers for the crisis in gender relations. The reasons men had for favoring this model are easy to comprehend—in making a case for the "natural order," they could relegate women who had begun demanding changes to their proper place in society. Nevertheless, women also identified with this model on several levels. One of the women's organizations of the GDVP, for instance, called itself the Association of German Women *Volksgemeinschaft* (Verband deutscher Frauen "*Volksgemeinschaft*"). It functioned basically as a self-help organization of impoverished middle-class women. The existence of this association points out how men and women were differently affected by impoverishment. The depreciation of the money earned, which put quite a few products and services beyond people's means, was matched by women working extra hours in their households in order to produce the use values needed. Husbands, therefore, never felt the total effect of the economic crisis.

Those women who came together in the Association of German Women *Volksgemeinschaft* tended to cope with the crisis collectively. This strategy was based on three assumptions: collective self-help was to be limited to "German" (and that meant "Aryan") women; the increase in time and energy needed to maintain middle-class standards in the home was not to be criticized; and that the household remain fundamentally the domain and responsibility of women was not to be questioned.

Indeed, the GDVP's female politicians tried specifically to secure women's access to political decision making by using the concept of home economics. They insisted that housewives be represented as an estate in their own right within the "Council of Estates," which was part of their party's program. On a preliminary level, the women of the GDVP planned the foundation of the Chambers on Home Economics (Hauswirtschaftskammern), representing the households. These chambers were intended, on the one hand, to demonstrate how important home economics were for the national economy, and, on the other hand, to develop a common consciousness of solidarity within each and every woman active in home economics, including female domestic employees. Through these chambers, middle-class housewives tried to avoid wage disputes with their domestic employees by symbolically enhancing the employees' status; they also aimed at integrating gainfully employed housewives into these institutions in order to create a specifically female form of participation in politics. Additionally, the concept of Chambers on Home Economics seems to have been appropriately and directly linked with the estate model of the GDVP. This linkage reveals that this model of gender-specific political domains only gained real ground within the context of the "organically" structured *Volksgemeinschaft* program. On the level of a gendered social division of labor, this model seemed to offer a way out of the frustrating competition between individuals who were simultaneously equal and unequal. By defining women's tasks as "organic," they could attain political relevance through their work performance without exposing themselves to either comparison to men or to competition with men, which would be hard to win.

Apart from that, the women of the GDVP claimed equal rights and equal education for women, just as their counterparts in the bourgeois liberal women's movement had done. This, of course, led to conflicts within their own party. To face these controversies, the women reformulated their demands for better educational opportunities for girls and women within the context of the racist "national struggle," which was such an important issue to their party. In order to prevent having only Jewish girls sent to the expensive private secondary girls' schools, the GDVP was supposed to support women's demands for public funding of secondary schools for girls as well as for an increase in the number of coeducational schools. These demands cannot be regarded as only a gender struggle with an unwilling male party leadership. Already in 1923, the Pan-German politician Maria Schneider gave top priority to the struggle for the *Volk* among the objectives of the women's movement. According to her, it was essential to understand "that the ultimate . . . objective of the women's movement was and is not university studies and suffrage; both are just the most outstanding means on the way to a revolution . . . that would favor women of the whole 'Volk.' This most fundamental struggle . . . for . . . the whole 'Volk' is really just beginning now."[16]

With the concept of the *Volksgemeinschaft*, women of the GDVP formulated a political objective that promised them a part within the imagined "whole" and therefore a way out of the crisis within the women's movement. This "whole," of course, was defined in a racist manner—in conformity with the ideology of the *Volksgemeinschaft*.

NATIONAL SOCIALISTS: THE GENDER CONFLICT AS A "RACE ISSUE"

The function of antisemitism in National Socialism as an ideological instrument for transforming social conflicts has already been mentioned. Analysis of this phenomenon normally focuses on the belief in the ostensible resolution of class antagonism within the *Volk* community, which was stabilized by establishing an imaginary countercommunity of the Jews.[17] However, this analysis can also be applied to the severe gender conflict that shook Austrian postwar society. The erosion of the social agreement on the division of labor between the sexes and the loss of bourgeois values in the gender relationship was not counterbalanced by consensus regarding a new framework. This imbalance presented itself as gender conflict in concrete situations although the sexes were not in opposition to one another in the same way the classes were as political groupings. Considerable problems resulted, especially for youths, who were to form their own gender identity in this situation. Certain groups of the youth generations that grew up in the two decades after World War I tried to escape the problems through a similar ideological transformation, which, this time, was used to translate not only the class antagonism but also the gender conflict into a "race conflict." This translation is evident when viewing the frequent use of the image of the raped or seduced "German girl" in the publications of youth organizations in the Austrian NSDAP and—in its wake—the concentration on questions of gender relationships under the terms of "virtue" and "moral decline."[18]

Most of the (partly anonymous) relevant texts represent a male perspective. In many cases, the background for these authors' political activity seems to have been impending or existing unemployment.

Consequently, marrying and settling down and thereupon entering legitimate relationships in the traditional sense with women was postponed to an uncertain future, and any grown-up gender identity was in large part only fictitious in nature. It was under these circumstances that these men were confronted in public life with representatives of a new self-assured type of professionally and politically independent women, who did not seem to need the sort of men they were, or the sort of help that they, in any case, were in no position to offer. This led to a conflicting mix of unsatisfied desires and fearful aggression, which the young authors found a way to deal with in the racist antisemitic motif of the "Jewish" stealing of "German girls." Moreover, they found a solution through projection, in which women appear as both the stolen and desired object as well as the "polluted" threat for the "German nation." Projecting a reason for these conflicting threats onto the Jews seemed to resolve the gender conflict and the already existing ambivalence toward women, by grouping women as either the sisterly "pure" or those "polluted by Jews."[19]

Female authors, in their texts, elaborated on the image of sexual attacks on German women by Jewish men. Such women writers confronted dangers that were real for them; the possibilities of being raped, of being sexually harassed at work, and of dealing with difficult developments in nonmarital relationships (unwanted pregnancy, "marriage impostors")[20] led many young women to regard relationships with men, in general, as menacing. It was also true for them that the projection of the threatening elements of the opposite sex onto Jewish men enabled them to see some of the men as "German" and familiar and thus as not dangerous. Problematic for the women was the aspect of the theory that reflected male aggression, particularly the theory's claim that women were a "danger" for the "Aryan race," and were therefore "lost" to the *Volk*, after even a single "wrong" sexual contact. Female anti-Semites moderated this judgment with the term "misdemeanor" and proposed possible "expiation" for it. They also moderated the status of victim that male authors attributed to them. While men mainly focused on the image of rape, women identified the menacing relationship as seduction. This enabled them to design their own identity in a way that put them in the decision-making role. The "other" in their design was no longer the "woman," as it was with the middle-class male, but the "Jew."

I have shown that the activities of the GDVP's female politicians concentrated on the problems of married women. Also, married middle-aged and elderly women, who had already accepted their specific gender identity, largely formed the members and adherents of the

GDVP's women's organizations, which in turn helped them to keep middle-class standards for their families even under conditions of economic crisis. These strategies didn't have much relevance for those girls and young women who grew up with the crisis and whose prospects of setting up a home were nearly as poor as their hopes for a good job. Instead, they were more likely to become members of Nazi youth organizations. Indeed, the social set-up of these organizations indicates that it was middle-class youths from German-national origins who were primarily attracted to them.

The ideology of the *Volksgemeinschaft*, however, formed the link between these two generations of women, and its force became apparent during the thirties. Seemingly apolitical clubs like the Association of German Women *Volksgemeinschaft*, which remained legal even when all political parties were forbidden in 1933, offered shelter for many Nazis and let them use their organizations as cover for illegal activities. At the same time, many a former member of these German-nationalist organizations became National Socialists themselves. In 1938, when Nazi Germany's troops invaded Austria, the president of the Association of German Women *Volksgemeinschaft* rejoiced over this "dream come true" and proudly declared that she felt "aware" of having fulfilled her "duty" by having served the "German *Volksgemeinschaft*" to the best of her "knowledge and belief."[21]

METAPHORS: GENDER, NATION, AND "RACE"

Gellner's motto that "Our nationality is like our relations to women . . ." can be viewed as an example of Joan W. Scott's interpretation of gender as "a primary way of signifying relationships of power." She asserts that gender is a reference by which political power is "conceived, legitimated and criticized."[22] Of course, such a metaphorical use of gender causes repercussions for gender relations, or as Scott puts it, "Politics constructs gender and gender constructs politics."[23] Hierarchical gender relations—if for no other purpose—have thus to be defended to fulfill their function of legitimating power.[24]

Santayana, the original author of the motto, apparently considers gender relations to be something quasi-natural. Gellner, however, who borrowed Santayana's words, deals with the other side of this comparison. He shows that the ubiquity of nationality is a modern phenomenon and maintains that the development of industrial societies required a process of modernization. It became necessary to abandon local cultures and restricted codes in order to construct and adopt elaborate national languages and cultures and to establish national educational systems. These had to produce universally educated rational individuals who were free of kinship commitments and who were flexible enough to change their jobs according to the labor market. Gellner posits that loyalty to a certain culture necessarily becomes the basis of modern identity. The nation-state, as he sees it, is the only power structure strong enough to establish and defend a national culture.[25]

Gellner's mention of the rational individual brings another process of modernization to mind: the process by which the modern gender system and the modern family were constructed. Many feminist historians have indicated the necessity of these institutions for industrial capitalist societies. The bourgeois family has been characterized as the structure by which the modern male individual—independent and moral—was produced and reproduced.[26] The two analyses complement each other. Gellner's theses about social genetics are incomplete in that he restricts his considerations to public education. Only if his theory on nation building is combined with feminist research on the history of the family can the interrelationship between the modern family and the development of the nation-state be understood.

If we consider the common and interrelated roots of the nation-state and the modern family, it becomes less astonishing that the gender system can be used as a metaphor for nationality: the modern rational individual is their common offspring. The question that remains unanswered is, Is it possible to reverse the gender roles in Santayana's simile so that "Our (the women's) nationality is like our relations to men . . ."? This, however, isn't possible. The background for this impossibility lies in the way the male individual constructed himself against the mirror of the female other. In this process, everything that the male individual was not able to grasp within his own self was projected onto women. Therefore, women were not only prematurely defined before they were able to determine their identity for themselves, they also lacked the mirror of the other sex, in front of which they would have been able to design their own selves.

Yet women have their mirrors. For instance, German-nationalist and National Socialist female politicians in Austria used nation and "race" for structuring their self-definition as (female) independent individuals. They participated in a concept of German identity that increasingly viewed the Jews as the universal other. In defining their identity, they could not simply use "the man" as the other. But the counterimage of the Jewish man seemed to allow them to create this self-image. In this way, gender was not only used to define nationality, but nationality and "race" were also specifically used to construct gender identity.

A main fault in this case is the imprecise distinction between nation and "race." The two appear to be the same, at least according to the Nazi definition. One must, though, make note of the fact that the ideology of the *Volksgemeinschaft* obtained its force not from certainty but from the ambivalent distinction of belonging to the *Volk*; in other words, belonging to those defined as being within the borders of the community. Ambivalence—whether "German" indicated "race" or "nation"—made it possible to construct an interior alien within the nation who had to be expelled in order to erect a *Volksgemeinschaft*. Moreover, as I already mentioned, it was only by making use of this concept of the interior alien that all political questions could be transformed into a national question.

The criteria of belonging are of utter importance to this specific kind of nationalism. In comparison, the question of aggressiveness seems quite insignificant. The considerable differences between the inside and the outside perspective cannot be overemphasized. Every form of nationalism defines itself as defensive. This, however, will seldom prove to be true when considered from an outside perspective. Taking the example of the Austrian-German-nationalists as represented by the GDVP and the National Socialists, the policies of the GDVP can certainly be defined as merely defensive: the party's ideology was rooted in an acute crisis of national identity. It was the way in which the ideologists, both male and female, of the GDVP constructed belonging to the community, however, that formed the basis for their transformation into National Socialists: the ideology of the *Volksgemeinschaft*.

NOTES

The following considerations are part of a research project on German-Nationalism and gender in Austria, 1918–1938, headed by Professor Dr. Edith Saurer of the University of Vienna. This project was commissioned by the "Jubil, umsfonds der Österreichischen Nationalbank." I would like to thank Whitney Haycock for helping me with the translation.

1. Cf. Ernest Gellner, *Nations and Nationalism* (Oxford: Blackwell, 1983).

2. Cf. Benedict Anderson, *Imagined Communities: Reflections on the Origin and Spread of Nationalism* (London: Verso, 1983), 14. Cf. also Andrew Parker, Mary Russo, Doris Somer, and Patricia Yaeger, eds., *Nationalisms and Sexualities* (New York: Routledge, 1992), 4–5.

3. Cf. Judith Butler, *Gender Trouble* (London: Routledge, 1990).

4. Copy at the Viennese police authority for the Ministry of the Interior, 13 July 1923. Archive of the Austrian Republic: BKA 38.808/23 (22/NÖ).

5. Cf. Christina von Braun, *Die schamlose Schönheit des Vergange nen. Zum Verhältnis von Geschlecht und Geschichte* (Frankfurt/M.: neue kritik, 1989), 81–112.

6. Cf. Brunhilde Wastl, "An meine deutsche Schwester," in *Der ju gendliche Nationalsozialist* 5 (1926).

7. Ibid.

8. Although other authors may not use quotation marks with the word

"race," I find it necessary to do so as an Austrian woman who has grown up and worked in a society where this word can be otherwise misused.

9. This chapter is based on two earlier works that contain more detailed bibliographical references: Johanna Gehmacher, "Antisemitismus und die Krise des Geschlechterverhältnisses" in Österreichische Zeitschrift für Geschichtswissenschaften 4 (1992), 424–48; Johanna Gehmacher, "Le nationalisme allemand des femmes autrichiennes et l'idéologie de 'communauté ethnique,'" in Marie-Claire Hoock-Demarle, ed., Femmes, Nations, Europe (Paris: Publication de l'Université Paris 7, 1995), 95–106. Cf. also Johanna Gehmacher and Gabriella Hauch, "Eine 'deutsch fühlende Frau.' Die großdeutsche Politikerin Marie Schneider und der Nationalsozialismus in Österreich" in Frauenleben 1945. Kriegsende in Wien (Wien: Historisches Museum der Stadt Wien, 1995), 115–132. I want to thank Gabriella Hauch for very helpful discussions on the issue.

10. Although the word völkisch is derived from the German word Volk which can be translated not only as "people" but also as "nation," völkisch does not mean the same as "national." (For further interpretation, see the chapter section headed "The Ideology of the 'Volksgemeinschaft' as Social Utopia," below.)

11. For further information on German-nationalism and National Socialism in Austria, cf. Rudolf Ardelt, Zwischen Demokratie und Faschismus. Deutschnationales Gedankengut in Österreich 1919–1930 (Salzburg: Geyer, 1972); Bruce F. Pauley, Der Weg in den Nationalsozialismus. Ursprünge und Entwicklung in Österreich (Vienna: Bundesverlag, 1988); Adam Wandruszka, "Das 'nationale Lager'" in Erika Weinzierl and Kurt Skalnik, eds., Österreich 1918–1938: Geschichte der 1. Republik, vol. 1 (Graz: Styria, 1983), 277–315; Emmerich Tálos et al., eds., Handbuch des politischen Systems Österreichs. Erste Republik 1918–1933 (Vienna: Manz, 1995).

12. For further information on the women's movement in Austria before 1918, cf. Harriet Anderson, Utopian Feminism. Women's Movements in fin-de-siècle Vienna (New Haven, CT: Yale University Press, 1992); Birgitta Zaar, Vergleichende Aspekte der Geschichte des Frauenstimmrechts in Großbritannien, den Vereinigten Staaten von Amerika, Österreich, Deutschland und Belgien, 1860–1920 (Ph.D. dissertation, University of Vienna, 1994).

13. For further information on the Austrian women's movement after 1918, cf. Hanna Hacker, "Staatsbürgerinnen," in Franz Kadrnoska, ed., Aufbruch und Untergang. Österreichische Kultur zwischen 1918 und 1938 (Vienna: Ueberreuter, 1981), 225–245; Gabriella Hauch, Vom Frauenstandpunkt aus. Frauen im Parlament 1919–1933 (Vienna: Verlag für Gesellschaftskritik, 1995); Edith Prost, ed., "Die Partei hat mich nie enttäuscht . . . ," Österreichische Sozialdemokratinnen (Vienna: Verlag für Gesellschaftskritik, 1989); Irene Schöffmann, Die bürgerliche Frauenbewegung im Austrofaschismus. Eine Studie zur Krise des Geschlechterverhältnisses am Beispiel des Bundes österreichischer Frauenvereine und der Katholischen Frauenorganisation für die Erzdiözese Wien (Ph.D. dissertation, University of Vienna, 1986).

14. Cf. Monika Bernold et al., Familie - Arbeitsplatz oder Ort des Glücks? Historische Schnitte ins Private (Vienna: Picus, 1990).

15. This process is referred to in German as "Familialisierung," which might be rendered in English as "familialization."

16. Mizzi Schneider, "Eine Volksgemeinschaftsaufgabe," in Deutsche Zeit, 16 June 1923.

17. Cf. Wolfgang F. Haug, "Annäherung an die faschistische Modalität des

Ideologischen," in *Faschismus und Ideologie,* vol. 1 (Berlin: Argument, 1980), 44–80, 73–74.

18. Cf. Adolf Bauer, "Dirnentreiben" in *Der jugendliche Nationalsozialist* 7 (1924).

19. See for example, T. T. T., "Deutsche Not," in *Der jugendliche Nationalsozialist* 7–8 (1926).

20. Translation of "Heiratsschwindler" refers to a man who promises marriage to a young, naive woman and then runs away with the money she has saved for her dowry.

21. Cf. Paula Krauß, "An unsere Mitglieder!" *Die deutsche Frau,* 15–June 1938.

22. Joan W. Scott, "Gender: A Useful Category of Historical Analysis," *American Historical Review* 91 (1986): 1053–75, 1069, 1073.

23. Ibid., 1070.

24. For theses about women as signifiers of ethnic/national differences, cf. Nira Yuval-Davis and Floya Anthias, eds., *Woman-Nation-State* (New York: Routledge, 1989), 1–15, and Introduction, 9.

25. Cf. Gellner, *Nations and Nationalisms.*

26. Cf. for example Gisela Bock and Barbara Duden, "Arbeit aus Liebe—Liebe als Arbeit. Zur Entstehung der Hausarbeit im Kapitalismus," in *Frauen und Wissenschaft. Beiträge zur Berliner Sommeruniversität für Frauen Juli 1976* (Berlin: Courage, 1977), 118–199; Claudia Honegger, *Die Ordnung der Geschlechter. Die Wissenschaften vom Menschen und das Weib 1750–1850* (Frankfurt: Campus, 1991).

12

Images of Sara Bartman

Sexuality, Race, and Gender in Early-Nineteenth-Century Britain

YVETTE ABRAHAMS

Sara Bartman was a Khoisan woman, born in the eastern Cape of present-day South Africa in the early 1790s. In 1810 she was brought to London, England, and there exhibited to the general public. The reason she was exhibited, that is, the primary object of interest to the general public, was what was perceived to be the abnormal size of her buttocks. This feature was thought to be a distinctive characteristic of the Khoisan of Southern Africa. The nature of the exhibition raised the ire of evangelical abolitionists who took Sara Bartman's keepers to court, both because of the indecent nature of the exhibition and because they suspected that she was being illegally kept as a slave. They lost their application to have Sara Bartman set free, but, despite the huge publicity it generated, the court case was apparently bad for business. Sara Bartman was removed from London and exhibited in the provinces until 1814, when she was taken to Paris. During her stay in the French capital, Sara Bartman also aroused enormous scientific interest. She was examined by a team of French scientists in early 1815. Upon her death shortly thereafter, at the age of approximately twenty-eight, she was dissected by Baron Cuvier and Henri de Blainville. The remains were preserved and, to the best of my knowledge, are still on exhibit at the Musée de l'Homme in Paris.

This chapter begins with a discussion of the historiography. It then centers on the exhibition in London in 1810 and the publicity surrounding the court case. It rests on the conviction that the various uses of Sara Bartman, the metaphor, underpinned and reinforced the relations of power in which the living woman was embedded. This chapter investigates two aspects of this process. First, it considers the rationale behind exhibitions such as Sara's. Naturally, I cannot fathom why people should pay to gawk at a semi-naked woman bereft of home and family; that is, I cannot explain individual motivations. But there is much to be gained from a description of the culture in which these motivations were shaped. Second, this chapter examines how Sara's exhibition marked a key change in the way Black people were represented in British middle- and working-class culture. It considers how this process emanated from struggles over changing definitions of gender, particularly within the middle class. Since the people who became scientists in the nineteenth century increasingly originated in the middle class, rather than the aristocracy, these struggles were not irrelevant to the "scientific" treatment of Sara Bartman's body, or the creation of a scientific metaphor of race based on the body.

THE HISTORIOGRAPHY OF SARA BARTMAN

There has been no survey of the literature regarding Sara Bartman. Until recently, most authors approached the topic as if they were the first. They sometimes cited previous authors in their footnotes, but rarely in their text. The result of this approach has been that each author repeats the same story and yet manages to hide his or her own lack of originality. The effect has been to isolate Sara Bartman, the living person, to deny the interconnections between herself and the world in which she lived, and to place her story outside both historiography and history. This chapter cannot give a full survey of the historiography, but a few examples of modern writings on Sara Bartman may serve to clarify this point.

Richard Altick may be called the modern rediscoverer of Sara Bartman. He wrote about her in the context of circuses and freak shows, although his account was, to say the least, markedly lacking in both racial and gender sensitivity. Words like "savage" and "Hottentot" were used without either quotation marks or a trace of embarrassment, and his approach is perhaps best exemplified by the fact that he called Sara Bartman a "heavy-arsed heathen."[1] It may be worth mentioning that, on both counts, Altick wrote in the absence of any evidence. The sources do not give any indication of Sara Bartman's religious beliefs prior to 1811, when she was baptized.[2] The concept of *steatopygia* (the Latin name given to big buttocks) has never been defined in any of the literature. Thus it would seem this phenomenon existed largely in the eye of the beholder.

Bernth Lindfors's contribution to the freak-show literature was noteworthy in that it specifically exempted Sara Bartman's body from the idea of manipulation:

> Thus, as black stage performances in England and elsewhere in the western world in the latter half of the nineteenth century increased, they also grew less representative of the African peoples they purportedly were meant to portray. Stereotyping and dishonest fabrication became the norm, truth the exception.[3]

In his eagerness to see a chronological development in dishonesty, Lindfors did not include Sara Bartman's exhibition in this general conclusion. Lindfors's silence on the multiple manipulations of Sara Bartman, the metaphor, meant the myth was kept intact by omission. Using a phrase as objectionable as Altick's, Lindfors called Sara Bartman a "fat-arsed female."[4] My own research has shown that there was in fact a considerable degree of manipulation involved in creating both the physical exhibit and the discursive myth.[5] That Lindfors chose to replace analysis with name-calling was fairly typical of the approach of white male academics to the study of Sara Bartman. Not one study was published that did not either repeat old insults or invent new ones.

Sander Gilman's article is perhaps the best known one on Sara Bartman. It differs little from the articles already cited. It repeats the same stories, cites the same sources, and shows the same astonishing lack of discussion of work that has gone before. As with preceding studies, Gilman's article does not put Sara Bartman at the explicit center of discussion, but uses her as an example, a "case" of something else. Gilman's discussion of nineteenth-century sexual icons was perhaps best summed up by Baker: "presenting yet again, and so dreadfully embarrassingly, a white male confessional. 'Look what we have done,' it naughtily delights, rubbing its hands and looking pruriently sidewise."[6]

We need to look at what they have done, not in a spirit of salacious inquiry, but in order to begin to dismantle the myths and see clearly their function in creating and perpetuating racial hierarchies. The entry of Black women academics into the historiography has accomplished precisely this. For instance, Paula Giddings makes a connection, to me the crucial connection, between slavery and the creation of Sara Bartman as metaphor:

> It is no coincidence that Sara Bartmann became a spectacle in a period when the British were debating the prohibition of slavery. . . . there, as in North

America, race took on a new significance when questions arose about the entitlement of nonenslaved blacks to partake of the fruits of Western liberty and citizenship.[7]

There is considerable evidence to indicate that Sara Bartman was in fact a slave, despite the findings of the court case of 1810.[8] Giddings's insight is important, therefore, because it offers a way to link the metaphor with the living person. Hortense Spillers, for instance, argues that what she calls "pornotroping" became part of the condition of slavery itself.[9] Certainly, Sara Bartman's fate becomes a lot easier to understand if one begins from the point of view that she was a slave. My own research on the period preceding Sara Bartman's birth and her early life in South Africa bears out the conclusion that the height of Khoisan slavery in South Africa also coincided with a period of intense pornotroping of Khoisan women.[10] Thus we may begin to trace causal connections between the fate of the living woman and the myths that were built around her.

It is in this context that Giddings's contention, that scientific racism developed as a means of countering the perceived threat to social stability created by emancipated Blacks, becomes significant. Giddings further argues that this racism was from its inception also sexist: "By the nineteenth century, then, race had become an ideology, and a basis of that ideology had become sexual difference."[11]

If Spillers is right about the link between slavery and the invention of a deviant, Black sexuality, then it comes as no surprise that the link between sexism and racism became further strengthened in scientific racism. As the physical bonds on Black people weakened, the discursive ones had to grow correspondingly stronger. Racism and sexism developed together and not separately.

A somewhat different conclusion has been reached by a white woman writing on Sara Bartman. Londa Schiebinger's book on theories of gender and race in eighteenth-century Europe argues strongly that

> neither the dominant theory of race nor of sex in this period applied to women of non-European descent, particularly black women. Like other females, they did not fit comfortably into the great chain of being. Like other Africans, they did not fit European gender ideals.[12]

Like Altick's work, Schiebinger's book is certainly marred by her usage of the term "Hottentot," without any quotation marks, to denote the Khoisan. Further, when arguing that dominant discourses on gender and race developed separately, Schiebinger ignores much of the evidence she herself presents on the way the Khoisan in particular had been characterized as sexually deviant from the inception of European colonialism of southern Africa.[13] To then end her discussion of Sara Bartman with the question, "Why, then, did anatomists and anthropologists privilege *male* bodies when investigating race and *European* bodies when examining sex?" is disingenuous.[14] This formulation ignores the way in which racist and sexist discourses were constructed around each other in the case of the Khoisan. What is important about the myths built around Sara Bartman is precisely how the myth building became an increasingly conscious, and public, process. Before the exhibition of Sara Bartman, sexual analyses of Black people may have been a minor theme in dominant discourses. Afterward, ideas about the essentially deviant sexual nature of the Khoisan spread to include all Africans.

A CAVEAT

Before continuing, one reservation must be made. I deliberated at length as to whether to include illustrations in this paper. After all, their inclusion does contribute to the dissemination of degrading images of Black women. However, it is crucial to remember that the illustration reproduced in this essay does not bear any relation to Sara Bartman as she was in real life. For instance, I have been unable to find in any of the sources that she was ever exhibited naked. On the contrary, there is anecdotal evidence to show that she in fact resisted long and hard any attempts to undress her completely.[15] Yet nude illustrations of her abounded, and eventually acquired genealogies of their own as copies were made of advertisements, which were copied in caricatures, which in turn were copied in penny prints. Thus their relationship to the truth was at best tortuous and obscure. The illustrations represent not Sara Bartman the living woman, but the minds of those who made and viewed them. Simon Schama makes a similar point about a series of Dutch bourgeois portraits of vagrants. He calls them "sketches from the nightmares of the propertied, rather than any reliable social document. . . . And they catered in lingering detail to the respectable citizen's hunger to know about the fiendish tricks, ruses and strategems of the outcast."[16] The illustration of Sara Bartman in this chapter could best be characterized as a sketch from the nightmares of the melanin-deficient. As such it may be upsetting. But it should not be viewed as a picture of Black people.

IMPERIALISM AND THE FREAK SHOW

The freak show occupied a niche all its own in British culture. Its appeal lay in its accessibility. Unlike the written word, or the visual conventions of painting and sculpture, the exhibition of oddities required little knowledge and no effort on the part of the viewer. The effect was both immediate and lasting: "They were, in fact, an alternative medium to print, reifying the word; through them the vicarious became the immediate, the theoretical and general became the concrete and specific."[17] It was the reification of the word that underscored the powerful symbolism of freak shows. The credulous came to gape, and having gaped, could return home in wonder at the oddities of the "other," thus reaffirming the enduring normality of their own world. Not surprisingly, the nineteenth century was the heyday of the freak show. After all, the industrial revolution had irrevocably changed the world of the British lower orders. The freak show, and its accompanying penny prints and advertising leaflets, was one of the many ways in which the disruption of the social fabric was made to seem a normal, almost an enviable, state of life.

There was an important racial dimension to this effect. As Paul Edwards and James Walvin argue, white freaks were always exhibited as oddities, whose value lay in the way they were distinguished from the rest of their species. Black people, on the other hand, were exhibited as typical of their race.[18] Thus the savage freak show functioned to create the requisite distance between the colonizing self and the colonized "other." It must be borne in mind that it was precisely from the lower ranks of British society that the foot soldiers of colonialism were recruited. Institutions such as the savage freak show were an important contributor to the psychological makeup that enabled these functionaries to rob, maim, and murder for the greater glory of the British Empire. In this sense, Sara Bartman was doubly a victim of British imperialism. Had it not been for the British colonization of the Cape, she would never have been brought to London. Once there, her perceived physical characteristics were pressed into the service of imperialism through the medium of the freak show.

A crucial part of the "othering" process was the way in which African freak exhibits were invariably presented as bestial, thus serving to reinforce the common perception that there was little or no distinction between Black people and animals:

> The Black freak could be used to blur this distinction, as . . . in the case of the Hottentot Venus, by placing members of an already degraded race in a position of further degradation and by reinforcing the conception of Africa as a place of monsters.[19]

Thus the savage freak show served to reinforce common stereotypes. Less than five years after the second British occupation of the Cape, Sara Bartman could be viewed as one of the spoils of war. She also provided an early object lesson, showing the state of the indigenes in Britain's newest colony. The contrived savagery in which she was shown created a generalized picture of the savage people that British troops were at that moment trying to "civilize"—all this without a word being said. That imperialism itself may have played some part in making Sara Bartman less human than her ancestors, and that a childhood in a war zone and a state of semi-naked slavery in London may have made her sullenness and ferocity less of a natural state than a social construct, were of course not obvious to the casual observer. On the contrary, the phenomenon of race as spectacle worked to contrive this "savagery" as something so natural and obvious it went unquestioned—in that certainty lay its strength and its meaning within the broader world of British imperialism.

However, the exhibition of Sara also marked an important change in the format of the savage freak show, in that the connection between bestiality and unbridled sexuality was made explicit. I have been unable to find that earlier popular representations of the savage included either women or representations of sexuality. Certainly the "Young Oranatu Savage," exhibited at Bartholomew Fair in 1752, was advertised as savage, but without any sexual overtones.[20] The penny prints circulated prior to Sara's exhibition were almost overwhelmingly male, and while they represented Blacks as poor and degraded, they did not stress Blacks' sexual nature.[21]

Of course, bestiality and sexuality may been have linked in popular consciousness, but earlier representations of Black stereotypes did not make that element explicit. Representations of Sara Bartman, however, pushed the boundaries of public decency. Thus, while she was never exhibited fully naked, her dress was contrived to look nonexistent: "she is dressed in colour as nearly resembling her skin as possible. The dress is contrived to exhibit the entire frame of her body, and the spectators are even invited to examine the peculiarities of her form."[22] This is interesting. For one thing, the dress was obviously intended to emphasize the peculiarities of her figure, and for all we know, may have created them through the use of a cinched waist, wadding, or buckram. For another, in an age where a glimpse even of female ankles was regarded as indecent, the exhibition of Sara Bartman's legs clearly set her apart from white females. The invitation to explore what lay beneath her thin dress thus acquired sexual overtones. All the illustrations of Sara Bartman during this period show that the response to this sexual invitation was overwhelming. It was not just that she became an object of sexual fantasies, but that the sexual objectification became inseparable from the public representations of her. Other illustrations took the sexual fantasy one step further, ignoring even the convention of dress and portraying her as naked (Figure 1). Here, while the white man and the Black woman are portrayed as equally abnormal in a physical sense, the man is fully dressed. Sara Bartman's status as freak, however, is underlined by her nakedness and the careful depiction of body parts such as nipples and ankles.

Thus, representations of Sara Bartman mark the turning point toward exhibiting the savage as raw sexuality. The obscure illustrations of travel writings became increasingly socially acceptable. Thus, while in 1790 an English translator of a French traveler omitted both the verbal description and the picture purporting to be of a naked Khoisan woman, by 1810 Sara Bartman's body was being widely publicized in London.[23] In effect, conventional norms of decency were to become inapplicable to women of color. The moral lesson was clear—as a journalist observed of one of Sara Bartman's successors, Tono Maria, the "Venus of South America":

> He whose gallantry thought little of our fair Countrywomen before, will probably leave the show "clean an altered man," and for life after pay the homage due to the loveliest works of creation, enhanced in value by so wonderful a contrast.[24]

If the freak show itself came to play an important role in underpinning an imperialist mind-set, the exhibition of the sexualized savage was equally important in imparting gender specificity to the dichotomy between colonizer and colonized. By far the majority of those who went to the colonies to aid the imperial effort were men. The image of the civilization they were called upon to spread became increasingly symbolized by their "fair countrywomen." This image was created and disseminated in a dialogue with the image of the sexualized savage.

WHITE WOMEN, BLACK WOMEN, AND MEN

The entry of the sexualized savage into images of popular culture may be seen as one of the effects of imperialism, but its popular acceptance is more likely to be due to developments inside Britain. By the 1770s, the Black population in Britain was larger than ever before, and overwhelmingly male. Thus, the most visible image of the Black was not a savage in darkest Africa, but a working man, or a street entertainer. Most of these Black men married or had casual liaisons with white women, "a fact which produced some of the most splenetic (and anti-plebian) outbursts from pamphleteers."[25] The increasingly visible presence of Blacks in Britain gave rise to a moral panic.

Figure 1. "A Pair of Broad Bottoms," by W. Heath. ©
British Museum. Reproduced from Richard Altick, *The
Shows of London* (Cambridge: Harvard University Press,
1978), 272.

This moral panic dovetailed neatly with the more hysterical arguments of the antiabolitionists. As the abolitionist debate gained in strength, so too did the debate on the sexual nature of Black men, and their seemingly irresistible attraction for white women. Much of this debate was marked by class snobbery. For instance, Edward Long complained, "The lower class of women in England are remarkably fond of Blacks, for reasons too brutal to mention."[26]

It was in large part due to the debate on slavery that the moral panic showed no signs of diminishing in the early nineteenth century, despite the fact that the Black population of Britain was by that time dwindling fast. The increasing representations of the sexualized savage must be seen as an intervention in this discourse. To people like Edward Long, the reason Black men had for over a generation been largely assimilated into white working- or lower-middle-class families could not be due to simple demographics. Instead, antiabolitionists created arguments about the sexual potency of Black men and their irresistible attraction for white women. These arguments defined a conceptual split between white female identity and Black.

Black men became the embodiment of the sexualized beast, which white, and particularly white working-class, women could not resist. Black women, however, were more savage than the men, so bestial that even their own men would choose a white woman in preference to them. This was the genesis of a process that culminated in the Victorian ideal of white womanhood. White women were to be increasingly denied sexual expression, while for Black women, sexuality came to be seen as a defining characteristic. Sara Bartman's exhibition marked a change that was crucial to the success of this process, namely the fact that public displays of sexuality became legitimate. In the late eighteenth century, these emotions had been "too brutal to mention." In the nineteenth century, their representation became increasingly allowable, provided the woman being represented was Black. There was a crucial class dimension to this process. The caricatures, for instance, were published in newspapers read mainly by the burgeoning middle class and the aristocracy. Had pictures of a near-naked white woman been published in such a context, there would undoubtedly have been a public outcry. The caricatures of Sara Bartman, however, seem to have passed without a ripple. The exhibition, as well, was not aimed at the lower classes. It took place in the gentrified precincts of Piccadilly, and the entry fee—two shillings—would have been beyond the reach of most workers. As striking as the protests of the evangelicals were, what is surely more striking is the broad acceptance of the exhibition among the middle class in general. Ironically, we have the spectacle of white middle-class women, themselves subjected to increasing expectations of chastity, indulging in the display of another woman's sexuality. What needs to be explained is how a feature that in Black women was seen as a sign of savagery became in later Victorian fashions in Britain a sign of beauty (see Figure 2).

There were reasons the savage freak show became legitimate for the middle class, of course, such as the spread of popular education and the move of science away from the hands of the aristocratic amateur. Thus the prurient interest in Sara Bartman's anatomy could be understood as motivated by an interest in "science." It should be borne in mind that, at the time, it was popularly believed that Blacks could not feel pain. This belief was encouraged by respectable scientists such as the Frenchman Louis Figuer, who after extensive experiments "found that blacks were endowed with thick skins and insensitive nervous systems, making them impervious to pain."[27] These "scientific" findings were disseminated through the press and public lectures, and the effect was to create a climate that validated racism. The people who went to see the exhibition of Sara Bartman could view themselves as indulging a perfectly respectable scientific curiosity. Their voyeurism implied an acceptance of the conceptual split between Black and white gender roles. Yet in accepting the validity of a racist science, they had to accept its sexist implications as well. As options narrowed for women in the domestic gender struggles that were to come, the split left the white woman, not just on her own, but in a racial sense on the side of the white man. Increasingly, the only alternative to the desexualized, domesticated gender role dictated for white women was to become the sexual savage made physical in the exhibition of Sara Bartman and the many "Venuses" of color who succeeded her.

THE SAINTS AND THEIR DEMONS

The relationship between redefinitions of Black and white gender roles becomes evident when we look at what must surely have been one of the more liberal sections of British society, namely the abolitionist movement. This movement was undoubtedly more conservative, in every way, by 1810 than it had been during the 1770s and 1780s. In the earlier period, abolitionists, together with radical political reformers, pioneered a political popularism that used tracts, pamphlets, lectures, and mass meetings to advance its cause. The connection with political radicalism, however, severely damaged the movement during the post-Revolutionary backlash, and the ongoing Napoleonic Wars exacerbated the conflict between political radicalism and patriotism. In conse-

Figure 2. "In Sunday Best." Reproduced from Cecil Willet Cunnington, *Feminine Attitudes in the Nineteenth Century* (London: Heineman, 1935), 212.

quence, the abolitionists moved away from radical populism and into parliamentary politics. This marked a separation from working-class politics that was to endure into the 1820s. The increasing social respectability of the abolitionist cause was accompanied by an increasing political conservatism.

Representations of Sara Bartman bear witness to the growing schism between populist politics and evangelicalism. Although the working class would not have had much access to Sara Bartman in the flesh, the original aquatint was used as a poster to advertise her exhibition in both London and Paris, where it would have been seen by any passerby. The trial in 1810 gave rise to numerous broadside ballads, which would have been sung by street artists and sold in penny sheets. Of little literary value, they were deeply conservative on both race and gender issues. For instance, one ballad draws a comparison between the abolitionists and the chivalrous knights of old, finding exquisite humor in the implicit contrast between Sara the savage and the gracious ladies of medieval times. It concludes,

> When speaking free from all alarm
> The whole she does deride
> And says she thinks there is no great harm
> in showing her b—kside
> Thus ended this sad tale of woe
> Which raised well I wot
> The fame and the revenues too
> of SARTJEE HOTTENTOT.[28]

It seems that the fact that the evangelicals came to Sara Bartman's aid did much to discredit her among the working class. Thus *The Ballad of John Higginbottom of Bath* is explicit in its lambasting of the Saints:

> A strange Metamorphosis !—Who that had seen us
> 'Tother night, would take this for the Hottentot Venus
> and me for poor Jack ?—Now I'm Priest of the Sun
> and She, a queer kind of Peruvian Nun;
> Though in our Novitiate we preach but so so
> You'll grant that at least we appear comme il faut
> In pure Virgin robes, full of fears and alarms
> How demurely she veils her protuberant charms !
> Thus oft', to atone for absurdities past
> Tom Fool turn a Methodist preacher as last
> Yet the critics, not we are to blame—for 'od rot em
> There was nothing but innocent fun at the bottom ! [29]

This excerpt was typical of most lowbrow ballads in that it seems less concerned with Sara Bartman herself than with the golden opportunity her trial offered to lambast evangelical hypocrisy. Of course, it may be argued that these ballads were not necessarily written by the working class. Nevertheless, their target market was quite clearly the lower orders, and they would have been written with some idea in mind of what the working class would consider acceptable and amusing.

The growing class conservatism in abolitionist circles was reflected in their ideas of race, as well. Their initial insistence on abolition as part of a broader claim to the inalienable rights of man to liberty was replaced by an evangelical sentimentalism. Crucial factors in this process were the moral panic caused by the increased visibility of Black men in Britain, the successful slave uprisings in Santo Domingo and Haiti in 1790 and 1792, as well as the drawn-out Khoisan wars in Britain's newest colony from 1799 to 1802. All these clearly contributed to a racial backlash in Britain itself. Class radicalism and racial radicalism became linked in the public mind—as William Wilberforce remarked, "People connect democratical principles with the abolition of the Slave Trade and will not hear mention of it."[30] As a result, the abolitionists quickly moderated their demands for an end to the slave trade. Paradoxically, this moderation did not cease as the domestic Black population disappeared, and as the colonies quieted down. Rather, the abolitionists wove objectifying pity and condescension into their arguments, encapsulated in the slogan posed as question, "Is he not a man and a brother?" Their arguments emphasized the helpless, childlike nature of Blacks rather than their right to liberty. This is evident in their defense of Sara Bartman's liberty in 1810. Consider the tone of the following:

> that wretched object advertised and publicly shown for money—the "Hottentot Venus." This, Sir, is a wretched object. . . . The poor female is made to walk, to dance, to shew herself . . . for the profit of her master, who, when she appeared tired, held up a stick to her, like the wild beast keepers, to intimidate her into obedience.[31]

The language appeals to sentiment without in the least allowing Sara Bartman to appear as a subject in her own right. The "wretched object," the "poor female," is objectified by sentiment as much as she would have been by hatred in the language of the most racist planter.

The abolitionist movement had become decidedly more conservative on gender issues as well. The new religious revivalism that took the place of political radicalism had powerfully conservative ideas of proper feminine roles in genteel and middle-class households:

> In addition to their roles as a vanguard of political conservatism, these revivalists also played a key part in the formation of Victorian sexual attitudes. The intense sentimentalization of the home which reached its peak in the mid-century had its beginnings in their promotion of a "domestic religion" centered around the "moral influence" of the wife and mother.[32]

The women freethinkers of a previous generation had no home in the evangelical movement of the nineteenth century. Rather, any potential gender radicalism among white middle-class women was displaced in the struggle to free the slaves. The methods of struggle differed as well—it was as wives and mothers that white women fought against slavery in the 1820s and 1830s, in parlor meetings and church halls. There was a peculiar class dynamic to this process, as the earlier radicalism was replaced by an emphasis on the gentrified concept of charity. Abolitionism became an expression of middle-class philanthropy. All these factors served not just to emasculate the struggle for racial liberalism, but to subvert potential feminist tendencies as well.

Victorian gender roles assumed that proper women had no sexual feelings. Yet from its origins in the early part of the century, this gender role was racially defined. Representations of Sara Bartman show that, as Black women began to be depicted in British culture, sexuality became not only an acceptable, but a crucial part of their social identity. To do the evangelicals justice, it is clear from trial records that they disapproved of any public expression of sexuality. Thus they tried to "impress the court with an idea of the offensive and indecorous nature of the exhibition. . . . But the details would not be fit for the court."[33] Despite these protests, it should be clear that the increasing conservatism within crucial sections of the middle class could not be combined with its puritanism. Instead, the racist and sexist images of Sara Bartman became weapons in white gender and class struggles. The evolution of scientific sexism meant that the sphere of influence of white women was to become increasingly limited in the nineteenth century. Meanwhile, the Black woman was left to face the fate awaiting her at the Musée de l'Homme.

NOTES

1. Richard Altick, *The Shows of London* (Cambridge: Harvard University Press, 1978), 269.

2. Percival Kirby, "More about the Hottentot Venus," *Africana Notes and News* 10, no. 4 (1953): 129.

3. Bernth Lindfors, "'The Hottentot Venus' and Other African Attractions in Nineteenth Century England," *Australasian Drama Studies* 1, no. 2 (1983): 100.

4. Ibid.

5. Cf. Yvette Abrahams, *'Ambiguity' Is My Middle Name: A Research Diary about Sara Bartman, Myself and Some Other Brown Women* (Cape Town, SA: !Xam Press, 1996), 48–50.

6. Sander Gilman, "Black Bodies, White Bodies: Towards an Iconography of Female Sexuality in Late Nineteenth Century Art, Medicine and Literature," in Henry Louis Gates, Jr., ed., *"Race," Writing, and Difference* (Chicago: University of Chicago Press, 1986): Houston A. Baker, Jr., "Caliban's Triple Play" in Gates, *"Race," Writing and Difference*, 387–88.

7. Paula Giddings, "The Last Taboo," in Toni Morrison, ed., *Race-ing Justice, En-Gendering Power: Essays on Anita Hill, Clarence Thomas and the Construction of Social Reality* (New York: Pantheon, 1992), 449.

8. Cf. Abrahams, "Ambiguity," 35–40.

9. Hortense Spillers, "'Mamas Baby, Papas Maybe': An American Grammarbook," *Diacritics* 17, no. 2 (1990): 67.

10. Yvette Abrahams, "The Great National Insult: Science, Sexuality and the Khoisan in the Cape and Britain: 1770–1815." Paper presented to the Women's History Workshop of the South African Association of Historians, Grahamstown, South Africa, June 1995.

11. Giddings, "The Last Taboo," 450.

12. Londa Schiebinger, *Nature's Body: Gender in the Making of Modern Science* (Boston: Beacon Press, 1993), 160.

13. Cf. ibid., 91, 115, 135–36.

14. Ibid., 172.

15. Cf. the description of Henri de Blainville, cited in Schiebinger, *Nature's Body*, 170.

16. Simon Schama, *The Embarrassment of Riches: An Interpretation of Dutch Culture in the Golden Age* (New York: Alfred A. Knopf, 1987), 580.

17. Altick, *The Shows of London*, 1.

18. Paul Edwards and James Walvin, *Black Personalities in the Era of the Slave Trade* (London: Macmillan, 1983), 183.

19. Ibid.

20. James Walvin and J. Walton, eds., *Leisure in Britain, 1780–1939* (Manchester: Manchester University Press, 1983), 19.

21. See illustrations of "Billy Waters—the Dancing Fiddler," and "Joseph Johnson, Black Sailor" in Edwards and Walvin, *Black Personalities*, 116–17. See also, the illustration "It is miserable legs which must bear poverty," in Schama, *The Embarrassment of Riches*, 581.

22. Cited in Altick, *The Shows of London*, 270.

23. Cf. Schiebinger's discussion of Le Vaillant in *Nature's Body*, 168.

24. Altick, *The Shows of London*, 271, citing from The Literary Gazette, 23 February 1822, pp. 123–24.

25. Edwards and Walvin, *Black Personalities*, 20.

26. Ibid.

27. William B. Cohen, *The French Encounter with Africans: White Response to Blacks, 1530–1880* (Bloomington: Indiana University Press, 1980), 241.

28. *The Story of the Hottentot Ladie and Her Lawful Knight Who Essaied to Release Her Out of Captivitie, and What My Lordes the Judges Did Therein*, cited in Edwards and Walvin, *Black Personalities*, 178.

29. Cited in Percival R. Kirby, "The Hottentot Venus," *Africana Notes and News* 6, no. 1 (1948): 57.

30. Cited in James Walvin, *England, Slaves and Freedom: 1776–1838* (Jackson: University Press of Mississippi, 1986), 117.

31. Letter to *Morning Chronicle*, 28 October 1810, cited in Edwards and Walvin, *Black Personalities*, 172.

32. Barbara Taylor, *Eve and the New Jerusalem: Socialism and Feminism in the Nineteenth Century* (New York: Pantheon Books, 1983), 13–14.

33. *Times of London*, "Report of Court Proceedings," 26 November 1810.

13

Sexual and Racial Discrimination
A Historical Inquiry into the Japanese Military's "Comfort"
Women System of Enforced Prostitution

SAYOKO YONEDA

Nineteen ninety-five marked the fiftieth anniversary of the end of the Second World War. As the world remembered the many tragic and important events of this period in our global history, Japan and the Japanese government were being reminded of an old injustice—the acts of sexual abuse, including rape and forced prostitution, committed by the Japanese military during World War II against women within the Japanese Empire's sphere of domination. Long hidden and denied, these acts were now becoming the focus of criticism and demands for restitution by the formerly victimized.

In December 1991, several Korean women who were so-called "comfort" women, that is, women who were forced into prostitution by and for the Japanese military, brought a suit against the Japanese government, seeking an apology and compensation for the harm they had suffered. Shortly afterward, the United Nations also addressed this issue. In March 1995, the United League of Korean Labor Organizations announced that, because these Korean women were forced into prostitution, which is a violation of the International Labor Organization's (ILO) rules regarding forced labor, the League was making an appeal to the ILO that there be an international protest "against the Japanese government's refusal to compensate" former "comfort" women.[1]

At first, the Japanese government denied any involvement in the coercion of Korean women into prostitution as "comfort" women. However, following the investigations of some Japanese historians and citizens that revealed that the government had participated in this co-ercion, the government expressed regret for what had happened.[2] On April 15, 1995, Prime Minister Murayama Tomiichi gave a speech on the occasion of the fiftieth anniversary, in which he expressed a "painful reflection and feeling of sincere apology" for the fact that Japan caused a great deal of damage and pain to other Asian countries through the war it had waged. But, at the same time, he claimed that Japan had no obligation to provide individual compensation to former "comfort" women.[3] Rather, the government implemented a plan to raise money privately from the general public to send to Korean women as a nation-al group. However, the former "comfort" women have strongly criti-cized the private Asian Peace National Fund for women[4] because it does not provide for direct compensation and because it does not hold the Japanese government legally accountable. As a recent South Korean activist's banner proclaimed, "We would rather die than accept this deceptive national fund, because it is a measure aiming to circumvent the Japanese government's legal responsibility."[5] The former "comfort" women protest that it is not merely the monetary compensation they seek but an official apology from the Japanese government that goes beyond mere expressions of regret.

In order to address fully the issue of "comfort" women, the Japa-nese government must officially take responsibility for its role in forc-ing these women into prostitution as "comfort" women during the war and provide them with an apology and compensation. However, the government has refused to admit its fault. Unfortunately, there are still politicians who deny the fact that Japan ever aggressively invaded other countries, and further, a number of politicians have made state-ments expressing approval of the military's use of "comfort" women. For example, in May 1994, the Minister of Justice Nagano Shigeto[6] stated that the Japanese army was framed for the Nanking Massacre, which occurred during the 1937 Japanese military invasion of Nanking and in which an estimated two hundred thousand Chinese civilians were killed. Moreover, he insisted that the "comfort" women could not be considered to be forced laborers because they were paid for their "work."[7] The minister was criticized for these statements, and he re-signed.

In his statement, Minister Nagano was trying to imply that the "comfort" women system was just like the governmental licensed prostitution system, and thus the "comfort" women were the same as licensed prostitutes who voluntarily became professional prostitutes. There are two basic misunderstandings inherent in this statement. First, these "comfort" women were clearly not "public prostitutes" working under Japanese governmental authority; they were women who were taken from Southeast Asian countries that were invaded and occupied by the Japanese army and who were made the target of sexual abuse by the army. Second, the Japanese system of licensed prostitution was in itself a system that impaired the dignity of Japanese women and was antithetical to their freedom. Nagano's statement indicates that there is no sense of regret or remorse toward the Asian women who were used as "comfort" women, nor toward the Japanese women who were turned into "public" prostitutes. People who share the same sentiments as Minister Nagano are not rare today in Japan. For example, one may hear statements like, "It is natural that rapes by soldiers occur because the army is made up solely of men"; or, "It is desirable that the government provide sexual recreation for soldiers in order to prevent rape"; or, "As long as they're paid for their prostitution, there's no problem."

Today, Japanese men often go on "sex tours" in Southeast Asian countries in order to buy sex from prostitutes. There have been reported cases of Japanese men who have gone to the Philippines, impregnated Filipina women and then simply left them.[8] As well, there are many cases where Thai and Filipina women have been brought to Japan and forced into prostitution.

This combination of ethnic, racial, and sexual discrimination exemplified by the treatment of Southeast Asian women by many Japanese people is rooted in Japanese history. With the Meiji Restoration in 1868, Japan began its modernization; yet, at the same time, it implemented intertwined policies of ethnic/racial and sexual discrimination both at home and as foreign policy. While all non-Japanese were treated as ethnic/racial inferiors, Japanese women themselves were discriminated against and sexually abused. The existence of this combination of ethnic/racial and sexual discrimination provided the context in which the "comfort" women sysytem was created. In order to ensure that a "comfort" women system will never again be implemented by the Japanese government, Japanese women, as members of a country that was a wartime aggressor against other Asian countries, have a responsibility to apologize to the women who were forced into prostitution as "comfort" women by and for the Japanese military, and they must strive to restore a sense of respect toward their own sex.

Although Japan has made great economic progress and is today an important economic power, it has not progressed much at all in terms of sexual discrimination and women's rights. Women's wages and social status lag behind those of men, women are restricted in many ways by stereotypical gender roles, and few women hold political office. This situation further hinders the resolution of the "comfort" women issue.

In this context, I discuss the historical process that led to the creation of the "comfort" women system, focusing on four main aspects of this process: (1) the modernization of Japan and sexual discrimination there, with a focus on the licensed prostitution system and the *ie* family system; (2) the escalation of rural poverty and the disintegration of rural communities, which gave rise to prostitution; (3) the inhumanity and systematic sexual discrimination demonstrated by the Japanese military; and (4) Japanese foreign policy toward other Asian countries, including the body of discourse advocating a rejection of other Asian cultures and any identification with them *(Datsu-a-ron)* and the policy of promoting the idea of Japanese domination *(Dai-to-a-kyōei-ken)* in the East Asian sphere of mutual cooperation.

MODERNIZATION AND SEXUAL DISCRIMINATION

The licensed prostitution system was a system in which Japanese women sold sex under governmental sanction and regulation. "Public" prostitutes have a long history in Japan. The most recent system came into existence shortly after the Meiji Restoration in 1868, which marked the end of the Tokugawa era and the establishment of a new government. The Meiji government feared censure by western countries because of the practice of governmental authorization of sex trade activities. Thus in 1872, it declared that all *shōgi* and *geigi* (traditional names for prostitutes) who had been forced into prostitution through the sex trade were to be liberated.[9] At the same time, however, the government gave official permission to those women who, out of their own free will, wished to become *shōgi* or *geigi*.[10]

The notion that these women chose out of their own "free will" to become licensed prostitutes is problematic. First, women who became prostitutes could not work independently or be their own bosses; they were required to register with agencies called *kashi-zashiki*.[11] It was customary for these agencies to lend the women large amounts of money until the women were deeply in debt, and then the women were not allowed to stop working until their debts were paid off. In addition, clothing fees *(kimono-dai)* and similar charges were used to increase their debts further. As a result, many women were just as bound as if they were slaves. (This system still exists today, though in a different form. Many Southeast Asian women come to Japan because they are told that they can find good jobs there. Once they get to Japan, they are usually already deeply in debt to whoever brought them and are forced to become prostitutes in order to repay their debts.)

Second, most of the women who "chose" to become prostitutes were poor, and in many of these cases, it was their parents who decided that they should become prostitutes. A daughter who became a prostitute under such circumstances was praised for her filial piety *(oya kōkō)* in being dutiful to her parents by helping to support them financially.

In light of these circumstances, one can say that the licensed prostitution system was not necessarily one in which women decided to engage in prostitution purely out of their own volition. Moreover, in addition to this licensed system, there was a private system of prostitution in which women were exploited in similar or worse ways. In either case, many women who became prostitutes exercised only a very superficial free will in "choosing" to enter the sex trade.

Governmental approval of prostitution encouraged Japanese men to consider using prostitutes as acceptable behavior. Men who were usually political opponents shared an unusual sense of agreement about licensed prostitution. For example, Itō Hirohumi, a high official in the Meiji government, and Ueki Emori, a leader of the democratic movement which opposed that government, thought that licensed prostitution was a good thing.[12] It was said that both sides were arguing politics while wallowing in the laps of prostitutes. Famous writers like Ishikawa Takuboku and Nagai Kafu were known to buy sex often.[13]

Structural aspects of the *ie* (family) system also contributed to the widespread acceptance of prostitution.[14] Under the *ie* system, the typical and most common marriage was *yome-iri*, which required that the woman become a member of her husband's family and that she discard her own family name and take on that of her husband. (After the Second World War, the *ie* system was abolished. However, today most women still change their family names to their husbands' family names when they marry. Furthermore, the keeping of separate names for husband and wife—that is, where both keep their family names—is not legally recognized.) According to the *ie* system, as the head of the family in the family register, a husband had absolute power over other family members. Women were expected to be virgins at marriage and to be obedient and faithful to their husbands after marriage. On the other hand, men were freer to engage in nonmarital and extramarital sexual relationships before and after marriage. Furthermore, while married women were subject to legal charges of adultery for any extramarital sexual relationships they had, married men were charged only when they had affairs with married women. A woman could request a divorce only after her husband had been convicted of adultery, while a man could divorce his wife by merely alleging that she had committed adultery.[15]

The licensed prostitution system (as well as the unlicensed prostitution which existed in the background) and the *ie* system were crucial factors in creating a widespread atmosphere of acceptance toward the many men who bought sex from prostitutes and toward the idea of sexual intercourse without love or affection. Because of their positions in society and the family, women were legally powerless to prevent their husbands from purchasing sex from prostitutes or to protest their doing so. Moreover, some women felt that there was no reason to complain about such behavior, because such nonpersonal sex was considered to be a kind of male recreation that was irrelevant to the marital relationship.

THE RISE OF PROSTITUTION

The licensed prostitution system and the *ie* system also functioned to hinder men and women from building intimate relationships of love and affection with each other. Under the *ie* system, the father (as the patriarch, or *koshu*) arranged the marriages of his children without their consent. Often, a woman would not see the face of her future husband until the day of her wedding. A civil law that existed at the time clearly stated that men under the age of thirty could not marry without the permission of their fathers. In general, young people encountered great difficulty if they tried to decide for themselves whom they would marry. Indeed, *ren-ai* (love matches) were portrayed as immoral.

In the villages of some rural areas, before the government began to strengthen these restrictions on *ren-ai* and independent marriages among Japanese citizens, men and women were allowed to choose for themselves whom they would marry. In these villages, young people between the ages of fifteen to eighteen lived communally in same-sex youth lodges—boys lived in lodges called *wakamono yado* and girls in lodges called *musume yado*. They farmed or fished during the day, and in the evening they listened to lectures given by elderly villagers about proper living. Young men, more so than young women, were free to choose their own spouses, rather than follow the orders of the family patriarch. The young men in the *wakamono yado* could visit young women in the *musume yado* (or at their homes), and they could propose marriage to whomever they pleased.[16] Furthermore, this youth lodge system provided the young men with opportunities to have sexual intercourse with young women from the same villages before marriage.

Thus, until the beginning of the twentieth century, it was common practice for village men under the age of twenty to have sex with other village women before marriage.[17] Japanese cultural historians generally hold that this type of village practice allowed youths to engage in premarital sexual relationships without the restraints of the *ie* system or reliance on licensed prostitution. This system did not involve the association of sex with money. Rather, it projected the image of young people freely choosing to associate with their peers. However, from a female perspective, there was at least one major problem with this youth lodge system—in reality, the women could not freely choose with whom they would associate.

For young women, the *wakamono yado* represented at best another form of marriage regulation in which young men had the primary initiative. Some historians argue that young village women (*musume*) were regarded as possessions in common of the village men and that they were absolutely dominated by young male villagers. Young women were free in the sense that they could, for example, date men of the same village without their parents' permission or supervision, but their partners were restricted to those men in their village. It was unacceptable for a young woman to marry a man from another village. Furthermore, women could not reject requests for sexual intercourse from fellow village men without great difficulty.[18] Thus, for these village women, true freedom of choice regarding their future spouses or sexual partners was not a reality.[19]

As Japan underwent the process of modernization, the communal youth lodge system began to disintegrate. In the late 1800s and early 1900s, Japan was still largely a rural country. During this time, the economic division between wealthy landholders and unlanded poor grew increasingly wider. Peasants who sold their lands to large landholders and then rented them back to farm became impoverished as rents rose higher and higher. No longer able to make a living by fishing or farming, many farmers left the villages to look for jobs in the cities.[20] Furthermore, as villages became poorer, young women were sold to urban prostitution dealers to work as *shōgi*, *geigi*, and *shakufu* (barmaids). This practice was called *musume miuri* (which literally means the selling of girls'/daughters' bodies) and is comparable to the slave trade.

In addition, in 1873, the government instituted universal military conscription for every male aged twenty and older. The government further curtailed the freedom of young people by implementing official youth groups to inculcate them with the virtue of loyalty to the government.[21] Young women were organized into groups called *shojo kai*, which were designed to inculcate them with official views of ideal Japanese womanhood.[22] As a result of all these changes, the *wakamono yado* system could no longer function effectively.

Although the government initiated these sweeping changes in the structure of the lives of young people, it did not discourage young men from continuing the practice of engaging in sexual relationships with multiple female partners. The existence of licensed prostitution, along with "private" prostitutes in the cities, allowed men to become accustomed to the idea of "buying" women. The government encouraged this practice and viewed it as a means to control and subjugate the newly drafted young men.

THE MILITARY'S INHUMANITY AND SYSTEMATIC SEXUAL DISCRIMINATION

Before the Meiji Restoration in 1868, Japanese society was divided into a class system called *shi nō kō shō*. In this system, the samurai were the ruling class and were the only ones who could assemble an armed force. The Meiji Restoration brought an end to the privileged status of the samurai class, and the 1873 universal draft created a modern military.

The new "Imperial Army" appeared to be an army designed to protect Japanese citizens and the Japanese nation, but in actuality it did not. First, the army was established for the benefit of the Japanese Emperor (*Tenno*). In 1882, the Meiji Emperor issued an order called the *gunjin chokyu*, in which he demanded that the military be absolutely loyal to him alone.[23] The Emperor was declared the Supreme Commander of the military and had the power to declare both war and peace.

Second, the Imperial Army was used to suppress popular protests and dissent within Japan, while abroad it was used to wage a war of invasion in other East Asian countries. After the army was established, Japan initiated the Sino-Japanese War (1894–95) and the Russo-Japanese War (1904–05), and forcibly annexed Korea in 1910. Meanwhile, within Japan itself, the army never hesitated to take suppressive action against Japanese citizens. During a mass protest in 1905 and during a popular uprising known as *kome sōdō* in 1918, it turned its guns on Japanese citizens.[24]

Third, the universal draft proved to be a great burden on farming and fishing families, as they lost crucial labor to the military for certain periods of time. For this reason, antidraft demonstrations were frequent.[25] In order to prevent the destruction of the *ie* system, the government created a draft exemption for the oldest son of each family, so that he could remain to succeed as head of the household. Therefore, in order to help men avoid the draft, the family register was often divided up to create new families so that there could be more than one *koshu* (family head). This practice was called *chōhei nogare*—evading the draft. The government also allowed men to avoid the draft by paying a certain amount of money.[26] As a result, it was usually only the second or third son of poor peasant families who actually had to serve in the military.

The army tended to consist of discontented, violent young soldiers. Violence was frequently used to discipline the soldiers and to exact obedience from them in the name of the Emperor. Soldiers had no freedom at all. In fact, there was a popular saying that the difference between conscription (chō-hei) and imprisonment (chō-eki) was only one word.

The military also used sex in their propaganda to make young men more willing to serve in the army. As described above, many of the young men who came to the army had already experienced sexual intercourse with women. According to a 1925 poll of soldiers stationed in Tokyo, 66.1 percent had engaged in nonmarital sexual relations.[27] Soldiers who were originally from Tokyo tended to have experience with geigi (prostitutes), while those from rural areas had experiences with musume (village girls). Furthermore, after being drafted into the army, soldiers had opportunities to have sex with prostitutes during their free days. Red-light districts (yukaku) run by pimps were always found around military bases. As a result, many men contracted venereal diseases after entering the army; in all, 30 percent to 40 percent of soldiers were so afflicted.[28]

The unpopular lifestyle and violent discipline that were characteristic of the army caused many soldiers to want to escape from military service. Thus, the government and high military officers made it a policy to encourage openly and approve of the use of prostitutes by soldiers as a way of keeping them in the army. Some soldiers said that the best part about the army was the "pleasure" of buying the women that it offered. The system of licensed prostitution further encouraged soldiers to feel no moral compunction in using prostitutes for sex. Thus, widespread tolerance and governmental approval of prostitution, coupled with the inhuman, imperialistic, and violent nature of the Japanese military served crucial roles in robbing soldiers of any sense of morality and sensitivity toward women and sex.

JAPANESE FOREIGN POLICY TOWARD ASIA

As Japan modernized, sexual discrimination was not abolished, but rather was practiced over and over again. The military that sprang from this modern Japanese nation was not able to escape its characteristic aggressive policies, its lack of respect toward women, and its tendency to strip sex of any sense of dignity and respect.

In its efforts to modernize, Japan disparaged other Asian countries for being undeveloped and tried to further its modernization by invading these countries instead of trying to work with them. This policy was partially the result of what Japan experienced when it began to deal with the United States and with European nations in the mid-nine-teenth century and was forced to sign unfair treaties with these nations. At that time, Japan also saw that other Asian countries such as India and China were being colonized and dominated by European countries, and it realized that it was in danger of suffering the same fate as China because of these unfair treaties. In order to deal with this critical situation, Japan attempted to maintain its independence and security by separating itself from other Asian countries.

Fukuzawa Yukichi was a prominent intellectual and scholar who introduced principles of democracy to Japan and who published a "Discourse on Japanese Women," which advocated a higher status for women. However, in 1885 he published the *Datsu-a-ron*, which argued that Japan could not maintain favorable relations with China and Korea because these countries did not accept western culture and could not discard their "old" ways. He was a strong advocate of breaking off ties with these countries.[29]

In 1910, following the Sino-Japanese War of 1894 and the Russo-Japanese War of 1904, Japan invaded Korea and began to colonize it.[30] Japan tried to justify its invasions of Korea and other Asian countries by pointing to political pressure from the United States and European nations and claiming the invasions were necessary to protect its independence and national security. The government put out propaganda that depicted Korea and China as barbaric countries which could not accept western culture and that promoted a sense of superiority over these countries in Japanese citizens. Later, this propaganda evolved into the ideology of *Dai-to-a-kyōei-ken*, which justified Japanese domination over all other East and Southeast Asian countries and peoples.[31] The group that was most strongly discriminated against was also the same group that Japan was trying to colonize—the Koreans.

Considering this context, one can see how the "comfort" women system was an outgrowth of a combination of sexual discrimination, which has repeatedly flourished in Japanese society, and racial/ethnic discrimination, which was cultivated as a justification for invading other countries.

THE CREATION OF THE "COMFORT" WOMEN SYSTEM

As discussed above, the Japanese army was a violent group devoted solely to the Emperor and was imbued with injustice and discrimination. Under these oppressive conditions, sexual "recreation" was thought to be necessary in order to keep up the soldiers' morale. Regardless of whether the soldiers were at battle in foreign countries or in training camps in Japan, sex was made available to them through the "comfort" women system.

Historian Yoshimi Yoshiaki described three reasons for the army's "need" for "comfort" women:

1. When Japan invaded China, which was the first country it invaded in modern times, the army wreaked terrible harm by repeatedly plundering villages, setting homes on fire and raping women. Because of this behavior, the Chinese hated the Japanese invaders and resisted them. For this reason, army leaders thought that having "comfort" brothels available to the soldiers was necessary in order to prevent them from raping civilians.
2. Army leaders thought of providing sexual recreation to soldiers as a way of compensating them for fighting in battles that had no justifiable purpose.
3. Because many "private" Japanese prostitutes had venereal diseases, military leaders feared that they would spread such diseases among the soldiers. Therefore, army-supervised "comfort" women were necessary.[32]

When Japan began its invasion of China in the 1930s, the "comfort" women that accompanied the soldiers were Japanese women. These women were professional prostitutes. In Japan, they were looked down upon because of their "ugly" job. But once the war started, they were asked to "serve" their country by going to China. Many of these women agreed to go because they wanted to establish a place for themselves in Japanese society.

However, the number of Japanese "comfort" women was insufficient to satisfy the army's needs. On the one hand, there were too few of them—the war had spread and the army was scattered over a large area. On the other hand, as mentioned above, many Japanese professional prostitutes had venereal diseases, and the army was afraid that they would spread the diseases among the soldiers. Thus, the army claimed that it needed a large number of young, healthy women who could satisfy the soldiers' sexual urges without spreading venereal diseases. For these reasons, the Japanese government and army began to consider using Korean women, since Korea was already under Japanese control.

The government and army never considered the idea of gathering young virgin Japanese women to work as "comfort" women. But this oversight was not due to any sense of propriety about sex, or out of a sense of respect for Japanese women. In a society where licensed prostitution was widely accepted and where men regularly engaged in premarital sex and after marriage could buy sex from women, there was absolutely no respect for women as people or for the sanctity of sex. At the same time, the Japanese government promulgated the notion that young unmarried women had a duty to remain chaste as a fundamental part of the *ie* system and that it was shameful for women to engage in premarital sexual relations. The government also put forth the idea that married women had a duty to act for their nation's welfare by producing as many healthy children as possible.[33] Thus, the government viewed women almost solely in terms of their sexual and reproductive capacities.

There is no doubt that this type of thinking about women and sex was a crucial factor in the government's and army's actions to coerce Korean women into being "comfort" women. Never once did the Japanese government or military consider how degrading this irrational defiling of Korean women would be. Acting on these principles of racial/ethnic discrimination against Koreans and sexual discrimination against women, the military treated Korean women as mere devices at the disposal of the soldiers for the satisfaction of their sexual demands, and did not treat them as human beings.

During the Japanese occupation of the Philippine Islands, Indonesia, and Singapore, women from these countries were similarly forced to be "comfort" women for the Japanese military. "Comfort" women stations were built in the Okinawa Prefecture in Japan itself, and both Korean and Okinawan women were forced to work there as "comfort" women.[34] The Japanese military began stationing troops in Okinawa later in the war, shortly before the Battle of Okinawa (April–June 1945), and built regional "comfort" stations there, some of which were even located in schools. Although they were Japanese citizens, Okinawan women were forced to work as "comfort" women out of racial discrimination—because they were not *hondo* (mainland) people, they were not considered to be truly Japanese.

CONCLUSION

The frightening and criminal nature of the "comfort" women system cannot be defended by the excuses offered by some, such as "War is simply a crazy time," or "Armies everywhere were doing the same thing at that time." Furthermore, the idea that the women agreed to be "comfort" women because they were paid to do it is clearly wrong. Yet these types of notions have persisted since Japan first began its journey toward becoming a modern nation. By setting up the Emperor as the ultimate ruler, the Meiji government oppressed its own people and created a system of rule that discriminated against women in particular. In addition, this government created an "Imperial Army" that was created not for the people's protection, but for their oppression. Then, it used this army to carry out policies of invasion and oppression of other Asian nations, justifying these acts with racist and sexist policies. Thus, we see the historical origins and development of the Japanese military's "comfort" women system, which was born out of an ugly and ignoble joining of racism, ethnocentrism, and sexism.

NOTES

1. *Asahi Shinbun*, 12 March 1995.
2. In January 1992, Prime Minister Miyazawa Kiichi visited Korea and expressed an apology.
3. *Asahi Shinbun*, 15 August 1995.
4. The Asian Peace National Fund for Women was established in July 1995. As of May 1996, the funds raised were 50 percent below the objective. The criticism of the government for not taking any responsibility is thought to be one of the causes for the low level of donations.
5. Eugene Moosa, "Japan's Apology to Women Falls Short," *Globe and Mail*, 16 August 1996, A13.
6. Japanese names appear with the family name first.
7. *Sanyo Shinbun*, 4 May 1994.
8. *Asahi Shinbun*, 28 March 1994.
9. "Shōgi Kaihorei" ("The Declaration of the Emancipation of Prostitutes"), reprinted in Ichikawa Fusae, ed., *Jinken (Human Rights)*, vol. 5 of *Nihon Fujin Mondai Shiryo (The Compilation of the Sources of Japanese Women's Issues)* (Tokyo: Domes Publications, 1978), 195.
10. Ibid., 197.
11. Ibid., 197–99.
12. For information on Ito Hirohumi, see Murakami Nobuhiko, *Meiji Joseishi (The History of Japanese Women in the Meiji Period)*, vol. 2 (Tokyo: Rironsha, 1972), 531–35. For information on Ueki Emori, see Ienaga Saburo, *Ueki Emori Kenkyu (A Study of Ueki Emori)* (Tokyo: Iwanami Shoten, 1960), 531–32.
13. For information on Ishikawa Takuboku, see "Ishikawa Takuboku 'Roma Ji Nikki,'" in *Ishikawa Takuboku Zenshu (The Complete Works of Ishikawa Takuboku)*, vol. 16 (Tokyo: Iwanami, 1961). For information on Nagai Kafu, see "Danchotei Nichijo," in *Nagai Kafu Zenshu (The Complete Works of Nagai Kafu)* (Tokyo: Iwanami, 1963–64).
14. *Meiji Civil Law, Family and Inheritance Clause*, reprinted in Yuzawa Yasuhiko, ed., *Nihon Fujin Mondi*, vol. 5, *Kazoku Seido (Family System)* (Tokyo: Domes Publications, 1976), 239–76.
15. Takahashi Kikue, Orii Miyako and Ninmiya Shuhei, *Fufu Bessei eno Shotai (Introduction to Separate Matrimonial Names)* (Tokyo: Yuhikaku, 1995), 156.
16. Sato Mamoru, *Kindai Nihon Shudanshi Kenkyu (A Study of the Collective History of Modern Japanese Youth)* (Tokyo: Ochanomizu Shobo, 1970), 111.
17. Akamatsu Keiske, *Hi Jomin no Seiminzoku (Sexual Culture of Non-Common People)* (Tokyo: Akashi Shoten, 1990), 145–55.

18. Kawashima Takeyoshi, *Ideology to shit no Ie Seido (Family System as Ideology)* (Tokyo: Iwanami, 1957), 303.

19. Ariga Kizaemon, "Nihon Koninshiron" ("History of Japanese Marriage"), in *Arig Kizaemon Zenshu*, vol. 16 (Tokyo: Miraisha, 1968), 195.

20. Hosoi Wakizo, *Joko Aishi (Working Women's Sorrowful History)* (1925; reprinted, Tokyo: Iwanami, 1954), 67–68.

21. Mamoru, *Kindai Nihon Shudanshi Kenkyu*, 54–56.

22. Chino Yoichi, *Kindai Nihon Fujin Kyoikushi (History of Japanese Women's Modern Education)* (Tokyo: Domesu Publications, 1970), 197–205.

23. Fujiwara Akira, *Tennosei to Guntai (The Emperor and the Military)* (Tokyo: Aoki Shoten, 1978), 83–88.

24. Inoue Kiyoshi and Watanabe Toru, *Komesodo no Kenkyu (A Study of the Rice Riot)*, vol. 5 (Tokyo: Yuhikaku, 1962), 7–112.

25. Aoki Koji, *Meiji Nomin Sojo no Nenjiteki Kenkyu (The Chronological Study of Meiji Farmers' Uprisings)* (Tokyo: Ohara Siseisha, 1967), 40–45.

26. Matsushita Yoshio, *Choheirei Seiteish (History of the Decision of the Conscription System)* (Tokyo: Satsuki Syobo, 1981), 156.

27. Ohama Tetsuya, "Heishi no Sekai" ("The World of Soldiers"), in Ohama Tetsuya, ed., *Kindai Minshu no Kiroku (The Record of Modern People)*, vol. 8 (Tokyo: Shinjinbuts Oraisha, 1988), 55.

28. Ibid., 60.

29. Fukuzawa Yukichi, "Datsua Ron," in *Ji ji Shinpo*, 16 May 1885. The essay is reprinted in Kato Shuchi et al., eds., *Nihon Kindai Shiso Taikei (Outline of Modern Japanese Thought)*, vol. 12 (Tokyo: Iwanami, 1988), 312–14.

30. Unno Fukuju, *Kankoku Heigo (The Annexation of Korea)* (Tokyo: Iwanami, 1995).

31. Hashikawa Bunzo, "Daitoa Kyoeiken no Rinen to Jittai" ("The Ideal and Reality of the East Asian Sphere of Mutual Cooperation"), in Asao Naohiro et al., eds., *Iwanami Koza: Nihon Rekishi (Iwanami Course: Japanese History)*, vol. 21 (Tokyo: Iwanami, 1977), 265–320.

32. Yoshimi Yoshiaki, *Jugun Ianfu Mondai Shiryoshu (The Sources of Comfort Women Issues)* (Tokyo: Ootsuki Shoten, 1992), 5–60.

33. Hayakawa Noriyo, "Senjiki no Boseiron" ("The Discourses on Motherhood during Wartime"), in Tokyo Rikishi Kagaku Kenkyukai, Fujin Undoshibukai (Tokyo Society of Historical Science, Board of Historical Studies of the Women's Movement in Japan), eds., *Onna to Senso (Women and War)* (Tokyo: Showa Shuppan, 1991), 57–60.

34. *Daigokai Zenkoku Joseishi Kenkyu Koryu no Tsudoi Hokokusho (The Report on the Meeting of the Fifth Annual National Exchange of Japanese Women's History)* (Okinawa: Tsudoi Jikkoiinkai, 1994), 16.

14

Vacations in the "Contact Zone"

Race, Gender, and the Traveler at Niagara Falls

KAREN DUBINSKY

Tourism is about difference. As British sociologist John Urry has established, the tourist gaze is constructed primarily "in relationship to its opposite, to non-tourist forms of social experience and consciousness."[1] Indeed, the quest for true difference and authenticity is written into the fabric of modern western tourism, as the designation "tourist" becomes increasingly a term of embarrassment, something almost everyone is and no one wishes to be. As Trinh T. Minh-ha notes, "one among some fifty million globe trotters, the traveler maintains his difference mostly by despising others like himself."[2]

Scholars of imperialism and culture have added to this discussion, expanding our understanding of the construction of difference in travel to include those on the receiving end of the gaze. Travel writing by Europeans has been identified as a key source that helped to produce Europe's "differentiated conceptions of itself in relation to 'the rest of the world,'" as Mary Louise Pratt has put it in her fine study, *Imperial Eyes: Travel Writing and Transculturation*.[3] A host of recent studies have probed the relationship—historical and contemporary—between travel, imperialism, and racism. In light of the research that has been done on the construction of Native North Americans as tourist attractions, the appropriation of indigenous cultures as spectacle and souvenir for the enjoyment of Europeans around the globe, the evocation of the "good old days" of colonialism in the mythologized "Polynesian" vacation available at Club Med in the 1950s and 1960s, the transformation of Chinatowns in North American cities from places of vice and crime to modern ethnic spectacles, the appropriation of whole land masses and economies in the Caribbean for European and North American tourism, and even the essentializing "quest of the folk" in poorer regions within North America (the Canadian Maritimes in particular), the popular cliché that travel "broadens the mind" seems rather difficult to sustain.[4]

I have been researching this relationship between travel and the creation of racial/ethnic difference at one specific tourist destination, Niagara Falls. Niagara has been, for almost 200 years, a popular elite and, later, working-class resort. It has always been an overwhelming spectacle, especially for nineteenth-century visitors; it summoned great feelings, and provoked discussions of its wider meaning. As one guidebook advised visitors in the 1890s, "It is not merely what we see, but what impression has been wrought upon the mind? What new idea and inspiration has arisen in the soul? . . . Sit! Ponder! Contemplate! This is no place for butterflies, but earnest thinking souls."[5] Fortunately for historians, a good many visitors expressed themselves in print, and through the volumes of published travelers' accounts, guidebooks, and other writings, it is possible to reconstruct the multiple and often-changing meanings of Niagara.[6]

At Niagara, as at many other notable North American tourist stops in the nineteenth and twentieth centuries, travelers not only encountered a powerful "natural" spectacle, which they tended to find both alluring and terrifying, they found many new human curiosities as well. Since at least the eighteenth century, travelers have been at once horrified and fascinated by the presence of "locals," particularly at natural attractions. As Ian Ousby has suggested, in reference to the tour guides and souvenir sellers who lived close to the caverns in the English Lake District in the mid-eighteenth century, the cult of the sublime reduces residents to "stage extras whose job is to make the drama which the tourist creates for himself more piquant."[7] So too at Niagara Falls, though this time with a racial twist; the spectacle of Niagara in the nineteenth century was presented by an almost wholly other cast of characters. As one particularly indignant tourist described it, "vendors of Indian beadwork, itenerant philosophers, camera obscura men, imitation squaws, free and enlightened negroes, guides to go under the Cateract—who should have been sent over it—spiritualists, phrenologists and nigger minstrals have made the place their own."[8] That North American Native people have long held a peculiar fascination for white visitors has been established. Less well known is how the everyday experiences of travel released Europeans (and white North Americans) into the shadowy world of the non-Anglo service industry, which provided visitors with food, lodging, and enough "local color" to fill volumes of guidebooks. Such encounters were described by Europeans in a variety of ways—in terms of fear, humor, sometimes pity—and it is important to stress that this research documents only one side of the conversation. But my point is that it was a conversation—even though one voice was louder—not a monologue.[9] The tourist experiences I will discuss take place in what Pratt has termed the "contact zone," the space in which "people geographically and historically separated come into contact with each other . . . usually involving conditions of coercion, radical inequality and intractable conflict." In the context of dramatic and unequal relations of power, the relationship between colonizer and colonized (or traveler and "travelee") is not one of separateness and apartheid, but rather "copresence, interaction, interlocking understandings and practices."[10]

Why was the spectacle of racial difference so interesting to white Europeans and North Americans? How can we explain the apparently paradoxical worldviews of the colonizers, who at once deplored the "savages" in their midst, while at the same time made them central characters in their museums, exhibitions, fairs, and literature?[11] Is western fascination with things "primitive," as Marianna Torgovnik has posited, really about "imagining us," a revelation of the self that is inherent in the act of defining the "other"?[12] An analysis of tourism is especially well suited to the exploration of these questions, for unlike the museum visitor or adventure-story reader, nineteenth-century tourists recorded their reactions.

Many scholars have identified travel writings as central texts in the discourse of Empire, and others have used such writing to ask feminist questions about whether European women and men constructed their relationship to the "other" differently.[13] Unlike some feminists writing on this topic, I see little evidence that female travelers rejected the voice of colonial authority or found a common identity with the other. Far more persuasive are the arguments of scholars, such as Antoinette Burton and Vron Ware, that nineteenth-century European women invented a voice of imperial female authority, disparaging the "other" in order to become part of the self. This helped to produce, in Burton's terms, "feminist rhetoric of the same Orientalist-imperialist dynamics that marked mainstream political and scientific discourses in the Victorian period."[14]

On the question of travel writing as a contribution to imperial discourse, visitors to Niagara proved remarkably faithful to colonialist convention. Examining a wide range of scientific, travel, and journalistic writing across the globe, literary scholar David Spurr has recently attempted to outline and codify a "repertoire of colonial discourse," suggesting a number of tropes or what he terms "rhetorical modes" that are common to western writers seeking to construct a "coherent representation out of the strange and incomprehensible realities of the non-western world."[15] Many of these tropes, conventions, and rhetorical modes appear in travel writing about Niagara. My approach to travel writing, however, is different from the literature on both women travelers and travel writing as colonial discourse. I have adopted a case study method, and thus have collected a variety of writings about one location, as well as researching the history of the tourist industry at this location. Thus, I am examining interactions between the colonizer and the colonized in what was, by the mid-nineteenth century, a well-established tourist industry. This context is an important one, for it helps us see that the reinforcement of racial hierarchies through tourism had a significant (and so far underanalyzed) material foundation; it was inscribed in the political economy and power relations of the tourist industry since its inception. In this chapter, I survey the rhetorical strategies of nineteenth-century visitors to Niagara—primarily British and Americans and Canadians of European descent—that helped render the natural and human wilderness of the New World knowable and thus able to be appropriated. These acts of appropriation were produced discursively, creating Niagara Falls as an icon of the untamed, *and* economically—entrenching racial and ethnic hierarchies into the "bricks and mortar" of the tourist industry itself.

THE SPECTACLE OF RACE: NATIVE PEOPLE AS TOURIST ATTRACTIONS

Contact with Native people was always a central component of the tourist experience of Niagara. From travelers' descriptions of the sight of their "first Indian," to the variety of invented stories of Native tragedy and sacrifice associated with the Maid of the Mist "legend," to the construction of an "authentic" Indian village in the 1950s, Native people have been woven into the natural history of the area. Along with waterfalls and wax museums, Native people were thus established as tourist attractions, extensions of the natural landscape. The tourist gaze, as Jonathan Culler has suggested, is constructed by signs, and the practice of tourism might be thought of as the collection of signs.[16] Throughout North American history, Native people have been particularly potent signifiers.

For several centuries of western culture, Native people signified wilderness, the opposite of civilization. Like European explorers, traders, missionaries, and invading armies, European tourists patrolled the civilization/wilderness border carefully. They had a firm sense of the side they occupied, but they also evinced a strong curiosity about what, and who, lay on the opposite shore. By the nineteenth century, the civilization/wilderness boundary had acquired a meaning specific to the project of Empire. Following McClintock, we can posit that a visit to the wilds of North America was understood as a trip through "anachronistic space: prehistoric, atavistic and irrational, inherently out of place in the historical time of modernity."[17] As Canadian historian Patricia Jasen has recently documented, the quest for "wild things" brought hundreds of thousands of tourists to Ontario in the nineteenth century.[18] Niagara was no different from many other nineteenth-century North American tourist destinations in this respect; it was tame enough to accommodate the standards of daily comfort demanded by the European upper class (by the mid-nineteenth century at least six luxurious hotels stood on both sides of the river), yet wild enough to be interesting. The Tuscarora Indians lived only ten miles away from the Falls, near Lewiston, New York, serving, as Jasen has noted, as "a place where visitors could assess the residents' capacity for civilization while picking up souvenirs at the same time."[19] This particular contact zone, then, gave European visitors a close-up look at one of the century's great binaries: the difference between "progress" and "degeneration." As McClintock has explained:

> The degenerate classes, defined as departures from the normal human type, were as necessary to the self-definition of the middle class as the idea of degeneration was to the idea of progress, for the distance along the path of progress travelled by some portions of humanity could be measured only by the distance others lagged behind.[20]

Thus the sight of one's "first Indian" on the shores of the Niagara River was regularly noted in travel writings, sometimes in a tone that rivaled the excitement at seeing the waterfall. As George Sala, traveling in 1863, wrote, "he was the first North American Indian, in his own land, I had seen," and as soon as composer Jacques Offenbach arrived at Niagara, his guide insisted, "you would like to see the Indians." William Russell considered that, "next to the purveyors of curiosities and hotel keepers, the Indians, who live in a village at some distance from Niagara, reap the largest profit from the crowds of visitors."[21]

Like virtually all travelers, both Sala and Offenbach were disappointed with what they saw. Indeed, in most accounts of first sightings of Native people, we can glimpse what I think of as the moment of "racial panic" as travelers let loose a volley of invective at the spectacle of race before them.[22] Travelers' accounts of Niagara's Native inhabitants ran the full gamut of nineteenth-century attitudes: the Natives were too ferocious or too tame, romantic figures or pathetic drunkards, uncivilized and unchristian or boring (or ridiculous) in their attempts to mimic white lifestyles. Indeed, by mid-century many visitors' sense of disappointment arose because they felt cheated; Ida Pfeiffer wrote in 1855 that Tuscarora was "now scarcely worth going to see, as the inhabitants, who have become Christians, go dressed like the whites, and build and cultivate their fields just like their neighbours."[23] This conflict between the assimilationist aims of government policy and the demands of tourism for difference and exoticism explains the popularity of stage-managed "Indian events" at Niagara Falls in the 1870s and 1880s, such as the "Indian burial ceremony" and the "Great Buffalo Hunt," organized by Col. Sydney Barnett, owner of the Niagara Falls Museum.[24] Such events, however, did not stem the tide of tourist disappointment and cynicism, and one way of presenting oneself as a knowing, world-weary traveler was to question the authenticity of the Indians one met. Offenbach, in 1875, wrote that he "expected to find savages, but they showed me pedlars, men who produced articles de Paris. . . . were they really Indian? I rather doubt it."[25] Edward Roper, visiting Niagara for a second time in the 1890s, noted, "there are the same Indians about as of old; they say the squaws come generally from 'ould Oirland.'" Many complained about "Irish Indians" or "Indian curiosities" made in New York (or England, or France, or, later of course, Japan), and, by the 1890s, guidebooks, such as the popular series edited by Karl Baedeker, advised readers that "the bazaar nuisance [at Niagara] continues in full force. . . . Those who wish Indian curiosities should buy from the Indians themselves."[26] From savage to boring to fake, Natives as tourist attractions generally disappointed, but they always drew.

The sight of Native people provoked more than the desire to gaze, however. While the European gaze itself, expressed in scientific and travel writing especially, is a proprietary one (the "master-of-all-I-survey," as Pratt calls it), visitors claimed possession through a variety of other gestures. The other was consumed both imaginatively, when Europeans wrote their own scripts for fantasy conversations, and literally—when Europeans purchased Native-crafted souvenirs. In both of these encounters—imagining Native people and buying from them—we can glimpse the two-sided nature of relationships in the contact zone: exchange and appropriation.

Consider, for example, Sala's long discussion with his "first Indian," which takes place, he claims, as the two are gazing at the waterfall together. Sala begins with a familiar diatribe: the Indian is a "shiftless and degraded vagrant, who does not wash himself, who is not at all scrupulous about taking things which do not belong to him, who will get blind drunk on rum or whisky whenever he has a chance." Yet after this outpouring, Sala returns to their mutual fascination with the waterfall, and the Native man changes from a human object of scorn to one of nature's victims. "I wonder what he's thinking, as we look at the Falls together; maybe he is thinking that all this used to be mine," Sala muses. Adopting the voice of what Pratt calls the anticonquest (in which European subjects "secure their innocence in the same moment as they assert European hegemony"), and Spurr calls the strategy of idealization (which "makes use of the savage in order to expand the territory of the western imagination, transforming the Other into yet one more term of western culture's dialogue with itself"), Sala narrates his Indian fantasy: "All this belonged to me, and now I am a vagrant and an outcast and the white man charges me for the birds I have slain." Sala ends his reflection with a return to the explicit imperial voice, but his tone has changed from disgust to pity: "Poor copper hued child of the wilderness!"[27] We might read this as imperial guilt, genuine compassion or the re-inscription of racism, but the point is that it's an exchange that can function only because of the imagined silence of one party.[28]

The passion for collecting Indian "curiosities" also signals the cultural commingling—within hierarchical relations—that characterizes the contact zone. Why were Europeans and white North Americans so fond of Native souvenirs, when they were clearly so ambivalent about the people who made the souvenirs? Indeed, most visitors to Niagara commented on the "grotesque and gaudy" style of Native handicrafts, even as they purchased them. (One visitor even claimed to have seen a "real scalp of an Indian, duly labelled and consisting of a triangular piece of skin" for sale in an Indian bazaar.)[29] This paradox has been answered by several scholars, who have identified souvenir shopping as a means by which the traveler tries to attain nativeness via a "transitional object."[30] Art historian Ruth Phillips argues that European fondness for Native souvenirs in North America reflects a "ritual displacement of aboriginal people through processes of commodification and consumption."[31] The effect on Native people of this exchange is less clear. Certainly most travelers thought the Natives were profiting greatly, and would have agreed with visitor J. M. Ferrie that the Tuscarora Indians "reap large profits" from the manufacture of souvenirs.[32] Historians have been more cautious about assessing the strictly economic effect of souvenir manufacture on Native communities. Both Phillips and Jasen note that women and children secured employment as makers and sellers of Native crafts. Jasen suggests that the participation of Native people in the tourist economy was one way for them to "make the best of a situation they had not created," while Phillips argues that the manufacture and sale of tourist commodities was a rearguard "marginal" defense against dispossession of land and assimilationist government policies.[33] It should also be noted that this desire to mimic, consume, and possess that which is despised was not limited to souvenir shopping. The 1926 American musical "Lelawala, or Maid of Niagara" featured a (European) cast costumed in Indian dress.[34]

While I see little evidence to suggest that female travelers displayed a sense of empathy or connectedness with the other, gender certainly framed such encounters. Europeans' notions of appropriate gender identities for Native people abound symbolically in their writings. The paradigmatic "first Indian," who caused a moment of panic and sometimes further reflection, was always male, which likely indicates more about Europeans' notions of fitting representatives of culture than the sex of the Native person whom the tourist actually first saw. European discussions and representations of Native souvenir sellers marked them almost always as female, which also increases the possibility that the tourist's "first Indian" would be a woman.

Native women were not, however, ignored by Europeans, as the centuries-old fascination with the Maid of the Mist "legend" at Niagara indicates. Dating (possibly) from a story, "commonly reported in the country" and circulated by a traveling fur trader in 1753, of an Iroquois man caught above the Falls in a current and swept over, the tale changed form through the nineteenth century to conform to European conventions of drama, romance, and sexuality. As literary scholar Terry Goldie has argued, "Indian maids" were popular characters in nineteenth- and twentieth-century European fiction, but the white male who is charmed by the Native woman is doomed, hence "the only escape from this situation is the usual one, the death of the indigene . . . in order for the white to progress towards the future and move beyond temptation and achieve possession of the land."[35] These stories are merely the nineteenth- and twentieth-century versions of a long-standing cliché of colonial history: the allegorization of colonialized Natives in terms of the female figure. The "uncertain continents," as Anne McClintock has termed Africa, the Americas, and Asia, were always eroticized by Europeans, and "travellers' tales abounded with visions of the monstrous sexuality of far-off lands . . . a fantastic magic lantern of the mind onto which Europe projected its forbidden sexual desires and fears."[36] In this case, the Iroquois man became an "Indian maid," named Lelawala, forced by her unfeeling father, the chief, to descend the Falls in a canoe to appease angry gods. Sometimes the father, in a moment of remorse, joins her; in other versions she is joined by her lover and rescued by him at the bottom of the Falls.[37] Various versions of this story have been told, in guidebooks, travelers' accounts, and tourist industry promotional literature, for centuries. The story has added, as I have argued elsewhere, to the commonplace nineteenth-century discursive practice of gendering the Falls female, and has figured centrally in the imaginary geography of Niagara as a place of romance, danger, and sexuality.[38] Many travelers, especially men, claimed that they could "trace in the outlines [of the waterfall] the indistinct shape of a woman, with flowing hair and drooping arms, veiled in drapery."[39] Those lacking in imagination were assisted by tour promoters; a 1915 Canadian Steamship Lines brochure, for example, invited tourists to imagine that "instinctively we see the Indian maid in her flower-bedecked canoe approach the apex of the Falls, her body erect, her demeanour courageous." Images of naked Native women going over the waterfall adorned postcards and promotional brochures, as well as "high" Niagara Falls art, through the nineteenth and twentieth centuries.[40] We can understand these images as yet another possessive feature of colonial discourse; as Spurr argues, such "erotically charged language . . . marks the entrance of the colonizer, with his penetrating and controlling power, as a natural union with the subject nation. Colonial domination thus is understood as having a salutary effect on the natural excesses and the undirected sexual energies of the colonized."[41]

SERVING COLONIALISM: WAITERS, DRIVERS, AND GUIDES

The contrast between civilization and wilderness was also played out in travelers' accounts of their perceptions of the Niagara labor force. While the waterfall itself was a beloved icon of the sublime, its "handlers" were detested. Complaints about the "disgustingly obtrusive civilization that crawls over its sides," were nearly universal at Niagara Falls, and almost every visitor had a story to tell of an importuning hackman or swindling tour guide.[42] The "hateful race of guides . . . miserable little peepshows and photographers, bird stuffers, shell polishers, and collectors of crystals" destroyed what many considered the proper appreciation of nature, and such concerns about the debasement of Niagara figured centrally in the campaign, waged by politicians, conservationists, and intellectuals, to "free Niagara" through the creation of public parkland in the 1880s.[43]

Disgust for local inhabitants who made their (usually paltry) living from the tourist industry has been present in travel literature in many countries and for many centuries, but Niagara's "obtrusive civilization" had a specific racial and ethnic configuration.[44] While the social history of immigration and racial/ethnic relations in the Niagara region has yet to be fully explored, Blacks were present from the earliest days of European settlement throughout the Niagara peninsula, including a community called Drummondville, near Niagara Falls, which was organized in the early nineteenth century. By the 1830s, Black men found steady employment in Niagara's hotel industry.[45] The visibility of Black, as well as Irish, men was startling to many visitors, and such racial conflicts contributed to what the local press acknowledged was the "bad name held by Niagara the world over."[46] Complaints about the "swindlers" at Niagara were not racially neutral. The chorus of disapproval, disgust, and sometimes fear that rose up to protest the dynamics of capitalism at the Falls had a specific racialized target: Jewish museum owners, "saucy Negro" guides, and "half-tipsy" Irish hack drivers.

Encounters with Black waiters at hotels, for example, sometimes caused tourists the same momentary racial panic as the sight of their "first Indian." One European hotel guest remarked that he "could not get used to the negroes' attendance, I am always afraid lest they soil all they touch." Others found them objects of novelty; "pleasant, funny creatures" (particularly when dressed in white servants' jackets), "good, grinning, curly pated Sambos." Some (especially the English) inverted prevailing racial hierarchies to contrast Blacks favorably with the Irish: "awkward, stupid, noisy and slow, I confess they [Blacks] are more bearable and amenable to counsel than their fair skinned brothers. . . . Irish waiters abound, and their character is by no means improved by being 'citizens of a free country.'"[47]

Just as the presence of Native people lent an air of drama and exoticism to the surroundings, the presence of Black tour guides, particularly at several dangerous excursions around the waterfall, intensified the experience of "doing" Niagara. Two of the most popular attractions through the nineteenth century were the Table Rock House and the Cave of the Winds tours, where travelers, suited up in an oilskin costume, could make their way through torrents of water to go, as it was advertised, "behind the Falls." Isabella Bird's experience at Table Rock in the 1850s is particularly revealing. She first recoils at the notion she must disrobe, and when she sees herself decked out in oilskin is shocked to behold "as complete a tatter-demallion as one could see begging upon an Irish highway." Her process of transformation is experienced completely in racial terms; she fails to recognize herself as English. As she leaves the dressing rooms, "a negro guide of most repulsive appearance awaited me," and she begins her (literal and metaphoric) descent. At the most difficult part of the passage,

> heavy gusts almost blew me away; showers of spray nearly blinded me. . . . I wished to retreat and essayed to use my voice to stop the progress of my guide. I raised it to a scream, but it was lost in the thunder of the cataract. The negro saw my incertitude, and extended his hand. I shuddered even there as I took hold of it, not quite free from the juvenile idea that "the black comes off." He seemed at that moment to wear the aspect of a black imp leading me to destruction.[48]

Later, however, Bird's moment of racial panic subsides and is transformed into a moment of deep reflection. She reaches her destination, Termination Rock, and, like many visitors to the Falls, experiences this triumph in religious terms. At Termination Rock she finds a "temple . . . formed by the natural bend of the cataract," the magnificence of which "makes a lasting impression on the mind. The temple seems a fit and awful shrine for Him who 'rides on the wings of mighty winds' and, completely shut out from man's puny works, the mind rises naturally in adoring contemplation to Him whose voice is heard in the 'thunder of waters.'"[49]

Bird is clearly proud of her achievement and devotes a considerable part of her description of Niagara to this event. It is at the end of her story, however, that we can see how gender converges with race to frame her narrative. Having already distinguished herself from Black men, she proceeds to set herself apart from white men, by downplaying and mocking the heroic quality of her experience. She writes in retrospect, "this achievement is pleasanter in the remembrance than in the act." Furthermore, she does not encourage others to follow her, and adopts the "innocent" voice of the anticonquest to rebuke those (male) writers who bragged about their similar accomplishments. "There is," she wrote, "nothing whatever to boast of in having accomplished it, and nothing to regret in leaving it undone. . . . After all, the front view is the only one for Niagara—going behind the sheet is like going behind a picture-frame."[50]

Male travelers who described their journeys behind the falls were also terrified by the torrents of water, and also expressed dismay at the presence of Black guides: "strapping specimen of negro or mulatto, in thick solid ungainly boots."[51] Niagara guides, whatever their color, loomed in the tourist imagination as rugged, hypermasculine creatures. Indeed, the complaints by a number of male visitors that Table Rock tour owner Saul Davis employed "negroes" who "used profane language and spoke very excitedly" in order to harass customers and extract more money from them led to the creation by the Ontario government of a Royal Commission, in 1873, to investigate "ill-treatment or extortion . . . practised upon visitors to Niagara Falls."[52] Yet, as Jasen has also found, with respect to Native steamship pilots and wilderness guides elsewhere in Ontario, the combination of human and natural dangers heightened the adventure for Europeans; the rushing water or roaring rapids were almost indistinguishable from the ferocious men who navigated them.[53] Male visitors' narratives of their passage through Niagara Falls reflect a clear sense of pride and pleasure, such as that of Frederic Almy, who spoke of the water

> foaming and rushing about your knees, and lugging at you with an invitation that is irresistible. I have seen grave men frolic in the water, their trousers and sleeves swelled almost to bursting with the imprisoned air. . . . To play so with Niagara brings an exhilaration that is indescribable.[54]

Others spoke of the "delightful, novel and strange sensation, of commingled terror and safety." Most agreed, even if they were less enthusiastic about the experience than Almy, that it was a "terrible ordeal, which no one should miss undergoing."[55] What is consistent in Bird's account as well as in those stories written by men is their positioning of the Black guide as an adversary to be negotiated and conquered.

CONCLUSION

Niagara Falls was a contact zone, located in anachronistic space. Tourists were no more inclined to recognize the irony of their position—that their comfortable existence at Niagara was facilitated by the presence of the waiters, guides, souvenir sellers, and drivers whom they despised—than were middle- and upper-class Europeans who encountered the "other" in their households, their workplaces, their Empires. The tourist gaze at Niagara was firmly trained on the boundary between civilization and wilderness, progress and degeneration, which let the European imagination roam freely, through fear, annoyance, hatred, desire, and always the assertion of power.

The spectacle of race was a potent commodity through the nineteenth century. Part of what made the Native North Americans of the nineteenth century such a spectacular attraction—to artists, writers, and anthropologists, as well as tourists—was, as Daniel Francis has put it, the widespread conviction that "they would not be around to see much of the twentieth."[56] When dire predictions that "progress" was bound to doom Native people to extinction failed to come true, twentieth-century tourists continued to see Native people as a colorful, timeless reminder of North America's tumultuous frontier. In the 1950s, a boom period for Niagara tourism, one of the many new attractions that opened was a Model Indian Village. The real Tuscarora community was deemed to be too far away from the other tourist attractions in this area, but of course "real" Natives on Reserves had long ceased to hold much exotic interest. The Tuscarora had been completely "tamed"; the Depression of the 1930s had devastated their farming economy and most people worked off the Reserve in Niagara-area industries. Even more problematic, from the perspective of the tourist industry, was the fact that there were limits to the commodification of the Reserve; an enterprising non-Native tourist entrepreneur could hardly put up an admissions gate. But Eric Jobst, a non-Native, could indeed charge admission to his Model Indian Village, which featured replicas of longhouses and teepees, and Natives (from the Six Nations Reserve near Brantford) who performed traditional dances and manufactured souvenirs. But his quest for nineteenth-century authenticity was, by twentieth-century standards, overdone. Soon, owners of neighboring motels were complaining to the Niagara City Council about the "continuous smell and smoke of the bonfire," and that the "beating of tom-toms, yelping and hollering" were scaring tourists' children.[57]

The symbols of Indianness—still imagined only as masculine, such as the feather headdress—became highly manipulable cultural markers. Throughout the twentieth century, they have been appropriated to market everything from motor oil to margarine, and even "real" Indians have found that the nineteenth-century fantasy Indian can be invented, and pressed into service, when necessary. In the 1920s, Clinton Richard of the Tuscarora Band became heavily involved in a campaign against discriminatory immigration law changes in the United States (which ignored centuries-old Indian treaty rights of unimpeded border crossing). He found that his iconic tourist status gave him an effective political weapon in this battle; he spent a summer donning traditional dress and visiting tourist camps at Niagara Falls, telling tourists about the unjust law and convincing them to support the Indian position—which eventually won the day.[58] Journalist Edmund Wilson, interviewing a politically active Mohawk chief near Niagara Falls in the 1950s, noticed a feather headdress in his livingroom. He asked Chief Standing Arrow if it belonged to him. It did not, replied the Chief, but, he said, "I wear it around when the tourists are here. They don't think you are a real Indian, you know, unless your wear one of these things."[59]

NOTES

For their wisdom and encouragement, I'd like to thank Yvette Abrahams, Roberta Hamilton, Ena Dua, and Ruth Pierson.

1. John Urry, *The Tourist Gaze: Leisure and Travel in Contemporary Societies* (London: Sage, 1990), 2. Other useful studies of the social meaning of tourism are Alexander Wilson, *The Culture of Nature: North American Landscape from Disney to the Exxon Valdez* (Toronto: Between the Lines, 1991); George Robertson, Melinda Mash, Lisa Tickner, Jon Bird, Barry Curtis, and Tim Putnam, eds., *Travellers' Tales: Narratives of Home and Displacement* (London: Routledge, 1994); and Rob Shields, *Places on the Margin: Alternative Geographies of Modernity* (London: Routledge, 1991).

2. Trinh T. Minh-ha, "Other Than Myself/My Other Self," in Robertson et al., *Travellers' Tales*, 22.

3. Mary Louise Pratt, *Imperial Eyes: Travel Writing and Transculturation* (New York: Routledge, 1992), 5. See also William Stowe's analysis of American travel writing about Europe which, he argues, helped Americans "construct and claim identities variously defined by gender, class, race and nationality," *Going Abroad: European Travel in Nineteenth-Century American Culture* (Princeton: Princeton University Press, 1994), xi.

4. See, for example, Kay Anderson, *Vancouver's Chinatown: Racial Discourse in Canada, 1875–1980* (Montreal: McGill-Queen's Press, 1991), 211–44; Ellen Furlough, "Packaging Pleasures: Club Méditerranée and French Consumer Culture, 1950–1968," *French Historical Studies* 18, no. 1 (Spring 1993): 65–81; Daniel Francis, *The Imaginary Indian: The Image of the Indian in Canadian Culture* (Vancouver: Arsenal Pulp Press, 1992); Patricia Jasen, *Wild Things: Nature, Culture and Tourism in Ontario, 1790–1914* (Toronto: University of Toronto, 1995); Keith Hollingshead, "White Gaze, 'Red' People—Shadow Visions: The Disidentification of 'Indians' in Cultural Tourism," *Leisure Studies* 11 (1992): 43–64; Ian McKay, *The Quest of the Folk: Antimodernism and Cultural Selection in Twentieth-Century Nova Scotia* (Montreal: McGill-Queen's Press, 1994); Catherine Palmer, "Tourism and Colonialism, The Experience of the Bahamas," *Annals of Tourism Research* 21, no. 4 (1994): 792–811; Ruth B. Phillips, "Consuming Identities: Curiosity, Souvenir and Images of Indianness in Nineteenth-Century Canada," David Dunton Lecture, Carleton University, 1991; Frank Fonda Taylor, *To Hell with Paradise—A History of the Jamaican Tourist Industry* (Pittsburgh: University of Pittsburgh Press, 1993); and Pierre L. Van Den Berghe, *The Quest for the Other—Ethnic Tourism in San Cristobel, Mexico* (Seattle: University of Washington Press, 1994).

5. Rev. J. W. Wilson, cited in Mrs. S. D. Morse, *Greater Niagara* (Niagara Falls, Ontario: Gazette Printing House, 1896), 12.

6. The social meaning of Niagara in the nineteenth century has been analyzed by several scholars. See, for example, Jasen, *Wild Things*; Elizabeth McKinsey, *Niagara, Icon of the American Sublime* (Cambridge: Cambridge University Press, 1985); Rob Shields, *Places on the Margin: Alternative Geographies of Modernity* (London: Routledge, 1991); Patrick McGreevy, *Imagining Niagara:*

The Meaning and Making of Niagara Falls (Amherst: University of Massachusetts Press, 1994); John Sears, *Sacred Places: American Tourist Attractions in the Nineteenth Century* (New York: Oxford University Press, 1989); and William Irwin, "The New Niagara: The Meaning of Niagara Falls in American Culture, from Discovery to 1820" (Ph.D. dissertation, University of Virginia, 1991).

7. Ian Ousby, *The Englishman's England: Taste, Travel and the Rise of Tourism* (Cambridge: Cambridge University Press, 1990), 167.

8. Captain William Butler, *The Great Lone Land* (London: Sampson, 1872), 25.

9. For the other side of the conversation, see, for example, James Axtell, "Through Another Glass Darkly: Early Indian Views of Europeans," in Ken Coates and Robin Fisher, eds., *Out of the Background: Readings on Canadian Native History*, 2nd ed. (Toronto: Copp Clark, 1996), 17–29; and George Sioui, *For an Amerindian History: An Essay on the Foundations of a Social Ethic* (Montreal: McGill-Queen's Press, 1992).

10. Pratt, *Imperial Eyes*, 6–7.

11. See, for example, Annie E. Coombes, *Reinventing Africa: Museums, Material Culture and Popular Imagination in Late Victorian and Edwardian England* (New Haven, CT: Yale University Press, 1994); Anne McClintock, *Imperial Leather: Race, Gender and Sexuality in the Colonial Contest* (New York: Routledge, 1994); Robert W. Rydell, *World of Fairs: The Century-of-Progress Expositions* (Chicago: University of Chicago Press, 1993); Catherine A. Lutz and Jane L. Collins, *Reading National Geographic* (Chicago: University of Chicago Press, 1993); R. G. Moyles and Douglas Owram, *Imperial Dreams and Colonial Realities: British Views of Canada, 1880–1914* (Toronto: University of Toronto Press, 1988); and Richard Kicksee, "Contested Liberal Commonsense and the Negotiation of 'Indian Participation' in the Canadian Centennial Celebration and Expo '67, 1963–1967" (M.A. thesis, Queen's University, 1995).

12. Marianna Torgovnick, *Gone Primitive: Savage Intellects, Modern Lives* (Chicago: University of Chicago Press, 1990), 11.

13. See, for example, Sara Mills, *Discourses of Difference: An Analysis of Women's Travel Writing and Colonialism* (London: Routledge, 1991); Billie Melman, *Women's Orients: English Women and the Middle East, 1718–1918* (London: Macmillan, 1992); Shirley Foster, *Across New Worlds: Nineteenth Century Women Travellers and Their Writing* (New York: Harvester, 1990); Dea Birkett, *Spinsters Abroad: Victorian Lady Explorers* (Oxford: Basil Blackwell, 1989); and Susan Brown, "Alternatives to the Missionary Position: Anna Leonowens as Victorian Travel Writer," *Feminist Studies* 21, no. 3 (Fall 1995): 587–614.

14. Antoinette Burton, *Burdens of History: British Feminists, Indian Women and Imperial Culture, 1865–1915* (Chapel Hill: University of North Carolina Press, 1994), 82; Vron Ware, *Beyond the Pale: White Women, Racism and History* (London: Verso, 1992). See also Nupur Chaudhuri and Margaret Strobel, eds., *Western Women and Imperialism: Complicity and Resistance* (Bloomington: Indiana University Press, 1992). My thanks to Yvette Abrahams for her insights on this point.

15. David Spurr, *The Rhetoric of Empire: Colonial Discourse in Journalism, Travel Writing and Imperial Administration* (Durham, NC: Duke University Press, 1993), 1–3.

16. Jonathan Culler, "Semiotics of Tourism," *American Journal of Semiotics* 1, no. 1–2 (1981): 127–40.

17. McClintock, *Imperial Leather*, 40.

18. Jasen, *Wild Things*.

19. Jasen, *Wild Things*, 42. On the fascination of the British with Native

culture, particularly in nineteenth-century heroic masculine adventure stories, see R. G. Moyles and Doug Owram, *Imperial Dreams, Colonial Realities: British Views of Canada, 1880–1914* (Toronto: University of Toronto Press, 1988), 37–60 and 167–86. On representations of Native culture generally in Canada, see Deborah Doxtator, *Fluffs and Feathers: An Exhibit on the Symbols of Indianness* (Brantford: Woodland Cultural Centre, 1992).

20. McClintock, *Imperial Leather*, 46.

21. George Sala, *My Diary in America in the Midst of the War* (London: Tinseley Brothers, 1865), 184, and Jacques Offenbach, *America and the Americans* (London: William Reeves, 1875), 74; William Howard Russell, *My Diary, North and South* (New York: Harper, 1863), 137.

22. I am using this term in the same sense that Eve Kosofsky Sedgewick has used the term "homosexual panic." Sedgewick suggests that in the use of the pathological psychiatric state "homosexual panic" as a legal strategy to defend gay-bashers—which implies that the perpetrator of violence is uncertain and insecure about his own sexual identity—we can see "how the overlapping aegises of minoritizing and universalizing understandings of male homo/heterosexual definition can tend to redouble the victimization of gay people." In other words, the effective use of this legal strategy relies on the notion that there is a distinct minority of gay people, and a second minority of "latent homosexuals." But at the same time, it needs a "universalizing force," to convince jurors, for example, that they may have acted in the same manner. "Homosexual panic," as Sedgewick points out, does not exist as a psychiatric category or a legal defense, which indicates "the difference between antigay crime and other-bias-related antiminority crime: the difference of how much less clear, perhaps finally how impossible, is the boundary circumscription of a minoritizing gay identity." The parallel I see to what I have called "racial panic" is in this permeability of boundaries, a central feature of relations between observer and observed in the contact zone. As Trinh T. Minh-ha suggests, "travelers' tales do not only bring the over-there home, and the over-here abroad. They not only bring the far away within reach, but also contribute . . . to challenging the home and abroad/dwelling and travelling dichotomy within specific actualities. . . . they speak to the problem of the impossibility of packaging a culture, or of defining an authentic cultural identity." Racial panic also reflects what Spurr calls the "classic position" of the western writer in the colonial situation, as the "conditions of access to colonized peoples also mark an exclusion from the lived human reality of the colonized." See Sedgewick, *Epistemology of the Closet* (Berkeley and Los Angeles: University of California Press, 1990), 19–22; Trinh, "Other Than Myself," 22; and Spurr, *The Rhetoric of Empire*, 14.

23. Ida Pfeiffer, *A Lady's Second Journey Round the World* (London: Longman Brown, 1855), 244.

24. Duncan McLeod, "Niagara Falls was a Hell-Raising Town," *Maclean's Magazine* (26 November 1955).

25. Offenbach, *America and the Americans*, 74.

26. Edward Roper, *By Track and Trail: A Journey through Canada* (London: W. H. Allen, 1891), 419; Karl Baedeker, *The United States* (1893; reprint, New York: Da Capo Press, 1971), 200.

27. Sala, *My Diary*, 184–85; Pratt, *Imperial Eyes*, 7; Spurr, *The Rhetoric of Empire*, 128.

28. It is also an exchange with enduring cultural significance in North America. On the legacy of blacks as visual but voiceless icons, from antislav-

ery images to Rodney King, see Houston A. Baker, "Scene . . . Not Heard," in Robert Gooding-Williams, ed., *Reading Rodney King, Reading Urban Uprising* (New York: Routledge, 1993), 38–48.

29. Moses Jackson, *To America and Back: A Holiday Run* (London: McQuordale, 1886), 131.

30. Barry Curtis and Claire Pajaczkowska, "Getting There: Travel, Time and Narrative," in Robertson et al., *Travellers' Tales*, 204.

31. Phillips, "Consuming Identities," 20. See also Ruth Phillips, "Why Not Tourist Art? Significant Silences in Native American Museum Representations," in Gyan Prakash, ed., *After Colonialism: Imperial Histories and Postcolonial Displacements* (Princeton: Princeton University Press, 1995), 98–125.

32. J. W. Ferrie, *The Falls of Niagara and Scenes Around Them* (Pennsylvania: A. S. Barnes and Co, 1878), 120.

33. Jasen, *Wild Things*, 81; Phillips, "Consuming Identities," 5. For an account of recent campaigns by Canadian Native people to protect their craft production from non-Native mass producers, see Valda Blundell, "Aboriginal Empowerment and Souvenir Trade in Canada," *Annals of Tourism Research* 20 (1993): 64–87.

34. George Murray Brown, *Lelawala, or, the Maid of Niagara* (Cincinnati, Willis Music Company, 1926). Unfortunately, I have only been able to locate the stage manager's notes for this production; the nature of the script is thus unknown. The stage manager's directions, however, are revealing in their discussion of how to "perform" the "other": for example, they note that "most of the dances are Indian in character, but do not try to imitate the Indian's manner exactly—this merely results in a foolish burlesque. . . . try to get your cast to feel as the Indians felt before you make them dance as the Indians danced," 10.

35. Terry Goldie, *Fear and Temptation: The Image of the Indigene in Canadian, Australian and New Zealand Literature* (Montreal: McGill-Queen's Press 1989), 71–72.

36. McClintock, *Imperial Leather*, 22. See also Spurr, *The Rhetoric of Empire*, 171.

37. One of many versions of the origins of this story is Col. Frederick C. Curry, "The Discovery of the Cave of the Winds," *Ontario Historical Society Papers and Records* 27 (1946): 19–22.

38. Karen Dubinsky, "The Pleasure Is Exquisite But Violent: The Imaginary Geography of Niagara Falls in the Nineteenth Century," *Journal of Canadian Studies* 29 (Summer 1994): 64–88.

39. William Howard Russell, *Canada: Its Defences, Condition and Resources* (London: Bradbury and Evans, 1865), cited in Charles Mason Dow, ed., *Anthology and Bibliography of Niagara Falls*, vol. 1 (Albany: J. B. Lyon, 1921), 318.

40. Canada Steamship Lines, *Niagara to the Sea*, 1915, 7. The recent fortunes of the "Maid of the Mist" legend are also telling. By the late 1980s, Native groups at Niagara were telling the press that they believed the story "was probably invented as an advertising gimmick for Maid of the Mist boat tours in the mid-1800s." Yet in 1991, a Native performing arts group in the area reappropriated the story, in the form of a modern dance piece. This version of the story, according to one of its creators, "offers up a picture of spirituality at odds with the rigidly hierarchical Judeo-Christian models," and, incidentally, ends happily. See "Research Sends Maid of the Mist Legend Tumbling," *Niagara Falls (New York) Gazette*, 23 August 1989; "Native American Production Sets Western New York World Premiere," *Buffalo Metro Community News*, 22 September 1991;

and "Dance Presents Native American Spiritual World," *Niagara Falls (New York) Gazette*, 19 October 1991. In 1996, after receiving continuous complaints from Native groups, the Maid of the Mist tour boat operators finally agreed to stop using the legend in their promotional material. "Metro Morning," CBC Radio, 17 September 1996.

41. Spurr, *The Rhetoric of Empire*, 172.

42. James Carnegie Southesk, *Saskatchewan and the Rocky Mountains* (Edinburgh: Edmonton and Douglas, 1875), quoted in Dow, ed., *Anthology and Bibliography of Niagara Falls*, 268.

43. Russell, *My Diary*, 136. On the Niagara preservation campaign, see Gerald Killan, "Mowat and a Park Policy for Niagara Falls, 1873–1877," *Ontario History* 70 (June 1975): 115–35; Alfred Runte, "Beyond the Spectacular: The Niagara Falls Preservation Campaign," *New York Historical Society Quarterly* 57, no. 1 (January 1973): 30–50; and Thomas Welsh, "The Early Years of the Queen Victoria Niagara Falls Parks Commission" (M.A. thesis, Queen's University, 1977).

44. Ousby, *The Englishman's England*, 134.

45. Robin Winks, *The Blacks in Canada: A History* (Montreal: McGill-Queen's Press, 1971), 146. See also Owen Thomas, *Niagara's Freedom Trail: A Guide to African-Canadian History on the Niagara Peninsula* (Thorold: Niagara Region Tourist Council, 1995), 15. American sources suggest that Black men accounted for approximately one-quarter of the restaurant labor force until the 1930s. See Dorothy Sue Cobble, *Dishing It Out: Waitresses and Their Unions in the Twentieth Century* (Urbana: University of Illinois Press, 1991), 18. Few references exist to the presence of Black women in the Niagara tourist industry, with the exception of an account of a trip to the Cave of the Winds in the 1880s, which suggests that a "bright eyed mulatto girl" worked at the change room. "Cave of the Winds," *Providence, Rhode Island Journal* (n.d., circa 1880s).

46. *The Complete Illustrated Guide to Niagara Falls and Vicinity* (Niagara Falls, NY: Gazette Printing Company, circa 1880s), 22.

47. Ivan Golovin, *Stars and Stripes, or American Impressions* (London: W. Freeman, 1856), 15; Frances E. Monck, *My Canadian Leaves* (London: Richard Bentley, 1891), 161; Thomas Hughes, *Vacation Rambles* (London: MacMillan, 1895), 150; and Samuel Phillips Day, *Life and Society in America* (London: Newman and Co., 1880), 150.

48. Isabella Bird, *The Englishwoman in America* (1856; reprint, Toronto: University of Toronto Press, 1966), 232–33.

49. Ibid., 233–34.

50. Ibid., 234. On the religious meanings associated with the Falls, see Patrick McGreevy, "Niagara as Jerusalem," *Landscape* 28, no. 2 (1985): 26-32; and McKinsey, *Niagara, Icon of the American Sublime*, 85-92. In light of the evidence uncovered by Sara Mills that "heroic feats" accomplished by women travel writers were often disbelieved—and even censored by publishers who feared they would undermine the author's credibility with a disbelieving public—Bird's reaction to her own accomplishment is even more interesting. Indeed, thirty years after her travels to Niagara, Bird herself was subject to censorship from her publisher, who considered her accounts of travel to Asia "unfeminine." What is also remarkable, though unstated here, is that Bird suffered all her life from a spinal disease, and had in fact been sent to North America for a rest under orders from her doctor. In this context, Bird's refusal to adopt wholesale the heroic voice of the conquerer, and her subtle ridicule of those who did, perhaps provides another perspective to evaluate what

Mills terms the different constraints women faced in the reception of their texts. See Mills, *Discourses of Difference*, 110–16, and Birkett, *Spinsters Abroad*, 14–15.

51. Russell, *Canada*, as cited in Dow, *Anthology*, 1:323.

52. Killan, "Mowat and a Park Policy," 115–35.

53. Jasen, *Wild Things*, 72.

54. Frederick Almy, "What to See," in William Dean Howells, ed., *The Niagara Book: A Complete Souvenir of Niagara Falls* (Buffalo: Underhill and Sons, 1893), 37.

55. *The Complete Illustrated Guide to Niagara Falls*, 33; Roper, *By Track and Trail*, 418.

56. Francis, *The Imaginary Indian*, 23.

57. *Niagara Falls Review*, 14 June 1960 and 28 June 1960.

58. Clinton Richard, *Fighting Tuscarora: The Autobiography of Chief Clinton Richard* (Syracuse: Syracuse University Press, 1973), 78.

59. Edmund Wilson, *Apologies to the Iroquois* (New York: Farrar, Straus and Giroux, 1959), 53.

15

Uprooted Women
Partition of Punjab 1947

APARNA BASU

Owing to the distortions resulting from colonialism, imperialism, and nationalism, population movements on a grand scale have become a common feature of twentieth-century history; but there have been as yet relatively few attempts to look beneath the surface of these mass movements of people and to disentangle the specific experiences of women. Until the mid-1970s, women were largely invisible in studies of migration and, when they did emerge, tended to do so within the category of men's dependents.[1]

In this century of the displaced person, India's Partition of 1947 still remains one of the greatest social upheavals. The Mountbatten Plan, by which the subcontinent was to be divided into Pakistan and India, was announced on June 3, 1947. West Pakistan was to consist of Sind, Baluchistan, the North West Frontier Province, and sixteen districts of Punjab. The remaining thirteen districts of Punjab were to be in India. Though the exact boundary line was not yet determined, migration started taking place even before August 15, 1947, when roughly ten million people were uprooted from their ancestral homes. Historians have mainly focused on the causes of Partition and have endlessly debated whether it was inevitable and who was responsible for it—the British, the Indian National Congress, or the Muslim League. The loss of lives and property and the widespread violence that accompanied

Partition have by now been well documented. Less well known are the large-scale abductions of women from all three communities: Hindu, Sikh, and Muslim. No official estimates exist of the exact number of such abductions, but it is safe to assume that there were approximately one hundred thousand. Of these women, roughly thirty thousand were recovered by police and social workers in both India and Pakistan between 1947 and 1982.[2]

The history of Partition is based largely on official documents as a history of government-to-government debate, concentrating on the differences between the Congress and the League and on the British policy of divide and rule. This history has ignored the dislocation of human lives and the loss, trauma, pain, and violence people suffered.

This chapter tries to explore the human dimensions of the Partition of Punjab. It draws mainly on two sources: the private papers of Mridula Sarabhai[3] who devoted six years of her life, from 1947 to 1953, almost entirely to the task of recovering abducted women and who influenced and shaped government policy because of her proximity to Mahatma Gandhi and Jawaharlal Nehru; and *Mool Sota Ukhdela (The Uprooted)*, the memoirs of Kamlaben Patel, a woman who spent her early years in the Sabarmati Ashram with Gandhi and who worked closely with Mridula Sarabhai.[4] Both these women were close associates of Gandhi and had worked with him and taken an active part in the freedom struggle. Mridula Sarabhai had been with Gandhi in the early months of 1947, walking from village to village in Bihar, trying to restore communal peace and harmony and confidence among the Muslims. Kamlaben Patel's memoirs are rich in detail and provide fascinating insights into the psychology of the abducted women and the officials.

As, in the millions, Hindus and Sikhs from West Punjab fled to India and Muslims from East Punjab fled to Pakistan, they were brutally attacked by armed mobs. Refugee trains arrived, often carrying only dead bodies. Women in this communal holocaust became the most vulnerable and least protected victims. The brutality that accompanied Partition deliberately targeted women, for the wounds inflicted on them scarred and tainted entire communities. Some women were forcibly abducted, while others were left behind and lost in the confusion as their families ran for their lives. Many committed suicide by jumping into wells. In Thoa Khalsa in Rawalpindi district, ninety Sikh women jumped into a well to save their honor.[5] Fathers killed their daughters with their own *kirpans* (the small ceremonial sword worn by Sikhs from the time they are baptized) or consigned them to the fire. At Harnoli, in

Mianwali district, hundreds of women threw themselves into burning houses to escape being molested. Beyond the horrors of self- or enforced immolation, there was the horror of abduction.

When women were forcibly abducted, sold, raped, or remarried, they suffered unimaginable cruelty and humiliation. Having been uprooted from their families and familiar surroundings, they had to struggle hard to recover a sense of continuity in their lives. Crossing a border meant that they had to reconstruct their lives in new circumstances and in an alien culture. The remaking of the self must have been a traumatic experience.

A large number of abducted women were sold, often several times. Sometimes they were sent as gifts to friends and acquaintances. After the unforgettable massacre of what came to be called the Kamoke train incident, in which three thousand male passengers were killed, the Station House Officer collected the young women in an open space and distributed them like sweets among the police, the national guards, and the local *goondas* (thugs). Women were sold or given away as gifts in the same way that baskets of oranges are sold or given as gifts.[6] The first-rate "goods" were shared out among the members of the police and the army; the second-rate went to anyone else.[7] The old women were discarded and abandoned. It must not have been easy to live through and survive such harrowing experiences.

For an abducted woman, there was nobody she could turn to for help. She had to live with a man who may have killed her husband, brother, or father, but she had no option. She may even have felt some gratitude because he had brought her home and given her security and respect. Her abductor believed that people of her community had killed members of his community and abducted their women. Hence, he had no sense of guilt. In fact, he took pride that he had taken revenge by abducting her.

The large-scale displacement of people created certain urgent problems that led to the formation of the Ministry of Relief and Rehabilitation in India. On November 24, 1947, a separate Women's Section was formed within the Ministry to organize relief for women and children, especially those who were unattached, and to help with the recovery of abducted women and children and with their subsequent training and rehabilitation. Mrs. Rameshwari Nehru[8] was appointed honorary director and Mrs. Hannah Sen[9] honorary secretary of the Women's Section. As the work of this section expanded, the number of honorary officers increased. Mrs. John Matthai was appointed as secretary; Mrs. Raksha Saran, joint secretary; Mrs. Man Mohini Sehgal, deputy secretary; and Mrs. Kamla Tandon, assistant secretary. All these women were well-known social workers. Mridula Sarabhai was appointed as special representative of the Women's Section and was given charge of recovery operations in West Pakistan and also supervision of recovery work in East Pakistan.

When Mridula Sarabhai heard about the communal riots in Punjab, as she was watching the historic hoisting of the national flag on Red Fort on August 15, 1947, she felt that it was her duty to proceed there. Jawaharlal Nehru agreed. Sarabhai had planned to go from Delhi to Amritsar by the Grand Trunk Road, but as it was blocked by violent mobs, the prime minister advised her to travel by plane to Lahore and contact the inspector general of police, Qurban Ali Khan, who had served in Uttar Pradesh (previously known as the United Provinces) in the pre-Partition days and knew many congressmen, and seek his help in crossing the border.[10] Sarabhai arrived in Lahore on August 19, 1947, but having failed to contact Khan, she found a ride with a convoy of vehicles going to Amritsar. The convoy was carrying terror-stricken Hindu and Sikh refugees who were in a state of panic because they did not know whether they would cross the border alive.

On reaching Amritsar, the same day, she found that total anarchy prevailed. There was a complete breakdown of law and order and communications, and both governments were trying desperately to cope with the millions of refugees. Sarabhai set up her office in the Amritsar Hotel on Mall Road, which had been the best hotel in the pre-Partition days. From early morning till late at night, group after group of dazed and bewildered refugees would flock to the hotel, pleading their case.

> Behenji [sister], our women and children are trapped on that side [Pakistan], please get them out. . . . What could we do? When trouble started in our area, we came rushing out to look for help and then we could not go back. . . . Now all of a sudden communications are broken off. Wild rumours are afloat about the terrible happenings. Please do something, come to our help. . . .[11]

Sarabhai listened to their stories with great attention and assured them that she would do her level best to get their women who had been left behind rescued as soon as possible. To rescue these helpless women from the clutches of the abductors now became her prime task. She was convinced that this was a humanitarian task of utmost importance and devoted the next six years of her life entirely to it. Anees Kidwai writes that Sarabhai understood the gravity of the situation and, being a woman of unusual courage and capacity for hard work, crossed the borders and fearlessly walked about in Pakistan.[12] "She went about the business of recovery of abducted women 'like a tigress with cats,'" writes Y. D. Gundevia, who had been assigned the task of helping her in the Ministry of External Affairs.[13]

The question of recovery of abducted women was seriously considered for the first time at an Inter-Dominion Conference held on December 6, 1947, when the machinery was set up for this purpose in both India and Pakistan. The primary responsibility for recovery was assigned to the local civil service and police, but a large number of honorary and paid workers were also recruited for this work. It was agreed at this conference that statistical information would be compiled giving particulars of women and children abducted; public appeals would be issued through press, radio, district publicity offices, and village headmen; evacuation parties would be formed in each district and state; transit camps would be organized at important centers; homes would be established in Amritsar and Lahore for the reception of recovered women from East and West Punjab, respectively; and weekly statements would be prepared showing the number of women recovered in each district and state and sent to East or West Punjab.[14]

It was difficult to set up all this immediately. The acquisition of transport facilities took a long time. The Women's Section of the Ministry of Relief and Rehabilitation, in order to expedite the work of rescue and recovery of women and children, recruited a number of honorary and paid workers. Mridula Sarabhai often chose them after interviewing them personally. Many of them were recent graduates of the Delhi School of Social Work. Four regional organizers and nearly forty district social workers were assigned to this work. Camps were set up in each district of East Punjab (except the district of Simla) and were under the direction of Miss Premvati Thapar. Twelve women social workers were attached to these camps from the Indian side and worked in association with women social workers from Pakistan. Eleven camps, one in each district of West Punjab, were established for the reception and interim relief of recovered women and were under the direction of women social workers. The districts of Rawalpindi, Jhelum, Sialkot, Gujarat, and Mianwali were, however, declared closed areas by Pakistan. In May 1948, recovery work was extended to these areas, but only Indian women social workers could enter under Pakistani protection. Indian civil servants, police, and military officers were not allowed entry.

In the North West Frontier Province (NWFP), because of lack of support from the provincial government, no machinery or camp could be set up, and little progress was made for recovering the large numbers of abducted women who were suspected of having been taken there.

Kamaladevi Chattopadhyaya[15] was sent to the NWFP by the Ministry of Relief and Rehabilitation of India. She stayed in Peshawar for two or three days and met several government officers, but her efforts yielded no result. According to the decision made at the Inter-Dominion Conference, the Pakistani authorities were to provide food, accommodation, and other necessary facilities, whereas Indian troops in Pakistan provided the necessary protection at the camps. The reverse was the case in the Indian camps. Mixed police from both the Dominions were to help in the recovery work. The social workers were responsible for the care and supervision of recovered women and children in the district camps. They also helped the police in the rescue work, in the escorting of recovered women to the district transit camps, and in the evacuation of recovered women to the base camps from which they were taken to India or Pakistan. The Lahore base camp, located in the Sir Gangaram Hospital, was placed by Mridula Sarabhai under the supervision of Kamlaben Patel.

Sarabhai contacted women of various political affiliations and impressed upon them the necessity of giving wide publicity to the work being done for the recovery of abducted women. As a result, a joint appeal was issued on January 28, 1948, by many leading women of India and Pakistan for expediting this work. A vigorous campaign was launched between February 16 and 22, 1948, which was observed as "Restore the Women and Children Week." Sarabhai made frantic efforts for its success. She visited Karachi twice after hearing a rumor that abducted women were being removed from West Punjab and the NWFP to Sind. She met the premier of Sind, Mr. Khurro, and requested that he issue the necessary order for their recovery. She also met the Pir of Manki Sharif, who promised her full support in the NWFP.

In East Punjab, most of the abducted women were hidden in villages. The majority of abducted women were rural women under thirty-five years of age. The abductors would come to know the moment a police vehicle entered a village and would run away and hide in a nearby field or forest, with the women. As the police raids on these houses proved abortive, the police decided that the best time to search a house was around sunset, when all the family members were likely to be at home. The recovery police staff would leave their vehicle and driver at the outskirts of the village, lest the abductors got a signal about the raid. To avoid detection, the police chose to go at twilight in separate groups of two or three. Often, they had to walk five kilometers. Generally, they were accompanied by an "informer," who led them to the house of the abductor. There was the danger that, if a woman was rescued from a village, the rest of the abducted women would be sold or killed. The abductor usually denied that the woman was abducted. Often he offered stiff resistance and had to be physically overpowered by the police.

The women were so frightened and unsure whether their original family members were alive and if so, whether the family would accept them, that often they refused to go with the police squad. In some cases, the women had sufficiently adjusted to their new situation that they did not want to leave. In either case, they had to be persuaded by the social worker and sometimes forcibly put into the van and taken to the camps set up for them. This was even more true of Hindu and Sikh women who had been abducted in Pakistan and who feared that their families would regard them as "soiled." A Hindu woman felt that she had been rendered impure, had become sullied, was no longer *pativrata* (faithful to her husband). And her fears were not entirely unfounded. Mahatma Gandhi and Jawaharlal Nehru repeatedly issued appeals asking people to take back these women as they had committed no sin and were "pure." According to Kamlaben Patel,

> Hindu women were often accepted by their families because of economic failure. People had come from Pakistan as refugees and had no money. They did not have a woman to do the housework—a housewife. But here there was a woman available. So forgetting everything, they took her. They accepted them out of helplessness, not broadmindedness.[16]

There were people who were prepared to rescue women if they were paid handsome sums of money. Mridula Sarabhai strongly opposed this, on the grounds that women were not commodities to be purchased: "This will ruin our work in the field of raising the status of women," she said in a note to Mahatma Gandhi, Prime Minister Nehru, and Lady Mountbatten.[17] At an emergency meeting of the Cabinet, the government decided that it was opposed to any financial transactions in the recovery of abducted women from Pakistan.[18] Gandhi was appalled at the idea that women could be bought, and made a reference to this in a postprayer speech: "Some *goondas* came forward to bring back the girls if they are paid Rs 1,000 per girl. Has this become a business then?" he asked.[19]

After they were rescued, the women were kept in the camps set up for them, often for months, till their cases were decided and genuine relatives found. The abductors seldom sat quiet. They tried all ways and means of getting back the women by going to the officers of the Recovery Organization and also to the camps. The camps were overcrowded, and lack of sanitation led to frequent outbreaks of epidemics. The approved budget of an Indian camp could provide for barely two square meals a day and two sets of clothes for each woman. There was no money for extras. Mridula Sarabhai gave her own money to buy soap, oil, *kumkum* (red vermilion), and occasionally fruit for the sick or biscuits and sweets for the children.[20]

On one occasion, when news came that Hindu and Sikh women and children from the Kunjah camp in Pakistan were being brought to the Lahore base camp, there was great jubilation, and preparations were made for their bedding and food. Truck after truck started arriving at 8:00 P.M., carrying women and children who looked more like skeletons than human beings. They said that they had not eaten properly for six months or more. They had been given a diet of one dry *chapati* a day and no salt in their food. They could bathe only once a fortnight, and no soap or oil was provided. Their hair and bodies were covered with lice and ulcers. They had not been given any water to drink during a journey of 190 kilometers from Kurja camp to Lahore. Kamlaben Patel and her coworkers were overwhelmed and did not know for some time how to deal with the situation.[21] As news of the arrival of the inmates of Kurja camp reached East Punjab, anxious relatives started arriving in hoards in search of their lost sisters, wives, daughters. Security guards had to be put at the gates to prevent people from rushing in at all hours.

Sarabhai came to the camps as soon as she heard of the state of the women and children, arriving with Raja Gaznafar Ali Khan, Minister of Refugees and Rehabilitation of Pakistan. The security guard stopped them and said that nobody could enter without Miss Patel's orders. Kamlaben Patel rushed to the gate and was most embarrassed, but Sarabhai pointed out to the minister that "maintaining discipline, law and order is not just the prerogative of men. You have seen today the authority that can be exercised by a Patel girl!" Gaznafar Ali Khan was ashamed to see the condition of these women who had been lodged for several months in a Pakistani camp, and immediately authorized money for the purchase of milk, fruit, and so forth for them.[22]

Recovery work was proceeding rather slowly, and so on November 11, 1948, an Inter-Dominion agreement was signed between India and Pakistan for recovery of abducted persons on both sides of the border. To implement this, the Recovery of Abducted Persons Ordinance was promulgated by the Government of India on January 31, 1949. Its aim was to provide, in pursuance of an agreement with Pakistan, for the recovery and restoration of certain abducted persons. It provided that provincial governments could establish camps for the reception and detention of abducted persons. If any police officer had reason to believe that an abducted woman resided at any place, he could search it without a warrant and take her into custody and deliver her to the nearest camp officer. He could also seek the help of any female officer. The abducted woman could be transferred from one camp to another for the purpose of maintaining health in the camps.

If a question arose whether a woman detained in a camp was or was not abducted, or should or should not be conveyed out of India, the case would be decided by a tribunal to be set up by the central government, and its decision was to be final. The detention of any abducted woman in a camp was not be questioned by any court. The ordinance expired on July 31, 1949, and was repromulgated.[23] When the repromulgated ordinance was about to expire, the Government of India introduced the Recovery and Restoration of Abducted Persons Bill in Parliament, which was passed and became Act 65 on December 28, 1949. Clause 1 of the Act stated that every effort must be made to recover and restore abducted women and children within the shortest possible time, and Clause 2 said that religious conversion of persons abducted after March 1947 would not be recognized, and all such persons must be restored to their original Dominion. The wishes of the women concerned were irrelevant, and consequently no statements of such persons were to be recorded. One of the principal features of the Act was that it adopted a more comprehensive definition of the term "abducted" than the one provided for in the Indian Penal Code. Another important clause reaffirmed the setting of tribunals consisting of one representative from India, one from Pakistan, and one neutral member in Lahore and Delhi to settle disputed cases of women unwilling to return to their original homes. A special tribunal was set up at Jullundur to dispose of such cases in accordance with the decisions reached at the Inter-Dominion Conference. The cases were decided on the following broad principles:

1.   Those women who had relatives in Pakistan or who wanted to go there should be sent to Lahore.
2.   Those women known or believed to have relatives in the Indian Union should be handed over to the Indian authorities there.
3.   Cases of those women whose relatives were not traceable and who were persistent in wanting to go back to their new homes should be decided on their individual merit by the tribunal in the interest and future good of the women themselves.[24]

Recovery work in Pakistan was going on at a much slower pace than in India. Mrs. Rameshwari Nehru held that a firm attitude should be taken against the Pakistani government, and if it did not speed up the recovery work, India should also go slow. Mridula Sarabhai disagreed, and thought that India's approach should not be retaliatory but conciliatory. Sarabhai believed that the recovery work in India should proceed at a fast pace irrespective of the number of Hindu and

Sikh women recovered from Pakistan. As the differences between the two women sharpened, Sarabhai tendered her resignation, but instead of accepting it, Jawaharlal Nehru put her in sole charge of the recovery work, transferring it from the Ministry of Relief and Rehabilitation to the Ministry of External Affairs, which was directly under his charge. Sarabhai was provided a new office, the Central Recovery Office, which was set up in Constitution House, New Delhi. The Central Recovery Office kept in close touch with the Recovery Organizations in India and Pakistan and helped them implement the government policy regarding the recovery of abducted women.

As the years went by, many abducted women settled down and were assimilated into the family and society of the abductors. The women gave birth to children, were treated as wives, and had adjusted themselves to their new surroundings and way of life. To many it seemed unfair and perhaps even cruel to uproot them again and make them face an uncertain future. Mrs. Rameshwari Nehru was among those who felt that abducted women should not be forced to return to their original homes. Mridula Sarabhai, on the other hand, subscribed to the view that the rescued women must be returned to their original families: "recovery was an effort to remove from the lives of thousands of innocent women the misery that is their lot today and to restore them to their legitimate environment where they can spend the rest of their lives with *izzat* [honor]."[25] She argued that when a woman refused to leave her new home, it was out of fear. Though a strong advocate of women's rights, Sarabhai, in this case, did not want to give women the freedom to decide their fate. She was convinced that if they said that they did not want to return, it was out of fear and a confused state of mind, and she was not always wrong.

For example, in the Shekhapura district camp in Pakistan, a twenty- to twenty-one-year-old woman claimed that the police had forcibly brought her to the camp. She claimed that, before the riots, she had fallen in love with a Muslim boy who had worked in her father's shop and had married this boy willingly and that hers was not a case of abduction. The Pakistani police supported her story. No one in her neighborhood could confirm or deny her story, as the population had completely changed. Later, a young man came to Kamlaben Patel's office in the Lahore camp looking for his lost wife. By this time, the twenty-one-year-old woman was in the Lahore camp and when the man saw her he recognized her as his wife. He ran to Kamlaben Patel to say that he had seen his wife. When the woman was brought to the office, sobbing, she fell into her husband's arms, and when asked about her previous story, she confessed that she had been lying all along out of fear. In truth, she had lost her parents as a child and had been brought up by an uncle who ill-treated her. Subsequently, she was happily married, but soon afterward the communal riots started. She and her husband started running to escape the mob but they were caught. Her husband was severely beaten, stabbed, and wounded, and she was told that he would be killed. She was sold for fifty rupees. The man who bought her was kind to her, and she believed that if she were sent to India, she would be sold again. The next day she appeared in front of the Tribunal and repeated her story. Mr. Rizvi, Superintendent of Police, even accused the Indian side of having produced a fictitious husband. But the tears of the couple convinced the Tribunal, and husband and wife were once again restored to each other.[26]

In another case, in a village in Multan district, a father appealed that his daughter Veera, who was in the house of a subinspector of the police, be restored to him. He provided the name, address, and all other details, and the district worker from the Indian side went and met her. Veera said that her father had willingly betrothed her to a Muslim, there was no question of abduction, and she did not want to go back to India. When this information was conveyed to her father, he insisted that his daughter had been forcibly taken away from him. To make sure that Veera was not under any pressure, Kamlaben Patel insisted that she should be brought to the Lahore camp and the Indo-Pakistani Tribunal should decide her case. After a great deal of pressure and persuasion, Mr. Rizvi finally yielded. As soon as Veera came to Lahore, she told the superintendent of the camp, "Are you not ashamed to forcibly drag a married woman like this to the camp? I want to stay with my husband. I have nothing to do with my parents." The Pakistani police wanted to take her back to her husband, but Patel firmly said that she would remain in the camp till the Tribunal met and decided her case. This was agreed to.

One night the camp's superintendent brought Veera to Kamlaben Patel. Patel called Veera to her bedside and said, "If you want to go back [to the inspector] then I will send you. If you don't want to go back to your parents, don't go, but tell me why." Veera broke down and weeping said, "Everyone in the camp says that there is a lady who wears *salwar kameez* (pants and knee-length tunic), has short bobbed hair and is very powerful and can get anything done in India. Even Pandit Nehru listens to her [this was a reference to Mridula Sarabhai]. If I tell the truth, will she help me?" Kamlaben replied, "Of course, she will." Whereupon Veera told her story. The subinspector had told Veera's father, "If you leave your daughter, thirty tolas of gold, and your house, I will ensure a safe passage for your entire family to an Indian cantonment." The father agreed to sacrifice Veera for the life and safety of the rest of the family. He gave his daughter, thirty tolas of gold, and his house to the subinspector. When the work for the recovery of abducted women started, the father immediately made an application for his daughter, because he knew exactly with whom and where she was. Veera said, "Behenji, what am I to tell you. I am not happy at the sub-inspector's house. As long as he is in the house I am alright, but as soon as he leaves on duty, his wife harasses me and calls me a kafir's daughter and so on. She makes me do all the housework as if I were her maid. The man loves me but he is under pressure from his family. But those parents who sacrificed me, I will never go back to them." Kamlaben Patel assured her that if she told her true story before the Tribunal, she would not be forced to go back to her parents, and Patel would try to arrange a marriage for her with a suitable Hindu boy.

On the next day, in front of the Tribunal, Veera declared that she was ready to go back to India and that her marriage had been forcibly performed. The subinspector, present in the court, was seething with rage. To Kamlaben Patel, it seemed that, if possible, he would have shot her and Veera. Veera asked for her thirty tolas of gold, but Patel explained to her that such behavior could not be expected from men who were like animals. "God will give you everything. It does not behoove you to ask anything from this man." Some time after her return to India, Veera was married to a Hindu man, and a few years later Patel met her in Amritsar, a happily married mother of two children.[27]

Another incident also makes this point. When Mridula Sarabhai visited the Kunjah camp, a few women vehemently opposed being taken to India. "We know our relatives are dead. They were killed in our presence," said some of the older ones with tears in their eyes. A group of younger ones shouted hysterically, "We changed our religion three years ago. Our whole family did so. . . . We are Muslims; what right have you [addressing the Pakistani colleagues] to hold us here and ask us to go with these kafirs? If that is what you feel, why don't you go over to Hindustan and leave us in peace?" The ringleader was a bright girl:

> You say abduction is immoral and so you are trying to save us. Well, now it is too late. One marries only once, willingly or by force. We are now married. What are you going to do with us? Ask us to marry again? Is that not immoral? What happened to our relatives when we were abducted? Where were they? They now tell us they are eagerly waiting for us. No, you do not know our society. Life will be hell for us. You may do your worst, but remember this: you can kill us but we will not go.

After a few days, this girl's mother came. The change in the girl's attitude was unbelievable. Not only did she change her mind and opt to return to India herself but she brought the rest of the girls with her.

That night she spent with her mother. The next day, the girl asked the Pakistani officers to forgive her. "I have no relatives here. Nor have the other women I know here. We are all mortally afraid." With the help of the press and government agencies and an all-out effort of Sarabhai's workers, within ten days the relatives of this group of women were tracked down, and the women were brought down from Pakistan to India.[28]

There were, however, cases of women who willingly intermarried. For example, Sudarshan was a young Hindu girl studying in a college in Lahore who was friendly with a Muslim boy whom she wanted to marry. They knew that Sudarshan's parents would never allow this. In the meantime came Partition and the communal holocaust, and Sudarshan had to go away to Delhi with her parents. But the boy followed her, and the couple secretly returned to Lahore. Sudarshan's father came to Lahore and claimed that his daughter had been abducted. Kamlaben Patel assured Sudarshan that if she wanted to return to her husband, Patel would help her. Sudarshan was forced to accompany her father to Delhi, but after some time managed somehow to escape back to Lahore and her husband.[29]

In another case, a beautiful young Muslim girl, the daughter of an army officer in Baramulla, married a Hindu *jawan* (a young boy), who worked as an orderly for her father. In the course of time, they had two or three children. The Recovery team found out and wanted to take the woman back to Pakistan. She did not want to go, and she and her husband successfully eluded the Indian authorities for several years. Finally, however, she was traced and persuaded to meet her mother and aunt. They somehow managed to convince her to go back with them, leaving her husband and children behind. The young man converted himself to Islam, followed her to Pakistan, and managed to get back his wife.[30]

There were several tragic cases such as that of Ismat and Jitu, a Muslim girl and Hindu boy who were in love in Lahore. Ismat escaped to Amritsar and married Jitu. Ismat was forcibly taken back to Lahore, as her family lodged a complaint of abduction. Mridula Sarabhai and Kamlaben Patel agreed to her going back to her family. Her family forced her to say that she had no relationship with Jitu and did not want to go back to him. Jitu was heartbroken and never recovered from this shock.[31]

Boota Singh, a fifty-five-year-old Sikh bachelor farmer, had purchased Zainab, a seventeen-year-old Muslim girl, from her abductors for fifteen hundred rupees in 1947. He married her, and they had a daughter. A nephew of his, having an eye on Boota Singh's property, reported the presence of Zainab to the authorities. The Recovery Organization took her away to a camp for six months and finally forcibly sent her back to Pakistan. Boota Singh tried all means of getting her back. He became a Muslim, went to Lahore with his daughter Tanveer, and, on being rejected by Zainab's relatives, in despair committed suicide.[32]

There were numerous cases when women from both Dominions did not want to return but were compelled to do so against their wishes. Some resorted to hunger strikes; others refused to change their clothes. Their protests were powerful. The experience of being abducted as Hindus, converted and married to Muslims, recovered as Hindus but forced to leave behind their children in Pakistan, or vice versa, made these women extremely insecure and unsure of their identities.

There was the case of Ahmed-un-Nissa who went on a hunger strike in Ambala in protest against the attempt to send her forcibly back to Pakistan. While her husband filed a suit in the East Punjab High Court against her forcible detention, her parents in Pakistan were pressing for her early repatriation.[33]

And there was the problem of children. In a recent article, Ritu Menon and Kamla Bhasin claim that an ordinance was passed by the Government of India that children born to abducted women in Pakistan after Partition would be left behind with their fathers, but those abducted women whose children were born in India could keep them. It was only after protests from social workers that it was decided that the Hindu and Sikh women could take their children up to the town of Jullundhur and would have fifteen days to decide whether or not they wanted to keep their children.[34]

The recovery of the abducted women operations were begun with a genuine humanitarian motive of rescuing women who had been forcibly abducted—Hindu, Sikh, or Muslim. In the early months and first year or two after Partition, these women obviously lived in fear and with the insecurities of adjustment to a new religion and way of life, added to which were the memories of the harrowing experiences they had already gone through. After a couple of years, though, many of them settled down. As we have seen, Mrs. Rameshwari Nehru and many others argued that they should not be forcibly uprooted again. Mridula Sarabhai believed that they should be brought back to their original Dominion and then asked to choose. Only then would they speak freely. Was it proper to uproot and unsettle them again? Kamlaben Patel's answer was that "they were never ever secure, had never put down their roots."[35] The wishes of the women were not always easy to ascertain. Many were afraid to speak; others were confused. A pregnant young Muslim woman from Alwar spent six months in a camp. Her case could not be decided by the Tribunal because no relatives of hers could be traced in India or Pakistan. When asked where she wanted to go she replied, "I have nowhere to go. I cannot make up my mind. I am all confused. I will do what you tell me."[36]

In any case, women lacked the decision-making power. They had been treated as a commodity, handed from one man to another to be used and abused. Who had ever asked them what they wanted? Sometimes tall, huge, bearded men would surround Kamlaben Patel in her office and demand that the women rescued from their Hindu and Sikh homes in India should be returned to them. When asked whether these women were Muslims, they would reply that by having had holy water sprinkled on them, the women had been converted. When she told the men that it was her duty to send the women back to Pakistan, they replied, "Well, if we cannot have these women, can we have some of the Hindu and Sikh women you have recovered from Pakistan?" Such was their attitude to women.[37] The old Hindu concept of a married daughter being *paraya dhan* (another family's wealth) is a succinct example of viewing women as commodities. The concept of women as independent human beings with a right to choose their future was alien to traditionalists of both communities.

Women's experiences of Partition and the physical and psychological scars abduction left behind have not really been written or spoken about by the women themselves. Many of them were illiterate, and even if they could write, they found the experiences were too harrowing to report. Women usually do not want to talk or write about rape and sexual assaults. But creative writers such as Sadat Hasan Manto in "Cold Meat"; Krishna Sobti in "Where is My Mother?"; Kartar Singh Duggal in "Kulsum"; and Rajinder Singh Bedi in "Lajwanti" provide us with some clues.[38]

What emerges from this brief exploration of the human dimensions of Partition is the agony and suffering of women as a result not only of the massacres and migrations but of abductions. So many people entered the new era of independence severely traumatized. It should be remembered that, "At the stroke of the midnight hour . . . when India awoke to life and freedom," thousands were being massacred and driven out of their homes, lives were being disrupted at all levels as families were destroyed, their members separated and scattered. For the women abducted and sometimes recovered, confusion, dislocation, and the severing of roots, the loss of place and property, but more so the loss of community and any network of stable relationships, as well as the loss of coherent identity constituted their experience, not "freedom at midnight."

NOTES

1. M. Morokvasie, "Women in Migration: Beyond the Reductionist Outlook," in A. Phizacklea, ed., *One Way Ticket: Migration and Female Labour* (London: Routledge and Kegan Paul, 1983).

2. Kamlaben Patel, "Oranges and Apples," in Mushirul Hasan, ed., *India Partitioned*, vol. 2 (New Delhi: Rolli Books, 1995), 122.

3. Mridula Sarabhai (1911–74) was the daughter of the well-known industrialist Ambalal Sarabhai of Ahmedabad and a close associate of Mahatma Gandhi and Jawaharlal Nehru. Aparna Basu, *Mridula Sarabhai: Rebel with a Cause* (New Delhi: Oxford University Press, 1995).

4. Kamlaben Patel, *Mool Sota Ukhdela* (*The Uprooted*), 2nd ed. (Ahmedabad: R. R. Seth, 1985).

5. For details of this incident, see Unvashi Butalia, "Community, State and Gender," *Economic and Political Weekly, Women's Supplement*, 24 April 1993, 14–16.

6. K. Patel, "Oranges and Apples," 128.

7. Anees Kidwai, *Azadi Ki Chaon Mei*, trans. Noor Nabi Abbasi (New Delhi: National Book Trust, 1990), 142–43.

8. Rameshwari Nehru (1886–1966) was president of the All India Harijan Sewak Sangh; founder and president of the Delhi Women's League, Delhi branch of the All India Women's Conference; and awarded the Padma Bhushan in 1955 and the Lenin Prize in 1951.

9. Hannah Sen was a lawyer and a cofounder and architect of Lady Irwin College, New Delhi; she was an active member and officer of the All India Women's Conference, the India Women's Education Fund Association, and the All India Council of Child Welfare.

10. Mridula Sarabhai to Ambalal Sarabhai and family, 18 August 1947. Mridula Sarabhai Papers, Archives of the Sarabhai Foundation, Ahmedabad.

11. Mridula Sarabhai, "The Recovery of Abducted Women," National Press Syndicate, 25 July 1948. Mridula Sarabhai Papers.

12. Kidwai, *Azadi Ki Chaon Mei*, 139, 142.

13. Y. D. Gundevia, *Outside the Archives* (New Delhi: Sangam Press, 1984), 35.

14. "Recovery of Abducted Women," up to 15 July 1948. Circular letter from Rameshwari Nehru, Director, Women's Section, Ministry of Relief and Rehabilitation, Government of India, New Delhi, n.d.

15. Kamaladevi Chattopadhyaya (1903–1988) was born in Mangalore and educated at Bedford College, London, and the London School of Economics. She was president of the All India Women's Conference in 1927 and took part in the Salt Satyagraha in 1930. She was instrumental in reviving handlooms and handicrafts in independent India.

16. Patel, "Oranges and Apples," 128–29.

17. Mridula Sarabhai, Note on Purchase of Abducted Women in Sargoda District, 17 November 1947. Mridula Sarabhai Papers.

18. Edwina Mountbatten, letter to Mridula Sarabhai, 28 November 1947. Mridula Sarabhai Papers.

19. *Collected Works of Mahatma Gandhi*, vol. 90 (New Delhi: Publications Division, Ministry of Information and Broadcasting, Government of India), 128.

20. Patel, "Oranges and Apples," 150.

21. Ibid., 99–101.

22. Ibid., 102–103.

23. Hans Raj, ed., *Encyclopaedia of Indian Parliament*, vol. 1 (New Delhi: Amol Publications, 1996), 76–77.

24. "Recovery of Abducted Women," Circular letter from Rameshwari Nehru.

25. Mridula Sarabhai, "The Recovery of Abducted Women."

26. Patel, *Mool Sota Ukhdela*, 141–42.

27. Ibid., 143–46.

28. Mridula Sarabhai, "The Recovery of Abducted Women."

29. Patel, *Mool Sota Ukhdela*, 56–61.

30. Mrs. Sheila Sengupta, interview with the author, February 1995, New Delhi. She worked with Mridula Sarabhai in her Central Recovery Office in New Delhi.

31. Patel, *Mool Sota Ukhdela*, 43–52.

32. Mridula Sarabhai, "The Recovery of Abducted Women."

33. Mridula Sarabhai, "The Recovery of Abducted Women," 15 July 1948. Mridula Sarabhai Papers.

34. Ritu Menon and Kamla Bhasin, "Recovery, Rupture, Resistance, Indian State and Abduction of Women during Partition," *Economic and Political Weekly, Women's Supplement*, 24 April 1993. No mention of such an ordinance could be found in the *Encyclopaedia of Indian Parliament*, which contains all the ordinances passed by the Government of India from 1947 onward.

35. Patel, "Oranges and Apples," 128.

36. Ibid., 120–21.

37. Ibid., 36–37.

38. These stories are reprinted in Alok Bhalla, ed., *Stories about the Partition of India*, vols. 1, 2, 3 (New Delhi: INDUS, 1994).

16

Politics and the Writing of History

HIMANI BANNERJI

The writing of history is not a transparent affair. In common with other forms of writing, the writing of history entails issues of representation, which in their own turn entail issues of epistemology and ideology. As an integral part of the project of writing history, "representation" presents us with a great deal of complexity. It has, virtually, a double edge to it. By claiming to re-present someone, some moment in time, some situation—in fact all three, all at once—through our reporting, recording, or narration, "representation" implies both epistemological and (re)constructive responsibilities. It occupies both the terrains of the formal-aesthetic and the ideological-political. This it does simultaneously through the same inscriptional act. On the one hand, it brings the absent to the present, the invisible into visibility—readers hear or overhear voices, see the worlds of social subjects or moments, who and which can mainly be seen, heard, or known of through representational inscriptional gestures. Distanced through time and space, subjects and moments can mainly enter into our knowledge through the historian/writer's work—her attempts at re-presentation. Thus, re-presentation both marks moments of absence and offers us a presence—obviously at the second level of construction.

Works of history, then, are not immediate forms and entities. As re-presented, constructed, narrated existences they are only too obviously discursive and perspectival. They involve epistemologies, ideologies, and aesthetics, all of which make the project of re-presentation a political matter. This is the moment of "on the other hand"—re-presentation as recovery, narrating, and construction. But the necessary modes of mediation, forms of construction, are after all not uniform, automatic, and all-inclusive. Without any negative intention on the historian/ writer's part, her ideological knowledge frameworks, her chosen forms of re-presentation, may or may not permit certain presences or visibilities.[1] Thus projects of recovery, of rendering visible, may continue, produce, and reinforce conceptual practices of power. It is this phenomenon that is challenged by feminist historians' thematic of "hidden in/ from history."[2] It accompanies the endeavor to be present or visible in "history" by forcing the level of representation to correspond to that of lives and events at the level of the everyday world.

To substantiate what I mean, I need only to signal to women, colonized peoples, working classes, gays and lesbians, and nonwhites in "race"-organized societies to make the fact of their representational absence visible. Even in the hands of major historians, one or the other group has often been rendered invisible through the historians' adoption of dominant discourses and epistemologies.[3] This puts them outside of the privileged purview of those whose interests and imaginations constitute powerful and effective communities, nations, and their states—both in their making and writing. In short, I am speaking about the relationship of history writing and history making to "relations of ruling" and their institutional/cultural discursivities and ideologies.[4] These relations of ruling and their forms of consciousness, which can be coded as gender, class, or "race" and as regulation of sexuality, are constitutively implicated in the works of the historian/writer and they forbid as well as resist "other" voices and presences—the "other" subjects of power.[5]

The chapters in this volume testify to the politics of historical representation. They speak to these very prohibitions and occlusions, to exclusions and absences, and to negative, distorted constructions or representations of presences. They question in diverse ways the dominant practices of representation, of established ways of writing history, and in that process rewrite it. Interrogations, investigations, and criticisms are extended to not only what is conventional to critique, namely narrations and constructions rooted in patriarchal colonialism and imperialism, but also to nationalisms—to the forms and ideologies in which resistances have been imagined and projected. This is worth noting since we, in the West, have become rather accustomed to a non-Marxist, that is, classlessly cultural binary version of critique of colonial discourse.[6] Unidimensional and essentializing, what Frantz Fanon has called "Manichean," forms of antagonisms have long dominated the critical stage.[7] This essentialized formulation, with its unified blocks of opposition, constructs undifferentiated social subjects and political agents. These seamless narratives abstract the social subjects from their sociohistorical specificities and project through default masculinist fables. These are about masculine and elite protagonists, and they suppress the exposure of social relations of power, of deeply antagonistic contradictions that create "differences."

The chapters of this book are written from perspectives of difference, and they submit both colonial and nationalist discourses to queries and critiques. They introduce the much wider and deeper question of hegemony and show how both of these types of discourses, though apparently opposed, actually perform the work of ruling. They deconstruct discursivities productive of reification and show how women, for example, become object sites for hegemonic contestations between the patriarchal male elites of the colonizer and the colonized.[8] They become "objects" through and of power struggles. By bringing women back into history, or more importantly, by performing a methodological critique that exposes their erasure, their reification, and (mis)construction, feminist historians the world over are engaging in a crucial intellectual and political task. In particular, I would like to draw attention to Indian feminist women historians, political scientists, and cultural theorists who have produced an impressive body of work in this direction. A few examples should suffice. Anthologies such as *Recasting Women*, *Women Writing in India* (vols. 1 and 2), and *Forging Identities* are important to name.[9] Historians such as Tanika Sarkar bring to the issue of nationalism, especially as manifested in Hindu fundamentalism, a trenchant feminist critique.[10] Cultural theorists such as Lata Mani and Gayatri Chakravorty Spivak extend an equally necessary feminist critique toward the critique of colonial discourse.[11] Thus, not only alternative but oppositional ways of questioning and framing representations of women are put forward. These critical enterprises bring us to the substantive nature of social and political agencies of women of both the colonies and the ex-colonies. They, the "objects" of colonial patriarchal representation, now as "subjects" of history question these former representations and represent themselves.

For this new critical representational work, we do need to forge categories of difference. But this "difference" cannot be constituted in simple or ontological identity terms. Rather, difference should be understood in terms of social relations of power and ruling, not as what people intrinsically *are*, but what they are ascribed as in the context of domination. We need also to expose and question the role played by the social location of the knower in the production process of knowledge, including in the notion of "location" not only a spatiotemporal but a politicolinguistic dimension.[12] If a feminist historian, for example, doing a critique of colonial discourse could summon to her aid the importance of understanding the effect of class and other social locations on the possible representational apparatuses of the knower and a fluency in the vernacular of the region, be culturally literate in the vernacular, how different would her work be from that produced solely within the parameter of neglect of the question of location and the colonized's history, language, and culture? If research can go beyond the written word to that of the spoken, sung, and/or otherwise signified representations, how much fuller becomes its contribution to understanding the world of African diasporic women, for example, and other migrant "others."[13]

The writing of history then is not only not a transparent affair, but it is not innocent either. Since at all times it is an epistemological and intellectual project, it also has an ideological-political dimension to it. And this is above and beyond intentionality. Fundamental questions arise, not only about representational efforts to make the past accessible to the present, about aesthetic problems of re-presentation and realism, but also, and crucially, about the relationship between the discursive (as forms of consciousness in the broadest sense) and the social.[14] To raise these questions is to put squarely in the middle of what appears to be a purely intellectual-academic enterprise the question of power and its object, of what Michel Foucault has called "power/knowledge."[15] It shades off into the existence of marginal knowledges, and raises the exciting or alarming, depending on our stakes, possibility of emergence of unsettling knowledge practices and forms from these very marginalized spaces. The work of Edward Said, for example, in *Orientalism*, offered us an anticolonial adaptation of this Foucauldian frame. But this critical exercise, so effective in baring "the Orient" as an imperial knowledge construction, itself enters another circle of seamless ideological closure. When held up to the critique of gender and class, Said's version of critique of colonial discourse proves to be susceptible to a type of nationalism whose ideological space occludes a view of internal social relations of power.[16]

This example, only one of many, which simultaneously contains critical acuteness and ideological occlusion, makes us ask how such absences and erasures come about? What epistemological, discursive procedures have become so naturalized that even in recuperative, critical tasks there are such absences and unawarenesses? What, again, creates in many or most western feminist works such utter silence about "other women," who are constantly present in their world?[17] How do the lives and works of Black women and women of color existing beside them in North America assume an invisible status? And when and how, one might ask rhetorically, and through whose agency, does this silence break? Who enters through the fissures of hegemonic discourse, from the "outside," to make their absence visible, their silence audible? The answer is only too obvious—the excluded themselves, in their own social substantiveness and agency, in the course of their struggles, create this epistemological corrective and change, not just expose, the politics of discourse. It should also be noted that these erasures, silences, and oversights are most often not a matter of actual, purposive acts of antagonism. In fact, if they were so, the situation would be far simpler and easier to deal with. It is much more interesting to explore why these obvious omissions or badly theorized problematics did not attract the attention of well-known progressive historians, feminists, Marxists, and nationalists.

Can we begin by asking, then, about the question of location, of the relationship between social ontology and epistemology? Is there a connection between an author's historical project, knowledge framework and the author's sex, class, and "race" privileges? Is it automatically "always already" the case that a knower's language and knowledge framework are unrelated to who she/he is? And even where that is the case, for example, when a working-class historian produces elite history, do we not have to examine those modes and conventions of the discipline itself through which this becomes possible? Do not academic disciplines, irrespective of an individual's choice, identify themselves through self-markings of discursivities and common senses, which themselves possess a social ontology? Is there, then, a shared set of routine intellectual practices, ideologies, and languages designating what is meant by doing or writing of history?

A notion of a "discipline," with its boundaries, its recognizable lineaments, seems to settle in place, articulating the practitioners in the field. Before we know, we are interpellated by it, and we replicate it through our own activities, for example through the notion and practice of "scholarship," occlusive and exclusive epistemologies.[18] Within these disciplinarian boundaries, objects and subjects of inquiry, the meaning and modes of what "inquiry" could mean, fall into place. Not that "history," for example, as a field of discipline, does not expand in topics through time. From the days of "decline and fall," through "world history" or "universal history" of the world historical spirit, "history" has moved on to other concerns and terrains. It has ramified into areas of state formation, military and naval actions and exploits, and trade and economics. With the development of organized class struggles, social history began to be written, while anticolonial struggles consolidating national cultural identities also created their new histories. But in spite of this expansion, many peoples are, or until relatively recently were, left out of "history." Black people, indigenous peoples, women, and gay men and lesbians, for example, did not feature in histories of working classes or national struggles.[19] Certain psychological and sociological domains that were demarcated as the realm of the "private," for example, did not, for the longest time, qualify as material for either the writing or the making of "history." Sex and sexuality, family lives, the body and morality, socialization of children, to name a few topics, fall or fell outside of history writing's disciplinarian purview.[20] Thus, invisibility and exclusion, sporadic presences through distortions, remain as endemic dangers in the disciplinarian mode. In the conventions of academic history writing, there appears to be a sublime indifference to issues of power, while in practice the discipline relies on social relations produced through power, which it must do to qualify as an academic discipline in a world so severely divided in classes, on mental and manual divisions of labor.

This naturalization of power/knowledge brings us to the notion of hegemony functioning as disciplinarian common sense. Here an ideological mode has been arrived at, thereby creating a sort of a practitioners' consensus. This mode has become so pervasive as to have been naturalized through grand metanarratives of history. In this mode of history writing, even critical categories such as nation, class, or gender, which may have initially challenged ideological bases of colonialism, bourgeois class power, or patriarchy, can end up in closures of solipsism or self-referentiality. Sociohistorical or economic-cultural relations of power that constitute historical concreteness of class, for example, may become not only subsumed but submerged in seamless, self-validating narratives. Specificities of all kinds are thus reduced to symptoms of each one of these governing categories or are overlooked and erased as immaterial to the plot lines of the main story. What is represented in and as history and how, then, become contingent to these foundational metanarrative urges. Joan Scott's critique of E. P. Thompson's otherwise wonderful book *The Making of the English Working Class* reminds us of the pitfalls of this symptomatic metahistory of genderless class.[21] Needless to say, we find an equal emptiness when we scrutinize the text from an anti-imperialist, antiracist stance. But interestingly enough, Scott's own critique does not pay attention to this absence, and does not consider the importance of "race" or the empire for class formation in England.[22] The chapters in this volume about appearances and disappearances of Black people in European or in North American history books speak to many perils of occlusive or hegemonic nationalist historiography. Eric Hobsbawm's history of capital's development, of industry and empire, with its indifference to women, gender, peasants, and issues of "race" and racism, provides us another classic example of writing history where the governing typology of "class" can exist independently of gender and "race."[23]

In this story of thematized continuity, theoretical impulses from Foucault and Foucauldians have been influential in introducing new spaces through breaks and ruptures. Specificities and particular histories, disruptive of the grand marches of metanarratives, have been introduced. Microhistories, which privilege the local sites of temporalities and bounded spatialities, have brought in other narratives that challenge the linear constructions of established academic history. Stories of empires, nations, and capital and class have been traversed by stories of women, colonized and displaced peoples, and marginally located "others," such as gays and lesbians. This sensitivity to power/knowledge and specificities, this lens of difference, has been strengthened by techniques of deconstruction. Together, as cultural and political critique, they have undone the fabric of metahistory. At this time, both the writing of history and the making of it have taken on the look of incomplete projects that approximate more closely the actual state of affairs—both epistemologically and politically. One such critical sweep that challenges "elite history" might be mentioned here since it has assumed much currency. This project is known as "subaltern history."[24] It was initiated by Indian diasporic historian Ranajit Guha and carried on mainly by Indian historians and the odd Indian political scientist. This was an attempt to dismantle two metahistorical frameworks at once. Both Marxist historiography and nationalist historiography were discredited as elite, teleological, and colonial, and thus repressive and unrepresentative of popular projects of history writing. But it is at this point, when we are most critical, that we have to be most careful. We need to be vigilant that our critical histories do not themselves end up by creating reified subjects and narratival closures.

With regard to "subaltern history," two absences are glaringly evident—namely, the absence of women as either subjects or agents of making or writing of history and, of course, of any gender analysis. As far as writing history is concerned, in the course of the almost fifteen years of the existence of *Subaltern Studies*, only two or three women have been published sporadically in the volumes. Once there was an appearance of a woman historian, Tanika Sarkar, and from time to time we caught a glimpse of Gayatri Chakravorty Spivak, who popularized the *Subaltern Studies* group in the West. Any interest in "the woman question" so-called is totally super-added, one essay by a political scientist of the group notwithstanding, particularly since the same essay has reappeared in slightly altered versions in a few places with no response to critiques offered by feminist historians and cultural theorists working in the same area of women and nationalism. But what is even more astonishing is that the subaltern named "woman," whom even the old Marxist Engels was pleased to recognize as "the proletariat of the proletariat," has no definitional space within the subaltern project. Furthermore, those who reject the metanarrative of "class" in their resistance to a Marxist teleological reading and representation of history are content with an abstract, homogenized, and undifferentiated notion of "the community." The ethnicizing, racializing, communalizing, and patriarchal possibilities and political uses of this notion are generally overlooked.[25] Class and gender in particular disappear in the black hole of "subaltern" theorization. Needless to say, the one subject, author, and agent of "history," both in the sense of writing and doing, that emerges from this historiographic venture in combatting Marxist history is male by default. Furthermore, the postulation of a cultural or political consciousness that is "subaltern" and yet independent of class, "race," and gender and removed from "elite consciousness," introduces into this subaltern project and politics an ahistorical and asocial form of political consciousness and unconscious. This stance elevates the subaltern consciousness in rebellion or upsurge as above society and criticism. The spontaneous sociopolitical expressions of subaltern males are not supposed to be tainted by dominant ideologies or characterized by practices of power internal to the "subaltern" group.[26] This makes it difficult to criticize male violence against women, such as that of rapes during communal riots, or the particular ways religious fundamentalists place women on their agendas. The theoretical framework of this project is such that subaltern males as heroes in and of history, as peasants, tribals, minorities, and so forth cannot be perceived as doing wrong.

To say this is not to make merely a theoretical critique of this historiography. It is especially important to state this now for an urgent political reason in the current environment of Indian politics when a violent, fascist, Hindu fundamentalist strand of nationalism is on the path of ascendency.[27] Its objects of violence are Muslims, women (both Hindu and Muslim), and the Left in any shape or form. It is dangerous to project this "nationalist" upsurge, marked by the demolition of the Babri Mosque in December 1992 and subsequent riots that spread all over the country, as "subaltern" and liberatory just because it is seemingly spontaneist in its violence. It is even more dangerous to shore up this spontaneist and fascistic version of history making by writing essays on "Indian tradition" and "Indian psyche."[28] The notion of "Indian," when formulated through this lens of "tradition," not only invents these traditions and their compound called "India," but Hinduizes India and dehistoricizes it by the same stroke. This neo-orientalism of traditional essentialism, in tandem with its opposite but equally pernicious spontaneism, ends up by supporting all forms of social and "epistemological violence," not the least of which is against women.

If these are some of the pitfalls of anti-elite "subaltern" history writing, we need to watch out also for the dangers of "microhistory." It too began with the intuition of challenging the erasures of metahistory. As we concentrate on the local, the particular, and the immediate in resistance to metanarratives, we need to be wary of the epistemological traps peculiar to empiricism. This may result in work that centers on single issues, localities, or groups to the exclusion of complexities that go into their making, which cannot locate where they lie in socio-historical-political topography. Thus it is possible to work on single issues, for example on "gender" or "class," as though they do not hold a mediating, constituting relationship with each other, or were not formal "congelations" of multiple social relations and forms of consciousness. In the same vein, the study on a locality or a community can become an enclosed sociohistorical venture, what Marshall Sahlins has called an "island of history." Even when a work is antiessentialist and thus attentive to difference, the value of the work as a representational endeavor lies in the way "difference" is understood and deployed as a notion. If difference is understood solely as an ontological and descriptive category, it is bound to end up in an ahistorical enclosure of identity. Historicization and socialization of "difference" take us away from empiricism or foundationalism, and mark difference as a signifier for relations of power and a cultural and political form of domination. Read in this way, "difference" or its related category "identity" ceases to create the dangerous possibility of becoming an ideological-political prison of the self. It is through such a segregated and reified reading that much work based on difference or identity becomes as static and empty of dynamism as that based on essentialism. This empiricism ends up by creating micro-metahistory, in which the very historicity of the formation of subject, self as a being in history, is lost. It is in this way that histories of different oppressions are written as though they have never heard of each other or know of the long chains that bind them. Thus, we can write of memories and experiences of Jewish or African-American women and not connect racism with antisemitism. This is not to say that each book must write everything, but it is possible to be alert to the fact that the theoretical framework of the work could admit of a complex social organization and multiple relations and constructive semiologies of power. What, for example, is one to say about books in recent-day Germany that can speak about the oppression of the Jewish woman without casting the theoretical net wide enough to make possible, in theoretical terms, the oppression of her Turkish sisters?[29]

I can only hope in conclusion that I have brought forward, even if minimally and superficially, problems of representation (political) and re-presentation (aesthetic-epistemological) as particularly connected with history. But we are still left with having to puzzle out how, in the process of criticizing, we create more and other closures, how a set of ideological concentric circles comes into being as we run out of our disciplinarian, regulating intellectual regimes. Some corrective speculations are in order here, and I will attempt some suggestions. One way of overcoming closures might be to ground the topics, issues, problems, and so on with which we are immediately engaged into the broader sociohistorical relations that constitute and extend behind and before them. This is to place and deconstruct an event, an experience, a moment—in short, a phenomenon—in the purview within which it arises. It is as though we were to study a wave as a stable form, as an arc of water, and yet be attentive to the vast mass of liquid from which it formed and into which it will decompose. This would mean not only studying the formative discourses themselves but the world that needs, gives rise to, and mediates its moments through those discourses. I suggest also studying and comparing discourses, their rise and fall— the birth and death of discourses. There is a need to compare accounts, to read one through another.

This proposal necessarily brings me to the edge of disciplines, to the point when boundaries must be broken. Feminist historians, among "other" historians, have long realized the impossibility, and absurdity, of "writing representation" without attending to the social and the cultural. Sociologists and anthropologists who are similarly engaged in "social research" realize the ludicrous nature of studying the social without history and culture and simply reducing it to demographics. The notion of "graphic" (as in ethnography) has shifted from the graph of applied statistics to that of graphic art, of images. Memories, experiences, daily practices, and oral histories now jostle with conventions of disciplines, allowing for recreations never seen before. Disciplinarian purity has finally and happily yielded to hybridities such as "historical sociology." But underlying these practitioners' art and choices is the deepest question of methodology—not simply as an instrument of digging and measuring—but in the sense in which Marx, for example, speaks of it in the preface of *Das Kapital*. This is a question of epistemology—that very conceptual framework of inquiry—within which any knowing takes place. This is where being and doing in time, in life, and in death, must be understood as socially organized moments and experiences that are structured on multiple, contradictory warps and wefts. Any conceptual device that allows us to frame or address that and helps us to inquire deeply into a social formation may be called our desirable method.

Ultimately, the note on which I want to end is political. This should not be an abrupt gesture, since from the very beginning I have kept politics in our peripheral vision. What I have tried to say so far is that in the end—in the "last instance," should I say?—the issue of critical and intellectual work (I do not only say "academic") is a political issue. Keeping in mind the possibilities of change and criticism, breaks and fissures that exist even within the scope of our disciplinarian hermeneutics, we have to face the fact that the impetus for radical intellectual criticism comes from the struggles in our lives, from the world in which we live. Our being in the world and the struggles that surround us mirror each other. From social movements that create both history and possibilities of critical knowledge from memories and experiences politicized as organizations and identities of people come our inspiration to write new histories. So our last and most important source for writing in oppositional ways comes from the political, and this politics, I insist, has to be deeper than skin or sex if it has to work for transformation of knowledge and society at once.

NOTES

1. Dorothy E. Smith, "The Social Organization of Textual Reality" and "Textual Realities, Ruling and Suppression of Disjuncture," in *Conceptual Practices of Power: A Feminist Sociology of Knowledge* (Toronto: University of Toronto Press, 1990).

2. Sheila Rowbotham is one of the first historians to have pointed to this in her two early women's history books, *Hidden from History* (London: Pluto Press, 1973) and *Women, Resistance and Revolution* (New York: Vintage Books, 1974). See also an early collection of feminist and women's history, Juliet Mitchell and Ann Oakley, eds., *The Rights and Wrongs of Women* (Harmondsworth, England: Penguin, 1976).

3. The historians I have in mind are Eric Hobsbawm, E. P. Thompsom, Christopher Hill, Rodney Hilton, and Perry Anderson, to name a few, who have been particularly empty on gender, "race," or sexuality issues, even when they have been left or progressive and written histories of class and state formation and class struggle.

4. See Dorothy E. Smith, *The Everyday World as Problematic: A Feminist*

Sociology (Boston: Northeastern University Press, 1987) for this concept, and for its feminist sociohistorical use, see Chandra Talpade Mohanty, "Introduction: Cartographies of Struggle: Third World Women and the Politics of Feminism," in C. Mohanty, Ann Russo, and Lourdes Torres, eds., *Third World Women and the Politics of Feminism* (Bloomington: Indiana University Press, 1991), 1–47.

5. This epistemological critique regarding erasures and distortions is made by antiracist and feminist scholars. See Himani Bannerji, "But Who Speaks for Us? Experience and Agency in Conventional Feminist Paradigms," in *Thinking Through: Essays on Feminism, Marxism and Anti-racism* (Toronto: Women's Press, 1995) for this process of silencing and construction of the reified other. See also Chandra Talpade Mohanty, "Under Western Eyes: Feminist Scholarship and Colonial Discourses," in Mohanty, Russo, and Torres, *Third World Women,* for a searching critique of methodologies of representation as applied to third world women, mainly with regard to "western feminist writers."

6. See Edward Said, *Orientalism* (New York: Pantheon, 1978) and Malek Alloula, *The Colonial Harem* (Minneapolis: University of Minnesota Press, 1986) for examples of this, for both original theorization and one of the earliest sustained applications. See also Aijaz Ahmad's critique of Said in "Orientalism and After: Ambivalence and Metropolitan Location in the Work of Edward Said," in *In Theory: Classes, Nations and Literatures* (London: Verso, 1992).

7. For a critique of a reductionist binary view, phrased as "Manichean," see Frantz Fanon, *The Wretched of the Earth* (New York: Grove, 1963).

8. For a discussion about women and the familial domain as sites for hegemonic contestation, see the introduction to Kumkum Sangari and Sudesh Vaid, eds., *Recasting Women: Essays in Indian Colonial History* (New Brunswick, NJ: Rutgers University Press, 1990). See also Tanika Sarkar, "Women's Agency within Authoritarian Communalism: The Rashtrasevika Samiti and Ramjanmabhoomi," in Gyanendra Pandey, ed., *Hindus and Others: The Question of Identity in India Today* (New Delhi: Viking, 1993); H. Bannerji, "Mothers and Teachers: Gender and Class in Educational Proposals for and by Women in Colonial Bengal," *Journal of Historical Sociology* 5, no. 1 (March 1992): 1–30; H. Bannerji, "Textile Prison: Discourse on Shame (*lojja*) in the Attire of the Gentlewoman (*bhadramahila*) in Colonial Bengal," in M. Valverde, ed., *Studies in Moral Regulation* (Toronto: Centre of Criminology, University of Toronto, 1994). Also see the anthology by Margo Hendricks and Patricia Parker, eds., *Women, "Race" and Writing* (London: Routledge, 1994), which offers the same critique from the standpoint of feminist anthropology regarding colonization and racialization of women in the colonies.

9. Sangari and Vaid, *Recasting Women;* Susie Tharu and K. Lalita, eds., *Women Writing in India,* 2 vol. (New York: Feminist Press, 1991); Zoya Hasan, ed., *Forging Identities: Gender, Communities and the State* (New Delhi: Kali for Women, 1994).

10. Tanika Sarkar, "The Hindu Wife and the Hindu Nation: Domesticity and Nationalism in Nineteenth Century Bengal," *Studies in History* 8, no. 2 (1992): 213–35, and "Rhetoric against Age of Consent: Resisting Colonial Reason and Death of a Child Wife," *Economic and Political Weekly* 28, no. 36 (1992).

11. Lata Mani, "Contentious Traditions: The Debate on *Sati* in Colonial India," in Sangari and Vaid, *Recasting Women;* Gayatri Chakravorty Spivak, "Can the Subaltern Speak?" in C. Nelson and L. Grossberg, eds., *Marxism and the Interpretations of Culture* (Urbana: University of Illinois Press, 1988).

12. For the importance of "location" as a defining element of knowledge

and representation, see Dorothy E. Smith, "A Sociology for Women," in *The Everyday World as Problematic*.

13. Mary Louise Pratt, *Imperial Eyes: Travel Writing and Transculturation* (London: Routledge, 1992).

14. Abdul Jan Mohammad, "The Economy of Manichean Allegory: The Function of Racial Difference in Colonial Literature," in Henry Louis Gates, Jr., ed., *"Race," Writing and Difference* (Chicago: University of Chicago Press, 1986).

15. Michel Foucault, *Power/Knowledge* (New York: Pantheon, 1980).

16. My criticism of Said is on the grounds of leaving out the issues of gender and class in his critique of colonial representation of the "other." This undifferentiated reading leaves us with a homogenized view of both the colonizer and the colonized, without offering any ground for assessing or criticizing nationalism, for example. See Julia Emberly, "Introduction: Articulating Difference(s)," in *Thresholds of Difference: Feminist Critique, Native Women's Writings, Postcolonial Theory* (Toronto: University of Toronto Press, 1993); see also Ahmad, *In Theory*, for a searching critique of Said on the grounds of history and class formation. For a critique of nationalism on gender and class grounds, see authors such as Partha Chatterji and Tanika Sarkar in Sangari and Vaid, eds., *Recasting Women*, as well as Jashodhara Bagchi, ed., *Indian Women: Myth and Reality* (Calcutta: Sangam Books, 1995).

17. This is discussed extensively in E. V. Spelman, *Inessential Woman: Problems of Exclusion in Feminist Thought* (Boston: Beacon Press, 1983), and in bell hooks, *Ain't I a Woman? Black Women and Feminism* (Boston: South End Press, 1981). See also "Sisterhood: Political Solidarity between Women," in S. Gunew, ed., *A Reader in Feminist Knowledge* (London: Routledge, 1991), and Patricia Hill Collins, *Black Feminist Thought: Knowledge, Consciousness, and the Politics of Empowerment* (London: Harper Collins, 1990). We have to consider that feminist history of class formation in England, for example, largely ignores themes of "race" and/or the empire. Examples of these might be otherwise excellent feminist histories. See note 22 below.

18. For these occlusive and exclusive properties of "discipline," see Dorothy E. Smith, "Ideological Practices of Sociology," in *Conceptual Practices of Power*. One could substitute "history" for "sociology" without any violation of her argument and see how the common practice of qualifying as a member of the "discipline" brings one into a positivist and an abstract, essentializing frame. See also H. Bannerji, "Writing 'India,' Doing Ideology: William Jones' Construction of India as an Ideological Category," *Left History* 2, no. 2 (Fall 1994): 5–36.

19. I use the category "Black" to code peoples of African origin living in diaspora. Others, formerly colonized, indigenous peoples, or those coming from the third world, have been named with their countries of origin—for example, Turkish women.

20. France has produced historians of moralities or "mentalities" or private lives, such as P. Aries and G. Duby, eds., *A History of Private Life*, 4 vol. (Cambridge: Harvard University Paperback Editions, 1992), and A. Copely, *Sexual Moralities in France 1780–1980: New Ideas on the Family, Divorce and Homosexuality* (London: Routledge, 1989). Histories of childhood, such as C. Steedman, *Childhood, Culture and Class in Britain: Margaret McMillan, 1860–1931* (New Brunswick, NJ: Rutgers University Press, 1996), and of sexuality and the body, such as T. Lacqueur and C. Gallagher, eds., *The Making of the Modern Body: Sexuality and Society in the Nineteenth Century* (Berkeley and Los Angeles: University of California Press, 1987) or J. R. Walkowitz, *City of Dreadful Delight:*

Narratives of Sexual Danger in Late Victorian London (Chicago: University of Chicago Press, 1992) are some examples of new types of history writing.

21. E. P. Thompson, *The Making of the English Working Class* (Harmondsworth, England: Penguin Books, 1968); see also Catherine Hall, "Feminism and Feminist History," in *White, Male and Middle Class: Explorations in Feminism and History* (New York: Routledge, 1992), 1–40, for a critique of genderless history.

22. Joan Wallach Scott, "Women in *The Making of the English Working Class*," in *Gender and the Politics of History* (New York: Columbia University Press, 1988), 68–90. See also Denise Riley, *"Am I That Name?": Feminism and the Category of "Women" in History* (Minneapolis: University of Minnesota Press, 1988). This lacuna in feminist history is present even in texts that otherwise devote themselves to unsettling such fundamental notions as "women." There is a remarkable absence of nuancing this notion with difference in a book such as Riley's, which otherwise raises such interesting issues. The same absence of the colonial enterprise or slavery, or the roles that they play in defining the rising bourgeoisie's sense of themselves, in their notions and practices of "family," marks such an otherwise influential text as Leonore Davidoff and Catherine Hall, *Family Fortunes: Men and Women of the English Middle Class, 1780–1850* (Chicago: University of Chicago Press, 1987). The same could be said of P. Levine, *Victorian Feminism: 1850–1900* (London: Hutchinson, 1987). These are two examples out of many where awareness of one oppression, or the attempt to put back in an erased population, does not open the authors' eyes to others belonging to the same category, nor do they see how influential the empire, colonies, and racialization were in creating the European subject, both male and female, of all classes. Ann Laura Stoler makes the point very strongly in *Race and the Education of Desire: Foucault's History of Sexuality and the Colonial Order of Things* (Durham, NC: Duke University Press, 1995).

23. Eric Hobsbawm, *Industry and Empire* (Harmondsworth, England: Penguin Books, 1974), *The Age of Capital, 1848–1875* (New York: Mentor Books, 1979), *The Age of Revolution* (New York: Mentor Books, 1962).

24. See Ranajit Guha, ed., *Subaltern Studies*, vols. 1–6 (Delhi: Oxford University Press, 1982–89). For a critique of "subaltern studies," see R. O'Hanlon, "Recovering the Subject: Subaltern Studies and Histories of Resistance in Colonial South Asia," *Modern Asian Studies* 22, no. 1 (1988): 189–224.

25. Gyan Pandey's *Construction of Communalism in Colonial North India* (Delhi: Oxford University Press, 1990) shows some of the problems of reading "communities" without specificities of class formation in a consistent and analyzed manner. This makes critiques of nationalism and identity politics largely solipsistic.

26. See R. Guha, *Elementary Aspects of Peasant Insurgency in Colonial India* (Delhi: Oxford University Press, 1983).

27. Hindu fundamentalism becomes an issue in Indian history, not as a passing political deviation or attitude, but actually as the party forming the government following the 1996 national elections. This rule lasted only thirteen days, but does give us a glimpse into things to come. For feminist and progressive critiques of Hindu fundamentalism and nationalism inscribed in it, see Madhusree Dutta, Flavia Agnes, and Nira Adarkar, eds., *The Nation, the State and Indian Identity* (Calcutta: Samya, 1996).

28. Ashish Nandi's work in this direction of reworking the concept of tradition is highly problematic. See *The Intimate Enemy: Loss and Recovery of Self under Colonialism* (Calcutta, 1988). See also D. Chakravarty's neoconservative view of gender and women's roles and status in "The Difference-Deferral of

(A) Colonial Modernity: Public Debates on Domesticity in British Bengal," *History Workshop Journal* 36 (Autumn 1993): 1–34.

29. See Nupur Chaudhuri and Margaret Strobel, eds., *Western Women and Imperialism: Complicity and Resistance* (Bloomington: Indiana University Press, 1992). This collection, and the framework discussed in the introduction, allows for much more inclusive, critical, and interesting possibilities of writing feminist history where white and nonwhite women can take part in discussing agency without erasures or "appropriation."

CONTRIBUTORS

Yvette Abrahams was born in Cape Town and grew up in exile. She completed her graduate studies at Queen's University at Kingston in Ontario and is now completing a doctorate in history at the University of Cape Town. Her essay "Ambiguity Is My Middle Name: A Research Diary about Sara Bartman, Myself, and Some Other Brown Women" will appear in *Hobby, Passion and Struggle: The Revival of Native South African (Khoikhoi) Culture.*

Karen H. Adler's doctoral thesis (University of Sussex) examined the politics and culture of race and gender during and after the Nazi occupation of France. She has published a number of articles on this period and its consequences in journals such as *Modern and Contemporary France* and *Feminist Review*, and in the recently published *The Liberation of France: Image and Event* (ed. H. R. Kedward and Nancy Wood, 1995).

Himani Bannerji teaches in the Department of Sociology at York University in the areas of anti-racist feminism, Marxist cultural theories, gender, colonialism, and imperialism. Her recent publications include *Thinking Through: Essays on Feminism, Marxism and Anti-racism* (1995), *The Writing on the Wall: Essays on Culture and Politics* (1993), and the edited anthology *Returning the Gaze: Essays on Racism, Feminism and Politics* (1993). She has also published two books of poetry, *A Separate Sky* and *Doing Time*. She is involved in anti-racist and feminist activism.

Aparna Basu is Professor of History at the University of Delhi. She is Vice President of the All India Women's Conference and the author of several books and articles on the history of education, women's history, and communalism in India. Her publications include *Growth of Education and Political Development in India, Essays in the History of Indian Education, Women's Struggle: History of All India Women's Conferences*, and *Women's Perspectives: India and Canada*. She is on the editorial boards of *Gender and History, Women's History,* and *Indian Economic and Social History Review.*

Gabriela Cano is a professor of history at the Universidad Autónoma Metropolitana–Iztapalapa. She is the author of several articles on feminism, women's citizenship, and women's higher education in modern Mexico.

Joanna de Groot works in history and women's studies with a particular focus on the cultural and political dimensions of gender and ethnicity in the era of colonial, imperial, and global structures of power, resistance, and interdependence since the eighteenth century. Her research and writing deal particularly with Iran in the nineteenth and twentieth centuries and with European constructions of exoticized and colonialized "others." Her publications include "Conceptions and Misconceptions: The Historical and Cultural Context of Discussion on Women and Development," in Haleh Afshar, ed., *Women's Development and Survival in the Third World* (1991), *Women's Studies in the 1990s* (with Mary Maynard, 1993), and "The Dialectics of Gender in Iran 1890–1930" (1993).

Karen Dubinsky teaches women's history at Queen's University at Kingston in Ontario. She is the author of *Improper Advances: Rape and Heterosexual Conflict in Ontario, 1880–1920s* (1993) and is now writing a book on the history of tourism and honeymoons at Niagara Falls.

Johanna Gehmacher is a lecturer and research fellow at the University of Vienna, Department of History. She is currently researching a biography based on the letters of a Viennese teacher, born in 1884, who was active in the Austrian women's movement. Her most recent book is *Jugend ohne Zukunft. Hitler-Jugend und Bund Deutscher Mädel in Österreich vor 1938* (1994).

Breda Gray is currently researching gender, emigration, and contemporary Irish identities at the Centre for Women's Studies and the Department of Sociology, Lancaster University. Her publications on this topic include "Irish Women in London: National or Hybrid Diasporic Identities?" *NWSA Journal* 8:1 (1996); "'The Home of Our Mothers and Our Birthright for Ages?': Nation, Diaspora and Irish Women," in Mary Maynard and June Purvis, eds., *New Frontiers in Women's Studies: Knowledge, Identity and Nationalism* (1996); and "(Dis)locating Irishness in the 1990s: The Views of Irish Women at Home and Abroad," in Jim MacLaughlin, ed., *Location and Dislocation in Irish Society: Multidisciplinary Essays on Emigration and Irish Identities* (1997).

Patricia Grimshaw is Max Crawford Professor of History at the University of Melbourne, Australia, where she teaches Pacific and American history and contributes to the women's studies program. She is the author of *Women's Suffrage in New Zealand* (1987), *Paths of Duty: American Mission Wives in Nineteenth Century Hawaii* (1989), and co-author of *Creating a Nation* (1994).

Professor **Dolores E. Janiewski** teaches American history at Victoria University in Wellington, New Zealand, where she is currently working on two projects: one explores the gendering of frontiers on the American continent and in the Pacific, and the other addresses issues of gender and race in North Carolina.

Cheryl Johnson-Odim is Associate Professor and Chairperson of History at Loyola University. She is a former Fulbright scholar in Nigeria, a former member of the board of directors of the African Studies Association (ASA), and is among the founding members of the ASA's Women's Caucus and Pan-African Caucus. She is co-editor of *Expanding the Boundaries of Women's History* (1992) and co-author of *For Women and the Nation: Funmilayo Ransome-Kuti of Nigeria*. She sits on the editorial boards of the *Journal of Women's History* and the *National Women's Studies Association Journal*. She considers herself an activist scholar.

Marilyn Lake holds a personal chair in the Department of History at La Trobe University in Victoria. She is co-author of *Creating a Nation*, a feminist history of Australia, and co-editor of *Gender and War: Australians at War in the Twentieth Century*. She is currently writing a history of feminist thought in Australia.

Sayoko Matusomoto (Yoneda) is Professor of Women's History at the Yamanashi Women's Junior College in Yamanashi. Her research focuses on modern women's history in Japan, especially on Japanese women's liberation.

Louise Ryan is originally from Ireland but has been teaching Sociology and Women's Studies in England since 1992. Her research is concerned with the Irish feminist movement in the early twentieth century. She is the author of *Irish Feminism and the Vote* (1996).

Tanika Sarkar is a senior lecturer in history at St. Stephen's College, University of Delhi. She has published *Bengal 1928–1934: The Politics of Protest* (1987), co-edited *Women and the Hindu Right* (1995), and coauthored *Khaki Shorts and Saffron Flags* (1993). She has published a large number of articles in Indian and international journals on nationalism, popular politics, gender studies, and contemporary politics.

Rosalyn Terborg-Penn is a pioneer in writing and teaching about African American and African Diaspora women's history. She is the co-editor of *Black Women in America: An Historical Encyclopedia* (1994), *Women in Africa and the African Diaspora: A Reader* (1996), and *The Afro-American Woman: Struggles and Images*, second edition (1997). Terborg-Penn is a professor of history at Morgan State University in Baltimore.

EDITORS

Nupur Chaudhuri, who teaches at Texas Southern University, is the co-editor of *Western Women and Imperialism: Complicity and Resistance*, and co-editor of a special issue on "Gender, Race, Class, Sexuality: National and Global Perspectives" for the *National Women's Studies Journal*. She has written extensively on gender and imperialism and her articles have appeared in *Journal of Women's History*, *Women's History Review*, and *Victorian Studies*.

Beth McAuley, a freelance editor, is the acquisition and series editor of the Women's Issues Publishing Program at Second Story Press, Toronto.

Ruth Roach Pierson, Professor of Women's History and Feminist Studies at the Ontario Institute for Studies in Education, is the author of *"They're Still Women After All": The Second World War and Canadian Womanhood*, and editor of *Women and Peace: Theoretical, Historical, and Practical Perspectives*. She is also co-author of *No Easy Road: Women in Canada 1920s to 1960s*, and co-editor of *Writing Women's History: International Perspectives*.

INDEX